CINEMA AND THE CULTURAL COLD WAR

A volume in the series

The United States in the World

Founded by Mark Philip Bradley and Paul A. Kramer
Edited by Benjamin Coates, Emily Conroy-Krutz, Paul A. Kramer, and Judy
Tzu-Chun Wu

A list of titles in this series is available at www.cornellpress.cornell.edu.

CINEMA AND THE CULTURAL COLD WAR

US Diplomacy and the Origins of the Asian Cinema Network

Sangjoon Lee

Cornell University Press

Ithaca and London

First published 2020 by Cornell University Press

Library of Congress Cataloging-in-Publication Data

Names: Lee, Sangjoon, author.
Title: Cinema and the cultural Cold War : US diplomacy and the origins
    of the Asian cinema network / Sangjoon Lee.
Description: Ithaca [New York] : Cornell University Press, 2020. | Series:
    The United States in the world | Includes bibliographical references
    and index.
Identifiers: LCCN 2020022546 (print) | LCCN 2020022547 (ebook) |
    ISBN 9781501752315 (hardcover) | ISBN 9781501753916 (paperback) |
    ISBN 9781501752322 (pdf) | ISBN 9781501752339 (epub)
Subjects: LCSH: Asia Foundation—Influence. | Motion picture industry—
    Political aspects—Asia—History—20th century. | Motion pictures—
    Political aspects—Asia—History—20th century. | Cold War—Influence. |
    Communism and motion pictures—Asia. | Motion pictures and
    transnationalism—Asia. | Asia—Relations—United States. | United
    States—Relations—Asia.
Classification: LCC PN1993.5.A75 L44 2020 (print) | LCC PN1993.5.A75
    (ebook) | DDC 791.43/6582825—dc23
LC record available at https://lccn.loc.gov/2020022546
LC ebook record available at https://lccn.loc.gov/2020022547

For Jungyoun and Bohm

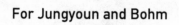

Contents

Acknowledgments

When I commenced a postdoctoral fellowship at the University of Michigan in 2011, my plan was to write a historical study that traced the network of motion picture studios in Asia—South Korea, Hong Kong, Taiwan, and Japan—during the 1960s and '70s. Everything changed, however, after a short research trip to Palo Alto in January 2012. It was a two-day visit to the Hoover Institution Archives at Stanford University, and I just wanted to check details about the Asia Foundation. But at the Hoover, I found a massive trove of the foundation's records. In particular, I discovered two big boxes of information on their motion picture project in Asia. This was my "Eureka!" moment. I had to postpone my initial publication plans accordingly. Between 2012 and 2016, I conducted extensive archival research at the Hoover Institution Archives, Yale University's Manuscripts and Archives, the C. V. Starr East Asian Library at Columbia University, the Margaret Herrick Library of Academy of Motion Picture Arts and Sciences in Los Angeles, East West Center at the University of Hawaii, National Film and Sound Archive in Australia, the Hong Kong Film Archive, Hong Kong University's Special Collections, the Korean Film Archive, the National Library of Korea, the Asian Film Archive, and the National Archive of Singapore. The first five chapters in this book are the outcome of this extensive archival research and were written mostly in 2015 and 2016. In 2018, I was fortunate enough to spend six months at the Australian National University (ANU) as a visiting scholar. Canberra was a quiet and peaceful city and the first full draft of *The Asian Cinema Network* was completed during my stay in Canberra.

I presented parts of this book at various film festivals, galleries, archives, conferences, and universities: the Busan International Film Festival (2019); the DMZ International Documentary Film Festival (2019); the National Gallery of Singapore (2018); the Korean Film Archive (2017); Society of Cinema and Media Studies (SCMS) conferences in Montreal (2015) and Seattle (2019); the Association for Asian Studies (AAS) conference in Toronto (2018); the Kinema Club Workshop at Harvard University (2010); the AAS-Asia conference in Taipei (Academic Sinica, 2015); the Korean Screen Culture Conference (KSCC) at the University of Copenhagen (2015); the Asian Studies Conference in Japan (ASCJ) at Meiji Gakuin University (2015); the Joint East Asian Studies (JEAS) conference at SOAS University of London (2016); the Cold War in Korean Films Symposium at Princeton University (2016); Cultural Typhoon conference at the Tokyo University of Arts (2016); the Asia Foundation Workshop at Columbia University (2017); the Korean Film History Workshop at UC Berkeley (2017); the Media Industries conference at King's College London (2018); the Association for Korean Studies in Europe (AKSE) conference at Sapienza University in Rome (2019); the International Film Festival Forum at Xiamen University (2019); Reframing Film Festivals conference at Ca'Foscari University of Venice (2020); Yonsei University (2016); Inha University (2016); Chung-Ang University (2017); the National University of Singapore (2017); University College London (2018); the Australian National University (2018); Monash University (2018); Deakin University (2018); and Ewha Woman's University (2019).

I remain indebted to those who read all or parts of the manuscript and offered me advice, comments, and feedback, which helped me improve this book tremendously: Dal Yong Jin, Hyangjin Lee, Nam Lee, Jinhee Choi, Roger Garcia, Yomi Braester, Ma Ran, Dina Iordanova, Ming-Yeh Rawnsley, Julian Stringer, Law Kar, Late Wong Ain-ling, Angel Shing, Kinnia Yau-Shuk-ting, Li Cheuk-to, Chalida Uabumrungjit, Jane Yu, Asako Fujioka, Lawrence Wong Ka-Hee, Alexander Zahlten, Kyu Hyun Kim, Nitin Govil, Brian Yecies, Seio Nakajima, Aynne Kokas, Miyao Daisuke, Hyunjung Lee, Christina Klein, Grace Mak, Chieko Murata, Tan See Kam, Charles Armstrong, Chung-kang Kim, Steven Chung, Jinsoo An, Hye Seung Chung, David Scott Diffrient, Emilie Yueh-yu Yeh, Darrell William Davis, David Desser, Roald Maliangkay, Aaron Magnan-Park, David Hundt, Kim Hong-joon, Kim Young-woo, Wing-Fai Leung, Sheldon Lu, Se-mi Oh, Henry Em, Soyoung Kim, Tim Bergfelder, Lee Soon-jin, Man-fung Yip, Lee Hwajin, Chung Jong-hyun, Lee Bong-beom, Kim Han Sang, Park Hyun Seon, Kim Shin-dong, and Xu Lanjun.

Throughout my academic career, I have been blessed with the finest of mentors. At UCLA, Nick Browne, Steve Mamber, and the late Teshome Gabriel, Lisa Kernan, and Peter Wollen showed me the spirit of film studies and intellectual responsibility. At New York University, Zhang Zhen was and is an extraordinary advisor. She has provided me unstinting intellectual inspiration and guidance, a debt that can never be repaid. This book owes the most to her. I have been extremely fortunate to have the support of such distinguished film scholars at NYU as Yoshimoto Mitsuhiro, Dana Polan, Jungbong Choi, Robert Stam, Bill Simon, Ed Guerrero, Antonia Lant, Richard Allen, and the late Robert Sklar. I am also indebted to Namhee Lee and Chris Berry. Namhee has always been my supporter, and I have learned from her how to think and write as a scholar. Chris taught me, not in his office in London but at the tables of coffee shops and restaurants in Beijing, Hong Kong, and Singapore how to navigate and survive in the intricate web of cinema and the transnational world. I am also grateful to my friends who helped me survive eight years of graduate studies in Los Angeles and New York City. I thank Jihoon Kim, Seung-hoon Jeong, Jeon Young-chan, Shin Young-jae, Hye Jean Chung, Hyunhee Park, Hieyoon Kim, Benjamin Min Han, Hyung-shin Kim, Brian Hu, Sachiko Mizuno, Andrey Gordienko, Lindy Leong, Nam Lee, Lee Hyunjin, Jae-eun Oh, Kia Afra, Wang Qi, Jina Park, Seo Jung-joo, Lee Sang-oh, Baik Hyo-sung, Lee Ji-won, Kim Hye-won, Kyung-joon Kim, Sueyoung Park-Primiano, Zeynep Dadak, Anuja Jain, Wyatt Phillips, Nathan Brennan, Cindy Chen, Alice Black, Dominic Hubert Gavin, Intan Paramaditha, Ami Kim, Rufus de Rham, An Ji-eun, Lee Soo Hyun, Molly Kim, Yuni Cho, Kim Young-a, Lee Jung-Ah, Ying Xiao, Jinying Li, Shi-yan Chao, Dan Gao, Chang Han-il, and Lee Soonyi.

At the University of Michigan, I received invaluable mentorship from Markus Nornes, Youngju Ryu, and Nojin Kwak. My colleagues in the Department of Screen Arts and Cultures, the Department of Asian Languages and Cultures, and the Nam Center for Korean Studies supported my family and me during our most difficult times. I thank Donald Lopez, Daniel Herbert, Christopher McNamara, Caryl Flinn, Mark Kligerman, Irhe Sohn, Philip Hallman, Mary Lou Chipala, Carrie Moore, Marga Schuhwerk-Hampel, Juhn Ahn, Hunjin Jung, David Chung, Kevin Park, Dae-Hee Kwak, Do-hee Morsman, Jiyoung Lee, Hoon Lee, Adrienne Janney, and Yunah Sung. My colleagues at Nanyang Technological University (NTU) are exceptionally supportive. I am immensely grateful for the kindness and support I receive from my colleagues at Wee Kim Wee School of Communication and Information, NTU. I am grateful most of all to my chairperson, Charles T. Salmon, who has been supportive of my research since my first day at WKW, but also to my cinema and cultural studies colleagues, Liew Kai Khiun, Stephen Teo, Nikki Draper, Ian Dixon, Sheersha Perera, Kym Campbell, Ella Raidel, Huh Chul, Ross Williams, Ben Slater, Ben Shedd, Nicole Midori Woodford, Kristy Kang, Chu Kiu-wai, and Ting Chun Chun, and to two of my senior mentors, Rich Ling and Gerard Goggin. I am deeply grateful to NTU's Korean professors—Jung Younbo, Nuri Kim, Hye-kyung Kim, Hyun-jin Kang, Myo-jung Chung, Won-sun Shin, Jin Cheon Na, Poong Oh, Kwan Min Lee, Joo-young Hong, Wonkeun Chang, Hajung Chin, Soo-hyun Lee—who have always been there for my family and me. They have made our lives in Singapore easier and more meaningful.

Earlier drafts of some material contained in this book have appeared in the following publications, and I am grateful to their respective editors and publishers for their kind permission to include this work: "The Asia Foundation's Motion Picture Project and the Cultural Cold War in Asia," *Film History* 29, vol. 2 (2017): 108–37; "Creating an Anti-Communist Motion Picture Producers' Network in Asia: The Asia Foundation, Asia Pictures, and the Korean Motion Picture Cultural Association," *Historical Journal of Film, Radio, and Television* 37, vol. 3 (2017): 517–38; and "The Emergence of the Asian Film Festival: Cold War Asia and Japan's Re-entrance to the Regional Market in the 1950s," in *The Oxford Handbook of Japanese Cinema*, ed. Miyao Daisuke (Oxford University Press, 2012): 232–50. I am grateful to those who helped me acquire the rights to reproduce valuable family and archival photographs, maps, posters, and official figures: Cho Junhyoung (Korean Film Archive), Amy Ovalle (the Asia Foundation), Jeannette Paulson Hereniko (Hawaii International Film Festival), Sean Bridgeman (National Film and Sound Archive of Australia), Suhan Pansha (Federation of Motion Picture Producers in Asia-Pacific), Melissa S. Mead (Rare Books, Special Collections and Preservation Department, University of Rochester), Hidenori Okada and Makiko Kamiya (National Film Archive of Japan), National Archive of Singapore, Chris Wong Han Min and Chew Tee Pao (Asian Film Archive), and Bobbi Johnson-Tanner, who allowed me to include a precious photo of her late father, Charles M. Tanner.

At Cornell University Press, I thank Paul Kramer, Michael McGandy, Bethany Wasik, and Clare Jones for their enthusiasm about this book and their professionalism. Allison Van Deventer, Julia Cook, Dina Dineva, and Jennifer Dana Savran Kelly offered amazing guidance in crafting the language of the manuscript.

This work would not have been possible without the generous financial assistance of several entities. I am indebted to the Nam Center for Korean Studies, the Department of Screen Arts and Cultures, and the Department of Asian Language and Cultures at the University of Michigan; the College of Arts and Social Sciences at the Australian National University; and the College of Humanities, Arts, and Social Sciences and Wee Kim Wee School of Communication and Information at Nanyang Technological University for their research support. The research for this book was supported by Nanyang Technological University's Start-Up Grant (M4081574.060) and the MOE AcRF Tier 1 Grant funded by the Ministry of Education, Singapore (MOE) (04MNP000412C440).

My closing words of thanks go to my family. My wife Jungyoun has supported my studies with patience, understanding, and love. It is impossible to put into words what she has meant to me. Our daughter Bohm came to us when we had just settled in Singapore. She is an inspiration who continues to enrich our lives. I dedicate this book to Jungyoun and Bohm, the two women I love most. Finally, I would like to thank my parents Lee Eui-Choon and Kim Sung-Ki and my two sisters Eun-Sook and Eun-Kyung, who have never stopped believing in me.

Abbreviations

AFPFL	Anti-Fascist People's Freedom League
AFL	American Federation of Labor
AMPP	ASEAN Motion Picture Producers Association
APEC	Asia-Pacific Economic Cooperation
ASEAN	Association of Southeast Asian Nations
CCF	Congress for Cultural Freedom
CEPA	Closer Economic Partnership Arrangement
CFA	Committee for a Free Asia
CFE	Committee for a Free Europe
CIE	Civil Information and Education Section
CMPC	Central Motion Picture Corporation
CMPE	Central Motion Picture Exchange
DPRK	Democratic People's Republic of Korea (North Korea)
ECA	Economic Cooperation Administration
ECAFE	Economic Commission of Asia and the Far East
ECOSOC	United Nations Economic and Social Council

ESA	Economic Stabilization Agency
FPA	Federation of Motion Picture Producers in Southeast Asia
GMP	Grand Motion Picture Company
HICOG	US High Commissioner for Germany
HIFF	Hawaii International Film Festival
ICC	East West Center's Institute of Culture and Communication
IFFI	International Film Festival of India
IFFPA	International Federation of Film Producers Association
KMPPA	Korean Motion Picture Producer's Association
KMPCA	Korean Motion Picture Cultural Association
MPAA	Motion Picture Association of America
MPEA	Motion Picture Export Association
MP&GI	Motion Picture and General Investment
MPPDA	Motion Picture Producers and Distributors of America
NATO	North Atlantic Treaty Organization
OPC	Office of Policy Coordination
OSS	Office of Strategic Services
PRC	People's Republic of China
RFA	Radio Free Asia
RFE	Radio Free Europe
ROK	Republic of Korea
SEATO	Southeast Asia Treaty Organization
SFIFF	San Francisco International Film Festival
SWG	Screen Writers Guild
TAF	The Asia Foundation
TCA	Technical Cooperation Administration
UNKRA	United Nations Korean Reconstruction Agency
USIA	United States Information Agency
USIS	United States Information Service
VOA	Voice of America
WBC	World Buddhist Congress
WFB	World Fellowship of Buddhists

CINEMA AND THE CULTURAL COLD WAR

Introduction

The Cultural Cold War and the Birth
of the Asian Cinema Network

We cannot expect that we can make all of the people of the world love us all of the time. In the interest of our security and world peace, from time to time we have to do things that some people do not like.

—Allen W. Dulles, Deputy Director of the Central Intelligence Agency ("Strengthening American Information Efforts," at the *Propaganda and the Cold War Symposium*, Princeton University, 1963)

SOS Hong Kong (*SOS Hongk'ong*, Ch'oe Kyŏng-ok, 1966), a Shin Films (South Korea) and Lankwang Pictures (Hong Kong) coproduction, begins with newsreel footage that displays the South Korean navy's heroic battles in Vietnam.[1] It is not widely known that between 1964 and 1972, South Korea dispatched over three hundred thousand troops to the Vietnam War, making it the second-largest contributor of troops to South Vietnam after the United States.[2] After the combat footage and a speech by President Park Chung Hee (1963–79) to the soldiers, the film's hero, a South Korean special agent named Paek Min (played by Pak No-sik), leaves for Hong Kong with a special mission to stop North Korean spies from selling information about the South Korean troops to China. Soon afterward, Paek reaches the Hong

Kong–based arms dealer Sha Lao-te through the courtesan Xianglan (played by Helen Li Mei), a queen of Hong Kong's nightclub scene who works for North Korea, and her vast network of social connections. Xianglan falls in love with Paek, her enemy, who in turn is falling for Taiwan's "Double Horse" agent, Maria (played by Ting Ying). Already consumed with jealousy and now perturbed by increasing pressure from her boss (played by Yi Min), Xianglan lures Paek and Maria to the nightclub, where their adversaries lie in wait. But she gets cold feet and puts her life at stake to pull Paek out of danger. Xianglan's boss, secretly in love with her, had proposed that they live together in Pyongyang, North Korea. Now deeply saddened, he asks Xianglan if she knows the consequence of betraying her country. She shouts with confidence, "Of course I know. But I realize it's meaningless to live without *freedom!*" Xianglan is shot by her boss and eventually dies. After her death, Paek returns to save Maria, and they seize the microfilm from the North Korean villains. Having accomplished his task, Agent Paek returns to South Korea.[3]

In South Korean espionage films produced at the peak of the genre in the mid-1960s, South Korean agents are almost always dispatched to Hong Kong. In many cases, as in *SOS Hong Kong*, they team up with female Taiwanese agents, their Hong Kong counterparts, or Korean American Central Intelligence Agency (CIA) agents. In other words, Hong Kong was the place where the communist forces of North Korea and China set up their secret units and operated covertly in underground bunkers to dismantle the capitalist societies of "Free Asia," namely South Korea, Taiwan, and Japan. The South Korean "James Bond," the nation's Cold War warrior, fought for South Korea's strategic and ideological allies.

Scarcely two decades earlier, however, the popular espionage novel *Typhoon* (*T'aep'ung*, 1942–43) showed a completely different world. Written in Chosŏn (the old name for Korea) by the novelist Kim Nae-sŏng and set in 1939, two years before the Pacific War, *Typhoon* depicts an intelligence war for the latest weapon of mass destruction, fought by Chosŏn, Japan, Germany, China, the UK, and the United States. *Typhoon's* protagonist, the young detective Yu Bulan (an homage to Maurice Leblanc, the French novelist who created Arsène Lupin), travels beyond the boundaries of colonial Chosŏn: to Marseilles, Liverpool, Delhi, Colombo, and Shanghai, working on behalf of the Japanese colonial power. The logic of Japan's Greater East Asian Co-Prosperity Sphere (*Dai toa kyoeiken*), which Japan used to instill a sense of bonding with and among its colonies, appears to have expanded the author's geopolitical imagination—after all, *Typhoon* was written in the wake of Japan's attack on Pearl Harbor in December 1941.[4] After Korea was liberated from Japan in August 1945, however, the geopolitical boundaries of the new nation left no room for Kim's transnational imagination. The world around the writer had changed completely. Japan had surrendered to the West. Korea was divided into two states—North and South. Moreover, the "evil forces" of the West were now the nation's new mentors. Kim's new country, the Republic of Korea, resided in the United States, the seat of the world order that had drawn the new map of "free Asia."

In the early 1950s, threatened by the expansion of communism throughout the region and particularly by the establishment of the People's Republic of China (PRC), the ascending popularity of communism in Southeast Asia, and the outbreak of the Korean War (1950–53), the US government believed it necessary to construct a military bulwark and a "free Asia" bloc in the region. Lazar Kaganovich, a Soviet politician and first deputy chairman of the Council of Ministers (1953–57), proclaimed in 1954 that "if the nineteenth century was a century of capitalism, the twentieth century is a century of the triumph of socialism and communism" and asserted that the Soviets' influence was spreading rapidly across Asia.[5] To counter this influence, the United States constructed the Western bloc, a term that refers to the countries allied with the United States and the North Atlantic Treaty Organization (NATO) against the Soviet Union and the Warsaw Pact (1955). As part of this bloc, the US-driven "free Asia" alliance contained vast networks of newly sovereign nation-states. Ranging from the Philippines and Indonesia to South Korea, Taiwan, and Japan, this anticommunist bloc was controlled by the new hegemonic regime, the United States, via financial and cultural domination that disseminated the American way of life. Bruce Cumings calls this bloc an "archipelago of empire" that effectively established a "territorial empire."[6] According to this logic, Japan emerged as an adopted and "enlightened" child of the United States and a financially self-sufficient "big brother" in the metastable regional entity. Remarkably, in just two decades, the animosity toward the Japanese empire during the occupation period had given way to fear of communism, resulting in a new consensus dubbed the anti-Red matrix. Within this new regional order, the cultural arenas of the various "free Asia" countries, and particularly their motion picture industries, were closely linked.

The first signs of a regional Asian film industry had in fact appeared in Japan in the 1930s and were deeply tied to Japan's imperial ambitions across the region. The "Greater East Asian Cinema" (*Dai toa eiga*) operated under the Japanese empire's "New Filmic System" design, in which each colony was linked to the others under the slogan of "the Greater East Asian Co-Prosperity Sphere."[7] This ambitious network ended with the Japanese surrender. The idea of creating a regional cinema network, however, was revived in the mid-1950s with a new outfit: the Asian Film Festival and its mother organization, the Federation of Motion Picture Producers in Southeast Asia (FPA). Founded in 1953, the FPA was the first postwar pan-Asian film organization. A year later, its annual event, the Southeast Asian Film Festival (renamed the Asian Film Festival in 1957), was held in Tokyo for the first time. The Japanese film executive Nagata Masaichi (1906–85), president of Daiei Studio, was the FPA's founding force and first president. Nonetheless, the FPA and its film festival should not be viewed as simply a perpetuation of Japan's unfinished colonial business. Instead, this new regional alliance was, in the words of Markus Nornes, tempered "by the legacy of Japanese imperialism and the overwhelming power of bilateral relationships with the United States."[8] In fact, the FPA was a platform of a US-designed "free Asia" motion picture network that I call the "anticommunist motion picture producers' alliance" in Cold War Asia.[9] This new network received financial and administrative support from US institutions, particularly a San Francisco–based philanthropic organization called The Committee for a Free Asia (renamed The Asia Foundation in 1954).

This book is a history of postwar Asian cinema. I am not, however, telling a comprehensive story of the films, filmmakers, and cinematic movements of the region. Rather, this is the first book-length examination of the historical, social, cultural, and intellectual constitution of the first postwar pan-Asian cinema network during the two decades after the Korean War armistice in July 1953. I argue that Asia's film cultures and industries were shaped by the practice of transnational collaboration and competition between newly independent and colonial states, with financial and administrative support from US institutions. More specifically, this book looks at the network of motion picture executives, creative personnel, policy makers, and intellectuals in Asia at the height of the Cold War and beyond. It shows how they aspired to rationalize and industrialize a system of mass production by initiating a regional organization, cohosting film festivals, coproducing films, and exchanging stars, directors, and key staff to expand the market and raise the competitiveness of their products. I claim that this network was the offspring of Cold War cultural politics and American hegemony. While providing financial and administrative aid to the film industries and supporting intellectuals and anticommunist cultural producers in Asia, US agencies—the Asia Foundation (TAF) in particular—actively intervened in

Figure 0.1. Official poster for the first film festival in Southeast Asia, May 1954. It was held in Tokyo from May 8 to 15. This film festival started as the Southeast Asian Film Festival and was subsequently renamed twice, first as the Asian Film Festival in 1957, then as the Asia-Pacific Film Festival in 1983. Photo courtesy of the Federation of Motion Picture Producers in Asia-Pacific (FPA).

every sector of Asia's film cultures and industries during the 1950s. The presence of the Asia Foundation is particularly important here. With a clear and consistent vision of "free Asia," the field agents of this philanthropic organization, founded in 1951, encouraged "native" film producers and directors to fight against the communist forces, with proper guidance from the foundation's motion picture officers and Hollywood's anticommunist veterans. The culmination of their efforts was the inauguration of the FPA.

The FPA was for at least its first two decades the single most important pan-Asian film industry organization.[10] Its annual event, the Asian Film Festival, was unique in that it was hosted in neither a single city nor a single country. Instead, this film festival adopted a peripatetic system that moved it from country to country each year; no member country was allowed to accommodate the festival in two consecutive years. From the beginning, then, the Asian Film Festival was not a conventional film festival, but rather a regional alliance summit for the region's film executives, accompanied by screenings of each participant's annual outputs, a series of forums, and film equipment fairs and exhibitions. Public screenings were not offered. Previous studies claim that the festival was primarily a "public relations event for the industries" and that its aim was "to become the Asian equivalent of the Cannes and Venice Film Festivals, a prestigious event at which filmmakers competed and made business deals."[11] These views have been echoed by other historians of postwar Asian cinema. However, by treating the history of the Asian Film Festival as a struggle between a few motion picture studios and executives in Japan and Hong Kong, previous studies have depoliticized the significance of the FPA and its secret alliance with the Asia Foundation. In fact, the underlying aim of the FPA was "to protect 'free Asia' from the invasion of the communist forces throughout cinema."[12] The Asia Foundation's clandestine financial backing of the FPA and many of its individual members is now coming to light for the first time.

Despite their historical significance, the FPA and its annual film festival have not received the scrutiny they deserve.[13] While preparing for the Asian Film Festival's fiftieth anniversary in 2005, Rais Yatim, Malaysia's minister of culture, arts and heritage (2004–8), lamented the paucity of available primary materials. He wrote that "no one man or entity keeps in store the 50 years struggle and the success of the festival."[14] Likewise, film festival studies in Asia, particularly of the pre-1990s period, have yielded few results. This is partly because the festivals do not fit comfortably within the rigid borders of national cinema studies; furthermore, film festivals in Asia are still a new field of inquiry.[15] Indeed, the Asia Film Festival, the FPA, and other

Figure 0.2. The official logo of the Federation of Motion Picture Producers in Southeast Asia (FPA). Photo courtesy of the Federation of Motion Picture Producers in Asia-Pacific.

equally important festivals and regional organizations in this period were seldom bound to a single nation. Most of them were regionally constructed entities, closely tied to nongovernmental organizations or the cultural policies of postwar US hegemony. In view of this situation, the present book sheds new light on the field of cultural Cold War studies.

Over the past two decades, much research has been published on the clandestine psychological warfare programs developed by the US government at the height of the Cold War. Kenneth Osgood and Laura A. Belmonte delve into the ways the Truman-Eisenhower administrations wielded propaganda and campaigns to influence public opinion.[16] The pivotal work in this area is Frances Saunders's *The Cultural Cold War*, which was published in 2000. Saunders examined how the CIA funded intellectual magazines, musical performances, art exhibitions, and the like to be used as "weapons" against the

Soviet Union and its allies.[17] A closely related body of work has since then documented the cultural conflict between the Soviet Union and the Western democracies. Greg Barnhisel, in his study of modernist art and literature's role in Cold War diplomacy, argues that "modernism" became a weapon in what has become known as the "cultural Cold War," the struggle for cultural prestige and influence between the Soviet-led Eastern and the US-led Western blocs. Cultural diplomats during the 1950s, Barnhisel argues, presented American modernism in painting, literature, architecture, and music as "evidence of the high cultural achievement of the United States."[18] The Eisenhower administration (1953–61) made use of the President's Emergency Fund for International Affairs to subsidize trade fair presentation by private industry, US national exhibitions in Europe and the Soviet Union, publications, and tours abroad by artistic groups. The US State Department's Cultural Presentations program likewise sent its finest performers of modern dance and ballet, classical music, rock 'n' roll, folk, blues, and jazz to Asia, the Middle East, Africa, and the Soviet Union to win the hearts and minds of the Third World and to counter perceptions of American racism.

In the realm of cinema and audiovisual studies, recent studies have provided new insights into US radio propaganda during the Truman-Eisenhower era by tracing the histories of the troubled existence of the Voice of America (VOA) and the CIA's clandestine sponsorship of Radio Free Europe/Radio Liberty. For their part, film historians have revealed how the CIA worked covertly with Hollywood during the Cold War. Tony Shaw, who works on the cultural Cold War and cinema, investigates the complex relationship among filmmakers, censors, politicians, and government propagandists in *Hollywood's Cold War* and discusses British cinema's contribution to Cold War propaganda in *British Cinema and the Cold War*.[19] Andrew J. Falk and John Sbardellati provide new perspectives on Hollywood's involvement with Joseph McCarthy and the House Un-American Activities Committee. Sbardellati uncovers the breadth and impact of the investigative activities of the Federal Bureau of Investigation (FBI) in the motion picture industry from 1942 to 1958, showing how the former FBI director J. Edgar Hoover became obsessed with the idea of subversion on the silver screen. It was Hoover and his FBI who decided that communists, anarchists, and other left-wing film artists were determined to turn Hollywood's ideologically "correct" films into propaganda vehicles. Falk tells a story of Hollywood and television artists who persisted despite this in expressing controversial views about international relations. These artists, whom Falk aptly names America's "new negotiators," used their influence in cultural affairs to address issues including the developing conflict with the Soviet Union, the atomic bomb, foreign aid, Palestine, anticolonial movements, and the United Nations (UN).[20] In highlighting how the US film industry functioned as one of the cultural sectors of the state-corporate network during the Cold War, a significant number of studies have scrutinized the Motion Picture Export Association (MPEA), formerly the Motion Picture Producers and Distributors of America (MPPDA), and its global businesses in the Soviet Union, Eastern Europe, Turkey, Germany, and Spain, along with the distribution of Soviet films in the United States during this period.[21]

Historians of Hollywood and European cinema might be surprised, however, to discover how little has been written about American involvement in Asian cinema during the cultural Cold War. Although the Cold War was by definition a global conflict and the United States confronted both the Soviet Union and China on the Asian periphery, Asia has often been glossed over in the cultural Cold War literature, most of which focuses on US cultural policy and is concerned with the European theater.[22] Scholarship on the Cold War in Asia has certainly been growing. However, very little of this scholarship deals with cultural matters, and film cultures and industries in Asia during the Cold War have largely been overlooked. Moreover, little attention has been paid to the significance of the Asia Foundation and its clandestine activities in the cultural fields. It is also true that the FPA's intimate network with the Asia Foundation, like the presence of the FPA itself, has been almost entirely omitted or simply forgotten in the emerging literature on the history of Asian cinema. Drawing on records of the Asia Foundation, the FPA, and the Asian Film Festival, this book is a novel attempt to reconstruct Asian film history. This history is not a linear narrative of the relevant nations' cinematic heritage or a close analysis of selected canonical opuses. Rather, it adopts a transnational and regional approach to the region's film cultures and industries in the context of new economic conditions, shared postwar experiences, Cold War politics, US cultural diplomacy, and intensified cultural flows in Asia.[23]

This pioneering study is divided into two parts, titled "The First Network" and "The Second Network." Each part aims at a different level of discussion, although the two levels are tightly connected. "The First Network" begins and ends with the Asia Foundation. Roughly from 1953 to the early 1960s, during the Eisenhower administration, this nongovernmental philanthropic organization surreptitiously supported anticommunist motion picture industry personnel, ranging from producers, directors, and technicians to critics and writers in Japan, Hong Kong, Burma (Myanmar),

Ceylon (Sri Lanka), South Korea, and the Chinese diasporas in Southeast Asia, as well as American and British motion picture producers in Malaysia and Thailand. What the Asia Foundation's motion picture project aimed at was to construct an alliance of anticommunist motion picture producers in Asia and to use the network as an anticommunist force to win the psychological war against the Soviet Union and China. The first part in this book, accordingly, identifies the cultural, economic, and political logic that gave rise to and modified the FPA and the Southeast Asian Film Festival. It argues that the history of the organization, at least in the first several years, was the product of US-driven Cold War politics that delineated the new map of "free Asia," an anticommunist bloc controlled by a new hegemonic regime: the United States.

More specifically, the Asia Foundation supported Japan's Nagata Masaichi, the producer of the Oscar-winning film *Rashomon* (Kurosawa Akira, 1951), in his bid to become a leader of the "free Asia" film industries. Nagata initiated the FPA, hosted the Asian Film Festival, and helped film producers and technicians in the FPA member countries train their peers in the latest film technologies, including color cinematography, developing, sound design, and modern acting skills. In addition, the experienced technicians of Daiei Studio received guidance from a Hollywood screenwriter chosen by the foundation's motion picture team. The Asia Foundation also produced a Burmese-language anticommunist film, *The People Win Through* (*Ludu Aung Than*, George Seitz Jr., 1953), and indirectly financed nine feature films in Hong Kong by pouring US dollars throughout the 1950s into Asia Pictures, the project of a local journalist, Chang Kuo-sin (1916–2006). South Korea was another beneficiary. South Korea's Korean Motion Picture Cultural Association (KMPCA), in fact, received almost the entire budget of the association's early operations.

With core motion picture projects in Japan, Hong Kong, and South Korea as well as small and ad hoc projects in Burma, Ceylon, and the Philippines, the Asia Foundation and its passionate motion picture officers—Charles M. Tanner (1919–2006), John Miller (1915–?), Noel F. Busch (1906–85), and James L. Stewart (1913–2006), none of whom had any professional training in the motion picture industry to speak of—invested enormous energy in Asia's film industries. At times, they brought in Hollywood Cold War veterans such as Cecil B. DeMille (1881–1959), Frank Capra (1897–1991), Frank Borzage (1894–1962), and Luigi Luraschi (1906–2002) as project advisors. The Asia Foundation's motion picture project team firmly believed that a little help from Hollywood would immensely increase the production quality of Asia's native films. Once improved, these films could travel to the American film market, which would ultimately benefit what they perceived as Asia's less-developed film industries. Using its San Francisco network, the Asia Foundation introduced select Asian films, particularly foundation-funded films, at the newly launched San Francisco International Film Festival, which had been started in 1957 by the local film exhibitor Irving M. "Bud" Levin (1916–95). The Asia Foundation saw the San Francisco festival as a gateway to Hollywood.

At the end of the 1950s, however, the San Francisco office of the Asia Foundation decided to decrease its involvement with the FPA and significantly cut the budgets for most of its motion picture projects in Asia. The Asia Foundation could not fully achieve its initial goals. Many factors contributed to the disappointment of its motion picture operations, but most important, the foundation's core collaborators in Asia were not capable of leading the regional organizations. Many of them had insufficient experience in filmmaking. Their films attracted neither local audiences nor Hollywood's sophisticated foreign film distributors. Furthermore, the film industries in Asia had been growing rapidly without America's direct help during the latter half of the 1950s. South Korea, Taiwan, and Hong Kong experienced a "Golden Age" of cinema in the 1960s, when each country churned out over two hundred films per year. The Asia Foundation gradually reduced the scope of its motion picture project and terminated the operation entirely in the early 1960s.

Nevertheless, the FPA network did not disappear. When the Asia Foundation's Cold War mission ended, a new network emerged. The new network, which I call the "Asian Studio Network," used the existing regional and interregional links that TAF and a group of anticommunist motion picture producers had vigorously struggled to create and maintain throughout the preceding decade. "The Second Network" begins at this critical juncture. This section argues that the new motion picture studio network in "East Asia"—Hong Kong, South Korea, Taiwan, and Japan—did not emerge out of the blue.

During the 1960s, the FPA gradually took a new direction. The most conspicuous change arrived in the form of state intrusion, especially from South Korea and Taiwan. The map of the regional film industry also changed. The once powerful Southeast Asian film industries largely disappeared from the Asian Film Festival's annual line-ups in the 1960s. Instead, East Asian film moguls—Run Run Shaw (1907–2014; Hong Kong and Malaysia), Loke Wan-tho (1915–64; Singapore and Hong Kong), Shin Sang-ok (1926–2006; South

Korea), Li Han-hsiang (1926–96; Taiwan and Hong Kong), and Henry Gong Hong (1915–2004; Taiwan)—came to dominate the festival and the FPA. Interestingly enough, none of them received any financial or administrative support from the Asia Foundation except Run Run Shaw. Manuel de Leon of the Philippines was likely the only influential Southeast Asian film producer still participating in the FPA during this decade.

The two chapters in the second part of this book, accordingly, examine the Asian studio network as a cultural and industrial phenomenon in Cold War, colonial, and postcolonial Asia. Chapter 6 explores Shin Films, which was the largest motion picture studio of its time in South Korea. During its two decades of operation, from 1952 to 1975, Shin Films was owned, controlled, and managed by Shin Sang-ok, who bore complete responsibility for all of the products that Shin Films distributed. Shin was a director, a producer, and a studio executive who was deeply involved with the military government's film policies. This chapter scrutinizes Shin Films' business and management structure, aesthetic styles, mode of production, political relations with the Park Chung Hee government, and transnational networks with the FPA. The seventh and final chapter continues where chapter 6 leaves off, expanding its temporal and spatial boundaries into the global sphere. With the unexpected success of the Shaw Brothers' medium-budget production *Five Fingers of Death* (*tian xia di yi quan*, Chŏng Ch'ang-hwa, 1972; also known as *King Boxer*) in the United States in 1973, American media conglomerates turned their attention to Asia. Seeking to maximize profits, they poured capital into this region to secure kung fu films for global distribution. Hong Kong, as a cultural producer of kung fu films, generated the so-called "kung fu craze" in the context of the political undercurrent of United States-China normalization, epitomized by Nixon's visit to the PRC in 1971.

By then, the powerful studios of the 1960s—Shin Films, Central Motion Picture Corporation (CMPC), Grand Motion Picture Company (GMP; Guolian), and Motion Picture and General Investment (MP&GI)—were all declining, for various reasons. MP&GI had to cut down its film production after the untimely death of its president Loke Wan-tho during the 1964 Asian Film Festival in Taipei. Li Han-hsiang left GMP in 1970, and Shin Films was forced to shut down its business in 1975. With the success of kung fu films worldwide, however, Shaw Brothers and the newly launched Golden Harvest studio finally found a way to reach out to the world beyond Asia. The Asia Foundation's motion picture team and most Asian film moguls had anticipated such an opportunity for decades. The desire of the Hong Kong film industry to expand into the global arena, beyond the traditional market of

Chinese-speaking communities in Southeast Asia that Shaw Brothers and MP&GI had controlled since the mid-1950s, led to the possibility of constructing a global identity. Shaw's desire to extend its market to non-Asian territory—that is, Hollywood—was finally fulfilled. But the opportunity didn't last long.

Competing with television and facing the waning of the kung fu craze in the global market as well as the unexpected death of Bruce Lee (1940–73), the Hong Kong film industry decreased its global collaborations considerably. Once affluent and influential, the Asian cinema network virtually disappeared in the late 1970s. Since then, the rich history of Asia's first pan-Asian film industry network, which lasted over two decades, has been largely forgotten—until today.

And the story begins now.

Part I

The First Network

Chapter 1

The Asia Foundation's Motion Picture Project

On December 17, 1953, Charles M. Tanner, the Hollywood liaison of the Asia Foundation (TAF), a San Francisco-based philanthropic organization, was having lunch with two Hollywood magnates: Frank Capra, a celebrated Hollywood director-producer, and Luigi Luraschi, the head of foreign and domestic censorship at Paramount Studios. Before this meeting, Tanner had convened with Hollywood heavyweights such as Cecil B. DeMille, Herbert J. Yates, and a group of first-tier Hollywood scriptwriters, including Winston Miller, Leonard Spigelgass, Allen Rivkin, and Morris Ryskind.[1] Carleton W. Alsop, an ex-CIA agent, acted as mediator.[2] The meeting had been arranged by Luraschi's office at Paramount.[3]

The Asia Foundation, formerly known as the Committee for a Free Asia, was a private non-profit organization incorporated under the laws of the state of California in 1951.[4] Its primary aim, according to its mission statement, was to make "a significant contribution to development in Asia and to Asian-American understanding and friendship."[5] Tanner, a former United States Information Service (USIS) motion picture officer, was working at TAF's headquarters in San Francisco. This was his second mission to Hollywood since he had been hired in May 1953. This time, TAF head office had given him the task of consulting with some of the American film industry's most powerful, gifted, and ideologically "appropriate" personnel to discover whether Hollywood was willing to support the TAF's newly launched project in the Asian motion picture industry. Tanner had a particular subject in mind: the Southeast Asian Film Festival, scheduled to be held in Tokyo in May 1954. The Southeast Asian Film Festival was an annual event of the Federation of Motion Picture Producers in Southeast Asia (FPA), a pan-Asian organization recently established by the Japanese film executive Nagata Masaichi, president of Daiei Studio in Japan. While meeting with Capra and Luraschi, Tanner asked them to help sponsor the Southeast Asian Film Festival by convincing the Motion Picture Association of America (MPAA) to donate the festival's first prize, a 35 mm Mitchell movie camera. In fact, TAF had already purchased the camera and was ready to ship it to Tokyo; apparently it was looking only for the MPAA's illustrious label.[6] Tanner also asked that some of the industry's celebrities be present at the festival as Hollywood representatives. Capra and DeMille were undoubtedly Tanner's top choices. Their fervent anticommunism has been well documented.[7]

As a film consultant to the recently created USIS and one of the founding members of the National Committee for a Free Europe, DeMille was a Cold War conservative who, according to Nora Sayre, firmly believed there was "a Red band encircling the earth."[8] Less than two years earlier, *Greatest Show on Earth* (1951), one of DeMille's signature extravaganza films, had been shown at the International Film Festival of India (IFFI), held in Bombay from January 24 to February 1, 1952.[9] Four other American entries, *An American in Paris* (Vincent Minnelli, 1951), *Alice in Wonderland* (Clyde Geronimi, Wilfred Jackson, and Hamilton Luske, 1951), *Bright Victory* (Mark Robson, 1951), and Jean Renoir's France-India-America coproduction *The River* (1951), had also been introduced to Indian audiences during the festival.[10] IFFI was the first international film festival held anywhere in Asia. It showed about fifty feature films and seventy-five documentaries from twenty-three countries, including Italy, Japan, China, the UK, France, the USSR, and the United States.[11] Other notable films screened at the festival were *Bicycle Thieves* (*Ladri di biciclette*, Vittorio De Sica, Italy, 1948), *Miracle in Milan* (*Miracolo a Milano*, Vittorio De Sica, Italy, 1951), *Rome, Open City* (*Roma città aperta*, Roberto Rossellini, Italy, 1945), *Orpheus* (*Orphée*, Jean Cocteau, France, 1950), *The Trap* (*Past*, Martin Frič, Czechoslovakia, 1950), *Yukiwarisoo* (Minoru Matsui, Japan, 1939), *The White Haired Girl* (*Bai Mao Nu*, Wang Bin and Shui Hua, China, 1950), *The Dancing Fleece* (Frederick Wilson, UK, 1950), *Mussorgsky* (*Musorgskiy*, Griogri Roshal, USSR, 1950), and *The Fall of Berlin* (*Padeniye Berlina*, Mikheil Chiaureli, USSR, 1950).[12] K. L. Khandpur, senior director of the film division in

India, characterized this event as historic, claiming that "it was . . . the first time that the Indian film industry was exposed to such a vast range of outstanding films of [the] postwar era."[13] Kishore Valicha argues that this "exposure" resulted in a "more serious and, in artistic terms, a more articulate kind of Indian film," such as Bimal Roy's *Do Bigha Zamin* (1953) and *Devdas* (1955) and Guru Dutt's *Kaagaz Ke Phool* (1959).[14]

At IFFI, Frank Capra, known as a "fighter against communism," represented the US film industry.[15] He gave talks on technique, organization, and story value during the festival.[16] At the time, Capra was a member of the President's Advisory Committee, which advised the State Department on how best to present the United States' image in the information media, including radio, television, and motion pictures. Capra saw the Cold War as "a death struggle between the free world and the slave world . . . a battle for the minds of men."[17] Chester Bowles, the US ambassador to India and Nepal, had solicited Capra to attend IFFI to help gauge the level of Soviet and

Figure 1.1. The first International Film Festival of India (IFFI) was held in 1952, and American director Frank Capra (a man wearing a gray hat in the front row) attended as a part of the US delegation. The IFFI was inaugurated by the Indian prime minister, Jawaharlal Nehru (middle of the front row), on January 24, 1952. *March of India* 4, no. 4 (March–April 1952): 5.

Chinese influence on India. Besides Capra, Ingrid Bergman and Gene Tierney had been invited, but at the last moment, they could not attend. Hence, it was Capra, Kenneth McEldowney (producer of *The River*), Harry Stone (an MPAA officer), and Floyde E. Brooker (audio visual chief of the Mutual Security Agency) who attended in their place as the American film industry representatives.[18] As Nitin Govil argues, Capra's attendance at the festival was "one of many coordinated displays of geopolitical friendship between the United States and India."[19] It also, however, suggests a new perspective on US cultural diplomacy in Asia at the height of the Cold War. Surprisingly, Capra was under scrutiny by the House Un-American Activities Committee (HUAC), having been blacklisted under suspicion of being a communist or communist sympathizer.[20] Just before IFFI, he was cleared of all charges.

For Capra, consequently, attending IFFI was a chance to display acts of patriotism that would prove his strong anticommunism. This was Capra's chance to go back to Hollywood. Capra noticed the presence of "commies" at the festival.[21] In his autobiography, he wrote, "I warned Festival officials I was not here to be sucked into any Commie plots. I was here to beat their brains out if I could and for no other reason."[22] Capra wrote afterward to DeMille, "The Russians have a large delegation of some 15 people here, and the Chinese about ten. Also there are delegates from Hungary and Czechoslovakia. . . . We need all the help we can get to hold our own here on their battleground."[23] Capra was likewise enthusiastic about the trip to Japan. He even suggested that "not one man should go but a team" to increase Hollywood's influence over the Japanese movie industry and to combat communist motion picture activities in Asia.[24] All in all, Tanner's mission to Hollywood promised to be fruitful, and it seemed certain that some of Hollywood's big names, like Capra and DeMille, would come to Japan to throw their weight behind the FPA.

Nevertheless, TAF's undertaking in Hollywood raises a number of questions. Nagata Masaichi and other film executives in the region had founded the FPA. Its objective, according to the FPA's official letter, was to "promote the motion picture industry in the countries of Southeast Asia and to raise the artistic and technical standards of motion pictures and ensure cultural dissemination and interchange of motion pictures in the Far East."[25] Given this objective, what was the logic behind Tanner's meetings with Hollywood producers, directors, writers, and executives in support of the FPA? For what purpose, likewise, did TAF become involved in the formation of the FPA and its annual film festival? Who was Tanner, and why were the Paramount executive Luraschi and prominent Hollywood directors like Capra and DeMille attached to TAF's activities? What were the consequences of TAF's motion picture projects, and how did the film industry in Asia respond?

Although TAF was ostensibly a private, nongovernmental foundation, in reality it was quietly subsidized in large part—perhaps even completely—by the US government and the CIA. Because of this support, it should rather be called a "quasi-nongovernmental organization."[26] TAF's CIA connection was not publicly acknowledged until 1967, when *Ramparts* magazine published a special report on the CIA's funding of various cultural and educational organizations. The *New York Times* simultaneously published a series of reports revealing the covert CIA sponsorship of "an astonishing variety of other US citizen groups engaged in Cold War propaganda battlefields with communist fronts."[27] The Congress for Cultural Freedom (CCF) was the *Times'* primary target, but TAF was also included, although it was considered less controversial than the CCF,.[28] Like other nongovernmental philanthropic institutions that operated in the battle for hearts and minds, such as Beacon, Kaplan, Appalachian, and the Borden Trust, TAF was a camouflaged association shaped and carried out by the CIA, following the direction of the US government's foreign cultural policy. Victor Marchetti, a former CIA employee, alleges that the foundation had the objective of "disseminat[ing] throughout Asia a negative vision of Mainland China, North Vietnam, and North Korea," and continues, "[The Asia Foundation] sponsored scholarly research, supported conferences and symposia, and ran an academic exchange program, a CIA subsidy that reached 8 million dollars a year."[29]

With a view to exploring how US government–led Cold War cultural policies influenced the Asian regional film industry in the 1950s, this chapter investigates how and to what extent TAF and its field agents covertly acted to construct an alliance of anticommunist motion picture producers in Asia. It also scrutinizes the ways TAF agents responded to the various needs of local film executives and negotiated with the constantly changing political, social, and cultural environments in the region during the project's early activities. Accordingly, this chapter begins with the origin of TAF, the Committee for a Free Asia (CFA).

The Committee for a Free Asia

The CFA was originally a creation of the executive branch, intended to advance US foreign policy interests in Asia. It was established on March 12, 1951, during the second Truman administration (1949–53), "by a group of

Californians who believed that a non-governmental American organization primarily focused on Asia could help to increase the desire and ability of Asians to resist Communism on their own soil."[30] The Korean War was then at its height. Besides its headquarters in San Francisco and offices in Washington, DC, and New York City, TAF operated more than fifteen field offices in major cities throughout the 1950s, from Tokyo and Manila to Karachi and Rangoon. The CFA's initial board of trustees was composed of twenty-two members with distinguished careers in professional fields. Most of them were entrepreneurs based in San Francisco. Brayton Wilbur (1896–1963; president of Wilbur-Ellis) joined first as chairman of the CFA.[31] Turner H. McBaine, a San Francisco corporate lawyer, was a secretary of the CFA's board of trustees. Charles R. Blyth (1883–1959; president of Blyth and Co.) and J. D. Zellerbach (1892–1963; an owner of paper mills in Canada and California) followed shortly. Other notable board members were S. D. Bechtel (president of Bechtel Corporation), T. S. Petersen (president of Standard Oil Com. of California), Alden G. Roach (president of Columbia Steel Co.), Walter A. Hass (president of Levi Strauss and Company), James K. Lockhead (president of American Trust Co.), and J. E. Wallace Sterling (president of Stanford University).[32] It is hardly surprising that none of the board members were associated with the political realm, as the CFA wished to conceal its intimate alliance with Washington policymakers and to present itself, both privately and publicly, as a nongovernmental philanthropic outlet.

The CFA board members' top priority was undoubtedly China. In a letter that Wilbur, Blyth, and Zellerbach—three core board members—sent to potential CFA donors, they expressed the CFA's aim clearly:

> This organization [the CFA] has been set up along somewhat the same lines as the National Committee for a Free Europe, headed by C. D. Jackson and its Crusade for Freedom under the leadership of General Lucius Clay. It will expect to do the same job in Asia as is presently being done in Europe, that is, vigorously to fight Communism with every means at its command. From the numerous refugees who have fled China for this country and other parts of the world to escape communism, we know there is in China a strong counter-movement against Mao Tse-tung and his Soviet-conceived police state. We feel that by proper propaganda methods, this committee can really be effectual in helping to crystalize the anti-communist movement, particularly in China.[33]

As explicitly indicated in this letter, the CFA was the Asian counterpart of the National Committee for a Free Europe (CFE).[34] The CFE was founded on June 2, 1949, at the beginning of the second Truman administration, under the laws of the state of New York. Joseph C. Grew, the former ambassador to Japan, was chairman of the board, and the veteran diplomat DeWitt Clinton Poole Jr. was executive secretary.[35]

The CFE's leadership structure was almost identical to the CFA's. Its initial board of trustees included mostly entrepreneurs, bankers, educators, filmmakers, and retired generals such as Frank Altschul (an executive of General American Investors Company), Adolf Augustus Berle Jr. (a lawyer and diplomat), James B. Carey (a labor union leader), Dwight D. Eisenhower (a retired general who became president of the United States in 1953), Charles P. Taft (a lawyer and politician), Cecil B. DeMille, and Henry Luce (a magazine publisher). An expert on psychological warfare, Charles Douglas Jackson (known as C. D. Jackson), became the CFE's first president.[36]

As a brainchild of the CIA's deputy director Allen W. Dulles (1893–1969), brother of John Foster Dulles (1888–1959; US secretary of state from 1953 to 1959), the CFE worked to spread American influence in Europe and to oppose Soviet influence. The CFE's international association of elite American

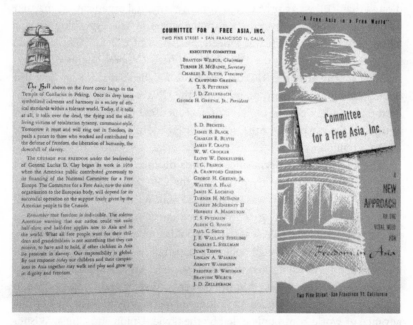

Figure 1.2. The CFA's information brochure. It clearly indicated that the CFA is the sister organization to the CIA's European body—the National Committee for a Free Europe (CFE). Asia Foundation Records, Hoover Institution Archives, courtesy of the Asia Foundation.

and European political and cultural intellectuals, the Congress for Cultural Freedom (CCF), was established in June 1950, with the inaugural conference held in West Berlin. Its aim was, according to Elena Aronova, "to combat communist ideology and to secure the ideological and cultural-intellectual support for the Marshall Plan in the sphere of culture and ideas."[37] The CCF held conferences and cultural festivals in many European countries and directly published or financed periodicals such as *Encounter*, *Der Monat*, and *Minerva*.[38] Some of the most important (and controversial) thinkers and public intellectuals in Europe, such as Arthur Koestler, Michael Polanyi, Hannah Arendt, Daniel Bell, Sidney Hook, and Arthur Schlesinger Jr., were delegates to the congress during its early period.[39] As Hugh Wilford has pointed out, the CCF, backed by massive CIA subsidies, rapidly evolved into the United States' "main weapon in the cultural cold war."[40]

One of the projects in which the CFE invested most heavily was Radio Free Europe (RFE). RFE, headquartered in Munich, West Germany, was a new anticommunist station whose broadcasts to Eastern Europe had begun in the summer of 1950. The Minnesota-based political scientist Robert T. Holt, in his comprehensive history of RFE, written in 1958, unequivocally indicated that REF was a private and nongovernmental organization and that "the voices that go out over the air are the voices of exiles speaking to their fellow countrymen." RFE was indeed the "voice of exiles."[41] The Crusade for Freedom, chaired by the World War II hero General Lucius Clay, was founded shortly after the RFE to raise funds for the station.[42] Clay was also one of the founding board members of the CFE. The CFE voluntarily undertook to underwrite the organizational expenses of the CFA during its first two years. On top of this, the Crusade for Freedom promised to contribute USD 1.4 million to the CFA.[43]

The CIA's recently declassified records on the CFA (under the project name of DTPILLAR) clearly prove that the CFA was initially launched by the CIA.[44] To be precise, it was Dulles and Frank Wisner (1909–65), the CIA's deputy director of planning, who designed the CFA.[45] Wisner's justification for the creation of the CFA was that it would combat international communism and promote US foreign policy "by assisting Asian groups and individuals to develop and strengthen their own societies and institutions in such a manner of the free world."[46] In other words, Wisner and Dulles aimed to create anticommunist sentiment among the population of Asia to stop the advance of world communism, led by the Soviet Union and China. Wisner had achieved a certain success with the CFE, and he wanted similar success in Asia. The CFA's initial aims and purposes were laid out in November 1950:

1. It [the CFA] will provide a medium for disseminating directly to the population of Asia via radio, newspapers, pamphlets, etc., information and ideas which do not seem identified with any governmental agency. In this respect, it will utilize its own name and, as the program develops, the name of whatever subsidiary committees in the area it may develop.

2. It will provide a means of disseminating information and ideas indirectly, through furnishing assistance and guidance overtly to other anti-communist groups.

3. Through activities utilizing its own name and those of existing groups, it will tend to create an impression of a widespread anti-communism throughout the area which will lend courage to those previously hesitant of expressing themselves and in time, enlarge the sentiment itself through a "bandwagon" effect.

4. Directly, and in cooperation with OPC [The Office of Policy Coordination]'s covert mission, it will serve to create new groups engaged in the fight against communism.[47]

5. It will provide to diverse groups a sense of unity transcending the specific interests of small groups and of "cause" to which they are all related. At the same time, it will give greater promise, through such unity, of success.

6. It will greatly simplify OPC's problem of making contact with existing or potential groups in the area.

7. Through selectivity, it will be able to lend support to groups whose total aims or activities may not be identical with our own.[48]

The CFA's primary target was China. But other areas were also considered. They were, in order of their importance, Southeast Asia, Japan, the Philippines, India, and Siberia.[49] Setting up regional branches in major Asian cities was considered but not actively discussed at this early stage. The project, however, encountered unforeseen obstacles. Finding the "right" person to lead this organization proved a difficult mission. Candidates for the presidency of the CFA had to have psychological warfare experience and established reputations as business executives. Moreover, they required a background in Asian affairs, which in the early 1950s was extremely rare. As Inderjeet Parmar notes in a study of the early development of Asian studies programs in the United States, American elites in the early 1950s found "woeful their own knowledge of Asian history, language, and cultures" and feared that America "would be unable to influence the development of Asia, leaving the way clear for communist control."[50] Accordingly, at the time there was no pool of Asia-experienced government officials in the United States. The CIA had much better options in the European theater, but none of these candidates were ideal for the CFA position. George H. Greene Jr., the CFA's director of programming, explained this to Brayton Wilbur, the first chairman of the board: "The field for the selection of this officer is extremely limited. Psychological warfare is a comparatively new subject of study in the United States. The principal direction of studies in that field among Americans has been toward Europe.... Conceivably, a man qualified in the European field of psychological warfare could accommodate himself to the oriental environment in time, but time is extremely important because of the advanced stage of communist infiltration in all countries of the Far East."[51]

Perhaps due to his insightful perspectives, Greene himself was appointed acting president in August 1951.[52] An alumnus of the University of Michigan, Greene had joined the National City Bank of New York in Shanghai in 1929 and served with the bank until 1949.[53] He worked with the Office of Strategic Services (OSS) during the war. Before joining the CFA, he was chief of the Industrial Reconstruction Division of the Economic Cooperation Administration (ECA) mission in China.[54] Under Greene's presidency, the CFA began aggressively recruiting, and approximately seventy of the projected 160 positions in the organization had been filled by the end of 1951. The CFA's association with the CIA had to be kept secret during and after the recruitment process.[55] Despite this difficulty, Greene strategically recruited several notable "China experts" to the committee, including James M. Henry (former president of Lingnan University in Hong Kong), Lester K. Little (former inspector general of Chinese customs), and William Zu Liang Sung (former president of St. John's University in Shanghai).[56]

Radio Free Asia

The CFA's core activities were divided into two projects: broadcasting Radio Free Asia (RFA) and supporting journalists, writers, and opinion leaders, encouraging them to fight against the communist forces in their respective countries.[57] RFA was the mirror image of RFE. As a weekly live broadcast aired from September 4, 1951, through April 15, 1953, RFA was the CFA's most ambitious and important propaganda activity. RFA distinguished itself from the Voice of America (VOA) by providing Asian—not American— viewpoints.[58] Instead of selling the American way of life to "the people of the Far East," RFA's basic aim was to provide "a platform from which free Asians can address their own people—in terms which are mutually understood."[59] Wilbur told the press, "Eventually RFA will beam towards the various parts of Asia programs on agriculture, health and other topics designed to assist the people of Asia and to maintain their courage and will to resist Communism."[60]

John W. Elwood (1897–1960), a retired San Francisco radio executive and former manager of KNBC in San Francisco, was appointed the first director of RFA. This was, according to Elwood, his "toughest and most challenging assignment."[61] RFA broadcast four hours a day, six days a week, in Mandarin, Cantonese, Hakka, and English. The broadcasts were short-waved at "the peak Asian listening hours," 7:45 to 11:45 pm, China Coast time.[62] They were carried to Asia via transmitters on Guam and in Manila.[63] In March 1952, Elwood opined, "A nongovernmental voice which speaks for free people everywhere can be the vanguard of a new and free life for the victims of oppression. It is difficult. It is expensive. But it is far less difficult and expensive than its alternative—total war."[64]

RFA did not thrive. Asian politics were far more complicated than Greene had initially thought. By its second year on the air, RFA was receiving a continuous stream of punitive criticism from Asia and even from within the United States. In a letter sent to Dulles, Philip Horton, the editor of the *Reporter*, called Greene's idea of RFA "extraordinarily naïve." He continued, "Most Asians are tired of hearing how good we are, and the history of our representative institutions has little bearing on their problems, for the conditions surrounding their evolution cannot be duplicated in Asia."[65] In March 1953, the CIA reviewed RFA's broadcasting operation. Admiral Harold B. Miller, president of the Crusade for Freedom, pointed out, "The Committee for a Free Asia is a different kind of operation. It works with and for Asian groups and individuals in free countries. Because of the delicate nature of any Western relations with Asian groups and individuals, particularly in those countries which have only recently become independent, the CFA's operation must be less militantly anti-communist."[66] It is not clear whether Miller's review had any meaningful impact on the CIA's judgment, but Wisner decided to stop broadcasting RFA shortly afterward. Wisner explained, "CFA has found that it can do its most effective work among youth and students, educators, writers and intellectuals, and civic, religious and women's organizations. It is worth noting that CFA's ability to work with these groups was enhanced in the past year by the termination in April 1953 of RFA, which attempted to stamp CFA in the eyes of Asians as a propaganda outfit directed at Asians."[67]

Alan Valentine

On January 2, 1952, the CFA welcomed its first president, Alan Valentine (1901–80).[68] A former Olympic gold medal–winning rugby union player, Valentine had served as president of the University of Rochester for fifteen years (1935–50) before being appointed as head of the Truman administration's Economic Stabilization Agency (ESA; 1950–51).[69] Valentine's shift to government work from the academic world, however, did not particularly suit him. He apparently had no experience outside academia. The CFA's existing officers gave him no more than a lukewarm welcome. Greene, the acting president, had been shocked to hear of his appointment. He had been expecting to be made the CFA's "official" president himself. Wilbur, the chairman of the board, however, had a different opinion of Greene. From the beginning, Wilbur did not consider Greene capable of leading the CFA. In a letter sent to the CIA in June 1951, Wilbur wrote, "George Greene is definitely a person who wears well. He is a man of genuine integrity who has intense zeal for his work and who thinks well. On the other hand, he is not too articulate and because of this near deficiency, he is not presently suitable for press conference, radio, or television appearances."[70] Wilbur wanted to recruit a nominal leader with a respectable career. Greene was upset about Wilbur's decision and went so far as to state that the appointment of Valentine was "ill-timed" and "ill-advised." He did not hide his resentment: "Valentine is being hired as a local public relations man and professional manager by the Executive Committee as a professional salary. He does not have the sense of a cause or of the devotion to duty which others of us have attached to the calling."[71] In fact, Valentine had earned a bad reputation while leading the ESA because of his "inflexible and introverted management style."[72] It is unfair to judge Valentine's capability based on Greene's letter alone, but at least one aspect of Greene's attack was fully justified: Valentine had absolutely no Asian experience or background, and his understanding of Asian geography, language, and culture was limited. Immediately after Wilbur's official announcement was made, Greene submitted his resignation and accepted the offer of a traveling fellowship to conduct economic studies in Southeast Asia.[73]

By the time Valentine took over the presidency, the CFA was already involved in multiple projects, including the *Young China Daily News*, a YMCA tour of Japan by Asian American students, a tour of US colleges by Father Liang, a translation of the Boy Scout Manual, initial research for the potential Hong Kong Bookstore project, and RFA—all initiated by Greene and his inaugural team.[74] Valentine's major contribution to the CFA, in contrast,

Figure 1.3. Alan Valentine (1901–80) in his office at the University of Rochester, a few years prior to his resignation in November 1949. Courtesy of Rare Books, Special Collections and Preservation Department, River Campus Libraries, University of Rochester, Rochester, NY.

was the establishment of overseas field offices in key cities in Asia. Besides its headquarters in San Francisco and an external office in New York City, the CFA had eight local offices by February 1953: in Tokyo, Taipei, Hong Kong, Manila, Kuala Lumpur, Rangoon, Colombo, and Karachi.[75] Offices were scheduled to open in Seoul, Bangkok, and Kabul in 1955. India and Indonesia were two exceptions; they saw the CFA, Valentine emphasized, as "a Cold War organization to which they do not want to be host."[76] The field officers were mostly college professors in Asian studies in major American universities, journalists, and former state officers.[77] F. Sionil José, a renowned Filipino novelist, reminisced, "Many of the foundation representatives were academics with extensive knowledge of the region and of the countries where they are assigned."[78] To avoid suspicion from local intellectuals, officers in certain countries represented themselves variously as a bookstore owner (Rangoon), a college professor (Taipei; faculty at Taiwan National University), and a seasoned journalist (Tokyo).[79] During Valentine's term, the CFA's annual budget increased significantly—from a mere USD 150,000 in the fiscal year 1951 to USD 3.9 million in 1953—largely due to its aggressive regional expansion.

Valentine decided to drastically revamp RFA under the new title *Voices of Asia*. This time the broadcast was intended not for Asians, but for American intellectuals and educated citizens. Supervised by Robert Goralski, the CFA's former Tokyo officer, *Voices of Asia* was a tape-recorded radio program designed to increase "goodwill for the foundation throughout Asian countries and to stimulate more American interest in the Asian viewpoint."[80] In contrast to RFA, *Voices of Asia* aimed to call Americans' attention to Asian affairs and to encourage Asia-America collaborations. Three to five half-hour panel discussions were recorded in each country, each featuring several English-speaking Asian leaders who discussed the cultural, economic, and educational problems uppermost in their countries. The program ended, however, after the weak and unpopular Valentine resigned in September 1952.[81] Two of his supporters, vice presidents Henry Siegbert and Ray T. Maddocks, submitted their resignation several days later. Valentine subsequently retired from the professional world.[82] Valentine's departure was not entirely unexpected. Just a month before his formal resignation, Valentine had expressed his deep frustration with the Office of Policy Coordination (OPC) and the CIA. He wrote:

> I have urged strenuously, but with good temper, that CFA should not be a subsidiary of OPC. An important member of OPC stated that CFA is such a subsidiary, and that . . . I [was] therefore technically subject to orders from him. That person is Deputy of the Chief of the Far East Division, who on the sponsors' chart is under the Deputy on Policy Coordination, who is under the Assistant Director of Plans, who is under the Deputy Director for Plans, who is under the Deputy Director, who is under the Director. This executive committee would, therefore, be taking its orders from a man six levels down. My apparently successful arguments against this may have given offense in some quarters; I do not know.[83]

In his resignation letter, Valentine did not hide his feelings. He wrote, "I see no hope that the situation will be altered sufficiently to offer a real chance to lead the Committee to success in terms of its original concept." Valentine, in a letter to Dulles and General Walter B. Smith, opined that Wilbur should not be allowed to continue as chairman of the CFA because, he wrote, "his leadership of the Committee has been demonstrably inept."[84] It is not clear what had happened between Valentine and Wilbur, but it is apparent that Valentine had lost faith in Wilbur. On September 15, Valentine submitted an important document titled "Analysis of CFA Future." This was probably his last contribution to the CFA, but it was one of his most important. Valentine suggested three plans that the "sponsor" (quite obviously the CIA) could follow for the future development of the CFA. The first plan was the "elimination of CFA." The second was the "integration of CFA with Sponsor," which meant the CFA would continue to exist as a private committee but "only as a completely window-dressing front" with no authority. The third option was that the CFA should become a "private committee concept"; this was the plan Valentine recommended. If the CFA were transformed into a private philanthropic organization, he emphasized, anticommunist propaganda would become "more effective" and would have "a great appeal to Asians, with their sensitivities, fears and dislike of open association with US government."[85] Apparently, the CIA took Valentine's advice seriously. The CFA was renamed the Asia Foundation in 1954. Wisner's reasoning for this name change was noteworthy: "The name 'Committee for a Free Asia' has proved an impediment in the establishment of the character desired for CFA. It has a political connotation and irritates Asians, proud of the fact that they are already free."[86] This is exactly the same reasoning that Valentine had laid out two years earlier.

Robert Blum and the Birth of The Asia Foundation

In July 1953, Robert Blum (1911–65) took over as president of the CFA. Finally, and "for the first time," in Wisner's words, they found a person in whom "the CIA, the Executive Committee of CFA, and the staff of CFA have the greatest confidence."[87] Earlier that year, Dwight D. Eisenhower (1890–1969; in office 1953–61), one of the founding members of the CFE, had become the thirty-fourth president of the United States. As an advocate of psychological warfare throughout his military career, Eisenhower put great emphasis on information activities, both overt and covert, and believed in the power of effective propaganda. Eisenhower was, according to Kenneth Osgood, "one of the earliest and most consistent supporters" of psychological warfare.[88] Eisenhower had developed his belief in the power of propaganda during World War II. After the war, he continued to support psychological operations against the Soviet bloc. While developing covert psychological warfare initiatives for the Truman administration (1945–53), Eisenhower actively communicated and collaborated with a group of "psy-war" believers—C. D. Jackson, Walter Bedell Smith, Allen Dulles, and Frank Wisner—who helped him launch the Crusade for Freedom.[89] Immediately after winning the presidential election, Eisenhower appointed C. D. Jackson as his special assistant for psychological warfare. He also staffed his administration with some of the other "psy-war" warriors listed above. His administration considered Blum the ideal person to lead the CFA. Blum understood the logic of psychological warfare well and alleged that propaganda could help challenge communist China and preserve the United States' international prestige in Asia. Most of all, Blum was one of the rare psy-war veterans who had wide-ranging experience in Asia and understood Asian affairs.[90]

A native San Franciscan, Blum lived in Japan for several years as a child and then received his PhD in international relations from the University of California, Berkeley, in 1936. For five years thereafter, Blum was on the faculty of Yale University.[91] During World War II, he acquired a distinguished record as an intelligence operative in Paris, London, and Washington, DC. He then stayed on with the OSS until its formal dissolution in 1946, whereupon he took up a succession of government posts, including in Cambodia and Laos. In 1950 and 1951, Blum was in Vietnam as head of a special technical and economic mission, and then served as assistant deputy for economic affairs in the office of the US Special Representative in Europe, stationed in Paris, until he joined the CFA in August 1953.[92] With the aim of supporting Blum, Wisner promoted James L. Stewart to director of programming. Stewart was essentially an Asianist. Born in Kobe, Japan, to Methodist missionary parents and raised in Hiroshima, Stewart studied journalism at Duke University and worked as an Associated Press correspondent in Chongqing (Chungking), China, from 1939 to 1944 and then as a war correspondent for CBS in the China-Burma-India theater after the attack on Pearl Harbor. In 1947, Stewart commenced a new post as a public information adviser to the US Army in South Korea and, two years later, became first a secretary and then a public affairs officer at the US Embassy in Seoul. In 1951, he and his family settled in San Francisco, where he began working for the CFA.[93]

Shortly after Blum joined the committee, it was renamed the Asia Foundation. Blum shifted the aims of the organization significantly. He opined that American "experts" should not force Asians to "adopt" but help them to "adapt" Western knowledge and techniques.[94] Accordingly, immediately after taking up his new position, Blum redirected TAF's cultural activities. He focused on influential noncommunist "leftist" and "naturalist" groups in Asia, mostly in Hong Kong, Japan, and Taiwan and in the Chinese diasporas in Southeast Asia, which were not easily reached by official US agencies.[95] Blum had a deep interest in popular media. He expanded the board of trustees: in addition to the powerful San Franciscan entrepreneurs, Blum invited educators, writers, media executives, and film industry personnel such as Raymond B. Allen (chancellor of UCLA, 1952–59), Robbins Milbank (a trustee of Smith College), James A. Michener (author), Paul G. Hoffman (president of the Ford Foundation, 1950–53), Barry Bingham (president of the *Louisville Courier Journal*), and Eric Johnston (president of the MPAA, 1946–63).[96] Following Blum's lead, TAF turned its attention to underwriting research, stimulating the distribution of noncommunist literature, sponsoring travel to key conferences, and helping various media publish "free world" news and, most of all, produce feature films. The "Motion Picture Project" became one of TAF's most invested-in operations, at least during its first several years.

The Asia Foundation's Motion Picture Project

Before Blum's arrival, TAF had already prepared to launch its motion picture program.[97] John Glover, director of programming, and Richard P. Conlon, director of plans, drafted TAF's first motion picture program plan in September 1952 and March 1953, respectively.[98] It was a year after TAF's first film, a self-introductory short documentary film called *The Truth Shall Make Men Free*, was completed in September 1951. Glover believed in the power of cinema in Asia and openly proclaimed that "no other media presently available could be developed and utilized to reach so many people in Southeast and South Asia in as short a time and for as low a cost as a soundly conceived motion picture production and distribution program."[99] In his draft, therefore, Glover illustrated three TAF-sponsored short films that were in production: (1) a newsreel short for overseas Chinese audiences; (2) *The Friendly Philippines*, aimed primarily at Filipino audiences; and (3) *The Living Buddha*, a documentary on the Second World Fellowship of Buddhists (WFB) in Tokyo.[100] *The Living Buddha* aimed to foster the existing Buddhist anticommunist movement in Burma, Ceylon, Thailand, and Malaysia as part of TAF's strategic support for pro-American Buddhist organizations.[101]

Glover suggested that rather than producing occasional "spot" features on an ad hoc basis, TAF should set up a broad and integrated program, with a regular production schedule, an organized distribution system, and a wide appeal to a mass audience. Glover was aware of the vast spread of communism in Asia, from Burma and Hong Kong to Japan, and believed it was essential to devise a new strategy in the field of motion pictures. Indeed,

TAF believed that high literacy rates had made motion pictures a popular medium of communication and entertainment in Asia, and that the enormous potential of movies as a means of conveying a Free World message was "far from fully realized."[102] Glover therefore requested the sum of USD 500,000 for the 1953/54 budget for motion picture operations. Thirty ten-minute short features, at an average cost of USD 10,000 each, with USD 50,000 allowed for contingencies, were proposed for production only, while the balance of USD 150,000 was intended to establish a distribution system to ensure the exhibition of TAF films.[103] This requested budget, which was a relatively large sum in comparison to the budgets of other major TAF programs (amounting to roughly one-eighth of TAF's annual budget), was authorized at the end of 1952, and TAF embarked on a new motion picture program in the fiscal year of 1953/54.

However, as Conlon's report suggested in March 1953, it was apparent that short propaganda films alone were not enough to attract significant notice from the motion picture world in Asia. To block the growing influence of "mass communism," Conlon believed, TAF had to adopt a new approach, distinctively different from that of the communists.[104] This approach would focus on three aspects of the motion picture industry: (1) motion picture industry personnel, (2) production, and (3) distribution. A focus on production and distribution was not particularly novel, but Conlon's recommendation to focus on professional workers in the motion picture industry in Asia is noteworthy. He argued that TAF "should stimulate and assist non-Communist screen writers, and the local production of pictures within the lines of our broad objectives." He continued, "We should consider exchange programs between Asian film groups themselves and with America, and promote the joint production of pictures."[105] Instead of producing propaganda shorts with American companies and distributing them in Asia, Conlon suggested exploiting the TAF's own networks and strengths: assisting young writers, supporting inter-Asian conferences and workshops, and dispatching American scholars, technicians, and field experts to Asia. To achieve this, Conlon suggested that a qualified motion picture professional with Asian experience be hired.[106]

That professional was Charles M. Tanner. He joined TAF in 1953 as a Hollywood liaison and motion picture program supervisor. Born in Salamanca, New York, Tanner had joined the US Air Corps in 1940 and served as a sergeant, second lieutenant, and then first lieutenant until his service with the Army was up in 1949. Within the State Department, he was made the motion picture officer in charge of restarting the film industry, first in South

Korea and then later in Japan. After the war, he became a motion picture officer and media director in the USIS in South Korea.[107] Blum highly valued Tanner's vast human networks and motion picture industry experience in South Korea, the Philippines, and Japan. Tanner was assigned to work at the CFA's San Francisco headquarters.

John Miller, a special motion picture officer in Tokyo, was appointed to assist Tanner and Noel Busch, the foundation's new representative in Tokyo. Miller, who had studied at Ohio State University, had a varied career in radio before the Pacific War. From 1941 to 1946, as a captain in the United States Army, he was involved in radio programs in Japan, the Philippines, and Korea. He produced the first program designed to teach the "principles of democracy" to the Japanese. He also served as field supervisor of all Armed Forces Radio Service stations in Asia. Just before he joined TAF, Miller was engaged as a writer, narrator, and director with Palmer Pictures, a San Francisco-based motion picture production.[108] Noel Busch, in contrast, was a seasoned journalist. He had worked for Henry Luce for over twenty years before joining TAF as its Tokyo representative. Busch had been a moving picture critic, a theater critic, a sports editor, and associate editor of *Time*,

Figure 1.4. Charles M. Tanner in the late 1940s, when he served as a motion picture officer in charge of restarting the film industry in South Korea. Photo courtesy of Bobbi Johnson-Tanner.

and he had written intermittently for all the other sections of the magazine. During the war years, as a war correspondent, Busch wrote many feature stories for *Life* magazine. Busch was known as a Japan specialist. He wrote *Fallen Sun: A Report on Japan* in 1948 based on his first-hand experience in occupied Japan.[109] He was also a senior editor for *Life* magazine before he resigned in 1952.[110]

The People Win Through

Shortly after Tanner and Miller took up their new posts, they embarked on their first motion picture mission: wrapping up *The People Win Through* (*Ludu Aung Than*, George Seitz Jr., 1953), the first TAF-financed feature film. It had begun production a year previously. *The People Win Through*, based on a play by the prime minister of Burma (now Myanmar), U Nu (1907–95; in office 1948–56), tells a story of Burma in 1950. Burma declared independence from Britain in January 1948 after a powerful political alliance, the Anti-Fascist People's Freedom League (AFPFL), won the 1947 general elections. Aung San, often considered the father of the nation, was set to become prime minister, but he was assassinated in July. In his place, U Nu became both the prime minister of Burma and the leader of the AFPFL. Soon, the new country plunged into an all-out civil war between AFPFL and the Communist Party's Revolutionary Burma Army. *The People Win Through* was written in the midst of this political turmoil and chaos. U Nu expressed the reasoning behind his writing in the foreword:

> Our union of Burma is standing at the cross-roads. One way leads us to the seizing of power by force. The other leads to the willing devolution of power by the masses to their representatives elected by fair democratic methods. The first is no new way for Burma. . . . This evil habit of seizing power by force is now rearing its ugly head in Burma. If this wickedness takes hold of our fair country, it will reduce her to a state of abject misery and subjection to tyranny that would beggar description. So we have staged this play, which I hope, will help you to decide which way to choose.[111]

The People Win Through, a morality tale, narrates the gradual disillusionment of the idealist revolutionary Aung Win, who has joined the communist insurrection. The play's message is that good democratic methods are superior to the evil totalitarian ways of the communists.[112] The play is rich in

Figure 1.5. A newspaper advertisement for *The People Win Through* (*Ludu Aung Than*, George Seitz Jr., 1953). The film was screened at Rangoon's two movie theaters, New Excelsior and Carlton. Asia Foundation Records, Hoover Institution Archives, courtesy of the Asia Foundation.

characters. More than fifty soldiers, villagers, politicians, children, and teachers cross the stage. But its main characters are clearly Aung Win and his childhood friend Aye Maung, who is now a pro-AFPFL politician. Through their voices, U Nu stresses again and again that governments should be determined by elections. In the beginning of the play, Aung Win claims that "freedom" is never won without fighting and that the AFPFL governments are under the power of the imperialists. In the final act, he regrets his choice after witnessing the communist leaders' inability to lead the revolution. He says, "It was a big mistake to rush into insurrection without proper preparation. Insurrection is not child's play. . . . I am not ashamed to admit that I didn't understand at first. Now I know. I realize it more and more every day."[113] Aung Win is killed by the brutal and ruthless communist leader Boh Tauk Tun. And so the play ends.

The play *The People Win Through* had its US premiere at the Pasadena Playhouse in California in October 1951. Cascade Pictures of California purchased the film adaptation.[114] A small, independent film production company that was incorporated in April 1949, Cascade Pictures had wide experience in the production of educational films, military training films, advertising shorts, and "message" films in the United States, and had branched out into the production of films for the State Department. It nevertheless had almost no experience in producing feature-length narrative films. Bernard J. Carr, Cascade's founder and president, was a native San Franciscan, an alumnus of the University of San Francisco. He was formerly a director of 20th Century Fox and Hal Roach Studio and had served in the US Navy during the war.[115] By the time Cascade began production of *The People Win Through*, the studio had already completed a short documentary, *The Living Buddha* (discussed in the next section), for TAF.

Michael Charney states that Cascade Pictures had "somehow gotten financing for the play, for which it wanted nothing in return, not even for the cost of filming it."[116] Charney does not specify who financed *The People Win Through*, but in fact it was clandestinely backed by TAF.[117] The official record reveals that the budget of the film was USD 203,029, and that the foundation's Rangoon office assumed the production costs.[118] From the very beginning, *The People Win Through* was TAF's project. According to the record, a contract was signed in November 1952 by TAF and Cascade for the production of a screen adaptation of U Nu's play.[119] TAF's aim was to distribute the film in Burma, Thailand, India, Hong Kong, Japan, and Taiwan, where five hundred million Buddhists constituted the majority of the population. TAF also considered distributing the film for a US audience.

Paul Gangelin (1898–1961), a Hollywood screenwriter, was hired by Cascade Pictures to do the adaptation of the play and was sent to Burma to obtain U Nu's approval of the script. Gangelin had begun his Hollywood career in the late silent era. His first screenplay was Pathe Production's *The Rocketeer* (also called *Love's Conquest*, Howard Higgin, 1929). Gangelin wrote several modestly successful scripts, such as *The Scarlet Claw* (Roy William Neill, 1944) and *My Pal Trigger* (Frank McDonald, 1946), but when Bernard Carr, the president of Cascade, approached him in January 1953, he had never worked with a major studio and had not produced a film script in several years. Cascade Pictures sent a film crew and its own filming equipment to Rangoon to begin shooting the film in the local language with an all-Burmese cast in February 1953.[120] A local English-language newspaper broke the news of the film's production procedure. "After weeks of screen tests and casting," the newspaper wrote, the ex-army captain Arthur Maung Maung Ta was cast to play the leading role in the film. "Hollywood" was very impressed with his "sensational performance." Ba Kho, an ex-army major, played a supporting role along with a group of professional Burmese actors. *The People Win Through* was filmed on location at the old army rest camp on Victoria Lake (Inya Lake) in Rangoon (Yangon).[121]

The People Win Through was shown at an initial test screening at Cascade Pictures. Carr and George Seitz Jr. (1915–2002), the film's director, introduced the film to TAF executives. The screening was disastrous. Tanner's letter reveals their frustration: "We are agreed that the film is disappointing; of less than top-notch quality; overly expensive; of doubtful use outside Burma, at least as is." He went on to say that "there is little that can be done at this stage to get the kind of film that we feel we should have." Tanner's suggestion was to complete the picture in the shortest possible time in order to keep the costs down.[122] Conlon, too, was offended by the quality of the film and didn't believe that the high cost of the film had been necessary:

> There were no high-paid stars. There were no elaborate sets. There were no scenes establishing large expenditures. There were no expensive costumes. . . . By American standards and the standards of the more sophisticated Asian audiences; the film could not be classed as good entertainment. If it were released in its present form for possible distribution in the United States, it is almost certain that there would be very few, if any, outfits that would undertake to screen the film. . . . It is hard to see how Cascade can realistically justify the expenditure of a quarter-of-a-million dollars."[123]

Cascade Pictures was asked to reedit the film. Carr, the president of Cascade, was not happy to hear this. He stated, according to Tanner, that "it was unfortunate that TAF had developed a critical and dissatisfied attitude toward Cascade, who [had] only been trying to help." Carr argued that Cascade had made *The People Win Through* faster than anyone else would have. He continued: "If TAF had given the contract to some other firm, TAF would not have a picture this year."[124] The reedited version had its first public preview at the New Excelsior Cinema Hall in Rangoon on December 26, 1953.[125] U Chan Htoon, the attorney-general and president of the Society for the Extension of Democratic Ideals, delivered a welcome speech at the premiere:

> The film [*The People Win Through*] which so vividly shows the contemporary Burma scene in which the people have been tortured and tormented by irresponsible insurrectionists will be shown in all countries of the world where democracy flourishes. The film will not only be important as a vivid portraiture of contemporary Burma, but, because it records so truthfully an important chapter of Burma's history, it will become an essential piece of historical data to be preserved for posterity. . . . The photography is

excellent. The acting leaves little more to be desired. The language is pure and potent Burmese. Sound is what the latest technical skill can produce. *The People Win Through* as a film will therefore be enjoyed by all in Burma and it will be able to hold its own in the world's film markets.[126]

TAF executives, however, were concerned about the film's reception in other countries, particularly India and Thailand. At one point, they considered adding songs and dances to increase the distribution potential in India, until they realized that Cascade Pictures was not capable of composing songs for the film. Having already spent a huge sum of money, TAF had to find a way to make the film visible. To raise US interest in the film, Tanner arranged a private screening for the *Christian Science Monitor*. Richard Dyer MacCann (1920–2001) wrote a favorable article about the strategic weight of the film that emphasized its value as a compelling "propaganda weapon" against the ever-increasing influence of communist propaganda in the Far East.[127] MacCann, a University of Kansas alumnus with a PhD from Harvard, was a staff correspondent for the *Christian Science Monitor* in the 1950s.[128]

Another private screening in Hollywood followed: Tanner arranged a screening of *The People Win Through* under a new title—*The Rebellion*—at the MPAA building in Culver City, California, in April 1954. He invited Luigi Luraschi, Cecil B. DeMille, and other powerful Hollywood film directors and executives in hopes that they would distribute the film in the United States. But DeMille dismissed the film and judged that it would lack commercial potential even if "it were to be edited down and English subtitles added."[129] Albert Deane, the manager of the department of censorship and editing of Paramount Pictures, saw both versions and harshly criticized the newly edited one: "The film is still bad because it cannot be anything but the same film. The bad parts of the film, such as over-drawn commie characterization, the unfortunate casting of Aung Win's wife, the long, tedious explanation of the story line by dialogue instead of action, etc., cannot be eliminated. They cannot be taken out because they are essential to the telling of the story. In order for *The People Win Through* to be a good picture, it would have to be re-done."[130] Deane affirmed that the film should not be distributed in the United States, not even "on the art circuits."[131] Worse still, despite the wide acclaim given the picture by the Burmese press, which called it the finest film produced in Burma to date, Tanner reported that *The People Win Through* had performed "poorly in Asia."[132] Having paid a high price for their lesson, TAF's executives decided to fold their ambitious plan for US distribution of

The People Win Through. TAF, however, had an even bigger project in the pre-production stage, tentatively titled *Life of Buddha*.

Life of Buddha

In October 1952, the second World Buddhist Congress (WBC; sponsored by the World Fellowship of Buddhists) was held in Tokyo, just five months after the effectuation of the peace treaty of San Francisco. The first congress had been held in Ceylon two years before. As Joseph M. Kitagawa points out, the WBC was the first event in the history of Buddhism to attempt "to unite and coordinate all the important Buddhist activities throughout the world."[133] The congress in Japan attracted 180 Buddhist delegates from eighteen countries, as well as 450 Japanese delegates. This 1952 event was followed by conferences in Burma (1954), Nepal (1956), Thailand (1958), and Cambodia (1961).[134] Dr. G. P. Malalasekera, president of the All-Ceylon Buddhist Congress (1939–57) and the first president of the WFB, claimed, "The Buddhists' flag now flies in every country as the emblem of World Buddhism."[135] It is a little-known fact that TAF's support allowed several key figures in Burma, Ceylon, and India to attend the 1952 gathering. Cascade Pictures, hired by TAF, made a twenty-seven-minute black-and-white documentary film about the WBC in Tokyo, titled *The Living Buddha* (also known under the title *Buddhist World Brotherhood*). It was produced in English, but a Singhalese version was also prepared.[136]

The effort to make a feature-length film about the life of Buddha began immediately after the Tokyo conference. Indeed, the Japanese film studio Daiei produced a lavish black-and-white film on this topic, *Dedication of the Great Buddha* (*Daibutsu kaigen*, Kinugasa Teinosuke 1952), and released it in Tokyo to celebrate the WBC. This film entered the Cannes International Film Festival's competition section in 1953. Hollywood, however, had never before considered producing a film about the life of Gautama Buddha. Cascade Pictures proposed the project to TAF, and within several weeks TAF approved it. Cascade then hired the Chicago-born novelist and screenwriter Robert Hardy Andrews to write the script, paid for by TAF.[137] The project was tentatively titled *Life of Buddha*.

Like *The People Win Through*, *Life of Buddha* was Valentine's project. Therefore, when Tanner received the script in August 1953—just a month after Blum's term began—he had little idea what the project was about.[138]

Tanner praised the quality of Andrews's script but criticized the basic planning of the project. It should have been clear, Tanner wrote, "what people with what goal in mind" would produce the film. To Tanner, this was a script written for Hollywood that would cost several million dollars to produce. His solution was to coproduce the film with India. In his letter to Stewart, Tanner explained his reasoning:

> It [*Life of Buddha*] must be made for Asians in general, Buddhists in particular. Such a film may have some market potential for America, but will a major production company in Hollywood risk a considerable sum on such a possibility? . . . A new playwright is wise to keep his cast of characters to a minimum. If Mr. Andrews had written it with an Indian producer in mind, I am sure the story essence would be exactly the same but the size and scope of the production would be greatly lowered. My recommendation is that we approach Hollywood with a plea that such a picture be produced by them in conjunction with some first class Indian company.[139]

James W. McFarlane, president of Freedom Film Corporation in New York, also read the script and was more enthusiastic about the project. He stressed that this film "will do more toward fighting communist propaganda and bringing peace and security to Southeast Asia than any single effort previously made by any group or individual."[140] As a film distributor with significant experience in India, McFarlane could estimate the size of the film's potential market. He suggested that if 25 percent of the six hundred million Buddhists in the world saw this production, *Life of Buddha* would generate a "handsome" profit. McFarlane thought Frank Capra should direct the film, as he had represented the US film industry at the International Film Festival in India just a year previously.[141] TAF's motion picture team moved fast. To kick off the project, however, they needed support from Buddhist groups in India, Burma, and Ceylon.

From its inception, TAF had maintained a close relationship with G. P. Malalasekera (1899–1973), president of the WFB, which, in the words of Eugene Ford, was the "most significant institutional expression of a new postwar pan-Buddhist solidarity."[142] By the early 1950s, US policymakers began to regard Buddhism as an emerging theater of international relations and Cold War competition. As Ford argues, advancements in communication and transportation technologies "brought Buddhists of different nationalities into closer contact, bridging ethnic and geographical divides."[143] Malalasekera was trying to find ways to bring young people into the temple and keep them there. As a UK-educated scholar of Sri Lankan literature, Malalasekera was also anxious to disseminate Buddhism to the Western world.[144] When he visited San Francisco and New York in 1953, he discovered that many Americans had never heard of the Buddha or, even if they knew the name, had very little knowledge of him or his teachings. More important, Malalasekera noticed the power of film and television for disseminating ideas, ideologies, and knowledge. As he recounted in an article for the *Buddhist*, he had "no doubt at all that the film had today become the most efficient means of participating knowledge." "But," he continued, "who would make the kind of film I had in mind? Where would the money come from, because a film, especially one made in Technicolor, would cost a great deal?"[145] Malalasekera named TAF as the most appropriate American institution to undertake this task—making a film about the Buddha—and mentioned a film production company in Culver City, California, which had for "many years produced nothing but educational films."[146] It is easy to conclude that this production company was Cascade Pictures.

In a meeting in Trisinhalarama, Katugastota in Ceylon (Sri Lanka), Malalasekera expressed his view that this film "would be of great value in spreading the religion."[147] His wish to produce an educational film, preferably a documentary film, about the life of Buddha was not shared by TAF's motion picture team. TAF wanted to stress the anticommunist theme in the movie to influence six hundred million Buddhists in Asia, at least where the WFB had dominion over more conservative groups.[148] However, a major concern of TAF executives was whether other religious groups in Asia would feel that TAF was favoring Buddhism over other religions by backing this film. Another problem was its exceedingly high budget. Tanner estimated a cost of roughly USD 1.5 million if the film was coproduced with an Indian company. It would be closer to USD 4 million if a Hollywood studio became involved.[149] Tanner, who had taken a dim view of *Life of Buddha* from the beginning, recommended that a Hollywood motion picture company be selected to solely produce the film, with TAF taking a consulting position. Tanner had by then lost his faith in the ability of Cascade Pictures to produce a feature film. Tanner, in his letter to Stewart, noted that "Cascade had naturally assumed that they were going to be assigned to do this film [*Life of Buddha*]."[150] But Tanner specifically stated that TAF should work with a Hollywood studio that possessed a "much higher status than Cascade."[151]

About a year later, after giving up on its production plan, TAF sold the rights to *Life of Buddha*'s script back to its original author, Andrews, for a sum of USD 20,000.[152] MGM then took over *Life of Buddha* (now called *The Wayfarer*), with a little help from Cecil B. DeMille. Malalasekera volunteered as a technical advisor in preparing *The Wayfarer's* story and first-draft screenplay. Christopher Isherwood, an acclaimed British novelist who wrote the scripts for the MGM movie *The Great Sinner* (Robert Siodmak, 1949) and the British film *I Am a Camera* (Henry Cornelius, 1954), joined the team to polish the shooting script.[153]

Within a week, however, *The Wayfarer* faced an unexpected attack from enraged Buddhist groups in Burma. The *Burman*, like many newspapers in Burma at the time, was hostile to this "Christian company" (MGM) and its "entertainment" production *The Wayfarer*.[154] One of its reporters claimed, "It is time for every Buddhist to raise his voice against all attempts of these Hollywood film producers who try to convert the life of the Buddha to a toy that would bring more money to their ambitious pockets."[155] The *Burman* also criticized Malalasekera, who had announced the news of the Hollywood production of *The Wayfarer* to the press. "It is surprising," the reporter continued, "that Professor Malalasekera cannot realize the dangerous state of affairs that can arise as a result of his trying to play the fool with public opinion, although he may be the President of the World Fellowship of Buddhists."[156] Mon Soe Min, a staff reporter for the *Burman*, specifically mentioned TAF and its secret intention to use the sacred teaching as "an anti-communist weapon."[157] Malalasekera, forced into a corner, had to deny that he was a consultant to MGM on the production of *The Wayfarer*. He also claimed that he did not approve of the production in his capacity as president of the WFB.[158]

Having been informed of the backlash against *The Wayfarer* in Burma, Andrews wrote to TAF, "I have deliberately held back any communication to the *Burman* or any other friendlier publication in Burma or elsewhere in Asia, on the principle of not adding fuel to the fire at this stage in preparation."[159] It is not clear whether the hostile responses from Burma and other parts of Asia actually influenced MGM's decision-makers, but the production of *The Wayfarer* was permanently suspended.[160] TAF subsequently ceased to collaborate with Andrews.

A New Direction in the Motion Picture Project

After witnessing the failure of two projects—*The People Win Through* and *Life of Buddha*—Blum wrote with great disappointment, "Financing the production of motion pictures would seem to be a method TAF should employ with great caution. We have therefore told our representatives that our activities in the motion picture field should generally be considered in the light of aid to Asian organizations making films as an organizing device and selective support to Asian commercial producers and distributors."[161] Rather than outsourcing productions to US-based film companies, TAF's motion picture project team implemented a completely new approach. At an executive committee meeting, Blum claimed, "In the motion picture field, the communists usually attempt to gain control of movie industries through domination of key production, distribution and exhibition organizations. In line with our over-all organizational objectives, we try to create healthy, sound organizations within the Asian movie industries to prevent communist control."[162] TAF's motion picture team also shifted its strategy away from Burma, India, and Ceylon to focus on the film industries of Japan, Hong Kong, and to some extent South Korea.

In fact, Japan was Blum's most important target. After the communist victory in China and the outbreak of the Korean War in June 1950, Japan was, in the words of Odd Arne Westad, "all the US had in the region in the 1950s."[163] The Truman administration had, in John W. Dower's words, identified Japan as "the key to the balance of power in Asia," and it aimed to rebuild Japan's economy and so prevent the country from falling to communism.[164] The key players in postwar American politics, especially Dean Acheson, George Kennan, and John Foster Dulles, hoped to situate Japan "in a world system shaped by the United States," as Bruce Cumings claims.[165] Starting with Japan, they planned to construct a "free Asia" bloc, a "great crescent" of anticommunist containment in Asia, which in the end would be more or less nonterritorialized colonies of the dominant United States. With the end of the US occupation in Japan in 1951, Japan finally reentered the international political system. What was behind the turnaround of the US policy toward Japan was, as Yoshimi Shunya emphasizes, the Chinese revolution. Yoshimi claims, "Japan would have been far less important to American policy if there was still a pro-American government in PRC to act as a bloc against the southward spread of Soviet Power."[166] In fact, W. W. Rostow, an economic and foreign policy advisor to Eisenhower, vigorously called on the Eisenhower administration to rectify its previous policy toward Asia. Rostow claimed that the situation in Asia was more complicated than that in Europe. In Europe, the United States needed only to worry about defending West Germany against the spread of communism from the Soviet Union, but in Asia, he stressed, "There is Japan on the one hand and the whole area of Southeast Asia on the other. . . . In Asia the threat would become virtually a reality; either Japan or Southeast Asia would be lost to the Free World."[167] By supporting Japan's role in Southeast Asia, therefore, the Eisenhower administration finally began to apply its new national security policy. Known as the "New Look," this policy took as its primary object in Asia and the Middle East in 1953–56 "to reduce the American burden in cost and manpower of holding the line around the periphery of the Communist bloc."[168] Therefore, Japan needed to recuperate its economic alliances with Southeast Asia.[169] Blum understood this necessity well.

Accordingly, TAF's motion picture professionals, Busch, Tanner and Miller, under the guidance of the program director James L. Stewart, launched four new projects in Asia. The first step was to support the FPA and its mastermind Nagata Masaichi, financially and administratively, with the goal of creating an anticommunist motion picture producers' network in Asia. Second, they intended to provide a leading Hollywood screenwriter who could teach Japanese screenwriters Hollywood-style advanced writing methods: narrative structure, characterization, and modern editing techniques. Third, they would collaborate with local film executives and creative forces in South Korea and Hong Kong to increase the visibility of the anticommunist film workers. Lastly, they planned to introduce and distribute foundation-supported motion pictures and anticommunist producers' products to the American market via commercial/art film distributors and film festivals. With this plan in place, TAF's motion picture team turned to its first major project: the FPA.

Chapter 2

The FPA, US Propaganda, and Postwar Japanese Cinema

Nagata Masaichi, president of Daiei Studio in Japan, and Kimura Take-chiyo, executive secretary to Nagata and his right-hand man, sat in a restaurant with Noel Busch, TAF's Tokyo representative, and John Miller, a motion picture officer, in Ginza, Tokyo in May 1953.[1] Nagata pitched the idea of founding the FPA and an annual Southeast Asian Film Festival. Busch and Miller instantly liked the idea. Nagata's proposal was precisely what they had been looking for: a byway to create a "healthy and sound organization within the motion picture industries in Asia" to counter the rapidly increasing anti-American sentiment and the growing number of communist sympathizers in the region.[2] Certainly, backing an inter-Asian motion picture organization led by Japan, arguably the most advanced film-producing country in Asia at the time, seemed a timely and appropriate step for the foundation to take.

Since the end of the US occupation of Japan in April 1952, there had been consensus among American foreign officers stationed in Asia that communists had infiltrated the Japanese film industry.[3] Many saw the activities of the "Reds" in the Japanese motion picture industry as a "threat" to the United States' strategic Cold War interests in the Asia-Pacific region.[4] Richard L-G. Deverall, the representative for Asia of the American Federation of Labor's Free Trade Union Committee, stressed that a group of red propaganda movies were "fanning racial hatred and giving an intellectually dishonest picture of America."[5] In his brief account of this phenomenon, Deverall discussed three films, describing them as "magnificent propaganda," "vicious," and "racist": *Children of the Atomic Bomb* (*Genbaku no ko*, Shindo Kaneto, 1952; also known as *Children of Hiroshima*), *The Tragic General Yamashita Tomoyuki* (*Higeki no shogun Yamashita Hobun*, Saeki Kiyoshi, 1953), and *Mixed Race Children* (*Konketsuji*, Sekigawa Hideo, 1953).[6] In line with this view, Theodore Richard Conant, who served as head of the United Nations Korean Reconstruction Agency (UNKRA) Film Unit during the Korean War, stated that there was an underlying pattern in communist-oriented films produced in Hong Kong, Indonesia, Malaysia, and, most actively, Japan.[7] The pattern was, Conant wrote, "the depiction of Americans as imperialist war-mongering barbarians."[8] Robert Blum and others in TAF's San Francisco office were fully aware of the Japanese film industry's importance to the motion picture operations of TAF in Asia. Miller believed that almost all major studios in Japan would be "unable to resist" the strong box-office power of the anti-American movies.[9] In fact, according to the *Oakland Tribune*, four of the ten best domestic films in Japan in 1953, selected by film critics in Japan, were thoroughly anti-American or based on communist novels.[10]

By the time Nagata proposed the idea of the FPA, TAF had in fact been searching for a long-term partner in Japan that would be a strong anticommunist fighter. Several months before the meeting at Ginza, Murao Kaoru, a Japanese film writer-producer and a former employee of the Civil Information and Education Section (CIE) of the occupation government in Japan, was commissioned to compile a list of communist leaders within Japan's motion picture industry.[11] Murao named seven film industry employees: Ito Takeo, Miyajime Yoshiise, Saga Zenbei, Iwasaki Akira, Kamei Fumio, Yamamoto Satsuo, and Yamagata Yusaku. Murao emphasized that many leftists worked with these leaders, and that the Toei and Shochiku studios were "often used by lefty film production units."[12] Daiei, according to the report, was the only company that had never produced an anti-American or procommunist film.[13] In Miller's words, Nagata was the "only outspoken anti-Communist leader" in the Japanese film industry.[14] Even better, Nagata was the producer of *Rashomon* (Kurosawa Akira, 1951) and one of the most powerful motion picture executives in Asia at the time.

Nagata's Southeast Tour

Right after the meeting with TAF, Nagata embarked on a tour of Southeast Asia to execute the idea he had proposed. TAF's field representatives in

Manila, Kuala Lumpur, Singapore, and Jakarta arranged meetings between Nagata and local film executives: Run Run Shaw (Malaysia/Singapore), Manuel de Leon (1915–2005; the Philippines), and Djamaludin Malik (1917–70; Indonesia). Based on the favorable responses he received during the tour, the first constitutional conference was held in Manila from November 17 to 19, 1953. TAF provided travel grants to the twenty-four invited delegates from seven countries. Japan alone dispatched six delegates. Nagata proclaimed at the meeting:

> The chief aim of this project [FPA] is to promote the motion picture industry in the countries of Southeast Asia, to raise the artistic and technical standards of motion pictures and ensure cultural dissemination and interchange of motion pictures in the Far East. It is not only to raise the standards of motion pictures produced in the various countries of Southeast Asia to a world standard but even to a higher level than this. . . . I believe in the near future we can obtain a world-wide market and other countries will recognize the quality and standard of pictures produced in Southeast Asian countries, and thus get leading positions in the world market.[15]

Nagata was unanimously elected the first president of the FPA. Run Run Shaw, president of Malay Film Production in Singapore, became vice president. The headquarters would be in Tokyo. Nagata appointed six members of the board of directors other than himself and Shaw: Malik (Indonesia), Ho Ah Loke (1901–82; Malaysia), Prince Bhanubandhu Yugala (1910–95; Thailand), de Leon (The Philippines), Yamazaki Shuichi (Japan), and Run Run's older brother Runde Shaw (1898–1973; Hong Kong).[16]

It is worth noting here that two Shaw brothers were listed as board members. Shaw's Malay Film Production was established in 1939. By 1955, the studio had churned out over a hundred films, mostly in local languages. Run Run Shaw, the youngest of the four patriarchs (Runje, Runde, Runme, and Run Run), managed Malay Film Production until he took over his brother Runme's film production company, Shaw & Sons, in Hong Kong in the late 1950s. In 1953, therefore, Run Run represented Malaysia/Singapore, while Runde covered Hong Kong. The Philippines had four vertically integrated studios, commonly called the "Big Four" (LVN, Premier, Sampaguita, and Lebran-Movietec), and it had been producing around a hundred films per year since the beginning of the 1950s. Due to this ever-increasing annual output, film studios in the Philippines were seeking to export their films. Manuel de Leon, a general manager of LVN, was very much interested in co-production, and was already finished the propaganda film *Huk in a New Life*

(*Huk sa bagong pamumuhay*, Lamberto V. Avellana, 1953), coproduced with the US government and based on the story of a Filipino independent activist, a leftist force (the Huk), and the endeavor of the United States to defeat this force.[17] Indonesia was experiencing the greatest political uncertainty, and its

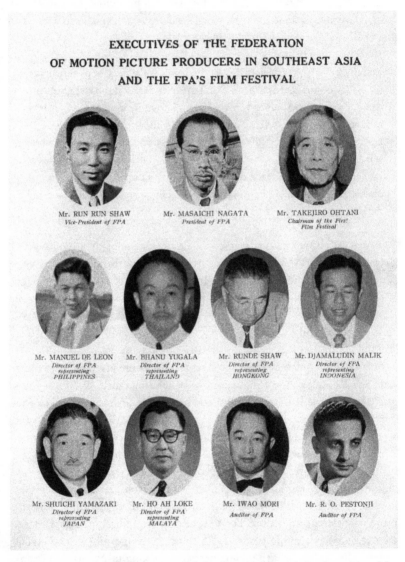

EXECUTIVES OF THE FEDERATION OF MOTION PICTURE PRODUCERS IN SOUTHEAST ASIA AND THE FPA'S FILM FESTIVAL

Mr. RUN RUN SHAW
Vice-President of FPA

Mr. MASAICHI NAGATA
President of FPA

Mr. TAKEJIRO OHTANI
Chairman of the First Film Festival

Mr. MANUEL DE LEON
Director of FPA representing PHILIPPINES

Mr. BHANU YUGALA
Director of FPA representing THAILAND

Mr. RUNDE SHAW
Director of FPA representing HONGKONG

Mr. DJAMALUDIN MALIK
Director of FPA representing INDONESIA

Mr. SHUICHI YAMAZAKI
Director of FPA representing JAPAN

Mr. HO AH LOKE
Director of FPA representing MALAYA

Mr. IWAO MORI
Auditor of FPA

Mr. R. O. PESTONJI
Auditor of FPA

Figure 2.1. Executives of the Federation of Motion Picture Producers in Southeast Asia and the FPA's film festival, May 1954. Photo courtesy of the Federation of Motion Picture Producers in Asia-Pacific (FPA).

two film moguls, Malik and Usmar Ismail (1921–71), were under heavy pressure from both the country's communist party and the government. Loke Wan-tho (1915–64)'s Motion Picture and General Investment (MP&GI, also known as Cathay Pictures) took the lead in Malaysia and Singapore, and the company was eager to acquire up-to-date technologies, especially cinemascope and color processing, to fill its vast theater chains in Southeast Asia. In sum, although all of the member countries had different purposes for participating in the FPA, they had three common aims: to coproduce films, to acquire modern technologies, and to sell their films to adjacent markets. At the conference, they decided to launch a film festival, the first Southeast Asian Film Festival, to be held in May 1954. Tokyo would be the host city.

It All Began with *Rashomon*

The renowned Japanese film critic Yomota Inuhiko called Nagata Masaichi an "idea man." Donald Richie and Joseph Anderson called him a "businessman's businessman." Kido Shiro of Shochiku Studio habitually called Nagata a "smooth-talking opportunist." At the official reception of the third Asian Film Festival in Hong Kong, Loke Wan-tho, president of MP&GI in Singapore, dubbed him the "Mr. Motion Picture" of Southeast Asia.[18] The Kyoto-born film executive first entered the film business as a studio guide at Nikkatsu Studio in 1926 and was promoted to production manager after ten years.[19] He became well known for his Machiavellian instinct to seize power after he surreptitiously sided with Kawazura Ryuzo, the chief of the Information Bureau in Japan. As the Pacific War took off in 1941, the Japanese government suffered a shortage of film stock. In response, Nagata persuaded the bureau to consolidate the entire film industry into three major conglomerates: Shochiku-Koa, Toho-Taiho, and Daiei-Nikkatsu. As president of Daiei, he brought Nikkatsu, his former workforce, under the umbrella of Daiei.[20]

Nagata's good fortune almost ended, however, with Japan's defeat in August 1945. The occupation forces led by General Douglas MacArthur (1880–1964) were on the hunt for war criminals, and this search extended even to the film industry. Nagata was placed on a list of war criminals and was later discharged from the industry for rehabilitation. As an "idea man," he kept busy with new projects and ideas. Due to his close alliance with Joseph Dodge, who had served as the Truman government's economic adviser for postwar economic stabilization programs in Japan from 1949 to 1952, Nagata traveled to the United States in 1949. Indeed, in Christopher Howard's

Figure 2.2. Nagata Masaichi (center), president of Daiei Studio, meets with Tatsuo Hirabayashi (left), a sound recording engineer, at Daiei Studio in 1951. Photo courtesy of National Film Archive of Japan.

words, Nagata was "the first Japanese citizen outside the military or civil service who had travelled to the United States during the Occupation."[21] During the trip, Nagata met executives of the Walt Disney and Samuel Goldwyn studios and took the opportunity to visit the Eastman Kodak Corporation in Rochester, New York. Daiei later licensed Eastman Color for use in the studio's production, which led to the studio's first Eastman Color film, *Gate of Hell* (*Jigokumon*, Kinugasa Teinosuke 1953). *Gate of Hell* won the Palme d'Or (Golden Palm) at the Cannes International Film Festival in 1954.[22]

In 1951, Daiei's medium-budget period drama *Rashomon* was submitted to the Venice International Film Festival and unexpectedly won the Leone d'Oro (Golden Lion), the highest prize.[23] The ramifications of this honor at the time were far greater than we might think now. It was, in fact, a sensation. The film critic Curtis Harrington, reviewing the Venice festival and its surprise grand prize winner, wrote, "Such a discovery was the memorable event of last year's Venice Film Festival; from Japan, a country whose film production has been largely ignored by the Western world for many years, came the brilliant *Rashomon*, a film that, thus called to the attention of the world by winning the grand prize in competition with the best of American, French, and Italian films, has since been playing successfully in all the capitals of the world."[24]

A year later, in March 1952, *Rashomon* won the award for Best Foreign Language Film at that year's Oscars, which elicited simultaneous respect and jealousy from other nations in the region.[25] With the unprecedented success of *Rashomon*, Nagata's presence in the Japanese film industry was rapidly established. On top of *Rashomon*'s success, Nagata's extravagant epic production *Dedication of the Great Buddha* was invited to the Cannes film festival in 1953. As a result, Nagata was elected president of the newly established Society for the Promotion of the Japanese Film Industry (*Nihon eiga sangyo shinkokai*), where his primary mission was to boost foreign sales of Japanese films. Nagata embarked on his Southeast Asian tour shortly thereafter.

Before turning to Nagata's expenditures, we should consider two factors. First, he had a significant acquaintance with two important figures, Mori Iwao (1899–1979) and Kawakita Nagamasa (1903–81). In 1937, Mori had become the studio chief of Toho Film Company, which was established in the same year through a merger of three companies: PCL Studio, JO Studio, and Toho Film Distribution Company. Mori had a close association with Kawakita, a Beijing-born Japanese citizen who had imported European films and distributed them through Mori's Toho.[26] Kawakita was a true cosmopolitan in Japanese cinema. He was a producer of the first

Japan-Germany coproduction, *The New Earth* (*Die Liebe der Mitsu / Atarashiki tsuchi*, Arnold Fanck and Itami Mansaku, 1937), and in 1941 was transferred to Shanghai to set up a national policy company, China Movie Company (Zhonghua dianying gongsi). In Shanghai, the sophisticated Kawakita aligned himself with Zhang Shankun (1905–57), the king of Chinese cinema, until the war's end.[27] Kawakita was known as a Chinese cinema expert in postwar Japan, and he maintained his friendship with his former colleague Zhang Shankun by coproducing films with Zhang's Xinhua (New China) company. Nagata, after resuming his status in 1948, joined Mori as a Daiei distribution partner.

Second, Nagata, Mori, and Kawakita were all interested in the global outreach of Japanese cinema. While Nagata traveled to Hollywood in 1949 in search of possible business contracts, Mori spent time in Hollywood and Europe between March and May of 1951. Mori met Joseph von Sternberg in New York for Kawakita's Japan-America coproduction *Anatahan* (also known under the title *Saga of Anatahan*).[28] As part of the efforts of Nagata, Mori, and Kawakita to reach outside Japan, they became the founding members of the FPA, although Kawakita stepped down at the last moment.

The End of the American Occupation

In the early 1950s, Hiroshi Kitamura states, the Japanese film industry was "finally regaining its momentum."[29] After Japan's surrender to the Allied forces in September 1945, the CIE, a suborganization of the General Headquarters (GHQ), the Supreme Commander for the Allied Powers (SCAP), controlled the entire film industry under its film production and distribution arm, the Central Motion Picture Exchange (CMPE). All Japanese films had to submit a translated script and synopsis before production, and the CIE and Civil Censorship Detachment censored them. A CIE official, David Conde, stated that the occupation government wanted the "Japanese film industry to pursue the principles of the Potsdam Declaration and help reconstruct Japan positively." He continued, "By abandoning nationalistic militarism in favor of developing individual liberties and human rights, Japan would never again threaten world peace."[30] Peter Duus argues that the Americans came determined to "transform their former enemy into a 'democratic' and 'peace-loving' country that would no longer threaten its neighbors and international peace," making it, as General Douglas MacArthur once remarked, the "Switzerland of Asia."[31]

CIE suggested desirable subjects when it distributed a list of thirteen prohibited subjects in November 1945. Anything related to militarism, revenge, nationalism, distortion of history, racial discrimination, approval of feudal loyalty and suicide, and antidemocratic opinions was forbidden. Simultaneously, 236 prewar and wartime films were banned. They were categorized as "ultra-nationalistic," "militaristic," and "propagating feudalism."[32] It therefore became almost impossible to make the popular *jidaigeki* (period films). *Gendaigeki*, films about contemporary life, however, became much easier to make, as they could incorporate the CIE's desirable subjects. Such films as *No Regrets for Our Youth* (*Waga seishun ni kuinashi*, Kurosawa Akira, 1946) and *The Victory of Women* (*Josei no shôri*, Mizoguchi Kenji, 1946) were produced under these circumstances. The CIE, and especially Conde, welcomed them.[33]

Kurosawa's *No Regrets for Our Youth* is the story of a woman whose father has lost his job and whose fiancé has died in prison for being leftist. She ultimately becomes a new leader of postwar Japanese society.[34] Yoshimoto Mitsuhiro argues that the film is marked by "ideological vacuousness" and is merely "a story that began with the rise of militarism and ended with the victory of democracy."[35] Likewise, *The Victory of Women*, produced by the Shochiku Ofuna studio, is the story of professional women in the legal courts. Departing from his prewar films, which were usually structured around "women's confrontation with a male-dominated, money-oriented society," in *The Victory of Women* Mizoguchi Kenji focused on Japan's "changing society."[36] The film dealt with the theme of women's unequal position in Japanese society and their struggle to survive intolerable conditions. Mizoguchi directed other "women's democratization films," such as *Love of Actress Sumako* (*Joyū Sumako no koi*, 1947), *Women of the Night* (*Yoru no onnatachi*, 1948), and *My Love Has Been Burning* (*Waga koi wa moenu*, 1949; also known as *Flame of My Love*), all of which were commercial and critical failures. His films, made following the authorities' guidelines, were met with the audience's indifference, unlike his popular wartime *chanbara* (sword fighting) films, such as *The Royal 47 Ronin* (*Genroku chushingura*, 1941). Within a few years, however, Mizoguchi overcame his postwar doldrums with his trademark *jidaigeki* films *The Life of Oharu* (*Saikaku ichidai onna*, 1952) and *Ugetsu* (*Ugetsu monogatari*, 1953), which ultimately brought him international fame.

In September 1951, the peace treaty between the United States and Japan was signed in San Francisco. The treaty granted Japan full independence with no reparations, no punitive economic restrictions, and no commitment to massive rearmament. At the same time, Prime Minister Yoshida Shigeru

(1878–1967) signed the Mutual Security Treaty with the United States. This treaty placed Japan "on the forward line of the American defensive perimeter in East Asia." It permitted US military bases and ports all over the country. The benefit Japan derived from these two treaties was economic; the American government gave "Japanese producers full access to the American domestic market."[37] As Hiroshi Kitamura comprehensively shows, CMPE, which had controlled and supervised the occupied territory's film production and distribution for nearly seven years, ended its operations on December 31, 1951, and "a new day of business dawned the following day."[38] No longer subject to the American occupation authority's cultural policies or government censorship, the content of Japan's cinema diversified. Genres that had previously been taboo—such as *jidaigeki* and war pictures—received an enthusiastic reception from Japan's new generation of audiences. Nikkatsu, after a long hiatus, reentered the market in March 1953, and competition among the major studios—Toho, Shochiku, Daiei, Toei, Shin Toho, and Nikkatsu—became fierce.[39] The annual output of domestic films rose throughout the 1950s and peaked in 1960 at 547. The domestic market was consequently already saturated in the early 1950s, and the resulting need for foreign markets turned the industry's attention to the exportation of films.

Japan's Reentrance into Southeast Asia

After the unexpected success of *Rashomon*, the number of Japanese film exports increased tremendously, and motion pictures rose to a prominent position among export articles. In 1953 alone, 675 films were exported to various countries, primarily in Europe, which was thirty times more than the number of films exported in 1947.[40] In other words, the Japanese film industry had become a "star of Japan's export industry" by the time the first Southeast Asian Film Festival began.[41] As Aaron Gerow argues, the Japanese film industry's "dream of export," which originated in the Pure Film Movement of the 1910s and '20s, was almost fulfilled.[42] To help mitigate the nation's trade deficit, the Japanese film industry was encouraged to export more films to new destinations, including Southeast Asian countries and, if possible, India.

The *Nippon Times* published a four-page special report on the Southeast Asian Film Festival and the Japanese film industry's current status, along with a celebration of the victory of another Japanese film, *Gate of Hell*, at Cannes. A reporter wrote in the special issue, "The Southeast Asian area being almost completely dominated by films of American origin, the indigenous movie industries were still in a very retarded stage of development. To foster these industries would contribute to a mutual exchange of motion picture culture as well as increase Japanese exports to that area. Therefore, it would be beneficial not only to Japan but also to the countries of Southeast Asia themselves if the Japanese movie industry, which was somewhat more advanced, were to take the lead in developing the film industries in this part of the world."[43]

Nagata's Southeast Asian tour in 1953 should be situated in the context of the Japanese film industry's recovery of its prewar condition and the general optimism of Japan's top film executives, particularly Nagata, whose supremacy within the industry reached its zenith around that time.[44] The establishment of the FPA therefore fulfilled a collective aspiration of the Japanese film industry to create an Asian market through a cultural event. The Japanese film industry's goal was to expand and secure the market for its products. Film executives, including Nagata, considered exporting Japanese movies a "patriotic act of earning foreign currency."[45] By hosting the Southeast Asian Film Festival and leading the FPA, the Japanese film industry thus attempted to expand and diversify its market.[46]

Here, four aspects of the Japanese film industry's reentry into the Southeast Asian market merit attention. First, it represented the continuation of Japan's unfulfilled imperial adventure. Nagata's Southeast Asian tour and the subsequent initiation of the FPA occurred in 1953, only eight years after the end of the Pacific War. Most Asian countries, including Indonesia, Hong Kong, Malaysia, Taiwan, and South Korea, were still hostile to Japan, and their wariness about a "second Japanese invasion" remained strong. Many of the region's intellectuals still vividly remembered the Japanese empire's *Dai toa eiga* (Greater East Asian Cinema) design that had linked the colonies under the banner of *Dai toa kyoeiken* (the Greater East Asian Co-Prosperity Sphere) during the total war in the 1940s. Nagata's idea of uniting the region's film producers was hardly new.

In 1940, as Kinnia Yau Shuk-ting reveals, the Japanese film industry established *Nanyo eiga kyokai* (the Association of South Asian Motion Pictures) with the assistance of the army, the navy, and the Information Bureau of the Cabinet. Shochiku and Toho, instead of Daiei, invested in this association, whose aim was to produce and release Japanese films in South Asia.[47] Kido Shiro became the first president, while Kawakita Nagamasa was appointed manager.[48] According to Yau, Dai toa eiga had three primary objectives. They were: 1) to open up Asian markets for Japanese movies; 2) to promote Japanese values throughout Asia; and 3) to improve the quality of Asian films in order to compete with

Hollywood.[49] Yau sees Dai toa eiga and the Japanese film industry's network with South Asian cinema as a historical precedent of the FPA. She argues, "It is obvious that the Asian film network initiated by Japan was designed to counter-act the powerful network set up by the American film industry."[50]

Second, the reentry of the Japanese film industry into the Southeast Asian market was a fulfillment of Nagata's personal goal. In 1944, Nagata had tried to form an organization similar to Nanyo eiga kyokai, but it failed to materialize because of Japan's surrender in August 1945.[51] This time, as a leader of the FPA, Nagata could be richly compensated while upholding his position in the domestic industry with ties to both Asia and the West. By screening films with technical superiority, Nagata and Daiei determinedly positioned themselves as the most modernized company in Asia. Daiei prof-ited from exporting film equipment and state-of-the-art techniques such as Eastman color cinematography and its lab processing, synchronous sound recording and shooting, and special effects, which lured Asian producers to Japan's laboratories for postproduction.[52] Moreover, Daiei could export genre films from the studio to other Asian countries by using Nagata's ex-tensive network of FPA members. As an apparent instance, during the sec-ond Southeast Asian film festival in Singapore, the second exhibition of film technologies and facilities was held simultaneously. The exhibition included a forum, lectures, test shooting sessions, and many other special events.[53] Consequently, Daiei's foreign sales, particularly to Hong Kong and Taiwan, increased rapidly, from forty in 1954 to seventy-four in 1956.[54]

Third, as discussed earlier, the Japanese film industry's entrance into South-east Asia was a brainchild of TAF's covert project to create a "healthy" network of anticommunist motion picture executives in Asia. Nagata fully understood what TAF expected from him. As president of the FPA, Nagata proclaimed in 1956, "We can say proudly, without any other ulterior motives of a political and ideological background, but only through self-reliance, we have overcome insurmountable difficulties in maintaining this project."[55] What Nagata meant by "political and ideological background" was the conflict between capitalism and communism. The Southeast Asian Film Festival would remain a politics-free event, Nagata implied, if its films came only from "free Asia."

Lastly, the Japanese government was being pressured by Washington policymakers through the Economic Commission of Asia and the Far East (ECAFE), a regional economic organization inaugurated in 1947, to reenter the Southeast Asian region to acquire raw materials and food while exporting the products of light industry. Needing to send a "goodwill" message, Japan used cinema to disseminate the image of the "reformed" colonizer. In view of this, Glenn Ireton, a Tokyo correspondent for Far East Film News, wrote in

1954, "The motion picture industry of Southeast Asia has succeeded where governments have failed. At the same time, this fact also illustrates one of the strongest arguments for democratic government. For imagine, if you will, the component parts of a commercial activity in six political entities, most of which don't have reciprocal and normal diplomatic relations, being permitted to band together to further common objectives, under anything other than a social and economic system founded upon free enterprise."[56]

The FPA was ideologically in line with ECAFE, which was a regional commission of the United Nations Economic and Social Council (ECOSOC). Oba Mie characterizes ECOSOC as "an arena wherein member nations could meet on a regular basis to exchange opinions on regional economic and social issues, and to assist in the economic reconstruction and development of Asia."[57] To be more specific, it is worth noting the official stipulation made in 1951: "Initiate and participate in measures for facilitating concerted action for the economic reconstruction and development of Asia and the Far East, for raising the level of economic activity in Asia and the Far East and for maintaining and strengthening the economic relations of these areas both among themselves and with other countries of the world." ECAFE was launched out of the United States' strong desire to seize hegemony in this "new" region, where each former colonizer's stakes clashed with those of each newly independent nation. It served, therefore, as a "laboratory" for America's new role in the world. From its third session onward, one of the most urgent agendas was to question the trade between ECAFE countries and Japan. E. E. Ward, in *Far Eastern Survey*, argued, "ECAFE countries should avail themselves of Japan's ability to meet some of their urgent needs, especially in exchange for raw materials, which the ECAFE countries could supply, provided no action taken by ECAFE usurped the functions of the Far Eastern Commission."[58] P. S. Lokanathan, an Indian economist who served as executive secretary of ECAFE, visited Tokyo in June 1949 and expressed his view that Japan should increase its trade with the rest of Asia, thereby "increasing her ability to buy from non-dollar areas and also enabling the rest of Asia to speed up its recovery and development."[59]

Japan–United States–United Kingdom

With the outbreak of the Korean War in June 1950, the Japanese economy achieved unprecedented growth. As Prime Minister Yoshida Shigeru (in office 1948–54) put it, "the war in South Korea was an unexpected gift of the gods."[60] Thanks to aid from the United States and the flourishing of the

Japanese economy with the help of the currency exchange rate policy, by the time of the Japan-United States peace treaty in 1951, Japan had emerged as a leading economic figure in Asia. Yet, as Japan's political economist Akira Suehiro notes, Japan, having lost the Chinese market, urgently needed alternative markets where it could export manufactured products and import raw materials and food, which had mostly been supplied by its "lost" colonies, such as South Korea, Taiwan, and Manchuria.

However, with this new regional map, Japan would have to carefully negotiate with the former imperial power over the region, the UK, to regain its lost terrain. In addition, in joining the regional economic organization (SEATO) and the UN, Japan would face hostile reactions from former colonies-cum-independent countries who feared Japan's reemergence and remilitarization. The UK's postwar policy objective in Southeast Asia was to regain colonial control of Malaysia, Singapore, Burma, and Hong Kong. However, it faced a number of obstacles in this attempt. First, growing anticolonial nationalism in Southeast Asia led to the waning of British power in the region, and the independence of India and Pakistan in 1947 practically ended Britain's imperial position. Second, the ever-expanding communist bloc led by the Soviet power threatened the region. In particular, the establishment of the PRC in 1949 and the communist insurrection in Malaysia created an emergency situation for the UK. Third, the UK's postwar financial difficulties deepened, and the country proved to be no match for the United States, the new regional power. Therefore, as James T. H. Tang has argued, the British postwar government aspired to create a "third force" in world politics.[61] However, it had no choice but to seek a close alliance with the United States in the Cold War confrontation.

British representatives in Southeast Asia, especially Sir Malcolm MacDonald (1901–81), the commissioner-general for Southeast Asia from 1948 to 1955, sought to use Japan as an "economic agent to help Britain shoulder its regional obligations." MacDonald stated, "Japanese 'return' to Southeast Asia should be viewed with friendly understanding . . . Japanese technical abilities, Japanese consumer and capital goods and Japanese influence might well prove to be a most important factor in the development and future stability of Southeast Asia."[62] Therefore, Tomaru Junko reasons, Britain and Japan entered into "co-operative relations vis-a-vis the region."[63] Nevertheless, Japan had to deal with countries where economic nationalism and fear of Japan's "second invasion" were strong. Suehiro writes concerning this problem and its solution that Japan made use of its "reparation payments" and "American economic aid to the region."[64] Prime Minister Yoshida, in his meeting with John Foster Dulles, asserted, "Reparations are a kind of investment. If we can contribute to the economic development of Southeast Asia in the name of reparation payment, we can help prevent the propagation of communism. With reparations, we can kill two birds with one stone."[65]

The Yoshida cabinet, through the Japan-United States economic partnership, launched a "scheme for the development of Southeast Asia" with high expectations. Riding on America's vast economic aid policy in the region and already operating the Colombo Plan, a United States-UK joint cooperative plan for economic development in South and Southeast Asia, Japan finally reentered Southeast Asia around 1953. As a result, many Japanese sectors also started to organize goodwill tours of Southeast Asia with the aid of government officials, Diet members, and entrepreneurs.[66] For instance, in August 1952, a Diet member of the Southeast Asian Economic Mission visited India, Pakistan, Ceylon, Thailand, Hong Kong, and Taiwan with the purpose of strengthening Japan's economic ties with these countries.[67] In accordance with all these economic missions, the *Ajia mondai chosakai* (Asian Affairs Research Society) was initiated and its monthly journal, *Ajia mondai* (Asian Affairs), was first published in 1953. Nagata, along with the Japanese government and many in the economic, political, and cultural sectors in the country, believed that cinema would become "Japan's cultural emissary." The film industry, per Richie and Anderson, "stuck to this concept with the evangelistic zeal of a true missionary."[68]

In an interview with the foreign press, Nagata proudly stated that "there has been an abundant flow of international amenity and *goodwill*, not to mention tangible accomplishments in direct assistance offered and received in joint production, in location facilities, in technical know-how and in production materials."[69] Nagata's statement reaffirms the aim and purpose of the Southeast Asian Film Festival and frames the event as an archetypical "flying geese" model, a theory of industrial development in latecomer economies in Asia that was coined by the Japanese economist Kaname Akamatsu in the 1930s.[70] Akamatsu's original article was later translated into English in 1962.[71] As the primary designer of the FPA, Nagata dreamed of leading the film industries of "free Asia." He aimed to kill two birds with one stone, uplifting the status of Japanese cinema in the region as a technically and artistically superior "big brother" and exporting genre films to the region to contribute to Japan's economy. But, as the following section argues, things were not so simple. Neither aim was successfully achieved in the end, because Nagata and TAF failed to untangle the intricate web of interregional politics.

The Battle for Control: The FPA's First Conference

As described earlier, the first constitutional conference of the FPA was held in Manila from November 17 to 19, 1953. Delegates from five countries, including Shaw, de Leon, Malik, and Nagata himself, joined the conference. For TAF's motion picture team, launching an alliance of anticommunist motion picture producers in Asia seemed within reach, considering the number of noncommunist film executives in the FPA. Paradoxically, however, the foundation's Manila representative, William T. Fleming, sent a bitter message to James L. Stewart, the director of programming, after the conference. Fleming lamented, "TAF-Manila sustained a considerable defeat at the hand of Communist influenced Asian film interests at the Manila planning conference."[72] What had happened to the conference? How and to what extent was the conference deemed a "defeat"?[73]

It was Djamaludin Malik, an Indonesian delegate and the president of Perseroan Film Indonesia (Persari), whose vehement opposition to the FPA's drafted constitution created unanticipated contention.[74] He challenged in particular its geographical scope, which excluded the PRC, North Korea, Burma, Vietnam, India, and Pakistan. No sooner had the conference begun than Malik cast doubt on the definition of Southeast Asia. Nagata responded that the Southeast Asian countries were those that bordered the Pacific Ocean, namely Burma, Malaysia, Vietnam, Thailand, Indonesia, the Philippines, Hong Kong, Japan, and Taiwan. "We have excluded," he underscored, "China occupied by the Communists, that is, Communist China." Nagata added that Burma and Vietnam were not invited, as neither country had produced enough feature films in the previous year. Malik objected: "I want to express my regret that the procedure of this conference is not properly done. I mean to say you exclude some countries just because of the reasons you have said. At least, we could send them invitations." He then suggested excluding the two Chinas altogether, "without discrimination whether it is free China or communist China." Indeed, Malik was a Sumatran businessman who during the war years had invested in theater companies. It is possible that TAF's office was not well informed about Malik and so was not prepared to deal with him; in fact, he had recently been working with various Chinese business interests, Indonesian as well as foreign.[75] Rafael Anton, a delegate from the Philippines, interceded in the heated debate by proposing that the board members vote on whether to receive a membership application from an organization of motion picture producers in the abovementioned countries, including the communist territories. Anton's proposition was difficult for Nagata to oppose and was accepted unanimously.

The FPA could not continue to exclude the PRC and North Korea from the organization while the voting members were advocating to receive their applications. Neither the Japanese film delegates (except Nagata) nor the Shaw family expressed any objection. They were, after all, entrepreneurs and concerned with their economic interests, not ideological stances. They all wanted to sell their films to the PRC, India, and possibly North Korea. This was the first unanticipated "defeat" Fleming noted. More contentious arguments followed when Nagata brought up the constitution for the film festival. Article 3, "participating films," was the most controversial because it reflected each film producer's own interests, fears, and desires. Article 3 was composed of seven paragraphs:

1. films shall be classified into the dramatic and the non-dramatic categories
2. the non-dramatic category includes the educational film, scientific film, documentary, cartoon, and cultural film
3. films should be exhibited in the country of origin during the year preceding the year of the film festival
4. films should not be exhibited at another international film festival
5. the number of participating films from each country should not exceed five in each of the categories
6. the film festival executive committee reserves the right to refuse participation of any film if it does not come up to the artistic or technical standards worthy of exhibition at the festival and/or hurts the national feeling of other countries
7. the dialogue should dubbed in the language of the host country.

The first five paragraphs and the seventh stipulated general rules for festival films and were passed unanimously. The sixth paragraph was the one that created controversy. Coupled with this disputed paragraph was a new addition proposed by Anton and Nagata: 6-B, "Films whose theme is contrary to democratic principles shall not be eligible to participate in the Film Festival." Nagata explained the term "democratic principles" as follows: "I think, and you all know, that the world is divided into two parts: one is the democratic group, and the other is the Communist group. There is no neutral country. That should be the case. Our conference or our Federation is in the democratic group . . . and if this Federation holds a film festival, it is under the auspices of the democratic group and when we say it is political and ideological, it means the other part, the Communist group."

Robert G. North (1913–54), an American film producer and a delegate of Thailand, seconded Nagata's proposition but went further. North claimed, "I have spoken with the Philippines delegates (Anton and de Leon) and I think we are all agreed that films of communist theme or origin should not be eligible to participate in the festival." Three Filipino delegates, Anton, de Leon, and Ricardo S. Balatbat, seconded his suggestion. Malik, predictably, disputed the motion and asserted, "If the majority of the representatives want to insist on that motion, we cannot stop them, but I only want to clarify our stand. If that paragraph is received by the body, then we won't hold ourselves responsible for this organization . . . I think that we should allow the Communists or whatever they are to express themselves." Chapman Ho, a Hong Kong delegate, petitioned to replace the motion with a more balanced one: "Films of political and ideological propaganda shall not be eligible to participate in the film festival." Both motions were put to a vote. Thailand and the Philippines supported North, while five board members from Hong Kong, Indonesia, Japan, and Malaysia cast their votes for Ho's petition, resulting in the addition of a new paragraph to Article 3, 6-B. With this new subsection, it fell to the hands of the committee to determine the ideological and political origin of submitted films. This was certainly the second "defeat."

Busch, Miller, and Tanner had assumed that the Thai and Filipino delegates were all anticommunist fighters and would stand with Nagata. Indonesia had been a headache for TAF from the very beginning of the FPA. But what put them in a real corner were delegates from Hong Kong and Malaysia, and even Japanese delegates who revealed ambivalence in their ideological and political outlooks. Contemplating this unforeseen setback in building an anticommunist alliance of film producers in Asia, TAF representatives realized that assuring enough voting members for their objectives would be a real challenge. Busch wrote to Stewart, "The threat of Communist penetration and eventual take-over of the Federation was a real one. . . . and the battle for control of the Federation has only started."[76]

After exchanging many letters and notes, their collective solution was to recruit every possible independent pro-American, anticommunist film company in the region to join the FPA in an effort to obtain more free-world votes.[77] TAF moved fast, as the first festival was slated to commence in just a few months. Stewart summoned all the TAF field representatives and briefed them on the FPA's precarious circumstances. The Taiwan representative, Ward D. Smith, had turned down the initial invitation from the FPA, but now he arranged a meeting with Peter B. T. Chang, the information director for the provisional government in Taiwan.[78] Smith stressed that he was working "every angle I can think of to see to it that Taiwan does join the Federation."[79] Robert B. Sheeks, the Kuala Lumpur representative, contacted the British film producer Thomas Hodge, the head of the Malayan Film Unit, who according to Sheeks was "capable, energetic, and believes strongly in the same principles that we do."[80] Hodge headed the Malayan Film Unit from 1951 to 1957.[81] Before Malaysia, he was director of the Film and Publications' Division of British Information Services in the United States from 1948 to 1951.[82] He was passionate about TAF's plan to construct an anticommunist film producers' network in the region. Hodge joined the federation hoping to diminish the influence of Run Run Shaw.[83] In the Hong Kong office, as will be discussed extensively in the fourth chapter, the TAF-financed motion picture studio Asia Pictures, operated by the former journalist Chang Kuo-sin, had completed its first Mandarin-language feature film, *Tradition* (*Chuantong*, Tang Huang, 1955), and it was ready to be submitted to the festival.

The Japan Writer Project

At the same time that it was aggressively intervening in the FPA by supporting anticommunist film producers in Asia, TAF's motion picture project team also embarked on a new operation in Japan for Nagata's Daiei Studio, officially named the "Japan Writer Project." This project was intended, in Blum's words, "to utilize American know-how to help the Japanese make a film which might be acceptable to American audiences, probably to be distributed through the so-called art circuits."[84]

Certainly, TAF's continuous support of Nagata was based upon a desire to help create "an economically stable non-communist motion picture industry in Japan which will see the necessity of forcing the communist producers out of business."[85] The motion picture project team of TAF assumed that the weakness of Japanese cinema lay in its script—that is, in a lack of Western-style "good storytelling." TAF believed that someone from Hollywood should "study the existing production problems" and come up with a story that might result in exportable films.[86] TAF hoped to see Daiei Studio's contract writers develop scripts, in cooperation with top US writers, that would be "acceptable to western audiences."[87] As discussed earlier, Nagata aspired to sell Daiei productions to the international film market and the American market in particular. He produced several films aimed at the American market. One example is *Girls Hand in Hand* (*Futari no hitomi*, Shigeo Nakaki, 1952), in which Nagata cast the former American child actor Margaret O'Brien, known for her memorable appearance in *Meet Me in St. Louis* (Vincent Minnelli, 1944). *Girls Hand in Hand* tells the story of an American girl (O'Brien) who visits her father, an American diplomat in occupied Japan. She makes friends with a war orphan (Hibari Misora) and helps her and her friends raise money to build an orphanage. But *Girls Hand in Hand* was unsuccessful even in Japan, and there is no record that the film had any theatrical release in America.

To choose a "teacher" for the Japanese screenwriters, Tanner met with a group of Hollywood A-list writers, including Richard English, Winston Miller, Leonard Spiegelglass, Allen Rivkin, and Morris Ryskind, in December 1953. Many of them were contract writers for Paramount. Afterward, he reported to Noel Busch, the Tokyo representative: "Spiegelglass is emotionally unstable, and is reputed to be a homosexual. Rivkin is undependable: off-on-wild drunks sort of thing in which he gets lost for days, etc. Ryskind is too arbitrary. He has deep political colorations which influence his thinking too much."[88] Tanner also thought that English was "too good for this project."[89] Tanner's vote went to Winston Miller, Busch's brother-in-law, since Miller, he thought, was more competent than the others. And most important, Miller was an anti-communist warrior. Tanner particularly liked Miller's recent script *Hong Kong* (Lewis R. Foster, 1952), an adventure film set in Hong Kong during the second phase of the Chinese Civil War (1945–49) in which Ronald Reagan (who later became the fortieth president of the United States) played an American adventurer who helped a Chinese boy and the daughter of an American missionary escape from the city.

The Japan writer project was customized to Nagata's needs. TAF paid the travel expenses, while Daiei covered Miller's salary. Daiei promised Miller 10 percent of the export revenue.[90] Miller arrived in Tokyo on March 30, 1954. *The Hollywood Reporter* described his role as "ambassadorial" and designed to "pave the way for closer cooperation between the American and Japanese film industries."[91] Given that his previous scripts, including the widely acclaimed *Home in Indiana* (Henry Hathaway, 1944) and *My Darling Clementine* (John Ford, 1946), were widely known in Asia, Miller was warmly welcomed by the Japanese film industry. Moreover, one of Miller's recent films, *Rocky Mountain* (William Keighley, 1950), was coincidentally released in Japan only a week before his arrival, proving his solid status in Hollywood. During his month-long residency, Miller closely examined a number of Daiei films, from *Rashomon* and *Ugetsu* (*Ugetsu Monogatari*; Mizoguchi Kenji, 1953) to the studio's latest Eastman Color production *The Golden Demon* (*Konjiki Yasha*; Shima Koji, 1953).

Miller believed that Japan's "greatest need" was for more modern and original stories. He devised a way he could play a role as an editorial agent by screening and sending synopses of stories to Japan, and Nagata was enthusiastic about his plan.[92] Upon returning to Los Angeles, Miller contacted the Screen Writers Guild (SWG) to receive its approval for this project. On May 10, 1954, immediately after the meeting, SWG circulated among its members a letter titled "Attention! SWG Members . . .: Possible Story Market" in which it solicited stories. In this letter, the SWG specified the length and contents of the stories. The stipulations were (1) that the plot concern modern-day people and problems, as the Japanese had an unlimited supply of historical and "legendary" source material, (2) that the submission be in synopsis form, no more than five pages long, and (3) that Daiei would pay $500 to $2,000 for each story accepted.[93] In less than a month, Miller received over twenty stories from SWG. He shipped eleven of the "better" synopses to Daiei in June. Miller admitted that "some of them [were] pretty bad," but "two or three of the stories were good." While editing the stories he received, mostly for "ideological content," Miller completed his own story for Daiei. To TAF, everything looked good and promising. In a speech at the general committee meeting, Blum said, "This [writer project] may be a windfall for Hollywood writers released by studio [sic] because of production cutbacks and ensures Daiei receiving [sic] it is from the original document good, original non-communist story material which has been the Japanese industry's greatest need. This new cooperation eventually could help the Japanese achieve their cherished goal of producing films suitable for the lucrative American market."[94]

To Tanner, Miller was a savior. Tanner wrote, "We have obtained more from this project than they hoped for at the beginning. It [the writer project] could win American acceptance for one or more Japanese films on the art circuit and earning dollars as a result accomplish what the Japanese government and film industry have sought vainly to do for some time."[95] Busch considered the writer project, with the promise of the MPAA's support, "the strongest weapon we could have in keeping the Festival in line." With these, he wrote, "The opposition does not win the fight for control."[96]

Chapter 3

It's Oscar Time in Asia!

On May 18, 1954, Frank Borzage (1894–1962), a two-time Oscar award winner for best director, arrived at Tokyo International Airport with his wife Juanita Scott to attend the first Southeast Asian Film Festival. He was the representative from the US movie industry.[1] Duke Wales, the director of publicity for the MPAA, described Borzage's arrival: "Japanese hospitality is creating practically an around-the-clock schedule of honors for Frank Borzage . . . [the] enthusiastic reaction to Hollywood's recognition of the festival started with the Borzages' arrival at Tokyo airport, where the red carpet was literally laid out, from the airplane to the custom office."[2] Borzage's participation in the festival had been arranged by TAF's Tokyo office.

Borzage was not on TAF's list of "most wanted." The organization wanted a big name Hollywood mogul. Finding prestigious Hollywood delegates, however, was not easy. Charles Tanner, the Hollywood liaison and a motion picture officer of TAF, had beseeched Frank Capra, Cecil B. DeMille, John Ford, George Stevens, Mervyn LeRoy, Henry King, and William Holden to attend, but none of them was available.[3] Capra showed a strong interest in attending the festival in Japan, but he could not change his production schedule. Borzage's lone presence at the Southeast Asian Film Festival stood in contrast to the immense Hollywood delegation sent to the third

Figure 3.1. Frank Borzage, an Oscar-winning Hollywood director, attends the first Southeast Asian Film Festival with his wife, Juanita Scott, as a US movie industry representative. Asia Foundation Records, Hoover Institution Archives, photo courtesy of the Asia Foundation.

Punta del Este International Movie Festival in Uruguay in January 1955.[4] In fact, Hollywood studios had little interest in the festival in the Far East. Asia was neither as sizeable a market as Europe nor was it considered an emerging territory for the Hollywood industry.

Borzage was emerging from a long hiatus.[5] It is not known what encouraged him to accept the invitation of the FPA, but it is worth noting that the Hollywood blacklist had forced him into a six-year period of inactivity after the release of *Moonrise* (1948).[6] Perhaps Borzage was desperate for a call from Hollywood. Before Tokyo, Borzage had joined a March 1954 tour to Argentina as a representative of the US motion picture industry. He had served on a jury of the inaugural Festival Internacional de Cine de Mar del Plata in Argentine, along with Mary Pickford.[7]

By the time Borzage arrived in Tokyo, the first Southeast Asian Film Festival (also known as the first Film Festival in Southeast Asia), which had started on May 8, was preparing to hold its closing ceremony on May 20. Six member countries—Japan, Hong Kong, Malaysia, the Philippines, Thailand, and the Republic of China (Taiwan)—sent fifteen feature films to the festival. Each of Japan's "big five" studios submitted its latest film: Shochiku's *The Garden of Women* (*Onna no sonno*, Kinoshita Keisuke, 1954; also known as *The Eternal Generation*), Daiei's *The Golden Demon*, Shin Toho's *The Grass-Cutters* (*Kusa wo karu musume*, Nakagawa Nobuo, 1954), Toho's *Sound of the Mountain* (*Yama no oto*, Naruse Mikio, 1954), and Toei's *Forsaken* (*Horoki*, Hisamatsu Seiji, 1954). In addition to the Japanese films, the Philippines' three major studios introduced five films: LVN's *Dagohoy* (Gregorio Fernandez, 1953), Sampaguita's *Inspirasiyon* (Armando Garces, 1953) and *My American Wife* (*Ang Asawa Kong Amerikana*, Eddie Romero, 1953), and Premiere's *Dyesebel* (Gerardo de Leon, 1953) and *Salabusab* (Cesar Gallardo, 1954). Thailand submitted *Santi-Vina* (Rattana Pestonji, 1954). Taiwan's entry was *Women in the Army* (Hsu Hsin-fu and Wang Yu, 1954), while Hong Kong and Malaysia sent *A Song of Romance* (*Gouhun yanqu*, Wang Yin, 1953; Shaw & Sons), *Tradition* (*Chuantong*, Tang Huang, 1955; Asia Pictures), and *Iman* (D. R. S. Sastry, 1953; Shaw's Malay Film Productions).[8] The Indonesian entry *After the Curfew* (*Lewat Djam Malam*, Usmar Ismail, 1954) was cancelled at the last minute for political reasons, and Djamaludin Malik and Usmar Ismail were absent from the festival.[9] The Indonesian delegates announced that "in view of the objections of the Indonesian government toward Indonesian-Japanese cooperation, even in the cultural field, pending the restoration of normal diplomatic relations between the two countries, they would not be able to take part in the Asian Film Festival."[10] *After the Curfew* was, however, shown at the second festival in Singapore a year later. In addition, at the first festival, twelve "cultural and educational" short documentaries from Japan, Malaysia, and Taiwan were screened during the twelve-day schedule. There were also four "special entries" from Ceylon (Sri Lanka) and India.

The magnificent Tokyo Kaikan (meeting hall), designed by Taniguchi Yoshiro in 1921, was the main venue for the festival. Facing the Imperial Palace, this opulent building was one of the architectural symbols of Japan's westernization. The introductory meeting was held in the elegant Rose Room on the fourth floor of the theater. Nagata, as president of the FPA, delivered his welcome speech:

> Being president of the Federation of Motion Picture Producers in Southeast Asia, I am very happy to note that the festival, at which best pictures produced by Southeast Asian countries contest for the highest honors that

are deserved for the most beautiful, harmonious, and elegant, will mark an epoch in the cultural history of Asia. The festival is not held merely to choose prize winners among entries but also to provide opportunities for participants to make a comparative study of pictures with regard to artistic value and technical standard. Moreover, the event is designed to better the quality of motion pictures, promote exchange of cultural achievements of each country in Southeast Asia and enhance friendly relations among the participating nations through the screening of choice products and free exchange of opinions on the entries.[11]

Certainly, film festivals in Nagata's time were conspicuously different from those we are familiar with now. As showcases of national cinema, most postwar international film festivals until the mid-1960s sent invitations to countries chosen by the festival committees. Which films were screened at the festivals was utterly dependent on the national committees' selection processes. Therefore, following the model of what Thomas Elsaesser describes as "the athlete who competes at the Olympic Games," each participant country sent what it believed to be its finest products, normally up to four films, and the festival jurors made the final decision.[12] The system by which the festival screened the selections, however, did not result in each "country's best and most representative motion pictures being seen at the festival," as Fred Roos, a film critic, complained of the Venice Film Festival in 1957. Roos also pointed out that the problem of the festival was that it had "too many films and too many prizes."[13] In most film journals of the time, especially during the 1950s, the films shown at festivals were reviewed not as individual filmmakers' works of art, but as products of countries.[14]

At the press conference of the first Southeast Asian Film Festival, Nagata expressed full confidence. *Gate of Hell*, the first Eastman color film produced by Daiei, had won the Grand Prix at the Cannes International Film Festival only a week earlier. This was certainly the peak of Nagata's career. Nagata boasted that "the worth of Japanese cinema has now been recognized . . . although Europe and America are important markets, Asia also holds a great future for Japanese movies."[15] No one could deny the artistic and technical superiority of the Japanese entries at the festival. Not surprisingly, Daiei's *The Golden Demon* walked away with the award for the best motion picture, and its producer, Nagata, took the trophy.[16] *The Golden Demon*, Daiei's second Eastman color production, was an adaptation of a classic novel that was originally published in serial form in the *Yomiuri Shinbun* (Yomiuri newspaper) and the literary periodical *Shinshosetsu* (New Fiction) from 1897 to 1903. It was, however, unfinished due to the unexpected death of the author, Ozaki Koyo (1868–1903), one of the pioneers of modern Japanese literature. *The Golden Demon* is considered one of the most successful and best-received novels of the Meiji Era (1868–1912). Daiei's screen adaptation tells the story of a woman who abandons her poor student sweetheart to marry the son of a wealthy banker. Years later, the poor man becomes a wealthy, cold-hearted loan shark. The woman, for her part, is miserable. Her husband treats her cruelly. She goes to her former lover to beg forgiveness, but he spurns her. The film finally brings them together, giving the audience a glimpse of hope in the end.

The special MPAA Mitchell Camera Prize was awarded to the Far East Film Company in Thailand for its Eastman color production *Santi-Vina*.[17] Tanner described the selection procedure in detail:

> The selection of the Mitchell award was well handled. The same jury that selected the Grand Prix was asked to choose the three films which they considered most completely fitted the specifications: the film which best disseminates Asian culture and increases understanding of Asia by the western nations. This they did. [Frank] Borzage then screened the three pictures and gave opinions concerning the three, after which the jury chose the winner of the award. Frank made it clear that in expressing his opinion he sought to assist the jury but definitely not to influence them in their choice. As it turned out he eliminated one immediately and said that *The Golden Demon* was obviously the best but in his opinion *Santi Vina* more completely filled the bill as to the specifications. *Santi Vina* was, of course, voted the winner.[18]

Santi-Vina was the first film produced by Far East Film Ltd. in Bangkok, a studio founded in 1952 by the self-taught filmmaker Rattana Pestonji (1908–70) and his American business partner Robert G. North. Pestonji also served as the cinematographer, while North penned the script. *Santi-Vina* was the only film written and produced especially for the first Southeast Asian Film Festival.[19] The Eastman Color negative development was done by Nagase Laboratories in Tokyo, and the printing, editing, and sound processing were completed in Bangkok. In receiving this special MPAA Mitchell Camera Prize, *Santi-Vina* became the first Thai film to win an award at an international film festival.[20] At the festival, the Royal Thai Ambassador his Excellency Luang Phinit Akson (in office 1954–58) received the trophy on behalf of the film's director Pestonji. He declared, "The Thai motion picture, while 30 years old, is still developing, and the picture *Santi-Vina*, which you have seen and honored, is our first picture to be exhibited in international competition. The fact is, you may be interested to know, that it is also the first 35mm color picture ever made in our country, and therefore, the achievement of Mr. Pestonji in winning the best photography award is the most remarkable."[21]

With the exception of *Santi-Vina*, the Japanese film industry dominated the festival, grabbing five major awards. Shaw Brothers was also awarded a special prize for Li Li-hua's (*A Song of Romance*) "most beautiful face and sweetest voice."[22] Luciano B. Carlos won the best screenplay award for *My American Wife*. An editorial in *Kinema Junpo*, a Japanese film magazine, wrote somewhat ostentatiously, "The quality of Japanese cinema justifies the Japanese film industry's dominion in the festival. To put it bluntly, we are questioning whether the festival still needs any competition categories."[23] After the ceremony, Nagata bragged, "I intend to follow the road I have chosen until I become king of the movie world!"[24]

Miller, after watching most of the films, committed himself thus: "It was quite obvious to Southeast Asian feature film producers that the Japanese were ahead of them and that there was a great need for them to increase artistic quality and improve techniques. . . . The first festival was a great success. It is encouraging to report that the festival was not held just for the purpose of mutual admiration but provided worthwhile opportunities for the participants to make a comparative study of each other's product."[25] He also emphasized that TAF's Mitchell Camera award would strengthen the foundation's position in the region.[26] Miller suggested that TAF should maintain an active behind-the-scenes interest in the federation. Miller was somewhat disappointed, however, that Asia Pictures' entry in the festival, *Tradition*, was the first to be excluded from any consideration due to its somewhat negative portrayal of a Japanese general. It was thought to meet the criterion for exclusion in article 6: "Films which are likely to hurt the national feeling of another country or territory." A documentary film from Taiwan (*Road to Freedom*) was also voted out of the festival on the basis of 6-B: "films of political or ideological propaganda."[27] Miller also mentioned that Shochiku's *The Garden of Women* caused controversy. Calling the film a "sneaker," he admitted its high production quality—it "could have been considered for the top award"—but it was, according to Miller, "the cleverest, more effective pro-Commie film yet produced in Japan." Armed with strong support from Tom Hodge, the head of the Malayan Film Unit, and Kukrit Pramoj, a writer and scholar from Thailand who later became prime minister, Nagata managed to exclude *The Garden of Women* from the festival's awards.[28]

Consequently, in his report to Blum, Miller evaluated key festival players whom he thought might line up with TAF at the second festival in Singapore:

Nagata Masaichi: President of the Federation; played a leading role in the festival but made no effort to dominate it; obviously striving for inter-Japanese and inter-federation harmony.

Kukrit Pramoj: Oxford graduate from Thailand. Publisher, writer, columnist, serviced as juror. Took a leading role in banning a communist-inclined film *The Eternal Generation* [*The Garden of Women*].

James Lawler: British subject. He is said to be politically naïve but while in Tokyo, indicated a willingness to go along with anti-communist efforts.

Thomas Hodge: Head of Malayan Film Unit. Career officer, British Foreign Officer. Strong anti-communist and one of the dominating members of the Asian jury.

Robert North: Former Vice-president of Far East Film, Bangkok. Former Hollywood scenario writer, Twentieth Century Fox. One of the dominant figures in the Federation; exerts a great influence on other Thailand members. North is an active anti-communist campaigner within the federation.

Run Run Shaw: Vice-president of the Federation. Vibrant, flamboyant leader of Shaw's film interests in Asia. Gregarious, egotistic; has a great interest in the welfare of the federation. He said to be a non-political opportunist.[29]

Nagata's Hollywood Tour

Nagata visited San Francisco, New York, and Los Angeles from June 16 to July 7, 1954. This trip took place only a month after the inaugural Southeast Asian Film Festival. Samuel Goldwyn, Lou Schreiber, Jack Warner, Walter Wanger, Borzage, and Luigi Luraschi were included in his full itinerary. Luraschi received a letter from Tanner before his meeting with Nagata. In this letter, Tanner disclosed Nagata's primary purpose in visiting America. He was blunt this time: "He [Nagata] needs money, especially dollars. His activities on behalf of the Federation of Motion Picture Producers in Southeast Asia and the Asian Film Festival have cost him a considerable amount of cash, and now he needs to recoup."[30] TAF facilitated communication between Nagata and the Hollywood independent producer Walter Wanger regarding Wanger's film project *Mother, Sir*, based on a novel by M. D. Blain about an American navy wife stationed in Japan during the Pacific War. Wanger wanted to coproduce the film with one of Japan's top studios, and TAF, as expected, recommended Daiei. Nagata met Wanger in Los Angeles during his visit to Hollywood. Wanger wrote to Tanner after the meeting: "I talked to Nagata when he was here but he was not interested in my proposition at all . . . so we got nowhere."[31] Wanger could not find a Japanese partner and had to shoot the film at Republic Studio in Los Angeles. Under the new title of *Navy Wife*, the finished film was released in 1956. Gary Merrill and Shirley Yamaguchi (1920–2014; also known as Yamaguchi Yoshiko, Li Xianglan, and Ri Koran) played the leading roles.[32]

Certainly, Nagata's intention on this trip was to make multiple deals to distribute two of his award-winning films: *Gate of Hell* and *The Golden Demon*. In leading the FPA, Nagata dreamed of expanding and diversifying Daiei's markets: he hoped to distribute popular genre films to Asia through the FPA network and films of high production value to major European film festivals and Hollywood, with the help of TAF.[33] Nagata believed that the West might be "receptive to a series of stories of old Japan told in a 'humanistic' style and with a delicacy of composition and refinement of gesture."[34] At the luncheon meeting with Warner and Goldwyn, Nagata jested, "A Japanese proverb states that the greatest compliment that can be paid to a teacher is for the pupil to surpass the one who taught him. I thought that compliment belongs to you [Warner] since I feel that in *Gate of Hell* the pupil had surpassed the teacher."[35]

RKO Pictures considered picking up *Gate of Hell*, but in the end the independent distributor Edward Harrison (1903–67) released both *Gate of Hell* and *The Golden Demon*. A former press agent and publicist for *Rashomon* at RKO, Harrison was one of the pioneering figures in the US distribution of Asian films. During the 1950s and '60s, Harrison distributed Japanese films and most of the early classics of the Indian director Satyajit Ray, including *The Apu Trilogy* (*Pather Panchali, Aparajito,* and *Apur Sansar*).[36] *Gate of Hell* was publicized as a new film of Kyo Machiko, who had achieved sudden international stardom as the heroine of *Rashomon*.[37] But Nagata soon realized that neither film would be able to penetrate the mainstream market, as Edward Harrison had released the films in just a handful of theaters in New York, San Francisco, and Los Angeles—on a much smaller scale than Nagata had initially expected. The film critic James Powers wrote a review of *The Golden Demon* for the *Hollywood Reporter*, declaring, "This picture

[*The Golden Demon*] is not for general run houses except where such Japanese imports as *Gate of Hell* and *Rashomon* played successfully. It is in the same tradition and of the same high caliber as these two, with the most beautiful imaginable color added."[38] Despite Nagata's hopes, selling films to the United States could not make up for his severe fiscal deficit. As Richie and Anderson point out, what made *Gate of Hell* important was "its incorporation of the most beautiful color photography ever to grace the screen up to that time" in the Japanese film industry.

Evaluating the international market, Nagata had confidently decided that the success of his films overseas lay in their exoticism and he resolved to produce more large-scale period films. But little by little it became clear that Nagata was heading in the wrong direction. Nagata failed to win any major film festival awards abroad, and many of his expensive films, including *Gate of Hell* and *The Golden Demon*, had only moderate success in Japan. Even worse, the Japanese critics were completely confounded by the foreign success of *Rashomon* and *Gate of Hell*. Daiei's policy of producing period films "that appeal to foreigners" resulted in a neglect of their bread-and-butter products and a consequent decline in general quality. *Gate of Hell* made no one's "best ten" list in 1953 in Japan and was completely ignored by many Japanese moviegoers. According to the *Asahi Evening News*, many Japanese film critics felt that "this type of production [*Rashomon* and *Gate of Hell*] tends to stress the barbarism of the orient to the exclusion of other features" and they felt ashamed that "the warlike barbarism of ancient times and the 'warrior spirit' which was encouraged by the militarists in more recent years, still remains the object of foreign interest." The article also claimed that Japan had suffered "a national insult." One critic in Japan even harshly characterized the motion pictures winning popularity abroad as "goods displayed in a souvenir shop, loud and flashy with no intrinsic value."[39]

Nagata initiated the first film coproduced by Japan and Hong Kong, *The Princess Yang Kwei-fei* (*Yokihi*), with Run Run Shaw in 1955. It was directed under Mizoguchi Kenji's eloquent touch.[40] Nagata needed a film that would win fame again from both the domestic market and international festivals, and this exotic product looked like a perfect opportunity, with its Chinese flavor replacing the Japanese exoticism that was already so familiar to Western critics. The film, however, proved nothing but a disaster both commercially and artistically. *Motion Picture Daily* criticized the plot for being "old fashioned to American audiences" and for "proceed[ing] with a funeral slowness."[41] No American distributors wanted *The Princess Yang Kwei-fei*, and its complete failure humiliated Nagata. Daiei had banked on the idea that there was a greater opportunity to make money on "big, quality pictures" that were successful abroad than on the biggest films at home, but this now appeared to be unwise.[42] Soon Nagata's status in the Japanese film industry was in trouble. Worse, despite TAF's assiduous backing, Nagata failed to gain a good reputation in Hollywood. Irving Maas, the vice president of the MPEAA, derided him as "a very ambitious and shrewd individual, who is very anxious for personal glory" and found him to be "a slippery customer."[43]

Apparently, the FPA connection did not help Nagata much either. The writer project made no progress. John Miller wrote to Blum on November 17, 1954, expressing his concern: "As you know, 22 scripts were received in July and August by Daiei and according to reports, one was purchased under difficult circumstances, for USD 700. Do the Hollywood writers feel that it is worthwhile to send stories here? If so, why did 22 arrive in July and August and none since that time? In an attempt to see if there is a more acceptable way for both parties to handle the project we will also attempt to determine Daiei's true opinions about its value to them."[44] It is not evident what Nagata had in mind and to what extent he was committed to the writer project. Tanner, Miller, and Busch regarded him as a strategic partner but never believed in him. Chase, in his letter to Stewart, advised caution in "any dealings with Nagata."[45] Worse still, *Escapade in Japan*, the script Winston Miller himself had developed for and handed over to Nagata, was never produced at Daiei.[46]

The Second Southeast Asian Film Festival

In April 1955, Kim Kwan-su (1905–?), president of the Korean Motion Picture Producers Association, received a call from Mary Walker, the administrative assistant of Philip Rowe, a representative of TAF's Seoul office.[47] By the time Kim arrived at TAF's newly constructed office in Kwanhundong, Seoul, the heart of postwar South Korea, Rowe was waiting for him. Rowe inquired whether he was aware of the newly launched FPA, and suggested that he be present at the Southeast Asian Film Festival, which would shortly be holding its second assembly in Singapore. South Korea had not been invited to the preceding year's inaugural event. TAF, Rowe stressed, would allocate three travel grants for attendance at the festival.[48] With the "greenbacks" given to him, Kim summoned another film industry power player in this war-ravaged country: Yun Pong-ch'un (1902–75), chairman of the Motion Picture Director's Association in South Korea. Cho Tong-jae (1921–2005), Rowe's project assistant, accompanied the observers as an interpreter. They embarked on the journey to Singapore. As Rowe indicated, this was the first link South Korean cinema had made with the region's film industry after the armistice that ended the ruinous Korean War just a couple of years before.

TAF had carefully arranged their trip. The three Korean men stopped first in Hong Kong and spent several days there to meet Chang Kuo-sin, the president of Asia Pictures, while waiting for their new tailor-made Western suits. Rowe's introduction of each observer to the Hong Kong representative is intriguing. He wrote: "Mr. Kim is an aggressive, cigar-smoking, producer type. Mr. Yoon [Yun] is quieter and less sophisticated. Mr. Cho's English is excellent." "None of the gentlemen," Rowe emphasized, "have spent time outside of South Korea other than in Japan."[49] The three South Korean delegates arrived in Singapore on May 13, 1955, just a day before the opening of the festival.

At the second festival, Irving Maas, the British filmmaker David Lean, and F. R. Simmons of London Films International attended as observers.[50] Japan dispatched the largest delegation, with twenty-six delegates from all six major studios: Toho, Shochiku, Daiei, Toei, Shin Toho, and Nikkatsu. The Philippines and Hong Kong followed, sending eight delegates each. The delegations from Taiwan, Ceylon, Thailand, and South Korea were rather small. The opening ceremony was staged at the Victoria Memorial Hall in Singapore. Completed in 1906 to commemorate Queen Victoria, the hall was also a site of an important political milestone in Singapore. The People's Action Party had been officially launched at Victoria Memorial Hall on November 21, 1954.[51] Indeed, the festival took place only six months after the founding of the new party. The opening address at the festival was given by Run Run Shaw, chairman of the organizing committee, followed by an address from Nagata. Ho Ah Loke, a local film magnate and president of Cathay-Keris Studio in Singapore, gave a brief summary of the films selected for the competition categories.[52] Then Singapore's Commissioner-General Malcolm MacDonald declared the festival open.[53]

During the festival, twenty-five features and fifteen short films were shown. Japan's "big five" studios, as they had done a year earlier, sent their "best" films, including Daiei's *The Story of Shunkin* (*Shunkin monogatari*, Itô Daisuke, 1955), Shin Toho's *Human Torpedoes* (*Ningen Gyorai Kaiten*, Soei Matsubayashi, 1955), Shochiku's *The Refugee* (*Bomeiki*, Nomura Yoshitaro, 1955) and Toei's *Bloody Spear at Mount Fuji* (*Chiyari Fuji*, Uchida Tomu, 1955). Toho's choice, *Madame Butterfly* (Carmine Gallone, 1954), caused a minor controversy during the festival as it was a Japan-Italy coproduction directed

Figure 3.2. Official poster for the second Southeast Asia Film Festival, May 14–21, 1955, which was held in Singapore. Photo courtesy of the Federation of Motion Picture Producers in Asia-Pacific (FPA).

by an Italian. Other than Japan, the Philippines (5), Hong Kong (3), Singapore (5), Taiwan (3), Indonesia (2), Thailand (1), and Macao (1) showed their films during the festival period.[54] It should be noted here that the presence of the Shaw Brothers, or at least the youngest Shaw, Run Run, stood out

At Keris Studios
12 Oct 1957:
With Ho Ah Loke
& Maria Menado

Figure 3.3. Ho Ah Loke (left), president of Cathay Keris Studio, and Maria Menado (middle), a Malay actress, at Cathay Keris Studio in Singapore, October 12, 1957. Courtesy of Asian Film Archive, Singapore.

at this Singapore festival. He was chairman of the organizing committee; he represented Singapore/Malaysia and Hong Kong; and he submitted, as a producer, four films: two from Shaw's Malay Film Studio, *Filem Merana* (B. N. Rao, 1954) and *Hang Tuah* (Phani Majumdar, 1956); and two from Shaw & Sons in Hong Kong, *Beyond the Grave* (*Ren gui lian*, Doe Ching, 1954) and *The Orphan Girl* (*Mei Gu*, Yan Jun, 1955). On the surface, the FPA was conceived as a Japan-led organization, but in reality Run Run Shaw had the most dominant presence at the event.

The Indonesian film industry was notably enthusiastic about the Southeast Asian Film Festival and formed a committee representing the nineteen member companies of the Indonesian Producers Association to select seven top films to submit the festival. The result was a kind of prefestival festival on a national level. The seven selected films toured from March 30 to April 5 in six major cities, including Jakarta and Surabaya, for the final judging. On April 17, the committee chose two films, *After the Curfew* (*Lewat Djam Malam*, Usmar Ismail, Pesari-Perfini, 1954) and *Tarmina* (Lily Sudjo, Pesari, 1955).[55]

Djamaludin Malik's participation posed a tricky problem for TAF. During the second festival, Malik replaced Run Run Shaw as vice-president of the FPA. Miller pointed out that "Indonesia's participation [would] assure the presence of at least one very clever communist agitator."[56] What Miller and TAF worried about was Malik's strong desire to host the next Southeast Asian Film Festival. Robert G. North, a cofounder of Far East Film in Bangkok, had been the Indonesians' "most formidable and outspoken antagonist" within the FPA. But his unexpected death a year earlier led TAF to be concerned about Indonesia's friendly relations with the PRC and India.

Unexpectedly, it was Kim Kwan-su, South Korea's delegate, who showed a strong objection to Indonesia. Kim was not afraid of speaking up against the ideas or opinions of those he believed to be "Red" producers or sympathizers in Asia. Kim, in an interview with *Kyŏnghyang shinmun*, a local newspaper in South Korea, boasted:

> At the [Asian Film] festival, we had a long discussion concerning which country will host the next year's festival. Indonesia was the most active among nations, but I refused because Indonesia seems to be a procommunist country. For example, Indonesia proposed including North Korea and Red China [People's Republic of China] in the festival's committee last year. As you know, this festival was established to promote the culture and ideology of free Asia to the outer world. How could such a communist country join the festival! Japan vetoed the proposal more strongly, and we, Korean delegates, followed Japan's opinion. We also refused a coproduction offer from one of the Indonesian film producers due to the same reason. We should not unite with such a procommunist country.[57]

Thanks to this surprise anticommunist warrior from South Korea, Hong Kong, instead of Indonesia, was selected to host the third Southeast Asian Film Festival. The Indonesian film industry, though, sent twenty-four delegates to Hong Kong a year later, the largest number among all participants—outnumbering even the Japanese film industry.[58] What should be emphasized here is less Kim's stalwart opposition to the Indonesian delegates than his firm alliance with Japan. During the Japanese occupation period (1910–45), Kim Kwan-su was a rather opportunistic member of the cultural elite who served as an executive officer of the Association of Chosŏn Theatre Culture, a pro-Japanese organization established in 1942. After the liberation in 1945, however, Kim precipitously reformed his ideological stance and became involved in the film industry. With his verbal fluency in both English and Japanese,

Kim seized a chance under the US occupiers and made his way to work with the United States Army Military Government in Korea (USAMGIK). Kim, paired with the respected film director Ch'oe In-gyŭ (1919-61), produced several anti-Japanese films right after the liberation, such as *Hurrah Freedom!* (*Chayu manse*, 1946), *An Innocent Criminal* (*Ch'oe ŏmnŭn ch'oein*, 1948), and *The Night Before Independence Day* (*Tongnip chŏnya*, 1948). A year after the armistice, in 1954, Kim donned a new outfit: anti-communism. This was only a decade after the formal closure of thirty-five years of Japanese rule in Korea. In a mere ten years, the fear of Japan's remilitarization in South Korea had been fully converted to the logic of the Red Scare.[59]

The awards ceremony of the second Southeast Asian Film Festival was held at Sea View Hotel in Tanjong Katong on May 21. Japan won six trophies, including the Best Film of the Year (*The Story of Shunkin*), Best Photography (*The Refugee*), Best Sound Recording (*The Refugee*), Best Art Direction (*The Refugee*), Best Actress (*The Refugee*), and Best Juvenile Actor (*Bloody Spear at Mount Fuji*). Nagata received the Best Picture trophy for the second consecutive year. The Filipino director Gerardo de Leon (1913–81) was awarded the Best Director prize with his *Ifugao*, which also won in the Best Screenplay and Best Actor categories. Hong Kong's Siao Fong Fong (Josephine Siao, b. 1947) won the Best Juvenile Actress award for her performance in Shaw & Sons' *The Orphan Girl*.[60] The MPAA Mitchell Camera Prize was, however, not given this time. In fact, this prize was never awarded after the first festival in Tokyo. Miller had already predicted the suspension of the MPAA prize as early as in January 1955. He wrote to Stewart, "He [Irving Maas] admitted that since there is a harder currency situation in Singapore, than in Japan, such arrangements may be difficult. Although Maas agreed that the American industry was enjoying great financial prosperity in Asia and rightfully should cover all expenses connected with MPAA and/or MPEA participation, he was not positive that funds could be made available. He did say that he was quite sure that the MPEA could not underwrite the costs."[61] As explained earlier, TAF, not the MPAA, had purchased the Mitchell camera used for the first festival. Outwardly, TAF wanted the MPAA label. But TAF headquarters did not want to continue purchasing the expensive Mitchell camera on behalf of the MPAA. Had it not been for TAF's expenditure, the MPAA would not have otherwise spent money on the Southeast Asian film festival.

After the festival, Miriam Bucher, who had attended the festival as an observer, submitted her report to TAF. Bucher and her husband Jules were American documentarists who were active from the early 1930s through the mid-1980s. They had extensive international careers, working largely for the US State Department.[62] When Miriam Bucher composed the report, the couple was living in Jakarta, Indonesia, helping the Indonesian government set up its film industry, Perusahaan Film National (Perfini) (PFN), under the leadership of Usmar Ismail. Under the Technical Cooperation Administration (TCA) program, a part of the Colombo Plan, PFN received USD 380,000 from the United States' Foreign Operations Administration to purchase new film equipment.[63] Moreover, ten American film technical experts were dispatched to Indonesia, and in the end they stayed for six years.[64] During the early 1950s, a group of employees of the government's film unit and several prominent film personnel were sent to the United States to be trained.[65] Interestingly enough, Malik, the most outspoken member of the FPA, was not included in the TCA program.

Bucher saw the festival as a "loosely organized trade convention" and therefore found there to be an "insufficient emphasis on films." She suggested that the participating countries should decide whether this festival was to be a genuine film festival or "a trade show."[66] More interesting, she called for TAF to contribute more actively to the festival. TAF's support was, Bucher wrote, "certainly not going to be a secret (witness the 'Asia Foundation Delegation from Korea') . . . I do not see why it cannot be open as has been other support from other foundations to various cultural endeavors."[67]

The Third Southeast Asian Film Festival and The Forum

At the Hong Kong festival, held June 12–16, 1956, Alexander Grantham (1899–1978), the governor of Hong Kong, gave a welcome speech at the opening reception in which he remarked, "It gives me great pleasure to open the 1956 Southeast Asian Film Festival, if for no other reason than that it teaches me some geography, for I had never realized before that Japan was part of Southeast Asia! But whether that is so or not I am quite sure that the inclusion of Japan, which has produced so many outstanding pictures, is much to be welcomed in a festival of this kind, and the Federation was wise to include her."[68] Whether or not his speech influenced the decision, the FPA's name was changed from the "Federation of Motion Picture Producers in Southeast Asia" to the "Federation of Motion Picture Producers in Asia" after the Hong Kong gathering.[69] Accordingly, the festival instantaneously became the Asian Film Festival. This name was maintained until it was renamed the Asia-Pacific Film Festival in 1983 to acknowledge the presence of

Australia and New Zealand. Actually, the fallacious geographical scope of the FPA had already been problematic. TAF's New York office had also raised this issue, expressing that "American movie men in New York have been surprised that India has been left out and puzzled as to why Japan should be included in Southeast Asia when Japan doesn't normally fall into that geographical term."[70]

India had been one of TAF's most contentious issues. India had the second-largest movie industry in the world, but Nagata, whether intentionally or not, had ignored the presence of India from the very first meeting in 1953. India sent three feature films to the third festival in Hong Kong and submitted its formal application to attend the festival as an observer a year later. South Korea, with TAF's financial support, dispatched three delegates to the Hong Kong festival, including Kim Kwan-su.[71] Interestingly enough, Kim again sided with Nagata in strongly disputing India's request, arguing that "the participation of Indian observers would lead to granting of the Federation membership to India and that India likely would propose that Red China and North Korea be admitted to the Federation."[72] Taiwan supported Kim. Kim's motion was defeated at the vote, but his views obtained considerable publicity during the festival. Kim's statement against India at the festival troubled TAF, who worried that the fact that Kim was sponsored by TAF could "easily embarrass [the foundation] in India." Jack E. James, the director of the program department, wrote to Lawrence Thompson, a representative of Seoul: "I would hope that at any future conferences Mr. Kim or any of his compatriots who receive Foundation travel assistance will see fit to take a less dominant role in such discussions."[73]

Robert D. Grey compiled a long evaluation report after talking with William A. Seiter, a director known for musicals and light comedies, who had observed the third event in Hong Kong as a Hollywood representative.[74] Grey was critical of the festival and Nagata's leadership:

> The federation itself is incapable of effective direct action on behalf of its member association. It has made no real progress toward the solution of major problems confronting the Asian picture industries, nor has it even established within its framework the organizational means for approaching work along these lines. . . . The Federation itself is still essentially a paper organization whose function, and value, is mainly to coordinate and to provide the framework within which cooperation among the member associations can more easily take place. Even this aspect of the Federation's contribution has been weak.[75]

Miller had already acknowledged this problem. After observing the second festival, he reported that communicating their ideas to the other festival delegates was the prime dilemma of Nagata and the other Japanese delegates. "This is a recurring problem," he pointed out; "once again the inability of the vast majority of Japanese film leaders to express themselves adequately in the English language (and the lack of qualified interpreters) severely handicapped them in an important international gathering; a gathering where the majority of representatives were, to a greater or lesser degree, prejudiced against them."[76]

One good example of Nagata's predicament is the forum held during the third Southeast Asian Film Festival in Hong Kong. During the event, a desire for coproductions, technical training, resources exchanges, and market expansion was expressed by the member countries. Indeed, the forum's major goal was to solve the problem of coproduction. Before this forum and festival in 1956, the Philippines–Hong Kong coproduction *Sanda Wong* was produced in 1955. Two active FPA members, the Cantonese film producer Chapman Ho and the prominent Filipino director/producer Gerardo de Leon, joined the project by casting Lola Young, a Hong Kong starlet, and the Filipino actor Jose Padilla Jr.[77] The president of the Philippines, Ramon Magsaysay (1907–57; in office 1953–57), attended the film's premiere in Manila. The film played in Tagalog in the Philippines and in Mandarin or Cantonese in the Southeast Asian market.[78] The film in fact opened the possibility of sharing the markets, since it made enough profits for both countries. Following the success of *Sanda Wong*, a number of coproductions appeared during this period: the Zhang Shankun–produced Hong Kong–Japan collaboration *Madame Butterfly* (*Hudie furen*, Yi Wen, 1956), the first Hong Kong–Thailand coproduction *The Autumn Phoenix* (*Qiu feng*, Wang Yin, 1957), the Hong Kong–South Korea coproduction *Love with an Alien* (*Igukchŏngwŏn*, Wakasugi Mitsuo, Tu Quangqi, and Chŏn Ch'ang-gŭn, 1957), and *Affairs in Ankuwat* (*Ankoru watto monogatari utsukushiki aishu*, Kunio Watanabe, 1957), a Hong Kong–Japan coproduction that starred Shirley Yamaguchi.[79] Few of the listed films had much success in local and regional markets.

Hong Kong, Thailand, Indonesia, Taiwan, Japan, the Philippines, and South Korea attended the forum held during the third Southeast Asian Film Festival, and, notably, two American representatives of the MPAA participated as well. The forum was opened by Ricardo Balabrat, a general manager of Premiere Pictures in the Philippines. He suggested a coproduced omnibus film, to be composed of five to six short films made by all of the member countries. He explained, "It is a sort of co-production that anyone

Figure 3.4. Thomas Hodge, head of Malayan Film Unit (MFU), is holding the awards won by MFU at the third Southeast Asian Film Festival, held in Hong Kong in 1956, including Best Documentary Film for *Timeless Temiar*, Award for Planning, and a Special Citation for *Valley of Hope*. Ministry of Information and the Arts Collection, courtesy of National Archives of Singapore.

of the member countries of the Federation may enter into with me or any other film makers in the Philippines on a co-production basis."[80] Balabrat stressed that he had gained confidence through his participation in a co-production with Japan, which had made a sound profit in the Philippines' domestic market the previous year. His proposal, however, soon proved its naivety as forum participants expressed concern about the different standards of filmmaking practices among FPA members, the language problem, and the issue of a "good story." The question of a "good story" in particular led to a heated argument. Kimura Takechiyo, the acting secretary general of FPA and executive secretary of Daiei, claimed, "Japan says that we have had many propositions from the various countries in this area to have a co-production with us, but we think that for a co-production it is more important first to find a good story, for which we have a mutual agreement, before we start a co-production . . . Without a good story on which we can mutually agree, we cannot say yes to a co-production."[81] Twice Kimura ignored Yugala's inquiry about Japan's previous experience in coproduction and he continually repeated his insistence on "a good story." In response to Kimura's discourteous attitude, Yugala pushed back gently: "The Japanese delegation does not understand clearly. You see there are many ways of coproduction: I merely want to know what is your line, your ideal, with regard to coproduction." Ismail added, "We [Thailand and Indonesia] would like to suggest to those who have actually done joint production to cite their experiences, and inform us on what they have done these co-productions; how the contracts were done, and any ills, so that we can remedy them . . . we would like to know how it was done in practice."

Kimura, however, was silent. He might not have wanted to be involved with any coproduction proposition made by participants in the forum. As a matter of fact, Daiei and Toho had done two big-budget coproductions with Shaw & Sons the year before. During the first festival in Tokyo, Run Run Shaw and Nagata Masaichi made an agreement to produce *The Princess Yang Kwei-fei*. A year later, Toho went on to coproduce *Madame White Snake* (*Byaku fujin no yoren*, Toyoda Shiro, 1955), a film based on a story that was well known not only in Japan and Hong Kong but in the Philippines and South Korea as well. Richie and Anderson denounce these films as "rather dull" and claim that Mizoguchi and Toyoda were largely "wasted" in them.[82] Both films ultimately failed to achieve an impact either on the domestic market or on the international film festival circuit. Daiei and Toho had gradually lost their interest in Hong Kong by the early 1960s. What Shaw gained from these experiences in coproduction, however, was know-how about color photography processing and Japan's rational division of labor system, which allowed the filming procedure to become faster and more reliable. Kimura's reaction to coproduction and his emphasis on a "good story" must be understood in the context of the Japanese film industry's disappointing experiences, especially of Daiei's and Toho's relationship with Hong Kong.

As a matter of fact, in the 1950s and 60s, by collaborating with the technically superior Japanese cinema, the rest of the countries were able to gain experience in the latest filming techniques. Since almost no directors and technicians in the region outside Japan were experienced or trained to film in color or to do lab processing of color photography, working with Japan constituted valuable "tutoring" for Asian film personnel. Peter J. Katzenstein's insightful study reveals that Asia's technological order has been defined by a "relatively hierarchical regional division of labor even though first Japan and other Asian states later have improved rapidly their technological profiles."[83] Postwar Japan extricated itself from a position of technological backwardness by instituting a strict government-guided screening system for importing foreign technology, especially from the United States and Western Europe.[84] As Japan mastered the techniques of color photography and development, widescreen process, synchronization, and cutting-edge special effects, the Hong Kong film industry, during the mid- to late 1950s, coproduced a number of epic films with Japan's Daiei, Toho, and Shochiku by making use of the FPA network. In tandem with the Hong Kong film industry, Shin Films of South Korea and Central Motion Picture Corporation (CMPC) in Taiwan were also in need of experienced hands. In line with this, Guo-Juin Hong wrote that "the CMPC had been sending technicians to Japan and the United States to learn color cinematography, but a color production completely independent of foreign, especially Japanese, technical support was not possible until 1963."[85] Thus Japan played a major role during the technical formation of these studios as well. With the "borrowed" technologies, Run Run Shaw built a massive motion picture studio and proclaimed that the studio had finally entered the age of color cinema in the early 1960s.

At the 1956 forum, the MPAA representative and veteran film director William A. Seiter (1890–1964) was equally unhelpful on the topic of coproductions, demonstrating how the United States viewed postwar Asia. Chang Kuo-sin, a pro-American intellectual in Hong Kong whose studio, Asian Pictures, was supported by TAF, asked Seiter's opinion on the issues of coproduction and a "good story." In response, Seiter stressed the need for education. He stated, "We [America] have now developed in three different colleges or universities, a school for motion pictures, which includes courses in writing, cinematography, art direction and editing, and this is a major course in the University of California, and the University of Southern California."[86] By stressing America's brand-new university courses on cinema, Seiter signaled the need among Asian cinema personnel for American education. His stance annoyed the participants, who were experts on filmmaking, each with at least a couple of decades of experience in the industry. Ismail and Yugala were among the most irritated by Seiter's proposition; Chang, however, responded to Seiter's point about education by suggesting they seek external help.

In the second half of the forum (which he led), Chang went even further. As an ardent supporter of "educating Asia," he suggested a scholarship to study in Japan and asked Kimura whether the Japanese film industry would allocate two- to three-month scholarships for other Asian film technicians, writers, or directors to acquire modern technologies in Japan.[87] Kimura was again hesitant. He reluctantly stated, "If member countries pay the travelling expenses and the staying expenses, then we will help with the other expenses which will be used in Japan. We will give that consideration as much as possible."[88] Kimura's uncompromising proposition provoked an instant reaction from the other members. Chang asked to make a clarification.

Chang: May I clarify this? Will you pay all expenses in Japan—board and lodging?

Kimura: no, no . . .

Chang: you will pay what?

Kimura: we will give consideration to the expense for the location, and to the materials and so on. So, the staying expenses and the travelling expense must be borne by their own studio, for the technicians who come from another country.

The Philippines then proposed two scholarships to its music conservatory for any member country that wished to develop its music and sound technology.[89] The forum ended, and the whole event finished in anticipation of the next festival, which would be held again in Tokyo in 1957.

The Decline of the FPA Project

Cho Tong-jae, the TAF-Seoul officer, composed a report after his participation in the fourth festival in Tokyo in 1957. He stated that many members of the FPA were utterly frustrated by a speech by Yasui Seiichiro (1891–1962), the governor of Tokyo Metropolis. Yasui's speech was, according to Cho, "strewn with all sorts of anachronous and dangerous expressions such as 'Great Asia' and 'The Asia Film Festival gradually expanding to influence world motion picture industries.' Things such as the above remind us of the old bitter days, and it was really a shocking experience."[90] What Cho meant was that Yasui's phrase "Great Asia" was the same wording the Japanese government had obsessively used while fabricating and exploiting an expansive cinema network in the colonized territory under the "Greater East Asia Co-Prosperity Sphere" in the not-so-distant past. Although Prime Minister Kishi Nobusuke (1896–1987; in office 1957–60) stressed that the Southeast Asian Film Festival should play a "large role in promoting world peace and raising cultural standards" as well as promoting "friendship with Japan through motion pictures," most East and Southeast Asian countries were still hostile to Japan and vividly remembered Japan's colonial venture.[91] Perhaps it was TAF members' ignorance of the region's complex history that made them put Japan forward as a "reformed" son and the region's financially self-sufficient "big brother."

Partly because of the Japanese producers' indifference to the organization and Nagata's incompetence as its leader, the San Francisco office began losing its faith in Nagata and the importance of the FPA. On top of this, the financial and administrative burdens these motion picture programs imposed "far outweighed useful results."[92] In 1957, John F. Sullivan, who had criticized TAF's motion picture programs, replaced Stewart as director of plan. Sullivan emphasized, "It appears that whether we like it or not we are in the motion picture business." "It is also fairly obvious," he continued, "we feel (now) we should not be in it, at least in a direct role."[93] Blum decided to decrease TAF's ties with the FPA and cut the budget significantly.

Three reasons for Blum's decision should be considered. First, the aim of TAF's motion picture project was to strengthen the influence of noncommunist motion pictures, especially in Japan and Hong Kong. While partnering with the FPA, TAF members believed that in Japan it achieved to some degree, if not completely, what it had initially aimed for. They soon learned, however, that the regional film industry was more complicated than they had thought. Moreover, joint production between the United States and Japan and the distribution of Asian films to the United States did not work as planned. The MPAA had consistently ignored TAF's request to support the FPA and its annual film festival. Worse still, contrary to expectations, the Japanese film industry executives were uncontrollable, and they participated in the festival only to expand markets for their products in Southeast Asia. Busch hoped to build a bridge between Hollywood and Japan to prove that producing noncommunist films could actually be profitable. Yet it became apparent that TAF's approach was rather naive. It was Tanner who understood this most acutely. He pointed out that the Japanese producers, Nagata included, were looking for something much more immediately promising:

the opening of doors into the rest of Asia for their films. "Certainly they would prefer to export to America," he wrote, "but they are well aware how difficult that project is to accomplish."[94] In fact, according to *Eiga Nenkan* (Film Almanac), in 1954, a total of 740 feature films were exported from Japan to the United States, Europe, and Latin America but only ninety went to Asia, mostly to Hong Kong and Taiwan.[95] Japan had few places in Asia to export its cultural products. South Korea had banned the importation of Japanese cinema; Taiwanese cinema was more favorable to Japanese cinema, but the whole film import business was under the control of its government; Indonesia had an authoritarian import-restriction system led by the government at the time; and the Philippines was still hostile to Japan, with a market that favored American cinema. Japanese film industry executives therefore became gradually disillusioned with the festival, and only Nagata evinced a strong desire to lead the FPA.

Second, by the third festival in 1956, TAF believed it had achieved its initial goal of constructing a league of anticommunist motion picture producers in Asia by lessening the power of the communist-inclined participants from Indonesia, India, and Japan. Nagata, backed by Hodge (Malaysia), Kim (South Korea), and Chang (Hong Kong), defended the exclusion of North Korea and China from the FPA. And TAF's decision to subsidize the Korean and Taiwanese delegates encouraged the rise of newly confident anticommunist groups. TAF had a major policy change in 1955, and its San Francisco office considered lessening its interest in the federation to avoid ideological conflicts among delegates.[96] Under the influence of the Eisenhower administrations' "People to People" campaign, instead of bringing "pre-conceived American ways of operating to Asians or telling them how to fight communism," Blum stressed, "we should strengthen local organizations and activities that are compatible with free world objectives." Blum also pointed out that this way "our [TAF's] help should not arouse as much suspicion."[97]

Lastly, TAF had turned its attention to the motion picture industries in Hong Kong and South Korea, beginning with Asia Pictures in Hong Kong in 1953 and South Korea's KMPCA in 1956. TAF's motion picture professionals, Busch, Tanner, and Miller, had launched two new projects to win the war of motion pictures in Asia: first, providing financial support to Chang Kuo-sin and his Asia Pictures to reverse the communist-dominated film industry in Hong Kong and the overseas Chinese communities; and second, supporting Kim Kwan-su, O Yŏng-jin, and the KMPCA in South Korea to help the wartorn new country's backward film industry and encourage them to be strong anticommunist "freedom" warriors of the FPA.

Chapter 4

Constructing the Anticommunist Producers' Alliance

The strategic significance of Hong Kong to TAF can be mostly attributed to its geographical, political, and economic weight among overseas Chinese communities in Southeast Asia, which were the main focus of TAF's operations in Asia. TAF's Overseas Chinese Study Project indicated that as of 1953 the overseas Chinese population "exceeds 12 million and constitutes the largest single group of nationalities abroad," and the foundation took note of the financial contributions of overseas Chinese communities to the homeland.[1] In the early 1950s, Hong Kong was a place of great influx, uncertainty, and anxiety. After the founding of the People's Republic of China (PRC) in October 1949, tens of thousands of Chinese people fled to Hong Kong in search of a better future. The population of the colony consequently skyrocketed from about 600,000 in August 1945 to 2.5 million in 1951. Many of the refugees still maintained close ties with the mainland. The new refugees, according to Lu Yan, regarded the territories under British jurisdiction as "a way station towards greater safety, a transit to a more permanent abode."[2] The new refugees brought with them a heavy load of ideological baggage. The entire British crown colony consequently became a fierce battlefield between two worlds.

Robert Blum understood the importance of Hong Kong as the primary center in Asia for the production of Chinese media in the Mandarin language. He wrote, "Throughout Southeast Asia it is apparent the communists have switched their strategy from using overt red publications, which have been losing ground, to non-communist media—especially newspapers, magazines, and movies. Floods of red propaganda materials aimed at the overseas Chinese are pouring into Asian countries, many in the guise of respectable publications. Since overseas Chinese look to Hong Kong as their intellectual and cultural center, The Asia Foundation believes that here lies a key to researching as many of them as possible in order to turn their support away from communist China."[3]

TAF's motion picture team accordingly believed that the film industry in Hong Kong had been heavily dominated by communist producers strongly subsidized by Chinese communist capital, and that the most successful Chinese films had "by and large been communist."[4] Such film production companies as Great Wall Pictures (Changcheng), The Phoenix Studio (Feng huang), Chung Lien, Kwong Yi, and Dragon Horse (Longma yingpian gongsi) had been markedly successful in local markets since the founding of the PRC in 1949.[5] Unsurprisingly, Great Wall Pictures was TAF's primary target. Great Wall Pictures was cofounded by Yuan Yang-an and, more important, Zhang Shankun, who had been called "the king of Chinese cinema in wartime Shanghai."[6] Zhang was very close to Kawakita Nagamasa, a head of Towa, during the Japanese occupation period in Shanghai. However, most of the leftist studios experienced financial hardship around the time TAF embarked on the motion picture operation in Hong Kong. The studios had to consider the Hong Kong, Singapore, and Malaysian markets and the films they produced were therefore considered "not strong enough propaganda-wise" for mainland consumption.[7] Even worse, the Taiwan market became unavailable, which imposed greater hardship on the studios. Consequently, the number of films produced by Great Wall dropped from ten in 1952 to six in 1954. TAF saw this trend in the film industry as a "green light."

"Pro-democratic films should be made in Hong Kong," Tanner stated, emphasizing that they had to be "really good, entertaining movies."[8] The San Francisco office, with the strong support of Stewart, had acknowledged the vast market for Mandarin films, including Hong Kong, Singapore, Malaysia, Indonesia, Thailand, Vietnam, and Taiwan (one third of the entire Chinese diasporas market). Miller estimated that there was a potential audience of over twenty million overseas Chinese. If TAF could help produce "good, entertaining" movies, then they would surely reach the majority of overseas Chinese living in Southeast Asia. The San Francisco office decided to assist a committed anticommunist journalist named Chang Kuo-sin, who aimed to offset the communist domination of the Hong Kong media and help stabilize the noncommunist portion of the industry. Chang had proposed a "Tri-Dimensional Project for the Battle for People's Minds" to TAF (then the Committee for a Free Asia) in November 1951.[9] The central aim of the "Tri-Dimensional Project" was to offset the "Red" domination of the Hong Kong media and help increase the noncommunist stake in the industry by setting up a publishing house, a film production company, and an intellectual club. All three components would mutually benefit each other, and together they could churn out books and magazines and produce films that would manifest the "traditional free values of China and the principles of the Free World."[10]

Project Hong Kong: Chang Kuo-sin and Asia Pictures

Chang was born in Hainan Island, China, in 1916. He grew up in Kuching, North Borneo, and finished his university education in 1945 at the National Southwestern Associated University in Kunming, China.[11] His professional career as a journalist started at the Central News Agency in Chungking (Chongqing) right after his graduation. A year later, he was sent to Nanking (Nanjing) and there, due to his excellent oral and writing skills in English, he was recruited by the American news agency United Press. In Nanking, Chang saw the fall of the city to communist forces in April 1949.[12] Upon arriving in Hong Kong for a new job, he began writing a series of articles and subsequently published a book titled *Eight Months Behind the Bamboo Curtain* in 1950.[13]

The Tri-Dimensional Project's publishing unit, the Asia Press, came first. It opened its doors in September 1952. The Asia Press went on to build an intricate configuration for the preparation, publication, distribution, and retail of anticommunist materials in Chinese. It published wide-ranging books, from academic works and investigative reports to novels, textbooks, and comics.[14] Some of the novels published by the Asia Press, such as Sha Qianmeng's *Long Lane* (*Chang xiang*) and Zhao Zifan's *The Semi-Lower-Class Society* (*Ban xialiu shehui*), were adapted for the silver screen and produced by Chang's own Asia Pictures.[15] Asia Bookstore, a retail outlet, launched in Hong Kong and Macau in 1952 and 1953, respectively. The Asia Press bookstore in Hong Kong, according to TAF's annual report, "serves as the center for distribution and is one of the most popular gathering places for writers, literary figures, students, and readers." TAF was very enthusiastic about expanding the bookstores. In 1956, they had branches in Singapore, Bangkok, and Jakarta.[16] The Asia Press also operated the Asia News Agency, which supplied Chinese newspapers in Southeast Asia with a weekly newsletter. Chang, in an interview with *The New Leader*, highlighted the objective of his venture: "Communist Literature fills many a bookstore here. Communist books and magazines are flooding Chinese communities throughout Southeast Asia. Unless we can produce creative and crusading literature, we will lose the Chinese outside the bamboo curtain to the Communists."[17] In the 1955–56 fiscal year alone, TAF allocated USD 80,000 to the Asia Press.

On July 11, 1953, Asia Pictures was incorporated. It took over the existing Yung Hwa motion picture company, Hong Kong's best-equipped company around the time, and officially commenced its productions. As Chang expressed, its aim was to "crusade against Communism, cleansing the Chinese movie land here of Chinese Communist influence, producing pictures promoting the principles of democracy and freedom and condemnatory of Communist totalitarianism, acting not only as film producers, but also as watchdogs of people's conscience and minds."[18] Evidently, Chang's primary objective was to beat Great Wall Pictures. Chang explicitly stated, "This is going to be our war-cry."[19] The close of the mainland market in 1949 had led most of the Hong Kong–based Mandarin film studios into near-collapse. Great Wall was one of the few exceptions; this pro-Beijing film company continued to sell films to the mainland.[20] A large group of Shanghai émigrés, such as the directors Yue Feng and Li Pingqian, the producers Zhang Shankun and Yuan Yang-an, and actors like Shu Shi and Liu Qiong, had long-term contracts with the studio. Yuan, a savvy businessman, launched the *Great Wall Pictorial* (*Changcheng huabao*), a sleek, popular monthly magazine, in 1950.[21] The *Great Wall Pictorial* was "the best-selling [magazine] in town and in the Far East" and was able to promote its pictures and stars successfully.[22] Chang saw the magazine as one of the key factors in Great Wall's commercial success. To create a counterpart to the *Great Wall Pictorial*, Chang introduced the *Asia Pictorial* (*Ya zhou hua bao*), to be published by the Asia Press, in 1953. It was, according to Chang, "a most important publicity weapon."[23]

In its inaugural issue published in May 1953, the *Asia Pictorial* led off with an article about America's first atomic bomb test (which had been conducted in March of that year in Yucca Flat, Nevada), as if to throw a cultural atomic bomb at communist-dominated Hong Kong. Throughout its first year, the *Asia Pictorial* delivered news of political and cultural affairs, mostly stories about anticommunist revolts in Eastern Europe, military training in Taiwan, the Asian tours of UK and US politicians and military generals, gossip about

Hollywood celebrities, foreign and regional film news, and tidbits about the affluent and independent lives of Western housewives.[24] The *Asia Pictorial* was, according to TAF's assessment in May 1955, a great success. It outsold "every other such publication on the market" and was "perhaps the most popular and effective medium in the magazine field in Asia."[25]

In January 1953, Chang recruited his "top lieutenant" in the movie project, Walter Woo.[26] Woo, who was Chang's close friend, was a Detroit-born, University of Michigan–educated Chinese American who had worked for Eastman Kodak and Paramount in America before joining Yung Hwa studio in Hong Kong as assistant general manager.[27] Woo was the ideal partner. His cultural background in the United States and his Hollywood career gained TAF's confidence. Soon afterward, Chang submitted an initial budget request of HKD 167,000 to the Hong Kong office for the movie project. Delmer M. Brown, the Hong Kong representative and a former University of California–Berkeley professor in Japanese history, was very supportive of Chang's new venture in the motion picture industry. Asia Pictures' first feature film, *Tradition* (*Chuan tong*, Tang Huang, 1955), began filming on October 17, 1953, and location shooting was completed in December of the same year. It was filmed in the Shaw Brothers' Hong Kong studio, the Nanyang Studio. Generally considered one of the earliest Hong Kong gangster films, *Tradition* is an epic about the battle between tradition—expressed in the Chinese code of loyalty—and the corrupting vices that come with modernity. As Miller and Tanner noted, *Tradition* is not an outright anticommunist film. In fact, Chang had resolved that Asia Pictures would not use a "direct attack" approach because "politically, propaganda pictures of any color are not permitted by the British censor. Besides, the Chinese public are extremely wary of openly-propagandistic pictures. We have to be more subtle and devious in our approach and do our job in an artistic and entertaining way. Generally, we should seek to hint at or imply and not point out. In political language, we should try to be diplomatic. The basic principle is that the best propaganda must at the same time be the best entertainment."[28] Interestingly enough, TAF generally maintained a hands-off approach. Tanner, Miller, and Stewart did not dictate content. One possible explanation is that they encountered language barriers. None of them could communicate with Asia's local film executives outside Japan without an interpreter. But, more important, the aims of TAF's motion picture officers were primarily to support non- (and particularly anti-) communist individuals, to provide opportunities for them to collaborate with each other, and to introduce their films to the US film market.

To fight against Great Wall Pictures and other pro-Beijing leftist film studios in Hong Kong, all members of the production, including filmmakers, performers, and even technical staff, were required to have no prior work experience with the communists. Delmer Brown and his TAF-Hong Kong office carefully researched the ideological background of each member of the production crew. Tang Huang, the director, started out as a newsreel editor with the CMPC in Taiwan. "Unlike many others in the movie industry here," Brown indicated, "Tang was never associated with the Communist producers, and thus there has never been any doubt about his loyalty to our cause."[29] Similarly, Wang Hao was chosen to play a protagonist because he had never appeared in "any of the Great Wall pictures."[30] *Tradition* was Asia Pictures' official submission to the first Asian Film Festival. It was, however, the first film to be excluded by the festival committee from any consideration. As discussed in the previous chapter, its negative portrayal of a Japanese general violated the festival's regulations.

Asia Pictures' second film, *The Heroine* (*Yang e*, 1955), was based on the well-known story of Xiang Fei, the Fragrant Concubine. *The Heroine* traces the life of a woman taken as a consort by the Qianlong Emperor of the Qing Dynasty during the eighteenth century. Chang explained: "I chose this story for its resistance against foreign aggression; loyalty to religion, country and husband; upholding of personal dignity; Xiang Fei's struggle for personal freedom from a love-sick and aggression-hungry Emperor and her being victimized by an ancient version of the Communist big lie. They lied to her that her husband was still living and for the rest of her life she lived under this false belief."[31] Chang's ambition for the subsequent two years was to churn out three films per year, each with a budget of USD 20,000. The budgets would be covered by TAF. This was a huge sum of money in comparison to TAF's overall budget allocation to Hong Kong. TAF's major concern, however, was to figure out how to distribute these TAF-financed films to target countries such as Taiwan, Singapore, Malaysia, Thailand, the Philippines, and possibly even the United States. Brown contacted all of the TAF representatives in these countries, with the result that *Tradition* had its first overseas release in Taipei's Great World Theatre and New World Theatre on April 26, 1954, and in the Cathay chains in Singapore and Malaysia several months later.[32]

Opening the gate to Hollywood for anticommunist film executives in Asia was the ultimate goal of the TAF motion picture project. The initial attempt, with *The People Win Through*, had been disastrous. *The People Win Through*, as illustrated in the first chapter, was produced by the

California-based Cascade Pictures. For TAF, therefore, introducing Asia Pictures' products to the United States was a delicate matter of vital importance. Tanner flew to Los Angeles and set up a special screening of *The Heroine*, which was, in Tanner's view, a better picture than *Tradition*. The screening was held at 8 pm on March 1, 1955, at a Paramount studio theater. In attendance were top-ranking Paramount technicians in the field of editing (Charles West), sound recording (Louis Mesenkof), camera (Jack Bishop and Walter Kelley), and script writing (Stan Carvey), along with a director (Frank Borzage) and two Paramount executives (Luigi Luraschi and Albert Deane).[33]

At the screening, according to L. Z. Yuan, a staff member at TAF's San Francisco location, Tanner stressed that "Asian movie people look upon Hollywood as the zenith of motion picture art and called on those present to offer constructive suggestions on how to improve Asian Pictures productions."[34] The initial responses from Paramount technicians were not, however, very positive. Charles West, the head of the Editing Department, criticized the film: "I don't know what kind of a market they are shooting at, but a picture of this nature would of course, never go in a market that we reach (the United States, Europe, South America, etc). The involved incidents, the great number of characters, the abrupt switch from sequence to sequence, of course, would not be acceptable to international distribution . . . what we have seen is not like an American picture. If they would like to follow our standards, they have missed the mark."[35] Other participants praised *The Heroine*'s costume design, cinematography, and production design. But its storytelling and editing were almost unanimously criticized, including by Frank Borzage, who pointed out three major problems—the laboratory processing, editing, and characterizations.[36] Crucially, Albert Deane also pointed out "the absence of suspenseful climax."[37] Hollywood-style effective storytelling was indeed what TAF believed to be Asian cinema's major weakness, as shown in the previous chapter's discussion of the Japan Writer Project. To help Asia Pictures overcome these difficulties, West suggested that Tanner bring Asia Pictures technicians over to Paramount Studio and let them observe the production procedure. Luigi Luraschi, the head of Foreign and Domestic Censorship at Paramount Studios, wrote a letter to Tanner only one day after the screening, agreeing with West's idea. He wrote, "I feel that the most important work we could do in helping our friends in Hong Kong would be to have a good constructionist and dramatist consult with their writers to show them some of the methods we use in developing our shooting scripts and in telling a story with the American type of tempo and suspense . . . I feel that at least their film cutters, if not their director, could profit by a long session with our men in the field, explaining the importance of dissolves, fades, time lapses, etc."[38]

Chang's responses to these critiques were sent to Tanner on April 28, almost two months after the screening held in Los Angeles. Regarding Asia Pictures' lack of facilities and technical skills, Chang stated,

> To put it bluntly, our industry here is years behind modern and western standards in picture-making. We are in need of the technical know-how and of the equipment. For instance, regarding many comments on our poor lab work, I am ashamed to confess that our processing was done by hand. . . . We don't have the equipment to make the dissolves, which are now being made by chemicals, as you had mentioned. We don't have a good editing machine like the latest western editor. We don't have a decent dolly or camera cranes. We don't have a portable magnetic recorder to do sound recording on location. We don't have good special effects men. We don't have good directors. There is another thing we don't have which is of great consequence—the will to learn and do a good job of it. Most people in our industry are loafing along and when I entered the movies I found one of my jobs was how to discipline these people.[39]

Instead of sending his technicians to Hollywood, which was a step too costly for Asia Pictures to take, Chang suggested sending them to Daiei Studio in Japan. His letter included numerous requests for TAF to purchase various items for Asia Pictures. Subsequently, Stewart became somewhat skeptical about Chang. Stewart expressed his doubt about Chang's capability as a producer and dispatched John Miller to evaluate Chang's studio and observe the communist activities in the film industry. Miller, after spending two weeks in Hong Kong, concluded that TAF should not hesitate to continue or even increase, if necessary, its subsidization. He emphasized that TAF's choice lay between giving the entire overseas Chinese film industry to the communists "by default" or "making what may turn out to be a costly effort to save it."[40] The San Francisco office was encouraged by Miller's strong recommendation. James Ivy even suggested that Asia Pictures be supported even more aggressively. He wrote, "I think we all now agree, with Asia Pictures firmly established on the company level and therefore in a position to lend support to Foundation efforts on a higher level, that the Foundation should re-direct its basic approach to extend its motion picture program to an industry-wide level."[41]

Figure 4.1. Full view of Asia Pictures studio in Hong Kong. Asia Pictures completed a new studio in November 1956. Asia Foundation Records, Hoover Institution Archives, photo courtesy of the Asia Foundation.

Figure 4.2. Asia Pictures held a reception party to mark the opening of the new studio and the completion of Asia Pictures' new film *Sisters Three*. The reception was attended by prominent figures of the Hong Kong film industry, performers, and civic and government officials. Left to right: Diana Chang Chung-wen (second from the left), an actress who plays the youngest sister in *Sisters Three*; Alexander Grantham, Governor of Hong Kong; Qin Qi, an actress who plays the eldest sister in *Sisters Three*; Chang Kuo-sin, president of Asia Pictures; Bu Wancang, director of *Sisters Three*. Asia Foundation Records, Hoover Institution Archives, photo courtesy of the Asia Foundation.

TAF had poured USD 69,000 into Asia Pictures in 1954/55, and another USD 63,800 in the 1955/56 fiscal year. By the end of 1955, it was agreed that Asia Pictures was ready to streamline the film production of Mandarin films.[42] After its first two productions, Asia Pictures had completed five more feature films, including *The Story of a Fur Coat* (*Jin lu yi*, Tang Huang, 1956), *The Long Lane* (*Chang xiang*, Bu Wancang, 1956), *Half Way Down* (*Ban xia liu she hui*, Tu Guangqi, 1956), *Life with Grandma* (*Man ting fang*, Tang Huang, 1957), and *Love and Crime* (*Ai yu zui*, Tang Huang, 1957). On November 2, 1956, Asia Pictures completed a new studio in Hong Kong. Loke Wan-tho's Motion Picture and General Investment (MP&GI) in Singapore took over the Yung Hwa studio for its Hong Kong production plan. At this new studio, Asia Pictures shot its eighth feature, *Sisters Three* (*San jiemei*, Bu Wancang; also known as *The Three Sisters*).[43] At the opening reception at the new studio, such celebrities as Peter Chen Ho, Grace Chang, and Diana Chang Chung-wen joined Chang Kuo-sin, Tang Huang, Bu Wancang, and Asia Pictures' staff.

TAF, on the other hand, was launching another motion picture project. This time it was in South Korea, aimed not only at winning the imminent fight against the communists but at lifting the standard of the country's backward motion picture industry.

Figure 4.3. A veteran actor Peter Chen-ho poses with other stars in Hong Kong cinema. Left to right: Peter Chen Ho, Grace Chang (Ge Lan), Qin Qi, Wang Lai, and Ching Chung. Asia Foundation Records, Hoover Institution Archives, photo courtesy of the Asia Foundation.

The Asia Foundation and Postwar Korea

The war damage to industrial offices, plants and equipment, public facilities, private dwellings, and transport equipment in the ravaged postwar South Korea was severe. The US government had poured USD 200 million into the decimated economy of the Syngman Rhee government (1948–60), which relied heavily on foreign aid, predominantly from America, for postwar reconstruction projects. In fact, between 1954 and 1959, about 70 percent of all reconstruction projects were funded by aid from the United States.[44] Surprisingly, however, South Korea as a whole was neglected by TAF. Perhaps the nation's recent war (1950–53) caused this desertion, but more important the nature of the strong anticommunism among the war-torn republic's intellectuals did not demand any immediate action from TAF. Tanner, for instance, confirmed this: "When thinking of Korea the first thought is that these people do not need to be persuaded away from Communism. They know its heavy hand too well."[45] TAF's Seoul office, accordingly, had a much belated inauguration compared to offices in other cities in the terrain.

Phillip Rowe became the first Seoul representative in 1954. Mary Walker was an administrative assistant of Rowe. They were assisted by six Korean full-time staff members, including Cho Tong-jae and Cho P'ung-yŏn (1914–91). Before joining TAF, Rowe was involved in the occupation authority's media policy in numerous ways as a director of the United States Army Military Government in Korea's (USAMGIK) special unit for radio, library, film, and publication. He launched a mobile motion picture operation that was alleged to have reached every county in Korea by mid-1948. In 1953, Rowe was transferred to the United States Information Service (USIS), a local branch of the United States Information Agency (USIA), which inherited the responsibilities of the World War II–era Office of War Information (OWI) and Office of Inter-American Affairs. S. R. Joey Long argues that the Eisenhower administration created USIA "to align public opinion abroad with US security objectives."[46] Kenneth Osgood calls the officials in the USIA "foot soldiers" in the battle for hearts and minds.[47] Indeed, as Nicholas J. Cull reveals, USIA began to target "opinion-formers directly through books, motion pictures, and personal contact."[48] USIA, therefore, maintained close relationships with the country's intellectuals, including Kim Kwan-su and other cultural elites in war-torn South Korea.[49]

The budget apportioned to the Seoul office, however, was low. The Seoul administrative team's 1954/55 expenditure was only USD 92,234, one fourth of what the Hong Kong office received during the same period. Brown, who transferred from Hong Kong to Tokyo in 1955, sent a letter to Blum to ask for more consideration for South Korea. Brown laid emphasis on the need for more financial and administrative support:

> A private organization like TAF has an important mission to help Asians gain a better understanding of, and to implement, those ideas and ideals that lie at the heart of a free way of life. Such work, on some counts at least, is more important in Korea than in some of the larger, wealthier, and more heavily populated areas of Asia, for South Korea (like Vietnam and Taiwan) constitutes a laboratory situation where, among the same people, the free way of life and the communist way are North [Korea] being tried. If in Korea, or in Vietnam and Taiwan, the intellectual situation is permitted to deteriorate to the point where people will turn to the communist solution, it will be interpreted throughout the Asian world, as strong evidence that the ideals and processes of the free way of life will not work in Asia.[50]

The budget for the Seoul office slowly but surely increased, reaching an expenditure of USD 165,000 in 1955/56.[51] The Seoul office paid particular attention to the cultural field, which was regarded as "an extremely important one in Korea."[52] The budget then increased further—to USD 220,000—two years later.[53] TAF's major projects were mostly in the arena of education, publication, and cultural matters. In the cultural sector, USIS-Korea had already been overseeing radio, library, film, and publication operations. Roughly twenty Americans and over 170 Koreans staffed USIS-Korea in 1954.[54] The means that USIS-Korea exploited to conduct its operations were fourfold: audio, audiovisual, experiential, and literary. In many aspects, its operations overlapped with TAF's core cultural activities. Moreover, the audiovisual section of USIS-Korea had constructed well-equipped motion picture studios in Chinhae and Sangnam, which were near the wartime capital, Busan. USIS-Korea hired Korean filmmakers and churned out localized propaganda films and the weekly newsreel film "Liberty News."[55] In 1954, according to Han Sang Kim, all the movie theaters in South Korea were showing USIS movies: shorts, documentaries, and news, seen by 3.75 million audience members every month. USIS even produced a theatrical feature-length film, *Boxes of Death (Chugŏm ŭi sangja*, Kim Ki-young, 1955).[56] TAF had to set up distinctive cultural programs to avoid unnecessary rivalry and so as not to be treated with suspicion or rejected by the nation's growing intellectual communities.

TAF's Seoul office, in consequence, focused on the local cultural elites and brought American educators, scholars, and technicians into the South

Korean cultural field. As Brown pointed out, "there [was] a deep interest, on the part of all Koreans, to learn about the Western (and particularly the American) way of doing things." After the civil war, Koreans were trying desperately to learn English, to read English books, and to learn about American life. In the first year of TAF's Seoul office, six English teachers were placed in five major universities as part of the English Teachers' Program in South Korea. In the category of publication, the Seoul office supported a huge number of literary magazines, including *Modern Literature* (*Hyŏndae munhak*), the oldest of its kind; *World of Thought* (*Sasanggye*); *The Literature and Arts* (*Munhag yesul*); and the first popular magazine for women, *Women's Garden* (*Yŏwŏn*).[57] "The Freedom Writer's Award" (Chayumunhaksang), which was given to writers who had fled North Korea and written books containing eyewitness accounts of their experiences there, was inaugurated in 1954. The first awardee, *Descendants of Cain* (*K'ain ŭi Huye*, 1954), by Hwang Sun-wŏn, became a national bestseller.

A significant portion of the budget was also allocated to the research center, where local university students and scholars could access English-language magazines and books donated by various American institutions.[58] Greg Barnhisel argues that books became "a central weapon" in the US cultural propaganda campaign, which was aimed at an audience of "elite opinion-makers" and sought to present "an image of the U.S. as a well-meaning liberal democracy whose civil liberties and democratic institutions ensured that it would mature past whatever shortcomings from which it might currently suffer."[59] The Seoul office also supported the National Museum, a project to transfer historical records to microfilm, and the Folklore Society in Korea. But the project it invested in most heavily in 1955 and in subsequent years was none other than the Korean Motion Picture Cultural Association (KMPCA).

The Korean Motion Picture Cultural Association

South Korea faced an abrupt influx of migrant workers after the Korean War. The number of Seoul residents spiked. The population of Seoul more than doubled to reach 1.5 million by 1955 from a mere 650,000 in 1951. Along with the overflow of migrant workers to the metropolis, postwar Korea faced a rapid influx of American culture in the form of "core" modernism. Charles K. Armstrong explains that the cultural arena "broadly conceived—from the realm of arts and letters to that of mass media and popular education—was the site of an intense political struggle in East Asia."[60] He accentuates that postwar South Korea was penetrated profoundly by American culture, perhaps on a level reached by no other country in Asia, and the position of the US government and its cultural agencies (including Christian organizations, Boy Scouts, the 4-H Club, and private foundations such as the Rockefeller, Ford, and Carnegie Foundations and TAF) were crucial to shaping attitudes toward American modernity.

Certainly postwar/postcolonial Korean people encountered material goods produced by an advanced capitalistic economy, and, as Chungmoo Choi argues, "the seduction of, desire for, and resistance to the power of fetishistic late capitalism weave the tapestry of the post-colonial nation's history."[61] A sudden arrival of Hollywood films with the alluring charm of what Miriam Hansen calls "vernacular modernism" fascinated postwar Korean civilians.[62] Hollywood cinema had immense popularity among Korean audiences, and many filmmakers and film workers dreamed of adopting the "advanced" Hollywood studio system. Under the strong influence of the American goods, way of life, and cultural products that flooded South Korea, the mass production ideal of Fordism was regarded as a norm to be adopted and followed to achieve modernization. South Korean film executives dreamed of constructing state-of-the-art soundstages, adopting a Fordist assembly line and an effective management system and borrowing modern technologies such as sound synchronization, color cinematography, special effects, and camera techniques. They lacked everything, however: equipment, sound stages, modern filming techniques, and, most important, money.

O Yŏng-jin (1916–74), a notable playwright, critic, and motion picture distributor, visited the United States from December 1953 to February 1954 on a tour sponsored by USIS. O visited Los Angeles, New York, and San Francisco to secure the South Korean distribution rights of Hollywood films and build relationships with American writers, critics, and educators. In San Francisco, O called on TAF. Tanner asked him about the current status and problems of the South Korean film industry. In a letter to TAF's director of program, James L. Stewart, Tanner cited O's response: "There is no production underway in South Korea. The only organizations equipped to carry on such activities are the UN and USIS. No Korean producers or any combination of them have equipment. However, there is a distinct need for motion picture production in South Korea for many reasons, one—at present there is little entertainment available for the people and this becomes a serious void when viewed in the light of conditions which exist there."[63]

After O's departure, Tanner and Stewart had a lengthy discussion, partly if not entirely inspired by O's bitter statements, about the ways TAF could help to resuscitate the South Korean film industry.[64] Stewart and Tanner, like TAF's Seoul representative Rowe, had served in Korea during the US occupation period and had dedicated themselves to bolstering the nation's cinema. They were passionate about this South Korea project. Miller was immediately assigned to conduct initial field research in South Korea. He spent two weeks there in January 1955. During this trip, he managed to convene with some of the industry's key players: O Yŏng-jin, Yi Pyŏng-il, Yi Yong-min, Kim Kwan-su, Yi Chae-myŏng, and Chang Ki-yŏng, the president of *Han'gug-ilbo* Publishing Company. Cho Tong-jae was a mediator, and the Seoul office arranged the meeting. Miller's preliminary recommendation was to provide basic motion picture production equipment to a nonprofit holding corporation in South Korea. Blum immediately approved Miller's proposition, and a new institution named the Korean Motion Picture Cultural Association was formed. Chang Ki-yŏng was elected KMPCA's first chairman of the board.[65] The founding officers and members of the KMPCA were as follows[66]:

Chairman: Chang Ki-yŏng (president of *Han'gug-ilbo*)
Managing Director: Yi Chae-myŏng (producer)
Auditor: Yi T'ae-hŭi (professor of law, Ewha Woman's University)
Members:

> Kim Kwan-su (producer)
> Yi Pyŏng-il (director)
> Yi Ch'ŏl-hyŏk (producer)
> Yi Yong-min (cameraman-director)
> Min Pyŏng-to (banker)
> O Yŏng-jin (critic and scenario writer)

Right after the third Asian Film Festival in Hong Kong in 1956, the motion picture project in South Korea finally took off. TAF's San Francisco headquarters had been decreasing the foundation's connection with the FPA, which contributed to turning its consideration to South Korea.[67] Moreover, and perhaps most crucial, Blum visited South Korea and had an engaging meeting with President Syngman Rhee (1875–1965) in October 1956. Rhee inquired whether TAF would bring an American motion picture expert to help the Koreans raise the standards and educational content of their motion pictures.[68] Shortly thereafter, the San Francisco office once again dispatched Miller to Seoul. This time, as a motion picture project advisor, Miller was committed to staying much longer. He ended up staying for six months, from

Figure 4.4. Robert Blum's visit to South Korea in October 1956. Left to right: Cho Tong Jae, program assistant, TAF (second from the left); Ko Chae-pong, mayor of Seoul; John Miller, motion picture officer, TAF; Blum; Chang Ki-yŏng, president of *Han'gug-ilbo* and chairman of board, KMPCA; Kim Kwan-su, director-producer of motion pictures and member of board, KMPCA; Mary Walker, the administrative assistant of Larry Thompson; Larry Thompson, a representative of TAF's Seoul office. Asia Foundation Records, Hoover Institution Archives, photo courtesy of the Asia Foundation.

July to December 1956. Upon completion of his duty in South Korea, Miller composed an exhaustive project report titled "The Korean Film Industry."[69]

In May of 1956, prior to his departure for Seoul, Miller made a short trip to Los Angeles to purchase necessary filming equipment for the KMPCA. TAF had approved a sum of USD 50,000, almost one third of the year's entire program budget for South Korea.[70] Consequently, one 35mm Mitchell camera and other technical equipment, including an automatic film developer and lighting facilities, arrived in Seoul in July 1956.[71] The facilities were, however, not given to the KMPCA as unconditional gifts. In an official letter to TAF on June 3, 1956, Chang Ki-yŏng clearly directed, "The Asia Foundation retains full legal ownership of the equipment and other materials made available to the KMPCA from the funds of The Asia Foundation."[72] Miller also specified that consideration must be given "to the aims and ambitions of the people who make or want to make pictures."[73] The KMPCA was now converted into a rental agency for the equipment. Since the South Korean film industry of the time seriously lacked filming equipment, the KMPCA's

Mitchell camera, one of very few in South Korea available for commercial pictures, became a dream of film directors in South Korea. The first film to be made using a Mitchell camera was Kim Ki-young's *Boxes of Death*.

Miller wrote in his report on "The Korean Film Industry,"

> During the unprecedented "boom" period of late 1956, many producers were handicapped by a shortage of production equipment. Lamps and cameras particularly were in short supply. It was not at all unusual to visit a set and see the crew and cast just standing around while the producer was out scouring the city in an effort to rent a production camera. This was caused primarily by a complete lack of coordination and planning. In fact, there are now available in Korea sufficient cameras to meet the normal production requirements of the industry. In addition to the Eymos, the Arriflexes, and the Russian made cameras which have been available since the end of the war, the OPI [Office of Public Information] has Japanese made "Seiki" which closely resembles the Mitchell NC. For some time the "Seiki" was the only studio type camera available in Korea. Recently, the OPI, through a UNKRA [The United Nations Korean Reconstruction Agency] grant acquired a 35mm Mitchell with blimp. The KMPCA too now has a Mitchell NC available for rental by producers. In the meantime, a few private individuals have acquired [French made] "Parvos" and new model "Bell and Howell" cameras.[74]

The situation in South Korea had been radically transformed. While he was staying in South Korea, Miller witnessed the South Korean film industry enter a crucial period of growth and development. In 1954, the Syngman Rhee government enacted a tax policy to support the movie industry, under which movie tickets for foreign films would be taxed at 90 percent while domestic films would be exempted. This gave a competitive edge to South Korean domestic films in terms of price, which served as a huge incentive for film production. The astonishing successes of *Chunhyang* (*Ch'unhyang chŏn*, Yi Kyu-hwan, 1955) and *Madame Freedom* (*Chayupuin*, Han Hyŏng-mo, 1956) in the domestic film market boosted the whole industry.[75] In 1953, only six films were produced, but in 1959, the number reached 111. In tandem with this phenomenon, USIS, UNKRA, and the US Military Aid Groups competitively allocated endowments to South Korean government agencies for the purpose of purchasing equipment and constructing motion picture facilities. Moreover, Hong Ch'an, a successful theater and motion picture producer, began construction of what would become the biggest motion picture studio in South Korea, with the support of the Syngman Rhee government.[76] Miller, however, emphasized that TAF's investment in the KMPCA would be used most appropriately in the ways he and TAF motion picture team approved. He wrote, "It is highly unlikely that private enterprise will be able to compete with government, when government has sufficient equipment to supply all the needs of the industry. Assuredly, present practices do not create a climate conductive to the development of private enterprise in equipment rental and laboratory activities. It may be proposed that the new equipment given to the various ROK [Republic of Korea] government agencies will not be used by film makers who are making commercial entertainment films."[77]

Miller, like Stewart and Tanner, truly believed that the entertainment film was one of the most powerful social, cultural, and political forces in the world. Neither the war-torn nation's intellectuals nor the government, in his view, paid much attention to the entertainment film, as they believed that films were for poor and unsophisticated civilians. "It never happened in Communist countries," Miller continued; "When a Communist regime takes over they immediately put all mass communications groups under their control. They are particularly interested in film making and film people . . . North Korean films are technically superior to the ones made in Seoul."[78] Supporting commercial filmmaking was, in the end, TAF's strategy to distinguish its motion picture project from other US state-led cultural programs in South Korea.

In 1957, the KMPCA received USD 10,000 worth of sound recording equipment on indefinite loan from the South Korean air force. TAF gave them USD 1,000 to restore and install it. In its three-year investment plan, TAF had bestowed approximately USD 61,500, making the KMPCA TAF's "most highly funded project."[79] TAF's principal aim, to assist in the production of one or two "technically acceptable" South Korean films for the Asian Film Festival through the KMPCA, was no different from TAF's objectives for Asia Pictures in Hong Kong. It refused, however, to provide financial support to individual film projects. Having been involved with and financed numerous films, from *The People Win Through* to *Tradition* and *The Heroine*, Blum had become skeptical. He wrote, "Past ventures of TAF in subsidizing or assisting individual motion pictures have almost invariably resulted in great complications and few successes. We have been working more and more toward the principle that we would not assist such individual ventures and the proposed Korean project would be a departure from this principle."[80]

The South Korean delegates could not submit a feature film to the third Asian Film Festival in 1956, but as soon as TAF's equipment donations to the

KMPCA were completed, Yi Pyŏng-il, a KMPCA executive member, commenced shooting for *The Wedding Day* (*Shijip kanŭn nal*, 1957), based on a play written in 1942 by O Yŏng-jin under the title of *A Happy Day of Jinsa Maeng* (*Maengjinsa taek kyŏngsa*). This classic postwar comedy critiques obsolete customs related to social class and marriage using humor and satire. *The Wedding Day* became the first official submission to the festival and won the Best Comedy Film award at the fourth festival in Tokyo in 1957. This was the country's first achievement at an international film festival. The whole country was caught up in the excitement, and one film critic proudly wrote, "Our [Korean] film industry has successfully proved that cinema can participate in the movement of rebuilding the country. Now it is time to move on and acquire dollars in line with the Rhee government's export-encouragement policy!"[81] The Korean film critic Yi Min, along these lines, proudly proclaimed, "South Korean cinema is now paving the way for the world, at least in Southeast Asia. South Korean cinema had a warm response at the 4th Asian Film Festival, which is the biggest achievement Korean cinema ever made. We can export our cinema to Southeast Asia, and, ultimately, acquire foreign currency."[82]

Acquiring foreign currency, especially US "greenbacks," was the ultimate goal for the Syngman Rhee government's decimated economy.[83] Having witnessed the achievement of *The Wedding Day* and subsequent local box office successes, the whole film industry in South Korea was given a boost, as Stewart and his motion picture team had anticipated. The city residents flocked to the films and these new patrons paved the way for what many film historians have collectively termed the Golden Age of South Korean cinema in the 1960s.[84]

An iconic director in 1960s South Korean cinema, Shin Sang-ok stood out beginning in the late 1950s. Shin produced and directed his first major commercial success, *A Confession of a Female College Student* (*Ŏnŭ yŏdaesaeng ŭi kobaek*), in 1958. Backed by the film's handsome profits, Shin Films, Shin's motion picture production company, built its own studio in 1959 (Wŏnhyoro studio), equipped with two sound stages, a recording studio, and an editing lab. Shin was not a beneficiary of TAF's motion picture projects in South Korea, but Shin Films grew into the most influential motion picture studio in 1960s South Korean cinema. It also became one of the most active members of the FPA in the 1960s.

By the late 1950s, most of the film executives and cultural elites in South Korea who had been secretly supported by TAF had failed to create any meaningful impact on the motion picture world. In 1962, one year after the *coup d'état* led by General Park Chung Hee (1917–79; in office 1963–79), TAF ended its motion picture project in South Korea and transferred ownership of the TAF-funded facilities and equipment to the KMPCA.[85] In that year, South Korea hosted the ninth Asian Film Festival. Shin Sang-ok, now the most powerful film director and producer in South Korea, served as the director of the festival.

Folding the Motion Picture Project

During the active operation of Asia Pictures and the Asia Press, from 1952 to 1959, TAF granted funds to both companies. The total amount reached almost a million US dollars.[86] However, TAF's most expensive project—to create a healthy, noncommunist Mandarin film industry in Hong Kong, led by Asia Pictures—came nowhere close to success. Chang produced nine theatrical films throughout the period of operations, but none of them stood out commercially in the 1950s Chinese diaspora market in Asia, although some of the studio's later films were better received than the earlier ones. Man-Fung Yip, for example, evaluates Asia Pictures' films positively, particularly in its later years, writing that *Sisters Three* (1957) portrayed Hong Kong's increasingly capitalist society and its culture of consumption and leisure "not with disdain but in a positive light—that challenged communism in a different way."[87]

What frustrated TAF the most was that Chang's two companies failed to strive for self-sufficiency and generate profits. Apparently, by the end of the decade, Chang and his companies had grown to be a burden to TAF, which found itself financially responsible for the two companies and their administrative deficits. John F. Sullivan, Stewart's replacement, had been critical of TAF's motion picture programs since its inception. Sullivan emphasized, "Asia Pictures' contribution to the Chinese cinema has been minor."[88] Asia Pictures was arguably TAF's worst defeat. John Grange, the TAF-Hong Kong Representative, wrote in October 1959, "Ever since I joined the Foundation in August 1957, I have heard the Asia Pictures/Asia Press complex referred to as one of our major 'headaches.'"[89]

TAF's earliest scheme was to endorse Chang and his two companies in the first two years and then retreat immediately once he became a self-sufficient and autonomous motion picture executive. But this initial design turned out to be calamitous. Chang considered himself an "agent" of TAF, whereas TAF regarded Chang as a "partner" and his two companies a "joint enterprise" dedicated to a common goal. Chang thus relentlessly requested subsidies for his corporations. J. F. Richardson, a successor of John Grange at TAF-Hong Kong, wrote, "As long as TAF in effect owns the two companies, Mr. Chang will depend and rely on us for additional investment to cover their deficits."[90] Chang, in a long and emotional letter to Grange, accused him of being behind many damaging third-party reports that had reached TAF and TAF officials. He complained, "I still don't know why the Foundation is so insistent that we stop the service. I think I am entitled to know exactly why they want to stop the service. We are here to fight the Communists. It is a tough fight and we have to throw in everything we have. If we can be convinced that the service is detrimental to our fight, we would stop it immediately."[91]

In March 1959, TAF supported Chang in constructing a second sound stage. On March 31, 1961, almost simultaneous with its withdrawal from the KMPCA, TAF irreversibly turned over ownership of Asia Pictures and the Asia Press to Chang.[92] L. Z. Yuan, however, emphasized that TAF's turning over of the complex to Chang would not mean "any diminishing of interest in keeping the overseas Chinese informed of the evils of the communist regime and rallying those 'Chinese-Chinese' to support Nationalist China."[93] Having struggled with financial deficits due to the constant failures at the local box office, Chang soon ceased the operations of Asia Pictures entirely. *The Shoeshine Boy* (*Ca xie tong*, Bu Wancang, 1959) was Asia Pictures' last production.

In 1959, Blum emphasized in his article for *United Asia*, published in India, the Asia Foundation's threefold purpose: of extending help in Asia, "of encouraging greater cooperation between Asian and non-Asian organizations, and of assisting in promoting a better understanding of Asia in the United States."[94] He then emphasized several major fields in which the foundation operated: education and research; science and technology; civic community development; youth and student outreach; the writing, publishing, and distribution of Asian-language materials; legal development; labor education and welfare; and activities in the United States. The motion picture project, the foundation's most heavily funded operations during the 1950s, largely disappeared in TAF's official and confidential documents. The HKD 200,000 the foundation had granted to Asia Pictures to construct a second sound stage was the foundation's last motion picture subsidization in Asia.

Three years later, Blum left TAF to direct a three-year project for the Council on Foreign Relations financed by the Ford Foundation, titled "The United States and China in World Affairs." On July 9, 1965, Blum died suddenly. He was only fifty-four years old. His book, *The United States and China in World Affairs*, was published posthumously in 1966. The foundation's motion picture professionals, Tanner, Miller, and Busch, all left the foundation one by one, and none of was working for the foundation by the late 1960s. Tanner left the foundation in 1956. As a dedicated Christian, Tanner, after directing and producing many Christian-themed plays, established the Covenant Players in his hometown of Oxnard, California. He wrote over three thousand plays before his death on March 11, 2006, and the Covenant Players became one of the largest professional theater companies dedicated to Christian-themed plays. Busch served two years as assistant to Blum in 1958 and 1959 and then became a staff writer for *Readers' Digest* in 1959, retiring in 1976. As a journalist, he wrote many books, including *Briton Hadden: His Life and Time* (1949) and *The Horizon Concise History of Japan* (1972). His last book, *Winter Quarters: George Washington at Valley Forge*, was published in 1974.[95]

Miller left the foundation in 1958 to pursue a motion picture career in the "real world." Unlike those of other TAF motion picture officers, however, Miller's career after TAF remains something of an enigma. It is fair to say that Miller was a truly passionate man who had abundant knowledge of and interest in the Asian motion picture industry. In a letter to Blum, Miller wrote, "I have a strong interest in doing a study of Asia's film industries for possible publication by UNESCO. I believe that useful conclusions can be drawn from the various individual country film studies, which I have made while working for The Asia Foundation. In fact, I have been told by every Asian film worker with whom I have discussed the possibility of a book on this subject, that a published account of the experiences and problems of other Asian film industries could be most helpful."[96] There is no record whatsoever of John Miller after his relocation to Los Angeles to work at Cinestar International in March 1962.[97] It is not known what happened in his life and career afterward. Miller's aspiration to write a book on the Asian film industries was, in the end, apparently unfulfilled.

In 1965, Stewart received the Order of the Rising Sun award from the Japanese government for his services to United States-Japanese cultural and educational relations. He then joined the Japan Society of New York in 1967 as executive director. Stewart, however, returned to TAF several years later. From 1970 to his retirement in 1985, he was TAF's representative in Tokyo. After his retirement, Stewart continued to work as a visiting scholar at the University of Washington and as a director of the Japan-America Society of the State of Washington. Stewart died in 2006.

Chapter 5

Projecting Asian Cinema to the World

Unheeded Cries (Shiptae ŭi panhang, 1959; also known as A Defiance of Teen-ager), by the South Korean filmmaker Kim Ki-young (1919–98), was screened on the afternoon of Sunday, October 30, 1960, at the Metro Theatre in San Francisco.[1] Unheeded Cries was South Korea's official submission to the fourth San Francisco International Film Festival (SFIFF) in 1960. It tells the story of postwar orphans in the slums of Seoul, which was destroyed during the Korean War, who live by pickpocketing and theft. The screenplay was adapted from an original story by O Yŏng-jin, a notable playwright and critic who was one of the founding members of the KMPCA. O also wrote the screenplay. Kim Ki-young was the first filmmaker to benefit from the KMPCA's film equipment support. Kim's debut film Boxes of Death was shot in 35 mm with a TAF-donated Mitchell camera. Boxes of Death was also partially financed by Liberty Production, a subsidiary unit of USIS.[2] The San Francisco Examiner heralded the screening of Unheeded Cries: "Interest aroused in the artistic life of Korea by recent contributions, such as those which were a part of the (Avery) Brundage collection of Asian art, should insure [sic] an audience for the motion picture from Korea entitled 'ship dae eui ban hang' or 'unheeded cries.'"[3] The initial reviews, however, were not remotely favorable. In his extensive report on the fourth SFIFF for Films in Review, the National Board of Review of Motion Picture's monthly magazine, Romano Tozzi compared the film to "our [Hollywood's] cheapest melodramas, which, alas, have obviously influenced the makers of this stupid mélange of violence, brutality, sex, prostitution and dope addiction."[4] *Unheeded Cries*, therefore, quickly disappeared from the year's film festival circuits.

One question lingers, however: How had *Unheeded Cries* been chosen to be screened at SFIFF in the first place? As SFIFF had held its inaugural event in 1957, only three years earlier, it was a very young film festival and consequently not widely known outside the California Bay Area. Indeed, SFIFF was regarded as a local event of "no particular importance" by most Hollywood people.[5] How, then, had the South Korean film industry acquired information about the existence of this rather "provincial" film festival? It is also noteworthy that *Unheeded Cries* was not the only South Korean film exhibited at an international film festival during this period. Several months later, in June 1961, Kang Tae-jin's *A Coachmen* (*Mabu*, 1961) was screened at the eleventh Berlin International Film Festival (the Berlinale). *A Coachman* follows the life of a poor widower and coach driver, Ch'unsam, who lives with his children in postwar Seoul, the capital of South Korea. Unexpectedly, it won the Silver Bear Award (Extraordinary Prize), which was the country's first achievement at a European film festival.

Since Yi Pyŏng-il's *The Wedding Day* was chosen as South Korea's official submission to the fourth Asian Film Festival in Tokyo, a significant number of South Korean films had been exhibited at international film festivals in both the East and the West. Curiously, though, three film festivals—the Berlinale, San Francisco, and Asian Film Festivals—consistently invited South Korean films to their competition sections during the first half of the 1960s. But why was this not the case with other festivals, such as Cannes, Venice, Karlovy Vary (held in Czechoslovakia), or Rotterdam? What was the logic behind these three festivals' rather enthusiastic attitude toward South Korean cinema? One simple answer is that they—the Berlinale and Asian Film Festival especially—were Cold War cultural battlefields, at least during the first decade. Both festivals had received significant financial support from the US government in either direct or covert ways. In other words, they were more or less "goodwill" events for US cultural diplomacy.

Marijke de Valck delineates several rationales for film festivals: politics, ideology, and restoring the national film industry (Berlin), off-season tourism (Venice and Cannes), and rebuilding run-down cities (Karlovy Vary and Rotterdam).[6] If we apply her categorization, the Asian Film Festival can be grouped with the Berlinale as a "politically charged institution" and the progeny of US-driven Cold War cultural politics.[7] Apparently, the Berlinale, at least in the first decade, was part of a US cultural diplomacy effort that was deliberately initiated to act against the thriving Karlovy Vary Film Festival, which became "a showcase for the Eastern Bloc after Soviet occupation."[8] Indeed, American authorities, and specifically the Information Services Branch of the Office of the US High Commissioner for Germany (HICOG), contributed financially to the Berlinale for at least the first five years, from 1951 to 1956. But the US involvement was never officially disclosed.[9]

The occupied force's cultural representative, Oscar Martay (1920–95), wanted to promote Berlin as the "Western cultural showcase of the East," whose image of a "revitalized Berlin" would "serve as proof of Western economic superiority and cultural dynamism."[10] As Heide Fehrenbach claims, Martay, a film officer of HICOG, was the single most influential person behind the birth of the Berlinale, and it is often said that the idea first came to his mind when he attended the Venice International Film Festival.[11] Both the United States and UK, which occupied seats in the festival committee, pressured other committee members to exclude Eastern European countries from the festival's invitation list. Accordingly, the Berlinale became a political front that explicitly placed its political and ideological messages in the spotlight.[12] The film critic Cynthia Grenier (*Film Quarterly*) criticized the Berlinale for being "industriously used to help influence people and make friends—usually those from Africa and Asia," claiming that the films of these friends "automatically lower the artistic level of the festival."[13] *Film Quarterly* stopped reviewing the Berlinale after Grenier's unfavorable review.

SFIFF, in contrast, was organized and managed by a local distributor, San Francisco's Irving "Bud" Levin, whose ultimate aim was to raise his profile to become an international-level figure. SFIFF was independent and was never granted any financial support from Washington. But SFIFF collaborated closely with TAF. Both institutions had headquarters in downtown San Francisco. More important, though, the president of the San Francisco Art Commission, the primary sponsor of SFIFF, was Harold L. Zellerbach, whose elder brother was none other than J. D. Zellerbach, one of the founding board members of the Committee for a Free Asia.[14] The screening of *Unheeded Cries* was, hence, made possible through SFIFF's close alliance with TAF. TAF attempted to use SFIFF to showcase non-communist and "ideologically correct" Asian films for mainstream American society.

The San Francisco International Film Festival

The first American international film festival, SFIFF was also described as "an Olympics of the screen world."[15] SFIFF held its first official event in

December 1957. The idea of having the international film festival in the Bay Area had started the year before, when a local theater businessperson, Irving M. Levin, organized an Italian Film Festival with the cooperation of the resident Italian consul-general, Pierlugi Alvera. The San Francisco–born Levin, often known as "Bud," had grown up in the theater business. His father, Samuel H. Levin, was a Russian immigrant who settled in San Francisco and established one of the early theater chains on the West Coast. Irving Levin, in a press interview held in 1960, recalled, "Naturally, I was always all wrapped up in the movie business. I can remember working at 14 years old at the old Coliseum theatre."[16] By age eighteen, Levin was managing the Harding and eventually inherited all of the theaters his father had built—the Balboa, Coronet, Galaxy, Stonestown, Coliseum, Alexandria, Metro, Vogue, and El Rey theaters.[17] At the Italian Film Festival, five films were screened, and Federico Fellini's *La Strada* (1954) won the Golden Gate Award (Best Picture). According to Traude Gómez's reminiscence, it was actually Alvera who suggested that Levin hold an international festival with films from all over the world "in the fashion of the famous Venice, Cannes, and Edinburgh festivals."[18]

Levin went on a ten-day trip to Europe in October 1957 and encountered film distributors in the UK, France, Italy, and Germany.[19] But the true mission behind this European tour was to obtain the official sanction of the International Federation of Film Producers Association (IFFPA).[20] In Paris, Irvin met the French film producer Jean-Pierre Frogerais, the president of the IFFPA. Irvin's meeting with Frogerais was not completely successful, but Frogerais told him that the IFFPA was watching the San Francisco experiments and "would probably get behind it officially in 1958."[21] Frogerais eventually kept his promise. The IFFPA endorsed SFIFF after its first festival.

On December 4, SFIFF began with fifteen features from twelve countries, including *The Captain from Köpenick* (*Der Hauptmann von Köpenick*, Helmut Käutner, 1956; Germany), *Il Grido* (Michelangelo Antonioni, 1957; Italy), *Kanal* (Andrzej Wadja, 1957; Poland), *Age of Infidelity* (*Muerte de un Ciclista*, Juan A. Bardem, 1955; Spain), and *Uncle Vanya* (John Goetz and Franchot Tone, 1957; USA)—the only American film in the lineup. Levin himself chose three features from Asia—from India, Satyajit Ray's *Pather Panchali* (1955); from Japan, Kurosawa Akira's *Throne of Blood* (*Kumonosu-jo*, 1957); and from the Philippines, Eddie Romero's *The Last Warrior* (*Huling Mandirigma*, 1956). All of the films were screened at Levin's proud Metro Theatre at 8 pm during the festival period, December 4 to 18, 1957.

A San Francisco film critic, Emilia Hodel, reviewed *The Last Warrior* somewhat positively, writing that "the cast employed a more exaggerated style of acting—similar to the Japanese—than that to which we are accustomed. It gave the film something of a dance ritual quality."[22] *The Oakland Tribune* heralded Kurosawa's *Throne of Blood* by predicting that it was "one of the festival entries which will play to good box office in the US after being released for regular theatre showings."[23] Among all of the Asian films at the festival, however, *Pather Panchali* had the most enthusiastic accolades. *The San Francisco Chronicle* wrote that it was "a remarkably sensitive picture, paced more leisurely than many, but constantly fascinating."[24] Having already won many awards at Cannes, Edinburgh, Berlin, and Rome, *Pather Panchali* grabbed two Golden Gate Awards—Best Picture and Best Director.[25] Ray himself received the trophies. Ray subsequently became a fixture on the international scene, particularly adored at SFIFF. From 1957 to 1972, not a single year passed without at least one Ray film showing at SFIFF.

Gavin Lambert (*Film Quarterly*) was excited to see that the United States was "the first of the three major filmmaking countries (India and Japan are the others)" to hold an international film competition on its own soil. He continued: "It is to be expected that when the San Francisco festival gains in prestige, distributors' and exhibitors' representatives will as a matter of course attend, using the festival as a source of foreign films, and as a method of judging potential audience reaction."[26]

Nevertheless, one important question arises here. Why was the first American international film festival held in San Francisco? Why not Los Angeles, New York, or Washington, DC? Certainly, there were fierce debates among Hollywood-based journalists, executives, and policymakers about launching an international film festival in a major city instead of in the rather remote San Francisco. Such big cities as New York, Chicago, Miami, and even New Orleans had been considered as hosts for an international film festival.[27] But to everyone's surprise, San Francisco was the city that got the show on the road. This initiative irritated Hollywood journalists and critics. Charles Einfeld was one of them. He strongly advocated in *Variety* that an American International Film Festival should be held either in Washington, DC, or in Miami, if not in Hollywood, arguing that San Francisco was "too distant a place for a full-scale festival."[28] However, creating a film festival in a "typical" city never worked out. Levin reasoned, "Who is going to pick the films to be shown? Who is going to pay the expenses? It will cost at least USD 250,000. The best thing for Hollywood to do is to join wholeheartedly in the San Francisco festival. We would welcome Hollywood support."[29]

From its inception to the mid-1960s, however, the Hollywood establishment completely ignored the presence of SFIFF. No major American film was screened at the festival during its early years. This was a significant problem. Stanley Eichelbaum, a local film critic, exclaimed, "Why is it that nearly two dozen countries—including Egypt and nationalist China—were willing to send important new films to the competition? On the other hand, the United States, which made 150 major pictures last year for world-wide distribution, apparently had nothing to offer but three low-budget movies submitted by unknown, independent producers."[30] In fact, Hollywood directors and executives were ignoring European film festivals as a whole. Mervyn LeRoy, one of Hollywood's most successful producer-directors of the time, expressed that he saw no value at all in festivals and that Venice and Cannes were merely "gimmicks for snaring tourists and publicity outlets for shamelessly extroverted stars."[31] Likewise, one Hollywood distributor stated, "I don't see the point of going into San Francisco at all. We would get nothing out of it at all. Even if our picture should win, it'd get no publicity to speak of except in the local papers. This is just a local promotion project and I can't see us getting into it."[32] Therefore, although Levin tried hard to bring Hollywood celebrities and respected directors to SFIFF—he even invited Orson Welles in 1957—he failed to gain any meaningful feedback from the Hollywood establishment. Instead of silver screen glamor, big studio moguls, stellar directors, and the MPAA proxy Eric Johnston, two delegates from the Screen Directors' Guild, Tay Garnet and Frank Borzage, attended the opening night of the first festival. Curiously, Borzage was also the Hollywood representative at the first Asian Film Festival in 1954.[33]

For the second SFIFF, Levin made initial contact with United Artists to invite Stanley Kramer's *The Defiant Ones* (1958). But the studio sent the film to Mexico instead, and then to the Berlinale, where it eventually won a Silver Bear for Best Actor. Having been screened in Mexico, *The Defiant Ones* became automatically disqualified by the rules of SFIFF, which specifically forbade the acceptance of films previously shown in the Western hemisphere. Consequently, no American film was exhibited at SFIFF in 1958. The San Francisco-based *Film Daily* stated, "An industry which enters its pictures in foreign festivals and fails to participate in a festival within its own borders invites criticism, regardless of the circumstances which occasioned the non-representation. Certainly, the lack of Hollywood interest in the SF affair will be noted overseas."[34] One critic at the *San Francisco Chronicle* wrote bitterly,

We now turn in bewilderment to the question of why Hollywood has ignored the festival. Hollywood was once set to enter the new film *Rally Round the Flag, Boys* until, at the last minute, word came north that a print was not ready. Yet the so-called "film capital of the world" must have other completed products worth putting up against the 15 films from 12 countries that are being exhibited. Whatever the reason, artistic timidity or commercial cupidity, the American film industry has made itself look idiotic by joining Russia in the corner reserved for noncompeting nations. Incidentally, three communist countries, Hungary, Poland and Yugoslavia have sent their offerings to the festival.[35]

But not everyone in Hollywood disregarded SFIFF. Its advocates included Edward Dmytryk, a Canadian-born Hollywood director best known for *Crossfire* (1947) and *The Caine Mutiny* (1954), who served one of the three jurors in 1959. Dmytryk returned to SFIFF a year later as one of the presenters at a symposium on "The Role of Films in International Cultural Relations," along with the Soviet director Grigory Chukhrai and the French master Jean Renoir.[36] Mary Pickford and her husband, Charles "Buddy" Rogers, also attended SFIFF the same year. In line with this interest, Fred Zinnemann published an open letter in *The New York Times* to general readers and Hollywood executives in 1961. He passionately pled,

> I have just returned from [a film festival] in San Francisco, which is promoted by a small group of dedicated people under the greatest possible difficulties and with almost no money to help them. Because of the enormous devotion of these people, this festival has managed to survive. It is stimulating, but that is not enough. It certainly is not a true representation of the importance of American filmmaking. I was deeply shocked to observe the total lack of interest, appreciation and awareness of Hollywood filmmakers, who have simply ignored this festival. I respectfully submit that everything possible should be done to help the San Francisco film festival become a true international event which would reflect the importance and the effectiveness of the American film industry.[37]

Without the presence of Hollywood, SFIFF had to rely on foreign films. San Francisco was, nevertheless, the ideal place for showing international cinema. Indeed, as Levin claimed, San Francisco had "more foreign-language theatres per capita than any other US city—even New York."[38] Certainly San Francisco's art film connoisseurs loved Japanese cinema throughout the 1950s. Kurosawa Akira's *Rashomon* had been picked up and distributed in San Francisco by RKO in 1952, and its reception was extraordinary. As Tino Balio claims, Japanese cinema was "the only non-Western venture to make a concerted effort to break into the mainstream US theatrical market during the 1950s."[39] In the late 1950s, San Francisco was about to face the waves of European and Asian art films, and therefore it was the ideal city to host an international film festival. Indeed, the San Francisco-based *Film Quarterly* opened its first "retitled" issue with Donald Richie and Joseph Anderson's article, "Traditional Theatre and the Film in Japan."[40] Likewise, *Films in Review* published a special Japanese cinema issue in March 1957, with three articles written by the influential film critics Henry Hart, Clifford V. Harrington, and Leona Protas Schecter. Hart, for instance, wrote in his review article on New York's Japanese Film Festival, "For of all the races of mankind, I think the Japanese are most likely to realize to the fullest the esthetic potentialities of the motion picture."[41]

Obviously, Levin wished to attract more Asian entries to his festival lineup. He was curious about Asian films produced outside Japan and India. Accordingly, he approached TAF's San Francisco headquarters in September 1957 to ask for recommendations for Asian cinema. This request came too late for TAF to obtain films from Asian countries before the festival was held. The TAF headquarters had a print of Asia Pictures' *The Long Lane*, but the film lacked English subtitles, which disqualified it from the competition.[42] TAF instead gave Levin a list of member producers of the FPA.[43]

The Asia Foundation and SFIFF

As explained in the previous chapter, TAF's motion picture officers, Noel Busch, Charles Tanner, and John Miller, had all left the organization by the end of the 1950s. James Stewart still had some interest in the motion picture industries in Asia, but Blum had decided not to involve TAF directly in the film industries. TAF's support for regional film activities had therefore been minimal since then. However, in 1958, TAF initiated a new venture—with the San Francisco International Film Festival. Interestingly, this happened around the time when TAF was stepping away from Asia Pictures, the KMPCA, and Nagata. In his letter to all TAF representatives, Richard Miller, the director of the Organization Relations Division, wrote, "Heretofore, Foundation activities in this field have been limited to the annual festival of the Federation of Motion Picture Producers of Asia. However, for some time now we have been giving thought as to how we might assist in not only gaining better recognition for Asian film productions, other than those from Japan and India, but also in creating opportunities for Asian film producers to better compete on the international market."[44] Miller's suggestion was to introduce selected Asian films, particularly "noncommunist" ones, to the newly launched SFIFF. TAF, using its vast network in Asia, carefully arranged screenings of Asian cinema at SFIFF to open a gateway for TAF-supported or ideologically "correct" films to enter the American film market. As discussed in a previous chapter, from the very beginning of the motion picture project, TAF had been pursuing this aim with local partners in Japan, Hong Kong, and South Korea. But this time the effort was taking place in San Francisco—TAF's home ground. Winning awards at SFIFF, TAF believed, should pave the way for Asian films to break into Hollywood. Bu Wancang's Hong Kong film *Nobody's Child* (*Kuer liulang ji*, 1958) was the first TAF-supported entry to the festival. Three South Korean films—*Unheeded Cries*, Shin Sang-ok's *The Evergreen* (*Sangnoksu*, 1961), and Yu Hyŏn-mok's *Aimless Bullet* (*Obalt'an*, 1961)—followed. TAF's primary focus now was apparently on South Korea and Hong Kong.

In March 1958, Margaret Pollard, an officer in TAF's Organization Relations Division, called on Hong Kong, Manila, Bangkok, Taipei, and Seoul representatives to see if they were interested in sending films to SFIFF.[45] She stressed that "the extent of assistance could vary from covering shipping costs of the entries to San Francisco to providing travel grants for the stars (feminine, preferably) of any film that is selected for the final competition."[46] Within a month, Levin sent out invitations to Hong Kong, Thailand, Taiwan, the Philippines, and South Korea through the local consuls-general in San Francisco.[47] Pat Judge, the TAF-Hong Kong representative, recommended *Nobody's Child* to SFIFF. Harry H. Pierson, the TAF-Bangkok representative, arranged a special screening of the Thai film *The Diamond Finger*, directed by Ratana Pestonji, that was attended by the king and queen of Thailand on September 12, 1958. In Pierson's letter to Pollard, he specifically mentioned that this short dance movie, twenty-seven minutes in length, was "to be shown" at SFIFF.[48] Pestonji was one of the pioneers of Thai cinema, and his feature-length film *Santi-Vina* was shown at the first Southeast Asian Film Festival in 1954. *The Diamond Finger* was screened not as one of the main competition films but in a special "short films" screening in that year.

As for South Korean cinema, the ad hoc screening committee for the South Korean entries for SFIFF selected *The Money* (*Don*; also known as *The Gambler*), by Kim So-dong (1911–88). Kim submitted his application for the Ministry of Education's approval as an official South Korean entry in the San Francisco Festival. But the Ministry of Education disapproved Kim's application on the grounds that the film showed "too dark an aspect of the

Korean farming village" and it would give "a bad impression to foreigners."[49] It was the film's second rejection from the Ministry of Education. *The Money* had already been declined once for its application to the Asian Film Festival, which was held in Manila in April. Instead of *The Money*, the ministry recommended *Hyperbolae of Youth* (*Ch'ŏngch'un ssang-goksŏn*, 1956), by Han Hyŏng-mo (1917–99), and *Forever With You* (*Kŭdaewa Yŏngwŏnhi*, 1957), by Yu Hyŏn-mok, for the year's official submission to the Asian Film Festival. With no submission from South Korea, Hong Kong's *Nobody's Child* was the only TAF-supported Asian film in the main section at the festival.

Nobody's Child and Josephine Siao Fong Fong

In February 1958, Pat Judge sent a letter to Blum requesting assistance for an independent film producer named Chu Hsu-hua, the president of the Kuo Phone Film Company. Judge wrote, "We are now desirous of providing a loan and we hereby request the activation of our 'Motion Picture Production Fund.' We specifically request that a sum of USD 10,000 be approved to be granted as an interest-free loan to the Kuo Phone Company."[50] The project Judge mentioned was titled *The Poor Child*. The English title was subsequently changed to *Nobody's Child*. The film was a screen adaptation of Hector Marlot's *Sans Famille*, which was first translated into Chinese in 1912 by Bao Tianxiao. The first silver screen reimagination, titled *Little Friend* (*Xiao pengyou*), was put out in 1925 by Shanghai's Minxing studio. Zhang Shichun directed this silent classic, which follows the original novel and features a boy.[51] The 1958 version, *Nobody's Child*, changed the child's gender. *Nobody's Child* tells the story of an orphaned little girl who wanders in search of her long-lost mother. At the beginning of the film, the girl is living with a loving mother who picked her up off the streets during the war. She is later sold by her heartless father to a street performer and becomes determined to look for her birth parents. Bu Wancang, the film's director, emphasized the orphan girl's strong will to survive her hardships.[52] Judge stressed that this film "stands as a symbol of a Chinese refugee from Communist fleeing from north to south." He continued, "The fact that Fong Fong herself is, in a sense, a fugitive, will serve to heighten the symbolism."[53]

Nobody's Child was part of Siao Fong Fong (Josephine Siao)'s "orphaned little girl" cycle, and her name weighed more than other factors. Fong Fong's cycle began with Shaw & Son's *The Orphan Girl* (1955). Siao's name became known to audiences when she won the Best Juvenile Actress Award at the second

Southeast Asian Film Festival in Singapore. The press often called her the darling of the Chinese silver screen. Between 1953 and 1965, Fong Fong appeared
in numerous films as a little orphan and in martial arts films as a younger sister-
in-apprenticeship. It was undoubtedly her name that prompted TAF to assist in
the production of *Nobody's Child*. But even more important to TAF than her
popularity among the Chinese diasporas was the fact that Fong Fong was contracted to the leading communist film company, Great Wall Pictures.[54]

Fong Fong was born in Shanghai in 1947. Her father was a German-
educated businessperson and her mother was a painter. In 1949, escaping
from the newly founded PRC, her family moved to Hong Kong. But no
sooner had they had settled in Hong Kong than her father's business went
bankrupt and her father died of cancer. Fong Fong and her mother descended
into poverty, and she began her acting career to earn money for food.[55] Fong
Fong first acted in a film called *Tears of a Young Concubine* (*Xiao xing lei*, Lee
Fa, 1954). Two years later, she became a superstar with the huge commercial
success of *The Orphan Girl* in 1955. She was indeed "the Hong Kong film
world's Shirley Temple."[56] Great Wall Pictures, TAF's major target in Hong
Kong, persuaded Fong Fong and her mother to sign a two-year contract in
which it was stipulated that Fong Fong would be paid HKD 600 monthly, a
very high sum for the time.[57]

In 1957, right after her contract expired, the Kuo Phone Company successfully signed a two-year, four-picture contract with Fong Fong, which
was, in Judge's words, "the biggest news of the year."[58] What came after their
"conversion" was a series of political events that Fong Fong and her mother
had to attend to prove their willingness to serve Free China (Taiwan). They
flew to Taipei, and during their two-week trip, Fong Fong went to Sun Yat-
sen Memorial Hall, visited military leaders, and broadcast in the Taiwan Central TV Station to announce to movie and stage workers in mainland China
that she had returned to Free China. The climax was her participation in
the celebration of the birthday of President Chiang Kai-shek (1887–1975).[59]
Chung Hsia wrote for *World Today* in February 1958, "Mrs. Siao [Fong Fong's
mother] was awakened to the environment she and Fong Fong had stayed
in during the past two years, a very desolate and horrible environment. One
can only feel the happiness of being healthy when he is sick. One truly real-
izes the happiness of freedom after his freedom has been lost. For the future
of Fong Fong, Mrs. Siao thought that she had no other choice except to take
her on the road of liberty. The opportunity to return to Taiwan to join the
celebration would be the best way to pledge their loyalty."[60]

With TAF's interest-free loan to the Kuo Phone Film Company, the filming of *Nobody's Child* was completed in July 1958. It then became Hong Kong's first official submission to SFIFF in 1958. It was one of four Asian films selected for the competition category in that year. The others were India's *Aparajito* (Satyajit Ray, 1958; winner of the Golden Lion award at the 1957 Venice Film Festival) and two Japanese films, *The Precipice* (*Hyoheki*, Masumura Yasuzo, 1958) and *Rickshaw Man* (*Muhomatsu no issho*, Inagaki Hiroshi, 1958; winner of the Golden Lion award at the 1958 Venice Film Festival). *Nobody's Child*, unfortunately, made little impact at the festival. It was completely overshadowed by *Aparajito*, which was the most-talked-about film of the festival. Satyajit Ray grabbed the Best Director award. Emilia Hodel stated that *Nobody's Child* "proved to be a charming, if somewhat naïve story about an orphaned little girl befriended by an old showman."[61] Paine Knickerbocker of the *San Francisco Chronicle* was harsher. He described the film as rather "primitive."[62] As TAF's San Francisco officer L.Z. Yuan wrote, it was "virtually a nobody's child."[63] He explained the challenges that the film had to deal with at SFIFF: "While many of the other entries enjoyed the sponsorship of their local communities and consulates, with cocktail parties and other events arranged before or after the performances, *Nobody's Child* found no such patronage." He continued, "The Chinese Consulates-General could not very well sponsor the film as it is a Hong Kong production. The British Consulate-General could not very well sponsor the film as it is a Hong Kong production. The British Consulate-General is itself busy with sponsoring the film from the United Kingdom. Also it arrives so late that little could have been done along this line."[64]

Nobody's Child was screened on Sunday afternoon, which was a bad time slot, and the theater was quite far from Chinatown. TAF's motion picture team had hoped to screen the film at the festival first and then secure the US distributor afterwards. If it won any awards, the film, they believed, could have a chance of "crashing into the so-called 'art film circuit' in America."[65] However, neither Paramount nor Columbia pictures agreed to handle the US distribution of the film. TAF's attempt to support *Nobody's Child* in breaking into the US film market failed in the end. But *Nobody's Child* was well received in Taiwan and Hong Kong. *Nobody's Child* received a first-rank prize, one of the "extraordinary" prizes, given by Taiwan's Kuomintang (KMT) government on July 14th, 1959. Siao Fong Fong was awarded a gold medal.[66] In less than a year, *Nobody's Child* was released in Hong Kong and instantly became one of 1960's box office successes.

Shaw Brothers

Interestingly enough, without TAF's support, Shaw Brothers had steadily begun submitting its prizewinning productions to SFIFF a year after *Nobody's Child* was screened at SFIFF. After its first submissions in 1959 of *The Kingdom and the Beauty* (*Chiang shan mei jen*, Li Han-hsiang, 1959) and *The Tragedy of Love* (*Tian chang di jiu*, Doe Ching, 1959), Ramona Curry writes, "Shaw Brothers appears subsequently to have won a kind of monopoly as a representative for films from Hong Kong, Taiwan, Formosa, or 'China,' as festival records and newspaper reviews describe the source of the subsequent Shaw entries."[67] Run Run Shaw was hungry for international film festival awards. His SFIFF debut in 1959 was, however, disastrous. Romano Tozzi wrote, "They [*The Tragedy of Love* and *The Kingdom and the Beauty*] combined to make four unbearable hours." He continued, "They didn't belong in a festival and can't possibly interest Occidental audiences."[68]

Several months later, Shaw Brothers dispatched a number of delegates to the 1960 Cannes International Film Festival with Li Han-hsiang's *The Enchanting Shadow* (*Qian nu you hun*, 1960), the most expensive costume film ever produced by the studio. Run Run Shaw aimed to expand his studio's limited market—at the time consisting of Hong Kong, Malaya, and Singapore—and sell films to the outside world. His reference was *Rashomon*. Shaw well understood the weight of European film festivals and knew that a single film could change the industry. His strategy was to emphasize Asian themes—music, costumes, dance, and production design, along with the historical background of medieval China, preferably the Ming dynasty. However, *The Enchanting Shadow* failed to attract significant attention either from festival participants or Euro-American distributors.[69]

The Enchanting Shadow played on October 23, 1960, at SFIFF. That year, South Korea's entry, *Unheeded Cries*, and Japan's *The Diary of Sueko* (*Nianchan*, Imamura Shohei, 1959) were the other Asian entries. Shaw attended the festival from its first day. He was present at the afternoon screening of *The Enchanting Shadow* with his wife and daughter.[70] The film was much more successful than Shaw Brothers' previous year's entries. *The San Francisco Examiner* delivered favorable news: "Run Run Shaw, the far eastern entrepreneur who produced the picture, was in the audience to hear applause for his retelling of a supernatural legend from ancient cathay. In limpid colour cleverly adapted to the mysterious mood, Shaw has composed a balanced, poetic, curiously modern ghost story."[71]

Shaw, however, came home empty-handed, while Akiko Maeda (*Sueko*) and Sung-Ki An (An Sŏng-gi; *Cries*) received awards under the category of "Honourable Mention for Acting by Child Performers." His efforts continued nonetheless. Shaw Brothers submitted three more films—*The Golden Trumpet* (Doe Ching, 1961), *The Love Eterne* (*Liang Shan Ba yu Zhu Ying Tai*, Li Han-hsiang, 1963), and *Between Tears and Smiles* (*Sun tai sil yen yin*, Lo Chen, 1964)—in 1961, 1963, and 1964 respectively. In all, Shaw Brothers submitted six films between 1959 and 1964 but received no awards from SFIFF. The company eventually stopped sending its productions to SFIFF. *Between Tears and Smiles* was Shaw's last attempt.

South Korean Films

In a letter to Robert Sheeks on August 11, 1960, Kim So-dong stated that *The Money* had been prevented from joining film festivals in Asia and San Francisco by Syngman Rhee's political power. Since Syngman Rhee had resigned after the student-led April revolution against the fraudulent presidential election in March 1960, Kim expressed his wish to resubmit *The Money* for the year's SFIFF.[72] Jack E. James, a TAF-Seoul representative, thought highly of *The Money*. He made an effort to help Kim but unfortunately could not reach him.[73] Stephen Uhalley, Jr., TAF officer in San Francisco headquarters, wrote a letter to Jack E. James about *The Money*.[74] Uhalley showed his disappointment: "It was indeed unfortunate that *The Gamblers* [*The Money*] didn't have a greater opportunity to enter the competition, for an official at the Film Festival indicated that had it been entered it might well have been selected. His remark was based upon information we could supply about its alleged content, particularly its realistic portrayal."[75]

While Kim failed to submit *The Money* to the festival, two South Korean entries were received by SFIFF. They were *Unheeded Cries* and Shin Sang-ok's *To the Last Day* (*I Saengmyŏng Tahadorok*, 1960). *Unheeded Cries* was selected and exhibited at SFIFF. Shin Sang-ok tried again in 1962. Shin's *The Evergreen* was chosen and premiered in 1962. Based on a novel written by Sim Hun in 1935, this screen adaptation follows two young university students, both from small towns, who want to help those in the countryside during the Japanese occupation period. The young woman, Yŏngsin, is especially passionate about educating children and goes to a village to teach. The young man, Tonghyŏk, returns to his hometown and builds a community hall to foster a sense of power over their future among the local young adults. Unfortunately, just as things start looking up, they both run into opposition from the Japanese officials and their supporters. At SFIFF, Martin Russell reviewed *The Evergreen* for *Variety*. He wrote, "Though technically a pleasant surprise, it is full of the idealistic naiveté that is greeted in the west with mild amusement . . . [T]he saga is thoroughly inundated with tears, which are not affecting. But, despite quite ingratiating performances by Choi Eun Hee [Ch'oe Ǔn-hǔi; 1926–2018] as the girl missionary and Shin Young Kyun [Sin Yǒng-gyun] as her rather nebulous lover, one comes to the sad conclusion that the sight of solid, unalloyed goodness at work is a trifle dull. It certainly isn't drama, though some may find an impeccable example uplifting."[76] Another critic, Michael S. Willis, expressed uneasy feelings about the film's strong strain of nationalism, going so far as to state that its entry in an international film festival seemed "inappropriate."[77]

Yu Hyǒn-mok's *Aimless Bullet*, however, had a better reception at SFIFF a year later. *Aimless Bullet*, often regarded as one of the best-made films in Korean cinema history, is the tragic story of a clerk at an actuary's office and his family. As Kelly Y. Jeong notes, *Aimless Bullet* "touched a nerve in the context of a nation slowly recovering from a destructive fratricidal war, now divided in the aftermath."[78] At SFIFF, a critic for the *San Francisco Examiner* wrote,

> Korea's contribution to the festival, *Aimless Bullet* is a bitter and despairing drama that protests violently against social injustice and unemployment, from the standpoint of the young army veterans who returned after the recent conflict to a shiftless life of poverty, slums and hopelessness. Their dilemma is aggravated by loneliness, particularly in the case of a glum, earnest and taciturn accountant, excellently played by Jingue Kim [Kim Chingyu], who was at the Metro with the movie's director Hyon Moak Yoo [Yu Hyǒn-mok]. The hero's crowded household is plagued with adversity—a factor that gives the film a relentless and almost fanatic gloom. His mother has gone mad, his sister prostitutes herself; his brother robs a bank; and his wife dies in childbirth. The movie has obviously been influenced by the Italian cinema's neorealism. And though it is generally a convincing and sophisticated work, done with admirable honesty, its dour outlook brings it down to a level of fiercely proselytizing social drama.[79]

The screening of *Aimless Bullet* at SFIFF was only possible with help from Richard Dyer MacCann (1920–2001), a former *Christian Science Monitor* staff writer and then a University of Southern California film school professor. TAF knew MacCann very well. As a matter of fact, many years earlier, in an attempt to raise US interest in TAF's first feature film, *The People Win Through* (1952), TAF had arranged a private screening for the *Christian Science Monitor*. MacCann, then a staff correspondent, wrote an explicitly favorable article for the newspaper about the strategic weight of the film against the ever-increasing influence of communist propaganda in the Far East. In a later article, "Films and Film Training in the Republic of Korea," probably one of the first academic pieces on South Korean cinema published in an American film journal, MacCann recalled how he "discovered" *Aimless Bullet*. In 1963, MacCann was an adviser and teacher, on a US State Department grant, for the Korean National Film Production Centre in Seoul. There he gave a two-month special course in documentary film for Chung-Ang University's program in film production. Yi Kŭn-sam (1929–2003), then a young playwright, was MacCann's interpreter and brought *Aimless Bullet* to his attention.[80] MacCann believed he had discovered South Korea's answer to *Rashomon*.

In an interview with the *San Francisco Chronicle*, MacCann confidently claimed that "a country's film can gain attention through the influence of one director" and continued, "*Aimless Bullet* is a high quality production which could lead the Koreans to a foreign language Oscar for their recently developed industry."[81] After all, *Aimless Bullet* had "a fantastic story" that the film festival community would love to hear—a story of film censorship and South Korean politics. *Aimless Bullet* was suppressed by the government for two years because of its depiction of "depression and hopelessness," which was considered a poor representation of the country, and also because of a refrain spoken over and over by the war-crazed grandmother: "Let's get out of here," which could be interpreted to mean "back to our home in North Korea."[82] MacCann's recommendation of *Aimless Bullet* to SFIFF, via the Asia Foundation, was eventually accepted by the festival committee. An invitation letter to the film festival in the United States resulted in a reversal of the government's decision about the film.

Aimless Bullet was released for screening in Seoul only a few weeks before the festival for the specific purpose of making it eligible for entry in the festival. Interestingly enough, Yu Hyŏn-mok, the film's director, said to the press, "I hope President Kennedy will see this film and continue aid to South Korea. Otherwise the poverty will become worse. I feel it is the last chance to preserve our country from aggression from North Korea."[83] However, contrary to MacCann's expectations, *Aimless Bullet* could not make a splash at the film festival. One critic at the *San Francisco Chronicle* expressed his dissatisfaction with the film, stating that "the story is repetitious, the action does not move. The robbery and chase are clumsily described and the dramatic structure of the film is faulty."[84] *Aimless Bullet* lost its chance to become South Korea's *Pather Panchali* or *Rashomon. Aimless Bullet*, though, later became a canonical postwar film that is generally regarded as one of the best-made films in South Korean film history.[85] In this regard, MacCann was not wrong.

The last South Korean film screened at SFIFF before the Korean New Wave in the 1990s was Shin Sang-ok's *Deaf Samryong (Pŏngŏri Samnyong,* 1964).[86] TAF was not involved with this selection. *Deaf Samryong* had already been invited to the Berlinale before the US screening at SFIFF in October 1965. In a festival program, an unknown contributor left an encouraging review of the film: "The progress of Korean cinema has been exceptionally haphazard, and past festival audiences have been bewildered by the naïve treatments of melodramatic domestic triangles or sentimental epics. Therefore, *Samryong* [Deaf Samryong] came as a surprise to the Berlin festival and its delicate observation of a mute servant's love for his employer's wife revealed a tragic, lyrical sense that was entirely unexpected."[87]

The New York Film Festival

TAF's strategic alliance with SFIFF ended in the mid-1960s. After the 1965 event, SFIFF included no further feature films from Hong Kong or South Korea until the mid-1980s. SFIFF screened Japanese films occasionally, but they did not gain critical attention from local and international critical circles. Continually ignored by Hollywood studios, Levin had struggled to expand the size of the festival, and SFIFF remained a regional film festival during the 1960s. Moreover, Levin had to deal with the second international film festival in the United States and the first festival held in a "typical" city, the New York Film Festival (NYFF), which was launched in September 1963. Two New York cultural icons—Richard Roud, a former film critic for the *Guardian* and programmer for the London Film Festival, and the legendary New York-based cineaste Amos Vogel—were its founding forces. NYFF cited "quality" as its only criterion. Round and Vogel proclaimed that their aim in initiating NYFF was "to present within a ten-day period a selection of the best films of the years—largely but not exclusively—garnered from the major festivals."[88]

Accordingly, during its first few years, NYFF ushered in such new cinematic movements as the Brazilian, Japanese, French, and Eastern European New Waves. Indeed, Susan Sontag reminisced, "There were new masterpieces every month" for New York's cultural connoisseurs.[89] Two Japanese films, *Harakiri* (Kobayashi Masaki, 1963) and *An Autumn Afternoon* (*Samma no aiji*, Ozu Yasujiro, 1962), were screened at the first event in 1963. Throughout the 1960s and into the early 1970s, many Japanese films and selected Indian films directed by Satyajit Ray were introduced to New York audiences. But what really caught New York art connoisseurs' interest was the Eastern European New Wave. Roman Polanski's *Knife in the Water* (*Nóz w wodzie*, Poland, 1962) was screened in 1963, and the film ignited a great interest in Eastern European cinema.[90] The curious cinephiles then discovered Věra Chytilová's *Daisies* (*Sedmikrásky*, Czechoslovakia,1966) and Miloš Forman's *The Fireman's Ball* (*Hoří, má panenko*, Czechoslovakia, 1967), not to mention the early Andrzej Wajda's *Ashes and Diamonds* (*Popiół i diament*, Poland, 1958).[91]

As Rahul Hamid recounts, early 1960s cinema had not yet achieved legitimacy on the still conservative American intellectual scene, and the NYFF committee, led by Roud and Vogel, had to struggle with the administrators of Lincoln Center and the city's cultural critics, who still favored the "high" arts.[92] With Roud and Vogel's concerted efforts and the support of the newly emerging cinephiles in New York, the NYFF committee received USD 150,000 from Lincoln Center, which reportedly made Levin jealous.[93] In contrast, SFIFF received a modest USD 10,000 annually from the Art Commissions of San Francisco, and all financial losses had to be borne by Levin himself.[94] SFIFF, at least by the late 1960s, was indeed the Levins' family business. Levin was also displeased about Hollywood's distrust of his motives. Levin said, "They [Hollywood] thought I was out to promote art house movies for my own benefit. The truth is that at that time I had only one foreign film theatre of 365 seats." He continued, "I also had 10 other theatres with 10,000 seats. I obviously wasn't going to profit from building up art films."[95] A year after NYFF's inaugural event, SFIFF was finally granted an "A" grade from the International Federation of Film Producers Associations.[96] At this critical time for SFIFF, after the 1964 event, Irving Levin and his wife Irma, who had worked by his side as hostess since 1957, left the festival.

Conclusion: The Asia Foundation's Motion Picture Project in Asia

The first five chapters of this book have mapped out how TAF's short-lived motion picture project aimed to construct an alliance of anticommunist film producers in Asia by supporting some of the ideologically "correct"—

prodemocratic and pro-American—motion picture executives in Asia, particularly in Japan, Hong Kong, and South Korea. As discussed earlier, what TAF's motion picture project team had hoped to do was to "minimize or eliminate the effectiveness of leftist anti-Free world influence" in the region's cinema and win the psy-war against the "ever-thriving" communist forces.[97] To achieve this mission, TAF supported the FPA and its mastermind Nagata Masaichi, Chang Kuo-sin and his Asia Pictures in Hong Kong, the KMPCA in South Korea, and selected Asian films that were introduced at the San Francisco International Film Festival.

Even with all of these efforts, however, TAF could not meet its initial expectations. The Asian film industry was much more complicated than the TAF executives had thought. What TAF overlooked was political instability, an intensifying nationalism that was often incorporated in communism or Red Scares, foreign currency regulations that made it difficult to purchase or borrow raw stocks and new and modern filming equipment from America, and the radical transformation of the film industry in the various countries. And, most important, TAF's strategic partners in the region, notably Nagata Masaichi, Chang Kuo-sin, and Kim Kwan-su, were either incapable of leading "Free World" organizations or lacked sufficient experience in the motion picture industry. Their blatant ideological stances often compromised the commercial values that were necessary to attract local audiences. By the late 1950s, TAF had stopped supporting them and, in a few years, ended its motion picture project completely.

Although TAF decided to cease subsidizing film studios in Hong Kong and South Korea, Run Run Shaw of Shaw Brothers in Hong Kong, the least politically engaged producer in the FPA, paradoxically achieved TAF's key goal—a healthy influence on the communist-dominated film industry in the overseas Chinese communities. Run Run Shaw, the youngest of the four Shaw brothers, was called an "opportunist" by Thomas Hodge, the director of the Malayan Film Unit.[98] Despite his lack of political engagement, his Shaw Brothers Studio probably benefited more than any other studio from the federation. After the first festival in 1954, Miller reported, "He [Shaw] is going 'all-out' to win the grand prize next year; does not care how much it costs, contemplates hiring Japanese director from Daiei to make the picture."[99] Indeed, Shaw Brothers had hired Japanese cinematographers, directors, composers, and costume designers and raised the quality of its products. One reporter for *Variety* wrote in 1960 that "the fact that Japan had to take a comparative back seat this year indicates that with the less developed nations becoming industrialized . . . the Asian picture is becoming more competitive."[100]

Shaw Brothers used the FPA, and particularly the Asian Film Festival, to promote its annual releases and as a meeting site for coproductions, firmly seizing control of the industry. Shaw, in the words of the veteran Hong Kong film critic Law Kar, "utilized festival awards to bolster the company's reputation in Southeast Asia."[101] What is more, the studio owned or was affiliated with over a hundred theaters and numerous amusement parks in Hong Kong, Singapore, and Malaysia, which allowed it to gain a majority of the voting rights at the FPA. In a similar vein, the Hong Kong film historian Kinnia Yau Shuk-ting, focusing on the role of Daiei and Shaw Brothers, claims that the history of the festival, especially between 1954 and 1969, demonstrates how Shaw "established its close tie with Japan's Big Five, and replaced them as the leading studio in Asia."[102]

Given all this, it is no surprise that in 1959, *Southern Screen*, Shaw Brothers' monthly magazine publicizing the studio's stars, business plans, and films, proclaimed it was "'Oscar' time in the Asian movie field!"[103] In that year, the Asian Film Festival was held in Kuala Lumpur, the capital of Malaysia, in May. Run Run Shaw chaired the festival committee. Shaw Brothers was operating its Shaw Malay studio, and three out of five festival entries of Malaysia were de facto Shaw Brothers products. Although the festival invited films from eight member countries—Taiwan, Hong Kong, South Korea, Indonesia, Japan, the Philippines, Singapore, and Malaysia—Shaw Brothers' films dominated three entries: those of Hong Kong, Singapore, and Malaysia. As expected, Shaw Brothers swept the festival by acquiring thirteen awards, including the Best Picture and Best Director awards for *The Kingdom and the Beauty*.[104] The seventh festival was held in Tokyo in April 1960. Shaw Brothers' *Back Door* (*Hou men*, Li Han-hsiang, 1959) won Best Dramatic Film out of twenty-seven entries. This was Shaw's third consecutive victory since 1958. The Shaw family was no longer the FPA's second-in-command. Run Run Shaw, in 1961, proclaimed, "Japan and Hong Kong are both leaders in Asian cinema. With Japan's profound relationship with Southeast Asia and the similarities we share in our cultural backgrounds . . . we will have to seek total collaboration with our Japanese counterpart."[105] Using the vast network of the FPA, Shaw Brothers had initiated multiple regional coproductions with Taiwanese, South Korean, Filipino, and Thai counterparts during the 1960s.[106]

Surprisingly, the FPA network did not disappear after TAF folded its motion picture program. It was successfully facilitated in the 1960s by nonpolitical motion picture executives in Hong Kong, Taiwan, the Philippines, and South Korea. From the mid-1960s onward, the region's two developing states—South Korea and Taiwan—and its regional media capital, Hong Kong, dominated the Asian Film Festival and the FPA. "To be perfectly honest," Li Han-hsiang recalled, "many awards at the [Asian Film] festival were dished out under the special maneuverings of producers, who were doing a lot of PR, taking people for meals, etc. The ulterior motive for organizing a festival was to cement connections and help each other sell films. That was exactly how the particular festival was formed, under the arrangement of Daiei's representative Nagata Masaichi, Run Run Shaw, Korean director Shin Sang-ok and several prominent producers of the Philippines."[107]

Nagata, in contrast, gradually lost his influence over the festival despite continuing on as president of the FPA until the end of the 1960s. The FPA network opened a new door for the region's ambitious film executives, and Hong Kong, South Korean, and Taiwanese cinema soon embraced each other's golden age of motion picture studios. In this regard, TAF's motion picture project contributed substantially to the Asian film industry. TAF, in other words, eventually played a significant role in the formation of the inter-Asian motion picture industry network, albeit in ways it had never anticipated.

Part II

The Second Network

Chapter 6

The Rise and Demise of a Developmental State Studio

By the beginning of the 1960s, five motion picture studios stood out in Asia: Shin Films in South Korea, GMP (Grand Motion Picture Company; Guolian) and CMPC (Central Motion Picture Corporation) in Taiwan, and Shaw Brothers and MP&GI (Motion Picture and General Investment; Cathay Pictures) in Hong Kong and Singapore. In the political, ideological, and economic sphere of the US-driven Cold War, South Korea, Taiwan, and Hong Kong formed a metastable geopolitical entity known as "East Asia." This was a "temporized regional order" (to borrow from Zbigniew Brzezinski) that had effectively subsumed, in the course of the Cold War, two preceding brands—"Far East" and "Greater East Asia"—that had been shaped by the colonial forces of Great Britain and Japan, respectively.[1] Each film studio in the region aspired to implement the rationalized and industrialized system of mass-producing motion pictures known as the Hollywood studio system.

The Hollywood studio system evolved in the United States to handle film production, distribution, and exhibition during the first three decades of the twentieth century. Like other American industries at the time, the film industry's production, distribution, and exhibition branches corresponded to manufacturing, wholesale, and retail activities. And like its complements, the motion picture industry was, according to Tino Balio, "vertically integrated in the main, with a handful of companies doing the lion's share of the business."[2] In this vertically integrated studio system in Hollywood, the major studios dominated film production, distribution, and exhibition, so that the studios made, released, and even owned the cinemas in which their films were shown. Its production has been characterized as a Fordian mass production system, and Janet Staiger describes it as an "assembly line."[3] The studio system had evolved into a highly efficient system that produced "interchangeable" and "standardized" feature films, newsreels, animations, and shorts to supply its mass-produced motion pictures to subsidized theaters.[4] To maximize its profits, the industry implemented the chain store strategy of mass-marketing.[5] Certainly Fordism, the famous American system of mass production, was what Michael Storper calls "a creature of particular American circumstances."[6]

To many Asian film executives, Hollywood was a place to long for and aspire to emulate. Since they lacked information about the creative personnel who worked in Hollywood, however, Hollywood modernity was for them an imagined modernity. Instead, the movie executives of South Korea, Taiwan, and Hong Kong turned to Japan, which had already adopted the Western system of movie-making. Each studio in the region, in fact, learned from and was stimulated by Japan's advanced film studios, which were far more reachable than those of distant Hollywood. Im Wŏn-sik, Shin Sang-ok's protégé and a Shin Films contract director, remembered,

> Japan had its unique system which was a hierarchal order back then. Under a director, there were chiefs who were first assistant directors. He [the director] normally led his own team composed of two to three assistant directors. Each assistant director had his/her area of expertise, like props, location shooting, production design, casting, and other miscellanies. When I first worked at Shin Films in 1959, Shin Sang-ok had already adopted this particular Japanese system. . . . This system worked very well, and we were proud of our scientific production process that other studios had never achieved.[7]

The motion picture studios in Asia were equipped with multiple large soundstages built exclusively for motion picture productions and had contracted stars and directors in their arsenals; they employed several hundred technicians, owned and managed state-of-the-art theaters and even movie palaces, and to various extents were associated with, supported by, or forcefully controlled by each newly independent or still colonial government.[8] Each churned out twenty to fifty films per year, with production peaking in the mid-1960s. The countries coproduced and distributed films with each other through the FPA, and each one aggressively attempted to expand its markets beyond its comfort zone.

This unprecedented regional phenomenon coincided ironically with the fading phase of TAF's motion picture project in Asia. TAF's motion picture project could not achieve its initial aim, and TAF pulled out of motion pictures completely at the beginning of the 1960s. The network it shaped, however, remained in place throughout the decade. An emerging group of nonpolitical regional motion picture executives took over the FPA platform and constructed the first inter-Asian motion picture studio network, with no financial and administrative support from TAF or any other US Cold War institution. The core members of this new network were Hong Kong's Run Run Shaw, Singapore's Loke Wan-tho, South Korea's Shin Sang-ok, and Taiwan's Li Han-hsiang and Henry Gong Hong. Except for Shaw, none of them had benefited from TAF's motion picture project.

This new network first emerged in 1962 with South Korea hosting the Asian Film Festival for the first time; it was in full swing during the mid- to late 1960s, showed significant signs of decline in the mid-1970s, and finally melted away at the end of the decade. This network, which I call the "Asian studio network," had a shared market; geolinguistic and geocultural terrain based on cultural proximities; a hierarchy built around a core, a semiperiphery, and a periphery that largely sustained the initial structure despite constant challenges; and a spatial-temporal boundary whose principal axes were Hong Kong, South Korea, and Taiwan.[9] Japan functioned as a parameter at every juncture. The logic that gave rise to the network is multifarious: it includes urbanization, the mass influx of American culture, the swift industrialization of each developing economy, laissez-faire economic policies, and a collective yearning to pull off a mass-production streamlining of cinema. In other words, the ultimate task of the film moguls in Asia in the late 1950s was to meet the needs of each ever-expanding local audience in the face of unprecedented rapid urbanization. The newly independent countries in the region experienced an abrupt influx of migrant workers. The number of city residents spiked, and these new patrons boosted the film industries.

Throughout the 1960s, management operations, business structures, human resources, distribution practices, genres, and the control of labor were discussed, shared, and adopted before and after the annual Asian Film Festival. A handful of passionate film executives, including Shaw, Shin, Loke, and Li, were competitors who simultaneously benefited from each other through their formal and informal connections with the FPA. One notable figure who was not included in the Asian studio network was Nagata Masaichi, the initiator of the FPA. For many decades, Japan had been the most advanced filmmaking country in Asia; its local film industry, as discussed above, had adopted the Fordist mode of scientific management of mass production. Nagata was one of the most influential figures in Asia throughout the 1950s—the belle époque of the Japanese studios. Thanks to Japan's postwar "economic miracle," the Japanese film industry grew with the larger economy throughout the 1950s. It started to decline, however, after that peak moment. This unanticipated demise was calamitous.[10] By the mid-1960s, Japanese filmmakers, and Nagata particularly, had lost interest in the FPA. Accordingly, Japan participated in the Asian Film Festival only as a passive member.

The Asian Film Festival in Seoul, 1962

South Korea hosted the Asian Film Festival for the first time in May 1962. It was the first international cultural event the new country had hosted under the military government's regime. Every cultural and political sector in South Korea was expected to contribute. Nearly every day, the nation's daily newspapers trumpeted the latest news about the festival, where Koreans would "proudly introduce our bright new country to the world."[11] To celebrate the one-year anniversary of the coup d'état led by General Park Chung Hee in May 1961, the festival was scheduled to be held in Seoul from May 12 to 16. Shin Sang-ok, then only thirty-five years old, was appointed to chair the festival committee. Shin was already becoming the nation's most powerful film mogul. His studio had swept the nation's own film awards—the first Taejongsang (Golden Bell Film Awards), held on March 30, just two months before the Asian Film Festival in Seoul—by receiving the awards for Best Picture for *Tyrant Yeonsan* (*Yŏnsan Kun*, 1962), Best Director for *The Houseguest and My Mother* (*Sarangbang sonnimgwa ŏmŏni*, 1961; also known as *My Mother and her Guest*), Best Actor (Sin Yŏng-gyun for *Tyrant Yeonsan*), and Best Actress (Ch'oe Ŭn-hŭi for *The Evergreen* (*Sangnoksu*, 1961)). His three winning films were chosen as the year's South Korean entries for the Asian Film Festival at the end of the *Taejongsang* ceremony.

Although Hong Kong and Japan complained that the Cannes International Film Festival was also to be held in May, the festival committee stuck with the planned dates, since the grand finale would be a celebration of what

Figure 6.1. Official poster for the ninth Asian Film Festival, May 12–16, 1962, which was held in Seoul, South Korea, for the first time. Photo courtesy of the Federation of Motion Picture Producers in Asia-Pacific (FPA)

the Park regime called "the May 16 revolution" (*5.16 hyŏk-myŏng*).[12] In April, the festival committee announced the full schedule. All participants were to visit the national army cemetery (Hyŏnch'ungwŏn), P'anmunjŏm, and the military academy.[13] Park, the new president, would attend the closing ceremony to present the highest award, the prize for best picture.[14] As evidence of the unpredictable direction of regional political transformation, however, Indonesia and Thailand pulled out of the festival due to each country's various internal and international political conflicts. In consequence, Seoul hosted only six countries: Japan, Hong Kong, the Philippines, Singapore, Malaysia, and Taiwan, which together sent approximately 110 delegates, directors, performers, jurors, and observers, along with twenty-five feature films.

Certainly the 1962 Asian Film Festival was an important turning point for many of its regional participants, as well as for the festival itself as an international sociopolitical and cultural entity. The Park administration had initiated a five-year plan for economic development in 1961, and all of the political, economic, and cultural sectors in South Korea had dedicated themselves to the new nation's economic development. The film industry was no exception. During the same period, the Shaw family relocated its motion picture headquarters from Singapore to Hong Kong; the completion of the new Clearwater Bay Studio, known as a "movie town," also occurred in 1962. Shaw Brothers wanted to boost the volume of its Mandarin-language costume dramas, which had been popular in Southeast Asia's vast Chinese diasporas, but Hong Kong was simply not suitable for shooting these grand-scale genre films with epic battle sequences. Working the 1962 festival like a business meeting, Run Run Shaw brought his right-hand man Raymond Chow and contacted Taiwan's CMPC, Japan's Daiei and Toho studios, and South Korea's Shin Films to make multiple coproduction agreements. In addition, recognizing that the Seoul festival would be a watershed moment for Japan's economic and political renormalization with the South Korean government, the Japanese cultural delegates were determined to show goodwill to Korean civilians. Okawa Hashizo, a chief executive of Toei, expressed in an interview with *Kyŏnghyang shinmun*, "I've been notorious for never attending film festivals but I'm here today. The reason I broke my dictum is to help normalize the interstate relationship between Japan and South Korea. I believe that cinema will play a major role."[15] In fact, Japan dispatched the largest number of delegates (thirty-three) of all the member countries.[16] Just before the festival opened, Nagata Masaichi announced that Daiei had decided to import a South Korean film, *Seong Chun-hyang* (*Sŏng Ch'un-hyang*, 1962). This was another Shin Sangok production and would be released in six major Japanese cities.[17]

During the festival, Shin's *The Houseguest and My Mother*, based on a best-selling novel by Chu Yo-sŏp, won the prize for Best Picture.[18] Through the eyes of an innocent six-year-old girl, Ok-hŭi, this postwar classic follows an exchange between Ok-hŭi's mother, a young widow (played by Shin's wife Ch'oe Ŭn-hŭi), and her houseguest Mr. Han (Kim Chin-gyu), who is a friend of the widow's brother-in-law. The "houseguest" awakens desires in the widow that she thought were long dead, or that perhaps she had never experienced. However, Ok-hŭi's mother becomes concerned about her mother-in-law and her daughter and rejects Mr. Han's confession of love. Mr. Han then leaves town. Park Chung Hee handed the trophy to Shin, the owner of Shin Films (Shinp'illim). The unexpected triumph of *The Houseguest and My Mother* caused a nationwide sensation. This was the first time a South Korean film had won the Best Picture award at an international film festival. Shin Films also secured three additional trophies: *The Evergreen* received the Best Actor and Best Supporting Actor awards, while *Tyrant Yeonsan* took the Best Art Direction award. Shin was undoubtedly the star of the festival's closing ceremony, and it marked the beginning of Shin's magnificent decade—the 1960s.

In the wake of this victorious outcome, local film critics, producers, and intellectuals continuously debated the present and future of South Korean

Figure 6.2. Shin Sang-ok (right) poses with Li Han-hsiang (center) and his wife Ch'oe Ŭn-hŭi (left) at the 1962 Asian Film Festival. Photo courtesy of Korean Film Archive.

cinema. The 1962 festival was indeed a contact zone for local film critics and film industry personnel, the place where they first encountered neighboring countries' contemporaneous films. In a roundtable discussion titled "Han'gukyŏnghwa ŭi mirae" [The future of South Korean cinema], various sectors of South Korean intellectuals expressed their visions, concerns, and perceptions of the obstacles to "modernizing" South Korean cinema. Yi Chae-myŏng, the former managing director of the KMPCA and the president of the Korean Motion Picture Producer's Association (KMPPA), observed, "Japan is still the most advanced country in terms of its cinematic techniques and artistic qualities; however, South Korea now became number two. We are a bit inferior to Japan but have almost reached the point of competing with Japanese cinema."[19] Shin Sang-ok, after listening to other influential figures in the industry, such as Yi Pyŏng-il and O Yŏng-jin, two of the founding members of the KMPCA, opined that South Korean cinema should begin by rationalizing the system of mass production. Requesting the government enact a law was one good way to achieve the modernization of the cinema industry. Yi Pyŏng-il, in line with Shin, remarked, "In sum, if we'd like to see the development of South Korean cinema, the most urgent mission is to acquire sufficient assets and to build a modern motion picture studio that enables us to experiment with synchronization, color photography, and other new cinematic techniques."[20]

To the South Korean intellectuals of the time, South Korean cinema was next to Japanese cinema in terms of artistic maturity. Compared to other national cinemas in Asia, South Korean cinema was thematically and aesthetically superior but lacked a modern production system equipped with state-of-the-art facilities. This perspective was maintained throughout the 1960s by most South Korean film critics and directors: once South Korean cinema became modernized and industrialized, it could surely surpass the standard set by Japanese cinema. In fact, Japanese cinema, not Hollywood, had long been the barometer used to gauge South Korea's degree of modernity. Most film personnel in the 1960s had begun their film careers during the colonial period and practiced film techniques in Japan. Shin was of this lineage, and for him, Japanese cinema represented the ultimate goal that South Korean cinema, and his own Shin Films, had to attain.

In 1963, a year after the Seoul Asian Film Festival, this collective self-assurance persisted. One critic predicted that this year's Asian Film Festival, which was scheduled to be held in Tokyo from June 11 to 15, would be "South Korea and Japan's match," and he added, "but one of those small rivals, Hong Kong, will challenge us. However, it will not be a big threat."[21] *Han'gug ilbo* predicted, "The Best Picture award will surely be awarded to either South Korea or Japan."[22] The film director Yi Pong-rae asserted, "Filipino cinema is less sophisticated than Japanese cinema in terms of its technical competency. Hong Kong cinema is less modernized and has a very slow tempo."[23] Yu Ch'i-jin, a renowned theater writer and a South Korean delegate to the Asian Film Festival in 1963, cautiously remarked, "We [Korean delegates] cannot be sure until the final moment but I predict that this festival will be surely a league of South Korea and Japan. However, although South Korean cinema has almost reached the level of Japanese cinema in terms of each film's thematic issues, morality, and good ideas, the cinematic techniques are, so to speak, still infantile due to our less developed photographic equipment."[24] At the 1963 Asian Film Festival, Japan's *Twin Sisters of Kyoto* (*Koto*, Nakamura Noboru, 1963) won the best picture award. South Korea received two acting awards—Kim Sŭng-ho won Best Actor for *Love Affair* (*Romaensŭ kŭrei*, Shin Sang-ok, 1963) and To Kŭm-bong won Best Actress for *Birth of Happiness* (*Ttosuni*, Pak Sang-ho, 1963).[25] But the real winner of the 1963 festival was Shaw Brothers. The studio's ambitious *The Love Eterne* (*Liang Shan Po yu Zhu Ying Tai*, 1963) swept five awards, including Best Director (Li Han-hsiang), Best Music, Best Art Direction, Best Sound Recording, and Best Color Cinematography.[26]

In 1964, Shin, after receiving the Best Director award for *The Red Muffler* (*Ppalgan Mahura*, 1964) at the Asian Film Festival in Taipei, confidently proclaimed, "There is no need to congratulate for this mere award. We should go out to the world. To compete with the world, South Korean cinema must conquer the Japanese market first. I will soon achieve this mission."[27] In this project, many local film directors and producers, including Shin, firmly believed that the most urgent task was "to build a modern motion picture studio that enables us to experiment with synchronization, color photography, and other new cinematic techniques."[28] What they aspired to do was to rationalize the system, enact the law, and inaugurate the modern motion picture studio; after all, this was what most industry people in Asia, not just in South Korea, had been trying to materialize since the 1950s. At this pivotal moment in the nation's film industry, Shin Films and its owner Shin Sang-ok entered the regional motion picture network—the FPA.

The Developmental State Studio

In analyzing Shin Films, this chapter uses the term "developmental state studio" to describe studios that were facilitated by the state's policies and simultaneously highly regulated and controlled by the state's trade, industrial, and investment policies. Alice H. Amsden argues that there are two models to explain late industrialization: an institutional model and a market-oriented model. Instead of banking on "invention" and "innovation," which fostered the early industrialization led by the West, Amsden claims, late industrializing societies "base their growth on learning, on borrowed technology that gains advantage from low wages, state subsidies, and incrementally increased productivity."[29] Partially inspired by Amsden, this section discusses Shin Films as an evident case of the developmental state studio. This chapter defines the developmental state studio's mode of production as a "late studio system" based on a "catching up" and "learning" process, which developmental state school theorists have extensively attributed to South Korean and Taiwanese economic development since the 1960s.[30]

The theory of the developmental state emerged out of the combined discontent of a group of economists and political scientists with the classic model of success of the East Asian economy, in which East Asian countries efficaciously climbed the ladder on the basis of free-market, free-trade policies, summed up by the economist Ha-Joon Chang as "the kind of policies and institutions that constitute the Anglo-Saxon model."[31] Viewed according to the classic model, post-1980s East Asian economic development was the end result of the belief that neoliberal economic policies were the primary engines of economic success. Therefore, unlike the "import substituting industrialization" of some Latin American countries, which failed to boost the economy in the end, the East Asian export-oriented model worked superbly and is considered a model case.[32]

Beginning in the 1980s, however, there emerged a group of thinkers who made an attempt at "bringing the state back in." As Peter B. Evans and Dietrich Rueschemeyer point out, effective state intervention is "assumed to be an integral part of successful capitalist development."[33] The state's role in economic development, particularly in late-industrializing countries such as Germany and Russia, had been discussed by a number of theorists before developmental state theory emerged in the early 1980s. Influenced by John Maynard Keynes, Alexander Gershenkron, and Karl Polanyi, Chalmers Johnson wrote his classic text, *MITI and the Japanese Miracle*, in the early 1980s. He is often considered a pioneer and he was the first theorist to rigorously conceptualize term "developmental state," establishing it as a third category alongside liberal (US) and Stalinist conceptions of the state. Johnson explains the absence of academic studies of such states by arguing that in Anglo-American countries, "the existence of the developmental state in any form other than the Communist state has largely been forgotten or ignored as a result of the years of disputation with Marxist-Leninists."[34] He distinguishes the communist economy from the Japanese economy by characterizing the former as "plan ideological" and the latter as "plan rational." In states that were late to industrialize, such as Japan, Johnson argues, "the state itself led the industrialization drive, that is, it took on *developmental* functions."[35] Johnson invokes the concept of the "developmental state" to characterize the role that the Japanese state played in Japan's extraordinary and unexpected postwar enrichment. Johnson was succeeded by Amsden, Robert Wade, and Woo Jung-Eun, who enlarged the theory of the developmental state and used the concept to interpret the cases of individual nation-states, such as South Korea and Taiwan. They identified the causes of these two late-industrialized states' success as corporatist politics and a guided market, a disciplined market, governed interdependence, and the control of finance.[36]

Certainly, developmental state theory has its drawbacks, or as Frederic C. Deyo argues, a "dark underside." While discussing South Korea, Taiwan, and Japan, theoreticians have paid only scant attention to the militaristic, gender-biased, and undemocratic rule and the lack of state welfare in these states, as well as the exclusion of workers.[37] In addition, developmental state theory has been criticized for ex-post facto rationalization and the theory's replicability to other newly industrialized states in Latin America and Africa is also being questioned. Still, the perspective of the developmental state is a strong tool despite its shortcomings, and the motion picture studios of South Korea and Taiwan can be analyzed aptly under this frame, which is not limited to the previous literature's conventional narrative that the military regime's "suppressed" and "brutal" cultural policies delayed the development of the film industry.[38] On the contrary, this chapter argues that film executives became involved in the state's film policies and, at least in the early 1960s, welcomed the state's intervention. The results were mutually beneficial, at least in the early honeymoon period. Therefore, by discussing Shin Films, the following pages will accentuate the relation between the studio and the government to elucidate the unexpected growth of the studio in postwar South Korea and its swift collapse, due to conflict with the authorities, after its brief glory in the second half of the 1960s.

Shin Films: The Beginning

What we now identify as Shin Films was continually renamed during two decades of motion picture business. Historically speaking, the lifespan of

"Shin Films" lasted from 1960 to 1970—exactly a decade. The famous logo, a flaming brazier, was shown onscreen during the 1960s; thus, Shin Films was truly an entity of the sixties. However, what this chapter discusses as "Shin Films" denotes a group of film studios: Shin Sang-ok Production, Anyang Pictures, Tŏk'ŭng Films, and Shina Films. These studios were operated, managed, and structured by the same executives, namely Shin Sang-ok, his two older brothers T'ae-sŏn and T'ae-il, Shin's wife and muse Ch'oe Ŭn-hŭi, and Ch'oe's brother Kyŏng-ok (b. 1933). The confusion in the studio names is the result of the nation's political, social, and cultural environments. In consequence, "Shin Films," in this study, designates all of the film companies run by the Shin and Ch'oe families between 1952 and 1975.

Yi Hyŏng-p'yo, a renowned director who was a technical supervisor for Shin Films' record-breaking *Seong Chun-hyang*, recalled, "Shin Films was basically driven by a kinship, not one but two families: the Shin family and the Ch'oe family."[39] As he pointed out, from the beginning, Shin Sang-ok and Ch'oe Ŭn-hŭi were ideal partners for the business. Ch'oe was one of the most popular actresses of the time and had a good relationship with the country's second-in-command, Prime Minister Kim Chong-p'il (1926–2018). When the studio began to extend its size and volume of production, Shin brought in his two elder brothers, and Ch'oe's younger brother Kyŏng-ok worked for Shin Films as a cinematographer. Of Shin's two brothers, T'ae-sŏn was involved more deeply in the studio's management. Before he joined the studio, T'ae-sŏn had worked for a construction company. He had no prior experience with cinema. The other brother, T'ae-il, had some relevant background, as he was a photographer. Both of the brothers, however, played supporting roles.[40] Shin Films was therefore fundamentally different from what Stephanie Po-yin Chung terms the "fraternal enterprise" of Shaw Brothers, which was based on "the very nature of traditional Chinese family business—being run by family patriarchs."[41] Unlike Shaw Brothers, where all four brothers shared the family's vast ancillary businesses, the logic of the Shin and Ch'oe families' involvement in movie management was to support Shin Sang-ok and help him seize total control of the studio.

Shin began his film career during the interwar period as an assistant director for Ch'oe In-gyu (1911–50) in 1948. Prior to his first appearance in the film industry, Shin gained his formal education in fine arts in Tokyo from 1944 to 1945 and came back to Korea shortly after the nation's independence from Japan on August 15, 1945.[42] His background in painting helped him to establish himself as someone who knew how to frame the perfect "angle," and Shin was often called a "master of *mise en scène*." Under Ch'oe In-gyu's guidance, Shin learned the ABCs of filmmaking: cinematography, editing, lighting, directing, and even acting.[43] During the Korean War, Shin formed the Association of Film and the Arts (Yŏngsang yesul hyŏp hoe) in 1952, and produced/directed his first feature film, *The Evil Night* (*Ag-ya*).

After the war, the South Korean film industry entered an especially fruitful period of development. As noted earlier, in 1954, the Syngman Rhee government moved to tax movie tickets for foreign films at 90 percent, while tickets for domestic films were exempt from taxes. This tax policy gave domestic films a distinct advantage and incentivized film production across the nation. The industry was also inspired by the dramatic domestic success of *Chunhyang* and *Madame Freedom*. Between 1955 and 1958, Shin Sangok directed four more films—*Korea* (1954), *Dream* (*Kkum*, 1955), *The Youth* (*Chŏlmŭn kŭdŭl*, 1955), and *Muyoungtap* (*Muyŏngt'ap*, 1957)—before launching Seoul Pictures in 1958. Shin met and fell in love with Ch'oe Ŭn-hŭi in 1954, while he was shooting the semi-documentary film *Korea*.

From his directorial debut *The Evil Night* to *Dream*, *The Youth*, *Muyoungtap*, *The Flower of Hell* (*Chiokhwa*, 1958), and *A Confession of a Female College Student* (*ŏnŭ yŏdaesaeng ŭi kobaek*, 1958), Shin consistently worked with the same group of staff: Kang Pŏm-gu and Ch'oe Kyŏng-ok (cinematographers), Yi Hyŏng-p'yo (screenwriter), Pak Haeng-ch'ŏl (production manager), and his wife Ch'oe Ŭn-hŭi (actress). In his early career, however, Shin was never a bankable figure. His films were often critically acclaimed but continuously failed at the domestic box office, which caused severe financial setbacks. His turning point came with his sixth feature film, *A Confession of a Female College Student*. It became a phenomenal success in postwar South Korea. With this success, Shin accumulated enough capital to produce more films simultaneously. In 1959, Shin directed four feature films: *A Sister's Garden* (*Chamaeŭi hwawŏn*), *Dongsimcho* (*Tongshimch'o*), *It's Not Her Sin* (*Kŭ yŏjaŭi chalmoshi anida*), and *La Traviata* (*Ch'unhŭi*); all of them made sound profits. This was Shin's "year zero" for the accumulation of capital. Backed by the films' revenues, Shin finally established Shin Films in 1960.[44]

To expand the size of the company, Shin Films opened the new Wŏnhyoro studio (Wŏnhyoro ch'waryŏngso; also called the Yongsan complex), which lasted until 1966. The Wŏnhyoro studio had a medium-sized soundstage, a three-story office building equipped with a recording room, a directors' room, and offices for the planning and production departments.[45] Shin implemented a Japanese-style hierarchical production system to achieve a more effective output. Therefore, from the very beginning, Shin Films operated and churned out films under Japanese influence, and it did so very effectively indeed.

The year 1961 marked a milestone for Shin Films. *Seong Chun-hyang* became the first South Korean film to break 300,000 viewers in Seoul, which
had only two million residents at the time. *Seong Chun-hyang* was not the
only box office hit of the year for Shin Films. Two Shin-directed films, *The
Houseguest and My Mother* and *The Evergreen*, reached 150,000 and 70,000
viewers, respectively, and Chang Il-ho's sword-fighting film *Iljimae* (1961),
produced by Shin, attracted a total audience of 150,000. In total, Shin Films
mobilized 700,000 patrons in Seoul with the four films the studio produced
and released in 1961. Ch'oe Kyŏng-ok recalled that they simply "could not
count how much money they earned. Every morning, several bags of cash
were delivered. We could do whatever we wanted."[46] In accordance with
this commercial success, Shin chaired the Asian Film Festival in 1962, where,
as noted earlier, he won the Best Picture award for *The Houseguest and My
Mother*. With this victory, his status in the South Korean film industry became unrivalled.

Motion Pictures as State Business

Shin Films should not be discussed as an entity separate from South Korea's
developmental government and its strong leader, Park Chung Hee. Starting
with the military coup on May 16, 1961, the Park Chung Hee government
accelerated the country's economic growth, urbanization, and modernization. The Park regime vigorously adopted anticommunist doctrine to guard
and uphold the militant dictatorship. In this political atmosphere, cultural
areas, including cinema, voluntarily or compulsorily served as an apparatus
to strengthen the state's ideological principles. The Park administration saw
the motion picture industry as a strategic industry, like textiles and light industries, that should be controlled, planned, and driven by the government.
Starting in October 1961, the Ministry of Public Information (MPI) took
charge of all cultural policies. The Motion Picture Law (Yŏnghwabŏp, MPL)
was launched in 1962 and subsequently revised four times (1963, 1966, 1970,
and 1973).[47] In 1961, sixty-four film production companies were consolidated
into sixteen.[48] Building a soundstage was part of an array of conditions that
had to be registered with the Ministry of Education and Information in order for a studio to become one of these licensed production companies. The
MPL governed production registration, censorship, import quotas, screening permits, and license suspensions. According to the MPL, only licensed
production companies could make films, and each studio was required to

release at least fifteen films per year. Under the law, independent productions could not exist, though they sometimes operated illegally. Thus, the law was advantageous just for a handful of film executives, and it was Shin who benefited the most. Many in the film industry believed that Shin was involved in formulating and enacting the MPL. Yi Hyŏng-p'yo, for example, stated, "What MPL required, a 200 P'yŏng soundstage, was, as a matter of fact, the exact size of Shin's Yongsan sound stage."[49]

With the support of the government, Shin Films accelerated the modernization of the system. Shin, in a 1965 interview with *Chosŏn ilbo*, claimed, "After the liberation, the primary mission of South Korean cinema has been to materialize the possibility of the industrialization of the film industry, which grew out of the underdeveloped system of cottage-like film companies that South Korea sustained until very recently."[50] To increase the volume of products the studio could manufacture, Shin recruited new directors and dispersed the power he possessed. In 1962, accordingly, Shin Films successfully released fifteen films. This time was also an incubation period for Shin Films' three representative genres: *Sagŭk* (historical dramas), melodrama, and comedy. Shin directed three "big-budget" *Sagŭk*, *Bound by Chaste Rule* (*Yŏllyŏmun*) and *Tyrant Yeonsan* (parts 1 and 2), and they were all considered the year's most important films. Pak Haeng-ch'ŏl claims that it was *Tyrant Yeonsan* that initiated the division of labor in Shin Films' production system. The film took only twenty-one days to complete, since *Tyrant Yeonsan* had to be released on New Year's Day (*Sŏllal*), the date when *Seong Chun-hyang* had swept the market the previous year. In 1962, the glory of *Seong Chun-hyang* was revived. *Tyrant Yeonsan* was the year's top grosser, and Shin became known as the "New Year's Day showman." Shin Films also introduced melodramas and comedies. These three representative genres were maintained throughout the entire span of Shin Films, but most of the profits came from *Sagŭk* that were directed by Shin and performed by Ch'oe.

In 1964, Shin Films released another thirteen films. Among them, two were directed by Shin, *Deaf Samryong* and *The Red Muffler*. Both films, along with the Shaw Brothers-Shin Films coproduction *Last Woman of Shang* (K. *Piryŏn ŭi Wangbi Talgi*, H. *Da ji*, Griffith Yue feng, 1964), were exceedingly profitable at the domestic box office. *The Red Muffler* alone drew 250,000 patrons in the Myŏngbo theater, where Shin Films had an exclusive contract.

Shin Films also began its foreign films import business as a benefit from the government in exchange for producing enough domestic productions.[51] They made a relatively good start and generated profits for Shin Films. However, the continuous predicaments that Shin Films was to suffer showed their first signs in that year. The biggest dilemma was the pool of talent in film direction. While Shin Films held a number of contract directors under its umbrella, Shin Sang-ok was the only one with verified box-office competence. The other films directed by the studio's contract personnel were, with few exceptions, mediocre at best, often flopping at the nation's box office. This was a recurring problem for Shin Films, and it was not solved before the studio's closure. Local distributors were willing to buy in advance if the film was to be directed by Shin. Shin Films had churned out one film per month since 1963, but only directed-by-Shin products made enough profits to run the company. Therefore, despite the prevailing success of *The Red Muffler*, *Deaf Samryong*, and *Last Woman of Shang*, Shin Films was in financial crisis by the end of 1964 due to the financial damages caused by the year's lineup. Shin craved a surefire success to compensate for the loss and sought ways to import more foreign films.

In the fall of 1962, the MPI had announced a new development plan for the domestic film industry that was an application of compensation trade

Figure 6.3. *Last Woman of Shang* was Shin Films' first major coproduction film. Sin Yŏng-gyun, a Korean actor, plays King Zhou of the Shang Dynasty. Da Ji (Talgi, Linda Lin Dai), in order to exact revenge, marries the king who killed her father (Yen Chun). Photo courtesy of Korean Film Archive.

policy (*Usuyŏnghwa posangjedo*).[52] Compensation trade is a form of "counter-trade" in which an incoming investment is repaid from the revenues generated by that investment. The Park administration created the policy to support the domestic light industries. With regard to the film industry, the MPI indicated that compensation trade policy in cinema would be enacted a year later, in 1963. If it was put into operation, there would no longer be a division between "production companies" and "import trade companies," which was a radical change. The momentum of this policy shook the whole industry.[53] Now one company could import and produce cinema simultaneously, and the more it exported films abroad, the more it could import foreign films. To import cinema, the existing import traders had to be transformed into production companies in a very short time.[54] In tandem with this compensation trade policy, the MPL was revised in 1963 to contain an "import rights" section.

This newly added section indicated that a licensed production company could apply for extra rights to import foreign films. During the 1960s and 1970s, South Korea had one of the strictest import quota systems in Asia. Fewer than 60 foreign films could be imported and distributed per year. Moreover, to get the rights to a foreign film, the studio had to do one of the following things: 1) export films to a foreign country and screen the film there for at least two months; 2) produce "quality" coproduction films chosen by the Department of Culture and Education; 3) win a major award at an international film festival (including the Asian Film Festival).[55] Consequently, after 1963, coproduction practice adapted to this method of importing foreign films. Hong Kong and the Asian Film Festival soon became the main battlefield for South Korean film executives. In this battle, Shin Films was in an ideal position. The studio outperformed its competitors and won far more awards than any other film studio. And Shin began negotiating with Hong Kong's Shaw Brothers to coproduce multiple projects.

International Adventures

Shin first met Run Run Shaw at the Asian Film Festival in 1962. Shaw commanded an army of talent—its "galaxy of stars" and directors. Shaw's five contract actresses, Lucilla Yu Ming, Li Hsing-chun, Yeh Feng, Tu Chuan, and Ting Hung, participated in the festival's "gala show."[56] Shaw certainly knew of Shin's status in the South Korean local film industry, and Shin and Shaw both instantly recognized their need of each other. They agreed to coproduce multiple films, which entailed the sharing of the budget, cast, direction, and production duties, and filed a contract immediately after the film festival. Due to the company's numerous markets, most Shaw Brothers films were dubbed in many languages. Hence, there were no language barriers for Korean performers. Run Run Shaw, in an interview with a South Korean newspaper, said that it was "very easy for Korean actors to play Chinese characters in the movie." He added, "We really hope that Shaw brothers make more films with Korea. By doing so, Korean cinema will also find a new market."[57]

Shaw deemed that epic films based on Chinese cultural heritage would hold a surefire allure for the large Chinese diaspora communities in the region, including Taiwan, as Li Han-hsiang's two preceding films, *Diau Charn* (1958) and *The Kingdom and the Beauty* (*Chiang shan mei jen*, 1959), had proved at the box offices in Hong Kong, Malaysia, and Taiwan.[58] Shin's primary concern was to streamline the process of churning out genre films and deliver more big-budget color films that would verify his competence as a movie mogul under the new military junta. Building a solid partnership with an international film company like Shaw Brothers provided an excellent occasion to make rapid advances. In addition, Shin could take advantage of Shaw Brothers' state-of-the-art studio facilities to produce multiple films concurrently, while Shin Films' contract actors could stay in Hong Kong for legitimate coproductions. Run Run Shaw wanted to produce more epic films to win the war against MP&GI. However, due to the loss of mainland China as a territory, Shaw needed a site for location shootings. Costume dramas based on Chinese history require castles, palaces, and vast fields for battle sequences that Hong Kong and Singapore could not provide.[59] Between 1960 and 1962, Shaw Brothers and its gem Li Han-hsiang had coproduced three epic films, *Empress Wu* (*Wu Tse-tien*, 1963), *Yang Kwei Fei* (1963), and *Beyond the Great Wall* (*Wang zhao jun*, 1964), with Japan's Toei, and shot most of the outdoor sequences, including a couple of major battle sequences, in the Kyoto area. However, due to Toei's strict work conditions and high wages, the project was repeatedly postponed and delayed.[60] By the time Shaw Brothers released these films, the studio's expenditures had outrun the likely profits. Before the studio signed the contract with Shin Films, Run Run Shaw also visited Taiwan and met Henry Gong Hong, the new executive director of CMPC. The two studios reached an agreement to coproduce *The Black Forest* (*Hei sen lin*, Chiu Feng Yuan, 1964).[61]

For Shaw, Shin Films was the perfect business partner. Shaw had less interest in the South Korean market than in using South Korea's historic sites, mountains, fields, and most of all its cheap labor. Hence, in Shin Films Shaw Brothers found an ideal partner who pledged to supply male actors and all expenditures for location shooting, in return demanding only exclusive distribution rights for local theaters. The two studios moved quickly. The agreement between Shin Films and Shaw Brothers was completed in September 1962. Although the contract is lengthy, five articles are worth noting here in their entirety.

3. The leading and major roles of the co-production motion picture films are to be given to SHAW and SHIN actors and actresses, subject to mutual agreement of the parties hereto.
4. The co-production motion picture film is to be directed by a director to be designated and appointed by SHAW.
5. The budget for the above-stated co-production is to be worked out and is to be accepted by the parties hereto upon mutual approval. It is also mutually agreed upon that the location filming of said co-production is to be undertaken by SHIN in Korea with all the necessary expenses to be advanced entirely by SHIN, while the studio filming of said co-production is to be done by SHAW'S STUDIO in Hong Kong with all the necessary expenses to be advanced entirely by SHAW.
6. The distribution of the above-stated co-production motion picture film in South Korea is to be handled by SHIN, and the distribution of said film in Southeast Asia excluding South Korea is to be handled by SHAW, while the distribution of said film in the world excluding the above-mentioned territories on either distribution or outright sale is to be decided by mutual agreement of the parties hereto.
8. It is mutually agreed upon that the negative of the above-stated co-production picture film shall be lodged with SHAW and that insurance of United States dollars fifty thousand (USD 50,000.00) shall be taken out on this negative by SHAW, for which SHIN and SHAW shall share the premium of fifty (50) fifty (50) basis.[62]

According to the agreement, two thirds of the net revenue derived from South Korea would be allocated to Shin Films and one third to Shaw. The net revenue derived from Southeast Asia, including Taiwan, would be divided in the same way: two thirds to Shaw and one third to Shin. However, Wong Ka Hee, a Shaw Brothers' physical production manager, divulged that the contract was drawn up to meet Shin Sang-ok's needs, and the net revenue share in reality was far simpler than described above. The South Korean market belonged exclusively to Shin Films, while Shaw grabbed all the revenues from outside Korea. Shin claimed the sole rights only in the South Korean market.

The script of *Last Woman of Shang* was not generated for the coproduction; it was a ready-to-shoot project for Shaw Brothers, since the script had already been completed over a year ago, under the interim title of *Fox Woman*.[63] *Last Woman of Shang* was supposed to be Shaw's next *The Kingdom and the Beauty*. It was a regional collaboration par excellence that brought together some of the finest creative personnel in both countries: Yen Chun and Linda Lin Dai of Hong Kong, Sin Yŏng-gyun and Nam-kung Wŏn of South Korea, and Nishimoto Tadashi (cinematographer) of Japan. The spectacular epic film was shot in color cinemascope, with the help of Nishimoto Tadashi, and was publicized in both markets as "the biggest-ever" movie extravaganza of the year. After the film's post-production was completed, the film pre-sold to Thailand, Laos, Vietnam, the Philippines, Cambodia, and Taiwan, where Shaw Brothers had not yet set up its direct-release distributors.[64] *Last Woman of Shang* premiered on August 26, 1964, at the newly opened Hollywood Theatre in Kowloon Peninsula, Hong Kong.[65] The film was distributed on August 27 at four of Shaw's major theaters in Hong Kong and on the Southeast Asian circuit.[66]

Outside of Korea, *Last Woman of Shang*'s box office revenue was less than stellar. It was not a major hit of the year in Hong Kong.[67] In South Korea, *Last Woman of Shang* was released under the title *Tal-gi* and publicized as a new film of the Korean veteran director Ch'oe In-hyŏn. *Tal-gi* was a huge success in South Korea, bringing 150,000 cinemagoers to the theater and ranking fourth in the end-of-the-year box office returns. Erasing any contributions made by Hong Kong, Shin Films publicized the film as "another Shin Films production." Although *Last Woman of Shang* was not a great success for Run Run Shaw, he did not want to break the partnership with Shin. Shaw still needed to produce more epic films and, after all, *Last Woman of Shang* had made a profit.[68] Shin Films and Shaw Brothers coproduced three more films, *The Goddess of Mercy* (K. *Tae P'okkun*, H. *Guan shi yin*, Im Wŏn-sik, 1966), *That Man in Chang-An* (K. *Hŭktojŏk*, H. *Wang Min Daai Hap*, Yan Jun, 1966), and *King with My Face* (K. *Ch'ŏlmyŏnhwangje*, H. *Tie tou huang di*, Ho Meng-hua, 1967). *The Goddess of Mercy* was a religious story based on the legend of Kwanyu, the Chinese bodhisattva of love and compassion. Li Li-hua, a silver screen goddess in the Chinese-language world, accepted the role of Kwanyu. Shaw Brothers pretentiously proclaimed that the film was "three times as expensive as *Last Woman of Shang;* this film will be an even bigger and more impressive spectacle in glorious Shawscope/ Eastman color."[69]

The Goddess of Mercy was by far the grandest production ever produced by Shin Films. For Shaw Brothers, the film was also the most anticipated production of the year. Shin Films poured 30 million *won* into it, which was four to five times higher than the usual budget for A-list films.[70] Im Wŏn-sik, Shin's protégé, took the helm under the supervision of Shin and Yan Jun.[71] To maximize profit, Shaw and Shin had agreed to make two versions of the film for two different markets.[72] The male leads were the same and the female performers were different—Li Li-hua for the Southeast Asian version and Ch'oe Ŭn-hŭi for the Korean version, while the male characters were played by the South Korean actors Kim Chin-gyu and Kim Sŭng-ho.[73] Both of the male performers were winners of the Best Actor's award at the Asian Film Festival, which made it easier to publicize the film to Shaw's Southeast Asian circuit. *The Goddess of Mercy* was one of Shin Films' prestige epic films, continuing the legacy of *Tyrant Yeonsan*. Most reviews praised the superior quality of the indoor set designs, which had "multi-dimensional textures and tones" and were "more realistic than other films."[74] *The Goddess of Mercy*, however, drew a mere 99,292 patrons, and ranked eighth on the list of the year's top ten films. The year's top-grossing film was Kim Su-yong's tear-jerker *Affection* (*Yujŏng*), which attracted 320,000 audience members.[75] The other two films, *That Man in Chang-An* and *King with My Face*, were less co-productions than the fruit of production cooperation on Shaw's films, in the form of Shin's investment and the loan of his actors to Shaw Brothers. *That Man in Chang An* was directed by Yen Chun, who had supervised *The Goddess of Mercy*, and *The King With My Face* was under the direction of Ho Meng-hua (1923–2009), a veteran Shaw director who made Li Ching an "Asian sweetheart" with the crowd-pleaser *Susanna* in 1967.[76]

Certainly, Shin derived many advantages from his work with Run Run Shaw. First, he obtained negative raw stock from Shaw Brothers. Prior to the coproduction, Shin Films and most other film producers in South Korea had to import negative stock from foreign countries such as the United States, Japan, or Italy. Since all imported products were charged heavy taxes and there was a limit on the importation of film stock, securing film stock was one of the main concerns of most South Korean film producers. Shaw Brothers relieved this headache. With off-the-record help from Shaw Brothers, Shin Films could covertly store the raw stock it needed in its storage facility. Second, by emphasizing Shaw's role as an international partner, Shin Films could claim that the studio exported its films to various Southeast Asian countries through Shaw Brothers' theater circuits. In this way, Shin Films gained the right to import foreign films. In other words, the more coproductions Shin made, the more he could import success-guaranteed foreign films such as Italian spaghetti Westerns, espionage thrillers, and American classics.[77] In sum, Shin had nothing to lose from the connection with Shaw Brothers, as Ch'oe Kyŏng-ok recalled: "Shin Films didn't lose anything but got many advantages."[78] By the mid-1960s, as one local journalist put it, Shin Films had become a "movie empire."[79]

The Empire

At the end of 1966, Shin was supposed to pop open a champagne bottle. His semi–vertically integrated studio was preparing a bigger-than-ever coproduction, *Romance of Three Kingdoms* (*Samgukchi*), with Japan's Daiei.[80] In May, Shin was again chosen to chair the committee for the 13th Asian Film Festival, which was to be held in Seoul from May 13 to 17.[81] Shin also had three coproductions with Shaw Brothers, *The Goddess of Mercy, That Man in Chang-An* and *The King with My Face,* in his year's line-up. Shin imported and released *For A Few Dollars More* (*Per qualche dollaro in più,* Sergio Leone, 1965), and it lured 350,000 moviegoers in Seoul alone. Finally, and most significant, Shin Films was in negotiations to consolidate the grandest motion picture studio ever built in South Korea, Anyang movie studio. The studio was constructed by Hong Ch'an, a media mogul, in 1957. Hong, with the support of President Syngman Rhee, was an ambitious media entrepreneur, and he was trying to build the biggest studio in Asia in his effort to become a movie tycoon. Hong did not understand filmmaking, however, and after the commercial failure of two big-budget films, he went bankrupt in 1958.[82] If Shin acquired the studio, he would be able to manufacture more than twenty films per year. When Shin Films took over the studio, it was equipped with two big soundstages, an underwater stage, a canteen, a public bath, and three Mitchell cameras, along with development and many other facilities. It seemed clear, at least for the first half of the year, that Shin had built an "empire" and finally achieved what he had long dreamed of—a major film company.[83] Shin recalled that his dream was the "rationalization and industrialization" of film enterprises. He added, "I thought that the stabilization of 'Korean-style major [studio] system' and cinema-intensive capitals were the most effective ways to leap forward."[84]

Figure 6.4. An aerial view of Anyang Film Studio in the late 1960s. Photo courtesy of Korean Film Archive.

However, shortly after Shin had successfully merged with Anyang movie studio in September 1966, Shin Films faced a financial crisis. All three Shin-Shaw coproductions failed to make profits, the Shin-Daiei project never materialized, most Shin Films line-ups for the year lost money severely, and Shin Sang-ok himself was accused of embezzlement, fraud, and tax evasion in the case of the Shin-Shaw coproduction *Journey to the West* (K. *Sŏyugi*, H. *Xi you ji*, Ho Meng-hua, 1966), one day before its scheduled release. Shin was investigated to detect whether the film was a true coproduction or merely a counterfeit one.[85] In the end, *Journey to the West* was deemed not a coproduction film but a Shaw Brothers product. Shin had, in fact, illegally brought an original negative print from Hong Kong and inserted some close-up shots of a South Korean actor, Pak No-sik (*SOS Hong Kong*), to disguise the film as a coproduction. On August 9, the prosecutor made a final adjudication that *Journey to the West* was an illegally imported Hong Kong film, and Shin Films was sentenced to pay a fine of 210 million *won*.

Even worse, the 1966 Asian Film Festival ended in a national scandal. The Best Picture award went to the Shaw Brothers Eastman color production *The Blue and the Black* (*Lan yu hei*, Doe Ching, 1966), and South Korea walked away with nine trophies out of twenty-seven awards.[86] But the real issue was

Yamamoto Satsuo's Best Director award for *The Burglar Story* (*Shonin no isu*, 1965).[87] Yamamoto Satsuo was a Japanese director known to have socialist leanings.[88] All of the South Korean festival jurors, including the commit-tee chair Shin Sang-ok, were summoned to court and investigated for viola-tion of an anticommunist law. Shin was interrogated by the National Intel-ligence Service and told that the committee should have rejected the film completely and deported the "communist" director.[89] This scandal should be understood in the context of South Korean politics at the time. The na-tion's involvement with the Vietnam War in 1964 and the massive dispatch of troops in 1966 mobilized the sense of "ongoing war" among civilians in this divided nation-state, which ignited the public's interest in international politics and the "holy" war against the communists.[90] The public view was that the Vietnam War was an extension of global communist expansionism, and as such, people believed, it had to be resisted. However, the more seri-ous question was about the nation's security.[91] Therefore, in 1966, the Park government needed to persuade both the opposing party and the public of its legitimacy. In other words, Park had to tighten its control of society using a strong anticommunist stance.

Last but not least, Shin's acquisition of Anyang motion picture studio proved a burden, and he soon faced a serious money shortage. Operating such a grand motion picture studio did not work as planned. Kang Pŏm-gu, who had done the cinematography for many of Shin Films' products during the zenith of the studio, recalls, "The reason Shin acquired Anyang studio was that Shin had strong confidence after his observation tour to Japan and Hong Kong. In those days, the major studios in Asia were all mass-producing films. I think that Shin expanded his company because he thought that Korean people were dexterous in manufacturing and crafting, and his company would easily outdo other Asian competitors."[92] Maybe Shin was hoping to earn foreign currency by promoting the studio's well-equipped soundstages to other Asian film ex-ecutives as an ideal shooting spot. "Much cheaper than in Taiwan" was Shin's motto at the Asian Film Festival's panel discussions, and he added, "You can hire our well-trained and experienced labor at a very reasonable price."[93] Pak Haeng-ch'ŏl reminisces that he and Shin, between 1969 and 1970, discussed countless times the construction of an indoor set designed specifically for Hong Kong *wuxia* (martial arts chivalry) films. For financial reasons, that blue-print did not materialize, but the outdoor set was frequently rented out to Hong Kong and Taiwan film producers, as well as local ones, during the 1970s.[94]

Shin Films, unlike Shaw Brothers, had a limited market. The studio sys-tem required a sustainable distribution and exhibition system. To operate its huge Anyang studio, Shin had to expand its market, which resulted in coproductions with Shaw Brothers and attempts to export its films to Southeast Asian markets. Owning and managing a big motion picture studio without exhibition outlets led Shin into a deep financial deficit. Ch'oe Kyŏng-ok reminisces bitterly, "It's all because of the foreign film festival [Asian Film Festival]. Success has turned his head, and Shin thought that Shin Films could surpass Shaw Brothers, and, to cope with Shaw, Shin wanted to have a big motion picture studio."[95] Later, Shin recalled the period. He wrote, "My utmost task was to build a modern motion picture studio. Once I completed the studio, more equipment and skilled labor were needed. I invested a large amount of money to purchase modern equipment whenever I could. To make the company run, I needed to produce movies continuously. The more films we churned out, the more theatres wanted. We could buy at least a couple of theatres; however, instead of purchasing movie theatres, I invested in more modern filmmaking gear from abroad. As a consequence, to keep the promise we made to theatres, I was stuck in a "catch 22" situation that meant I had to provide success-guaranteed films constantly. Otherwise, they would leave for other companies."[96]

In 1967, only a year after Shin's acquisition of Anyang Studio, the third revised MPL stipulated that each production company should produce no more than five films per year. Shin Films, now with Anyang Studio, was severely damaged by this revised law. To work within the new system, Shin had no choice but to divide the company into four mid-sized production companies: Shin Films, Anyang Pictures, Tŏk'ŭng Films, and Shina Films. To save the studio, Shin once again became prolific and directed four films in a row in that year alone. As the track record proved, "directed by Shin" films were success-guaranteed. *Tender Heart* (*Tajŏngbulshim*) and a remake of his own *Dreams* brought huge profits to the studio, and two more films, *Mountain Bandits* (*Majŏk*) and *Traces* (*Ijojanyŏng*), broke even. However, except for Shin's four films and *The King's First Love* (*Imgŭmnimŭi ch'ŏtsarang*, Yi Kyu-ung), the remaining thirteen films distributed in 1967 were flops, and just a handful of them barely avoided deficits. Shin now needed foreign films more than ever. Exporting South Korean films was the easiest way to get the quota for importing foreign films. If the studio provided a verified letter of approval from a South Korean foreign trade office confirming that the studio's films were screened in a designated country for two or more months, one import per film was given to the studio as compensation.

Between 1967 and 1972, Shin Films sold the distribution rights to thirteen films to Shaw Brothers. Wong Ka Hee reminisced that those films were not received well in Shaw Brothers' theater chains but were enough to make profits, since Shaw Brothers had bought them in bulk at an extremely low price.[97] In return, Shin imported and distributed in the local market a series of Shaw Brothers' *wuxia* films,[98] With the revenues generated from the success-guaranteed Hong Kong martial arts films, Shin Films could continue to produce local films. After all, Shin was not a savvy businessman like Run Run Shaw. He was, in the end, a film director. In this aspect, Shin Sang-ok was in many ways comparable to Li Han-hsiang, who in 1963 established GMP, another example of the developmental state studio in Taiwan.

Grand Motion Picture Company (GMP)

In 1963, at the acme of his career, Li Han-hsiang left the Shaw Brothers studio, where he had been under contract since 1956. Born in 1926 in Liaoning, China, Li started his movie career in Hong Kong in 1948. He joined Shaw Brothers in 1956. At Shaw, Li became the studio's most productive and bankable director by churning out such classics as *Diau Charn* (1958), *The Kingdom and the Beauty* (1959), *The Enchanting Shadow* (1960) and *The Love Eterne* (1963). In addition, Li received numerous awards from the Asian Film Festival. Without a doubt, Li was Run Run Shaw's number-one asset.

Li's most successful film was *The Love Eterne*. It created a sensation in both the Hong Kong and Taiwan markets. In forty-seven days of showing in Taipei alone, *The Love Eterne* grossed NTD 8,383,077, a phenomenal record that approximately doubled the previous record set by William Wyler's *Ben Hur* (1959). Nearly two thirds of the capital city's population saw the movie.[99] Taiwan's Union Pictures, MP&GI's Taiwan distributor, pledged its financial backing if Li, who was not happy with Run Run Shaw's monarchical style of management, established a studio in Taipei. Li sought greater independence, artistic control, and financial rewards. Like Shin Sang-ok, Li envisioned the creation of a "director system." This particular system meant, according to Janet Staiger, that one specific director and his skilled crew established "sort of a team which entirely aimed to produce a single director's opuses effectively."[100] At the end of 1963, Li moved to Taiwan with his staff members and launched GMP, which was "a vertically integrated studio that also allowed for the mode of independent production."[101] Loke Wan-tho, the president of MP&GI and one of the most powerful film moguls in Southeast Asia, had a keen interest in advancing into the Taiwanese market. He poured millions of dollars into both Union and GMP in 1964.[102] Union Pictures was based on the distribution-exhibition business but, due to thriving Mandarin film production in the territory and now *The Love Eterne* phenomenon, the company turned its attention to production. Li was unquestionably the perfect partner.

Taiwan was a suitable replacement for the mainland, which had closed its doors to most Hong Kong studios since the inception of the PRC in 1949. However, there were two significant barriers for Hong Kong producers hoping to penetrate the Taiwanese film market: strict currency controls and a high exchange rate. Stephanie Po-yin Chung writes, "Taiwan was enforcing tight currency control and Hong Kong films not only had to apply for a foreign currency permit but also pay a 20% 'defense tax,' cutting profit by a third."[103] Emilie Yueh-yu Yeh argues that participating in coproductions could thus reduce tax burdens, and that "cheap labor and land as well as the wide variety of locations made Taiwan an attractive place for an off-shore studio."[104] With all these factors in mind, instead of recruiting Li for MP&GI, Loke Wan-tho let him form his own studio in Taiwan and fronted the capital for GMP. Hence, as Yeh claims, GMP was ostensibly a local company but was in fact "part of a transnational operation."[105]

The mid-1960s was a blossoming period for Taiwan's motion picture studios. CMPC's new leader Henry Gong Hong, who brought the Asian Film Festival to Taipei in 1964, initiated a series of films belonging to a new genre called "healthy realism." This was a type of melodrama "with a strong civic message of conscientiousness, charity, hygiene, and environmentalism," according to Yeh.[106] And, as Guo-Juin Hong argues, Gong Hong who was the key figure who promoted healthy realism as a "priority."[107] Li Hsing's two films, *Oyster Girl* (*Ke nu*, 1964) and *Beautiful Duckling* (*Yang ya ren jia*, 1965), are some of the most representative films of this kind, and *Oyster Girl* received the Best Picture and Best Director (Li Hsing) trophies at the Asian Film Festival in 1964, held in Taipei. Under Gong Hong's management, CMPC's production output numbers increased to over twenty per year, which opened a new age for the motion picture studio. GMP, in this context, was uniquely positioned, as it was not owned, controlled, or supported by the Kuomintang (KMT) government but had been launched by transnational capital, mostly from the Singapore-Hong Kong nexus, and it brought diverse genres (costume, sing-song, comedy, melodrama, and thrillers) to Taiwanese cinema, even it had only been operating for a relatively short time.[108] In terms of its business structure, GMP was, in the words of Emilie Yeh and Darrell William Davis, much like "Shaw Brothers in miniature—an integrated, self-contained production complex."[109] GMP was more democratic, however, because of Li's style of decision-making. He gave more chances to young and inexperienced directors and put more time and energy into producing films precisely and meticulously.

However, in 1964, during the Asian Film Festival in Taipei, Li lost his major patrons. In a calamitous plane crash, Loke Wan-tho and Taiwan Studio's director Long Fang were both killed. Cathay Organization, the mother company of MP&GI, reorganized the company after Loke's death, and the investment in GMP had to be cut off. Li found himself in a bind as he looked for ways to survive. Between 1964 and 1970, the studio made only twenty-two films. Among them were six directed by Li, including the lavish epic film *Hsi Shih: Beauty of Beauties* (*Xi Shi*, 1965), the most expensive Mandarin film ever made in Taiwan at that time and a box-office sensation.[110] It received four trophies (Best Film, Best Director, Best Actor, and Cinematography) at Taiwan's Golden Horse Awards in 1965. Li's talent lay in directing historical films, not in business, and he had already overspent on the studio's outputs. GMP thus faced a severe financial crisis due to Li's mismanagement, the lack of a distribution and exhibition network, and overinvestment in the production department, all problems that Shin Films also faced. In 1970, GMP ceased its operations. A year later, Li returned to Hong Kong and directed an epic comedy *The Warlord* (*Da jun fa*, 1972). It was produced by Shaw Brothers.

Although GMP and Shin Films had many features in common, there were two definite disparities. First, Shin Films had a strong bond with the Park regime and benefited from informal relationships with the nation's top politicians. GMP, in contrast, was backed by Loke and failed to make contact with Taiwan's KMT government, unlike CMPC, which received state support. Second, Shin aimed to become a major company that could compete with Shaw Brothers and Japan's major studios. Shin had gradually shifted his company's mode of production from the "director system" to the "central producer system" by the mid-1960s.[111] However, unlike Shin, Li wanted to manage an independent production company in which each director could devote himself to producing high-quality films. Li left Shaw Brothers because he disliked the working conditions there. In light of these two differences, Shin was more similar to Run Run Shaw than Li was, but he never forgot his roots as a film director. Shin wrote, "People tend to distinguish Shin Sang-ok the film director from Shin Sang-ok the producer. However, that is not correct. Shin Sang-ok as a producer is just the other side of the coin."[112]

The Downfall

Anyone who looks closely into the history of Shin Films might well be perplexed when it comes to the 1970s. Shin Films produced and released thirty-five films in 1969, an all-time high in South Korean film history. Even today, no film studio in South Korea has yet reached this degree of productivity. But just a year later, the number plunged drastically to seven films. What happened to Shin Films? How could one extremely prolific studio be reduced to a mere medium-sized company in just one year? Two factors must be considered here. First, the third revised MPL, which was announced in 1970, specified that the foreign film import quota would no longer be given to studios that received awards from international or domestic film festivals. Instead, the quota was allocated to certified "foreign film import and export companies" with reliable track records of exporting films abroad.[113] Thus, Shin Films could import only two films in 1970, which severely damaged the studio's financial status. Second, the number of audience members in South Korea decreased considerably in 1970, and has continuously declined over the years since then. The whole industry faced difficulties. Many historians have already pointed out that television in the 1970s dominated the nation's cultural sphere, quickly absorbing civilians in their favorite series at home. Shin Films received a fatal blow, since the most popular television series of the time belonged to its representative genres: *Sagŭk*, comedies, and melodramas. *Sagŭk* in particular was frequently produced and aired on television. Shin Films had to find a way to weather this crisis. To stabilize the studio's finances, Shin opened a new movie theater in the heart of Seoul, Chong-ro.[114] Hŏriudŭ (Hollywood) theater, Shin Films' first movie theater of its own, opened its doors in early 1970. Ch'oe Kyŏng-ok became the chief manager of the theater.

Shin had a keen sense of Asian popular cinema and its industry. He had predicted the unfavorable conditions of the 1970s. To compete with television, Shin Films had to provide something television would not be able to present. Shin thought Hong Kong martial arts films could be the answer. In addition, to import success-guaranteed foreign films, Shin Films needed to export films. Thus, he invented an unprecedented business model that could kill two birds with one stone.

In 1969, Shin Films dispatched a group of newly contracted young performers to Hong Kong. To support the studio's ever-expanding volume of output, Shin Films—the most powerful motion picture studio in South

Korea—had conducted a major campaign to recruit young talent a year earlier, in 1968. The competition was fierce, and eventually thirteen actors were
chosen. They were called "Shin Films apprentices" (*Shinp'illim yŏnsŭpsaeng*)
and were trained, under the guidance of Ch'oe Ŭn-hŭi, to perform in a wide
variety of genres, such as martial arts, melodramas, and historical epics, the
stable repertoire of Shin Films. They even practiced horseback riding. But
all of a sudden, they were dispatched to Hong Kong. They stayed there until Shin Films' official closure in 1975, in the meantime starring in some of
Shaw Brothers' first and second-tier genre films. Chin Pong-jin (b. 1942),
one of the actors who was chosen in 1968, recalled, "One day, Shin Sang-
ok ordered me to obtain a passport. I didn't know what the purpose was.
A couple of months later, Shin asked me to come to his office. He gazed at
me for a while, and said, 'Pong-jin, you've got to go to Hong Kong. We [Shin
Films] are going to make many coproduction films with Shaw Brothers, and
you and your colleagues will stay a couple of years in Hong Kong.' I was so
happy. Who wouldn't be? It was Hong Kong! Since I haven't been abroad in
my life, I was so excited to go. For me, Hong Kong was a land of beautiful
ladies, exotic landscapes, and economic prosperity."[115]

Chin, Kim Ki-chu, Hong Sŏng-chung, and six other rookies arrived in
Hong Kong in the summer of 1969. They stayed in small, packed apart-
ments in Tsimshatsui, Kowloon peninsula. Shin Films had a small office
in Tsimshatsui, and a representative of Shin Films acted as a go-between.
About half a year later, Chin played a supporting role in one of Shaw Brothers' A-list films, *Finger of Doom* (*Tai yin zhi*, Pao Hsueh-li, 1971). Since Chin
could speak neither Cantonese nor Mandarin, he had to rely on the script as
translated by the Shin Films representative, whose name was given simply as
"Mr. Kim." As explained earlier, the Hong Kong film industry used dubbing
instead of synchronization due to the vast distribution circuits in Southeast
Asia. Thanks to the studio's dubbing policy, Chin spoke in Korean while
shooting the film. *Finger of Doom* was one of the year's major successes, and
Chin became a stable supporting actor at Shaw Brothers after that.[116] *Finger
of Doom* was released in South Korea in February 1971 under the new title
ŭmyangdo, and under the name of a new director, Ho Meng-hua, who was
not involved in the film at all. *ŭmyangdo* was publicized as a coproduction. It
drew a hundred thousand audience members and made a handsome profit
for Shin Films.[117]

By lending out its performers, Shin Films brought Shaw Brothers films
with their stars into South Korea as coproduction films.[118] Shin Sang-ok was
clever at working around the MPL. According to the MPL, to be approved

as full coproduction films, at least two main actors or actresses and two major staff members, including the screenwriter, director, or cinematographer, were needed. These minimum qualifications were easy to meet. Shaw Brothers benefited from the practice as well, since the studio was in dire need of more performers. In addition, the salaries of these actors and actresses were paid by Shin Films. Shaw Brothers, therefore, had nothing to lose and everything to gain, and was willing to issue any official documents that Shin Films wanted.

From 1970 to 1973, approximately twenty Shaw Brothers films were distributed in South Korea under the banner of Shin Films. The first set of these "counterfeit" coproduction films consisted of *The Rescue* (K. *Okchungdo*, H. *Xue sa tian lao*, Shen Chiang, 1971), *Six Assassins* (K. *Ch'irinüi hyŏpkaek*, H. *Liu ci ke*, Chŏng Ch'ang-hwa, 1971), *The Assassin* (K. *Taep'yogaek*, H. *Da ci ke*, Chang Cheh, 1967), *Venus' Tear Diamond* (K. *Yŏnaedojŏk*, H. *Zuan shi yan dao*, Inoue Umetsugu, 1971), *Finger of Doom*, and *Lady with a Sword* (K. *Ch'ŏllangja*, H. *Feng fei fei*, Kai Pao Shu, 1971). Exactly half of the Shin Films outputs in 1971 belonged to this category. They were all "made in Hong Kong" products but were distributed as coproduction films by adding a couple of Shin Films performers in supporting roles. All of the actors received salaries, as Chin recalls, from Shin Films by way of "Mr. Kim," while Shaw Brothers was only required to pay living expenses in Hong Kong. Shin Films did not participate in the production of those sixteen films aside from lending out its performers.[119] Shin, however, went further. In 1972, Shin Films released *Diary of a Virgin* (*Ch'ŏnyŏŭi such'ŏp*) with his name listed as the film's sole director. In reality, the film was a Japanese director Inoue Umetsugu's Shaw Brothers film *We Love Millionaires* (*Woai Jin guixu*, 1971). The film was poorly received at the box office. Shin did this once more with another Inoue Umetsugu film, *The Venus' Tear Diamond*.

Shin Films benefited tremendously from this bizarre business model of exporting cultural workers. The studio imported the Shaw Brothers' lucrative second-tier genre films in very affordable ways, sneakily avoiding the government's notorious foreign film import quota, and acquired quotas by falsely reporting to the government that the studio had coproduced films, exported them, and earned foreign currency—the last of which was the primary concern of the Park regime. With the quota Shin Films earned, Shin Films legally imported Shaw Brothers A-films, mostly directed by Chang Cheh and Ho Meng-hua, and profit-guaranteed Hollywood movies. In 1973, Shin Films welcomed another major partner, Golden Harvest. Chŏng Ch'ang-hwa (b. 1928), a South Korean director who had directed many *wuxia* films for Shaw Brothers, including *Five Fingers of Death* (*tian xia di yi quan*, 1972), left the studio with Raymond Chow and established a new "Post-Fordist" horizontally integrated studio, Golden Harvest. With the tremendous success of the Bruce Lee films, Golden Harvest began to threaten Shaw Brothers, and soon dominated markets worldwide with its urban-setting kung fu films. Chow approached Shin, and the two studios made *When Taekwondo Strikes* (*Hŭkkwŏn*, Huang Feng) in 1973, starring the South Korean Taekwondo master Rhee Jhoon Goo (Jhoon Rhee), who was known in South Korea as Bruce Lee's master.[120]

Shin Films' counterfeit coproduction practice ended in late 1974, when Shaw Brothers' major genre shifted to kung fu. Shaw Brothers now needed martial arts experts to mass-produce kung fu films, and thus there was no further need to work with Shin Films' actors. After the end of the decade-long collaboration with Shaw Brothers, Shin went to Hong Kong in search of a new partner but was able to find only minor independent producers. Shin produced a few more coproduction films before the studio's official closure.[121] After Shin Films was disassembled, the "Shin Films apprentices" became deterritorialized orphans. Some remained in Hong Kong, some moved to America, and the rest returned to South Korea. The story of the "Shin Films apprentices" has long since been forgotten, and their names and careers are found nowhere in the official history of South Korean or Hong Kong cinema.

In the early 1970s, a series of bad decisions and reckless management combined with Shin's perpetual quandary, the lack of talent in the company, drove the studio to the verge of bankruptcy. Shin's protégés Im Wŏn-sikand Sim U-sŏp all left the studio, and Shin Films no longer had contract directors under its umbrella. Instead, Shin Films focused on producing Shin Sang-ok films and hired directors on a "film-to-film" basis.[122] At the same time, Shin had left Ch'oe Ŭn-hŭi to live with a young actress, O Su-mi, who gave birth to his first child. This had far-reaching effects, since Ch'oe was not just Shin's wife—she was his most important business partner. In leaving Ch'oe, then, Shin lost his most powerful guardian.[123] Shin Films finally closed its operations in 1975 after publicly releasing an unapproved (uncensored) film *Rose and a Stray Dog* (*Changmi wa tŭlgae*, Shin Sang-ok). *Rose and a Stray Dog* was Shin's last film with his lover, O. When Shin Films shut down, Shin Sang-ok had fewer than ten employees. By that time, it was merely an independent production company called Shin Production, having left the glorious past behind.

For over two decades, the history of Shin Films epitomized the rise and fall of the South Korean film industry, which saw a sharp increase in mass production from the late 1950s to the mid-1960s. Shin Films was located at the core of the nation's film culture and industry. The studio actively interacted with and benefited from the Park Chung Hee government's motion picture policy, known as the MPL, but was forced to cease its operations in the end. Therefore, Shin Films was a quintessential example of the "developmental state studio," a state-sponsored and state-supported movie studio that benefited from and at the same time was heavily regulated by the state.

Epilogue

In 1978, Shin, desperately seeking his missing ex-wife Ch'oe, went to Hong Kong. There he was mysteriously kidnapped by North Korean agents. In the Democratic People's Republic of Korea (the DPRK, or North Korea), with the strong support of Kim Jung Il (1941–2011; in office 1994–2011), Shin and Ch'oe—who had already been abducted—formed their own movie studio, again called Shin Films. Shin directed eight films and produced more than twenty films under the banner of the new Shin Films from 1984 to 1986.[124] Ch'oe Ŭn-hŭi starred in seven of the eight films Shin directed. Moreover, interestingly enough, two of his last films in North Korea, *Hong Kiltong* (Kim Kil-in, 1986) and *Pulgasari* (Shin Sang-ok, 1985), were coproductions with Hong Kong and Japan, respectively. *Hong Kiltong*, based on a story popular in both South and North Korea, is the only martial arts film ever produced in the North. To make it, Shin invited a whole team of martial arts choreographers from Hong Kong, along with some stunt actors.[125] The film was a national sensation and was exported to many Eastern European countries. In particular, it took the Bulgarian box office by storm in 1986. For *Pulgasari*, a monster movie, Japanese technicians who had worked on *Godzilla* (*Gojira*, Honda Ishiro, 1954) stayed at Shin Films North for several months in 1985. In the North, as Shin recalled, he had total control over his studio. Kim Jong Il, who had written a book on film aesthetics, was very enthusiastic about the development of North Korean cinema.[126] In this totalitarian state, Shin finally materialized his dream, a "director-centered" vertically integrated studio system. There he produced, wrote, directed, and even distributed his films.[127]

Shin and Ch'oe escaped from the North in 1986, just a year after *Pulgasari*'s release in North Korea. They began their new career in Hollywood in the late 1980s. In Los Angeles, Shin began filmmaking in 1991 under the banner of Sheen Productions, where he wrote, produced, and directed a series of low-budget action films. Shin's filmography in Hollywood, under his English name Simon S. Sheen, includes *3 Ninjas* (John Turteltaub, 1992; producer), *3 Ninjas Kick Back* (Charles T. Kanganis, 1994, writer/producer), *3 Ninjas Knuckle Up* (Shin Sang-ok, 1994, producer/director), *The Legend of Galgameth* (Sean McNamara, 1996, producer/writer), *3 Ninjas: High Noon at Mega Mountain* (Sean McNamara, 1998, producer), and *The Gardener* (James D. R. Hickox, 1998, producer). After the commercial failure of *The Gardener*, Sheen Production ceased its operations and Shin and Ch'oe returned to South Korea in 1994. Shin Sang-ok died in 2006.

Chapter 7

Hong Kong, Hollywood, and the End of the Network

The Hong Kong film industry has been guided by what Steve Fore calls the principle of "positive non-interventionism."[1] Shaw Brothers was built under the Hong Kong version of laissez-faire economic policy in the 1960s. The corporate tax rates were low, there were no restrictions on the movement of currency, and customs procedures were quick and efficient. During that time, Hong Kong had what was probably the most lenient censorship system in Asia. Indeed, the flexibility and relaxed atmosphere led the studios to experiment with diverse genre films, and the Hong Kong film industry's unique need to satisfy transnational Chinese communities in East and Southeast Asia helped it quickly gain "global currency." Therefore, Shaw Brothers slid easily into the model of the market-oriented studio. Michael Curtin has branded Hong Kong a "media capital," a "site of mediation, locations where complex forces and flows interact."[2] He adds, "Hong Kong is one of these competing media capitals, as a consequence of its status as a nexus for economic and cultural flows within and between Chinese societies through the 20th century. The city benefits from a relative lack of censorship and from open trade policies, both of which encourage transnational alliances of talent and resources."[3]

According to Curtin, Steve Fore, and most scholars of Hong Kong cinema, the commercial success of Hong Kong cinema relied on the city-state's economic policy, and Shaw Brothers benefited the most from the policy. In fact, the unprecedented growth of Shaw Brothers in the 1960s paralleled the city's rising status as a financial center in the region. Catherine Schenk argues that Hong Kong emerged as an International Financial Center (IFC), like its precursors, London, Tokyo, and New York, in the late 1960s. The explanation for Hong Kong's ascension to the status of an IFC is surprisingly similar to the reasons for the success of its film business. Schenk singles out three elements: "Hong Kong had all three of the classic attributes of an IFC: political stability, infrastructure and regulatory freedom. In addition to these defining attributes, Hong Kong benefited from its commercial past, which left a legacy of financial expertise and institutions."[4]

The Hong Kong film industry had all three of these characteristics, and it took advantage of them. However, Hong Kong had not yet acquired its status as a media capital in the late 1950s when Shaw Brothers was starting out. At this time, Singapore was still the headquarters of the Chinese diasporas' film industry, and the production centers were dispersed in Malaysia, Singapore, and Hong Kong. The major source of Shaw Brothers' and MP&GI's competitiveness lay primarily in their enormous distribution and exhibition networks, which extended to major capitals in Southeast Asia such as Kuala Lumpur, Jesselton (Kota Kinabalu), Johor Bahru, Singapore, Saigon, and Hong Kong. It was not until the mid-1960s that the signs of Shaw Brothers' regional domination appeared.

This chapter explores the ways Shaw Brothers, a market-oriented studio, exploited its intimate network with the FPA member executives and transformed the regional film industry in the 1970s through transnational collaborations with film studios in Europe and Hollywood. The aim of this chapter is not only to draw attention to Shaw Brothers' vigorous endeavors to expand its regional market but also to scrutinize this specific moment and mode of production in Hong Kong film history. There are multiple ways to explain the sudden mushrooming of transnational collaborations among Hong Kong, Europe, and America in the 1970s: as a product of Hollywood's cultural imperialism in Asia, the new international division of cultural labor, Hong Kong cinema's global outreach, the hybridization of cinematic genres, the American film industry's deep recession in the 1970s, or the transformation of Hong Kong's political-cultural sphere. In addition, Nixon's visit to China opened a new chapter of the Cold War in the region. The following pages will discuss the network that linked Hong Kong, Europe, and Hollywood by using the rubric of the global film industry, in which the more advanced cinema industries' quest for cheap labor drove the increasingly transnationalized division of labor in every film city in the world. This chapter argues that Shaw Brothers was not a victim of the inevitable shifts in the capitals, but an active participant that aspired to penetrate the Western market by using the city-state's already established regional film industry hierarchies, as evidenced by Shaw's aggressive involvement with the FPA members in the region during the 1950s and '60s.

According to this logic, this chapter will trace the emergence of the global kung fu phenomenon in the 1970s, discussing how the kung fu craze started; to what extent Shaw Brothers, Golden Harvest, and Warner Brothers interacted with and competed against each other; and why and how the Asian studio network rapidly receded in the late 1970s. The following section traces the history of Shaw Brothers' entrepreneurial trajectories before venturing into the soaring 1970s.

Shanghai, Singapore, Hong Kong: The Shaw Brothers Story

Stephanie Po-yin Chung, a Hong Kong-based historian, asserts that although Shaw Brothers, or "Shaw Enterprise," transplanted the Western industrial model into Asian culture, the studio retained the nature of the "traditional Chinese family business—being run by family patriarchs."[5] She terms this particular type of business a "fraternal enterprise."[6] Emphasizing the role played by the four patriarchs, Runje (1896–1975), Runde, Runme (1901–85), and Run Run Shaw, Chung explains how Run Run, the youngest brother, took over the family's motion picture business in the late 1950s and adopted Hollywood-style vertical integration. Adopting the vertical integration system helped Shaw Brothers achieve hegemony in the region in the 1960s and 1970s. Convincingly arguing that Shaw Enterprise was ultimately a Chinese merchant, Chung states that "as émigrés of China, many of these self-made Chinese merchants worked their way up through hard work, frugality, and strong personal networks in coastal China and Southeast Asia."[7] The case of Shaw Brothers is evidence of this development.

Accordingly, the history of the Shaw Brothers studio spanned Shanghai, Singapore, and Hong Kong and should be closely examined in the context of the history of the three cities. The Shaw Brothers studio originated in Shanghai as Tianyi Film Company in 1925, founded by the four Shaw brothers. Tianyi's business principles were low costs, fast production, and big turnout, with a goal similar to that of Hollywood studios—making profits. The business leaders in these studios sought riches associated with market domination and monopoly power. Therefore, the Tianyi studio was also eager to establish its own distribution and exhibition network, which distinguished it from its competitors. Between 1928 and 1935, before the Tianyi studio moved to Hong Kong, Run Run and Runme went to Singapore to recapture the Chinese diaspora market. They successfully built a strong theater chain in Singapore and soon expanded it into Kuala Lumpur, Jesselton, and Hong Kong. In 1936, Runme returned to Tianyi to replace his brother Runje, who went back to Shanghai to look out for the family interests. Tianyi was renamed the Nanyang (Southeast Asia) studio, and its new name clearly reflects the company' new strategy and geographical identity. As a transnational film studio, the Nanyang studio had its production studio in Hong Kong and was operating huge theater chains in Singapore and Malaysia by the end of the 1930s.

During the Second World War and the Japanese occupation period, the Nanyang studio was seized by Japanese troops, and most of the company-owned theaters in Singapore and Malaysia were destroyed. After the war, the Southeast Asian market was in ruins, and while Run Run flew to Europe to study new film technologies in the late 1940s and the early 1950s, the Shaw brothers' theater chains were renovated and extended. Thus, in 1956, the Shaw family owned more than a hundred theaters in Malaysia, Singapore, North Borneo, Vietnam, Thailand, Taiwan, and Hong Kong.[8] To meet the demands of its theater circuit, the Shaw family had to stabilize its supply. Shaw Malay Production had come to dominate the Singapore and Malaysia markets by the mid-1950s as the sole major studio in the region.[9] However, with the infiltration of MP&GI, the competition took off. Feeling pressure from the family's rivals, Run Run Shaw decided to come to Hong Kong in 1957. His move was primarily aimed at securing the overseas Chinese audiences in Southeast Asia. Kean Fan Lim notes that the "power of Southeast Asian financier-cum-distributors was so strong that Hong Kong producers ceased to make Cantonese pictures."[10] In their place, to meet the swelling demand, most Hong Kong producers were coerced into manufacturing Mandarin pictures. Shaw Brothers was no exception.

Instead of making local cinema in vernacular languages, Shaw Brothers began to produce numerous Mandarin films for the thriving overseas Chinese communities. Hong Kong was a legitimate base camp for making Chinese films because the eldest brother, Runde, and his sons had already been operating a small-scale film production company, Shaw & Sons Ltd., since 1950. While Runde was in charge of the studio's Mandarin films, made by Shaw & Sons, he was less enthusiastic about filmmaking than about real

Figure 7.1. Capitol Cinema at the junction of Stamford and North Bridge Roads in Singapore. It was Shaw Organisation's flagship cinema after they purchased the Capitol Theatre (later renamed Shaws Building) in 1946. Ministry of Information and the Arts Collection, courtesy of National Archives of Singapore.

estate, a highly profitable business due to the skyrocketing land prices in postwar Hong Kong and Malaysia.[11] Between 1957 and 1959, Runde and Run Run set sail on a far-reaching expansion venture, the so-called theater-a-month project in the newly independent Malaysia.[12] The project was to construct twenty-two new, modern movie theaters in twenty-four months.[13] By 1962, Shaw Brothers owned nine amusement parks and 127 theaters in major cities in Southeast Asia.[14]

Nevertheless, Runme and Run Run were not content with their elder brother's tedious, cheaply made Mandarin films. MP&GI was producing a steady stream of box office triumphs with its well-made films, which featured modern subjects such as changing family values and women's rights coupled with Western songs and dances and references to the crazes of American culture. Run Run Shaw decided to stay Hong Kong to take over feature film production in the British Crown Colony, while Runme remained in Singapore to take care of Shaw Malay Production. In 1958, Shaw Brothers Ltd. was founded with Run Run Shaw as president. Although

Shaw Enterprise was divided into two production locations, Hong Kong and Singapore, the family did not make clear distinctions between the brothers' roles. On the contrary, they worked closely with each other. Shaw Enterprise had a wide chain of movie theaters, modern leisure parlors, and immense real estate under the family name. In 1959, Run Run Shaw recruited two non-family-member newcomers, Raymond Chow and Leonard Ho. They were both well educated, had good track records in the movie business, and spoke fluent English, Cantonese, and Mandarin. Chow took charge of the studio's publicity department, while the physical production was controlled by Ho. Chow had an astute sense of international business, and he was behind most of the firm's international coproductions. Chow would later leave the company to start Golden Harvest, a strong competitor of Shaw Brothers in the 1970s.

By 1960, MP&GI films were solidly ahead of Shaw Brothers films in Southeast Asia. MP&GI, like Shaw Brothers, entered the industry as a distributor, with numerous modern cinemas across Southeast Asia. The company was based in Singapore. MP&GI had a colossal success with the musical film *Mambo Girl*

Figure 7.2. Loke Wan Tho (far left), president of MP&GI in Singapore, poses with Singapore-Malay actors and actresses at the 6th Asian Film Festival, which was held in Kuala Lumpur, in May 1959.; Left to right. Wahid Satay, a Singaporean-Malaysian actor, comedian and singer; Latifah Omar, a Malay actress, Ho Ah Loke, president of Cathay Keris Studio in Singapore; and Maria Menado, a Malay actress. Courtesy of Asian Film Archive, Singapore.

(*Manbo Nülang*, Evan Yang, 1957) and commanded the two mega-stars Grace Chang and Linda Lin-dai, the rising starlet Lucilla Yu Ming, and "the Asian Cary Grant" Peter Chen Ho. The studio president Loke Wan-tho's keen sensitivity to the latest vogues in the region and the preeminently sophisticated scripts of Eileen Chang led the company to outstrip the rest of the industry. The Oxford-educated Loke, who was born and grew up in Kuala Lumpur, favored tales of contemporary Southeast Asia. MP&GI's refined stories of love, family ties, urban cityscapes, and the strong influence of Western cultures appealed to the postwar generations in Kuala Lumpur, Bangkok, Singapore, Hong Kong, and Taipei. As Poshek Fu states, Loke sought to build "a *modern* venture around the *modern* entertainment of motion pictures which he believed would both prove his entrepreneurial spirit and modernize the everyday culture of Southeast Asia."[15] Likewise, MP&GI's series of coproduction films starring Linda Lin-dai, a jewel of the studio, was filmed in Japan and had a Japanese flavor, as shown in the three Linda Lin-dai cycles *Miss Kikuko* (*Juziguniang*, Yan Jun, 1956), *Merry-go-round* (*Huanle niannian*, Griffith Yueh Feng, 1956), and the coproduction *Hong Kong-Tokyo Honeymoon* (*Tōkyō Honkon mitsugetsu ryokō*, Nomura Yoshitaro, 1957), a Shochiku-MP&GI collaboration.[16] A few years later, MP&GI produced a trilogy of MP&GI-Toho coproduction films: *A Night in Hong Kong* (H. *Xiang gang zhi ye*, J. *Honkon no yoru*, Yasuki Chiba, 1961), *A Star of Hong Kong* (H. *Xiang Gang zhi xing*, J. *Honkon no hoshi*, Yasuki Chiba, 1962), and *Hong Kong-Tokyo-Honolulu* (H. *Xiang Gang Dong Jing Xia Wei Yi*, J. *Honoruru-Tokyo-Honkon*, Yasuki Chiba, 1963).[17] All of these films starred the Japanese actor Takarada Akira and the Hong Kong starlet Lucilla Yu Ming. This trilogy was wildly successful in both markets and led Yu Ming into transnational stardom.[18]

Starting in 1957 and continuing through its initial opening in 1962 to its completion in 1967, Run Run Shaw built an ambitious motion picture studio in Clearwater Bay in Hong Kong known as "Movie Town." It had twelve sound stages, dubbing and processing studios, canteen and staff quarters, and a color process laboratory. As Run Run Shaw clearly shared the mindset of the Hollywood-type modern studio system, he had more than five hundred resident contract staff members.[19] Among them were fifteen screenwriters, twenty-four general writers, and many technicians. The completion of "Movie Town" meant that Shaw Brothers had created a vertically integrated production, distribution, and exhibition network.[20] With a huge and stable Southeast Asian market, Shaw Brothers could now monopolize the Chinese-language "world" outside the mainland.

Shaw's objective in the 1960s was to raise the standard of Shaw Brothers' productions. To compete with the rival studio MP&GI in Singapore, he longed to improve the output's production quality. To do so, Shaw Brothers desperately needed to recruit talented filmmakers to work in Movie Town. Shaw also aimed to release one film a week, and this meant he needed more people—skilled ones. Accordingly, Shaw hired filmmakers from South Korea, Taiwan, Singapore, Malaysia, and Japan. Shaw wanted to diversify the studio's genres to bring young audiences to the theaters and upgrade the inefficient and rather slow production procedure. To do this, he turned to the FPA network.

Shaw's Japan Connection

Run Run Shaw was eager to learn the mechanism behind the Japanese studios' high productivity. Japan's major studios had developed a system of churning out several hundred pictures per year. In addition, Shaw felt the need to diversify the studio's rather limited genres. During the late 1950s and early '60s, Shaw Brothers sent many production crew members, such as cinematographers, editors, production designers, and later actors and actresses, to Japan. Predictably, the next step was to bring Japanese film workers to his studio in Hong Kong. Between roughly 1966 and 1975, a number of Japanese film directors worked at Shaw's Movie Town. Shaw hired Japanese directors for two purposes. He was not aiming to achieve artistic superiority by hiring art film directors from Japan. Instead, his first goal was to achieve efficient craftsmanship that would fill the studio's theater chains and improve the still inefficient Hong Kong production system.

Second, Shaw hoped that Japanese directors would bring new genres to Southeast Asian audiences. The former core audiences of Cantonese films, women and the working class, were losing ticket power as they grew older, and a new audience had emerged: the postwar generation.[21] Throughout the 1960s, Hong Kong's manufacturing economy boomed. Huge amounts of capital and labor moved from the mainland to Hong Kong after the war, and Hong Kong's economy, like those of Taiwan, Malaysia, and South Korea, prospered from labor-intensive industries such as textiles, wigs, and plastics. However, this drastic economic prosperity created social inequality, which, in combination with corruption, the lack of representative democracy, problems with colonial law enforcement, a lack of public services, and a host of social problems (gambling, opium, prostitution, and organized crime), gave rise to major problems in the city.[22]

Foreign influence was also extremely strong in the 1960s. Western movies (mostly from the United States), TV series, books, and magazines were very popular. The Beatles came to Hong Kong in 1965, and Western pop music was absorbed by teenagers and college students, playing an extremely important role in forming local culture. Hong Kong's new Kai Tak International Airport, with its 8,350-foot runway, was completed and began operations in 1962. It represented, as Tan See Kam highlights, a "'coming-of-age' for Hong Kong's postwar modernity."[23] Hong Kong's Cathay Pacific Airways (CPA) began in 1946 as a small and unscheduled operator. It extended its capacity as a genuine regional airline and finally opened the "jet age" by purchasing Lockheed Company's prop-jet *Electra* in April 1959. It frequently flew between Singapore, Bangkok, Manila, Hong Kong, and Seoul. In August 1960, CPA began flying *Electra* to much more distant destinations: Tokyo, Osaka, and Sydney.[24] "We can see," Leung Ping-kwan writes about this period, "not only was the city's outlook changing, but the lifestyle and the way people thought about themselves were changing as well."[25]

Under the influences of the global movement of youthful uprisings, particularly the student movements in South Korea and Japan, the postwar generation, which had been better educated than older generations and was also influenced by Western culture, united and organized the decolonialization movement. Together with mainland China's Cultural Revolution (1966–76) and Kowloon's mass demonstration, these student movements sometimes turned into riots when they failed to mobilize popular support, and they sustained many casualties.[26] These so-called youth problems affected the film industry as well, especially the Cantonese production companies. In order to bring young people to the theater, new genres began to appear. During the mid- and late 1960s, films that portrayed juvenile delinquency, social disaffection, drug addiction, sex crimes, the rock 'n' roll craze, and the generation gap were actively produced by Cantonese production companies in Hong Kong. Shaw Brothers, however, was not particularly strong in any of these topics. Run Run Shaw needed new blood.

In response to this need, Shaw hired Chua Lam as the studio's representative in Japan. He was the son of Shaw's production manager in Singapore, Chua Boon Suan. At the time of his hiring, Chua was still a student in the film production program at Nihon University, Tokyo, which was the hub of Japan's avant-garde cinema movement in the 1960s. Chua's mission was to buy commercially competitive Japanese films that could appeal to Hong Kong's new generation. In fact, the mid-1960s was the last gasp of Japanese cinema's golden age. Each studio kept huge numbers of film prints in its library, and each studio wanted to sell them. This was the perfect time to buy Japanese genre films. Chua bought them in bulk, except for new and prestigious films. Chua remembered, "The head of Nikatsu's foreign trade department said it was pointless keeping the films and so sold Shaw the rights at USD 500 each."[27] Accordingly, Chua bought Nikkatsu *yakuza* films, Toei's *Jidaigeki*, and Daiei's *Zatoichi* series. Those Japanese action movies were well received among young Southeast Asians.[28]

In early 1966, Nakahira Ko and Inoue Umetsugu signed a contract with Shaw Brothers. Four more directors followed: Furukawa Takumi, Shima Koji, Murayama Mitsuo, and Matsuo Akinori. They worked mostly for Nikkatsu and Daiei, and all of them were well-known genre-film directors in Japan.[29] Most of them had shown films at the Asian Film Festival. For instance, Shima Koji, one of the first batch of Shaw recruits, impressed Shaw when he received the first Best Picture award with *Golden Demon* in 1954. To the Shaw Brothers, Japanese directors represented a model of technical, economic, and creative advancement, a standard to which they aspired. Compared to other Asian contract workers, therefore, Japanese film workers had a different status. The hired Japanese directors worked incredibly fast. As soon as the contract was ready, Inoue Umetsugu came to Hong Kong in March 1966, where two films were already simultaneously under production. He made *Operation Lipstick* (*Die wang jiao wa*, 1967), an espionage comedy, as his first Shaw movie.[30] Inoue's working style stunned the other Shaw directors. He completed the film in a month and began to shoot the second film, *Hong Kong Nocturne* (*Xiang jiang hua yue ye*, 1967).[31] By November, Nakahira Ko was producing another espionage film, *Interpol* (*Te jing 009*, 1967).[32] The trend yielded the first Shaw-Nikkatsu espionage film, *Asiapol Secret Service* (*Ya zhou mi mi jing tan*, 1966), which was produced in two versions, Wang Yu acted in the version produced for Hong Kong and Nitani Hideaki in the Japanese version, under the direction of Matsuo Akinori.[33]

Before being hired by the Shaw Brothers, the extremely prolific director Inoue had produced over seventy genre films that ranged from jazz musicals, espionage thrillers, and comedies to *taiyozoku* (sun tribe) films.[34] Furukawa Takumi directed the first *taiyozoku* film, *Season of the Sun* (*Taiyo no kisetsu*, 1956), and Nakahira Ko made *Crazed Fruit* (*Kurutta kajitsu*, 1956). Both films were based on the stories of Ishihara Shintaro, and his younger brother Ishihara Yujiro starred in them. Inoue worked with Ishihara Yujiro on many memorable films, including *Man Who Causes a Storm* (*Arashi o yobu otoko*, 1957), *The Eagle and the Falcon* (*Washi to taka*, 1957), and *Tomorrow Is Another Day* (*Ashita wa ashita no kaze ga fuku*, 1958).[35]

It is evident that one of Shaw's aims in hiring these directors was to recycle Japan's youth pictures from the past decade. As Inoue later recalled,

Shaw himself was a "keen viewer of Japanese movies," and he was also well aware that people in Hong Kong had "no concept of copyright."[36] Since Japan's youth culture of the mid-1950s could easily be adopted into Hong Kong society ten years later, Shaw saw the market potential of *taiyozoku* films. Most of the Japanese "hired hands" reworked their already proven Japanese youth films by changing the original scripts and settings to fit into Hong Kong's locations and suit its audiences. For instance, Nakahira Ko, who made the critically acclaimed *Crazed Fruit* in 1956, worked for the Shaw Brothers between 1967 and 1969 under the Chinese name Yang Shuxi (Yang Shu-shih).[37] He directed four films for the Shaw Brothers: *Inter-pol*, *Trapeze Girl* (*Fei tian nu lang*, 1967), *Summer Heat* (*Kuang lian shi*, 1968), and *Diary of a Lady-Killer* (*Lie ren*, 1969). *Trapeze Girl* was the only one of these films that was not a remake of one of his previous films in Japan. Inoue also remade his *Man Who Causes a Storm* into *King Drummer* (*Qing chun gu wang*, 1967) with Ling Yun and Lily Ho.

In addition to the Japanese forces, Shaw recruited action genre directors from South Korea. Chŏng Ch'ang-hwa (Cheng Chang-ho) joined Shaw Brothers in the glow of the impressive box office returns of *Special Agent X-7* (*Sun' gan ŭn yŏngwŏnhi*, 1966) in Hong Kong. Shaw picked up this South Korea–Hong Kong coproduction film and distributed it at his company's theater chains in September 1967. Shortly after the film's release, Shaw offered Chŏng a five-year contract. Chŏng arrived in Hong Kong in December 1968. His first work with Shaw was the urban-setting, female character–driven thriller *A Temptress of a Thousand Faces* (*qian mian mo nu*) in 1969. No one, however, expected that Chŏng's medium-budget kung fu extravaganza *Five Fingers of Death* would conquer the world in three years.

The aggressive endeavors to upgrade the system and to raise the annual output were eventually rewarded with a haul of forty-three films in 1967, more than doubling the previous year's number. Among them, three films were coproductions with Shin Films (*The Goddess of Mercy*, *That Man in Chang-An*, and *The King with My Face*), and five films were made with Japanese directors. Along with those international projects, Chang Cheh made his first mark with *The Trail of Broken Blade* (*duan chang jian*, 1966), and a year later, he opened a golden age of *wuxia* with the landmark film *One Armed Swordsman* (*Du bi dou*, 1967). Loke Wan-tho died, and MP&GI no longer threatened the Shaw family. Li Han-hsiang experienced financial disaster in Taiwan, and it became very clear that the Taiwan market was now dominated by Shaw Brothers. Shaw set up a branch studio in Taipei in 1968 to use local talent for the production of four to six films specifically targeted to the Taiwan market. Shaw Brothers finally paused; it began to focus more on the quality of individual films than on competition and expansion. In 1970, Wang Yu's *The Chinese Boxer* (*Long hu dou*, 1970) dominated the year's box office in the Hong Kong and Southeast Asian markets. This was the zenith of Shaw's regional dominion. In 1970, nine out of ten box office successes in Hong Kong were Shaw's martial arts films, including *Brothers Five* (*Wu hu tu long*, Lo Wei), *The Heroic Ones* (*Shi san tai bao*, Chang Cheh), *Vengeance!* (*Bao chou*, Chang Cheh), and *Valley of the Fangs* (*E lang gu*, Chŏng Ch'ang-hwa).

Cantonese Comedies, Adult Films, and European Coproduction

As the Hong Kong film industry entered the 1970s, Shaw Brothers had to face unexpected challenges. The advent of TV in the early 1970s transformed the industry as a whole. As Yingjin Zhang explains, the household ownership of television sets in Hong Kong grew "from 12.3 per cent in 1968 to 72 per cent in 1972."[38] The first transmission by Television Broadcast Ltd. (TVB) on November 18, 1967, signaled a new era in Hong Kong. The increased popularity of television in the early 1970s radically "undermined the importance of popular, previously dominant forms such as Cantonese films."[39] In 1970, a total of thirty-five Cantonese films were released, but in the following year, only one Cantonese film was released.[40]

With his well-honed instinct, however, Run Run Shaw noticed the potential for a revival of the Cantonese cinema market. The postwar generation, born in Hong Kong after the establishment of the PRC in 1949, had become a major force in Hong Kong society. Cantonese was their mother tongue, and they wanted to see their stories onscreen. To meet the demand, Shaw hijacked elements of Cantonese TV, in which the Shaw family had invested heavily from the beginning of TVB. Suddenly Shaw Brothers began producing Cantonese film versions of popular TVB programs. Chor Yuen, who had shown an impressive track record in the Cantonese cinema industry during the 1960s, was recruited to produce films that appealed to local people. Chor directed *The House of 72 Tenants* (*Qi shi er jia fang ke*) in 1973, bringing in TV entertainers because "the audience liked them."[41] The film broke box-office records. Chor Yuen recalled, "The success of the film owed much to the initial success of the stage play. My only contribution was to make it more localized."[42] Riding on the success of *72 Tenants*, Chor then directed a series of films adapted from TV. *Hong Kong 73* (*Xiang Gang qi shi san*, 1974) was another triumph, reaching second place in the year's box office. Meanwhile, Shaw had signed a long-term contract with Michael Hui, a widely popular TV comedian.[43]

Along with Cantonese comedies, Shaw Brothers began distributing adult films, which had already proven extremely popular. Run Run Shaw imported and distributed the Danish adult film *Swedish Fly Girls* (Jack O'Connell, 1971) in the Hong Kong market. Since Singapore, Malaysia, and Taiwan had more strict censorship policies, Hong Kong was the only legitimate market for distributing softcore comedy films. *Swedish Fly Girls* belongs to the short-lived group of early 70s stewardess-ploitation movies such as *The Stewardesses* (Alf Silliman Jr., 1969), *Fly Me* (Cirio Santiago, 1973), and *Blazing Stewardess* (Al Adamson, 1975). *Swedish Fly Girls* was very successful, and as a savvy businessman, Shaw instantly recognized the market potential of such films. The Shaw Brothers cast the film's heroine, Birte Tove, a Danish actress, in the studio's new production *Sexy Girls of Denmark* (*Dan Mai jiao wa*, Lu Chi, 1973). It was shot almost entirely in Copenhagen.[44] After wrapping up the shooting in Copenhagen, Tove came to Hong Kong to appear alongside Shaw's Lau Wai-yue and Kong Oh-oi and Shin Films' contract performers Yi Hye-suk, Ko Sang-mi, and Na Ha-yŏng in Kuei Chi-hung's "women in prison" film *Bamboo House of Dolls* (*Nu ji zhong ying*, 1973). The "women in prison" film, a subgenre of the sexploitation film in the 1970s, started with two Roger Corman–produced sexploitation films, *The Big Doll House* (Jack Hill, 1971) and *The Big Bird Cage* (Jack Hill, 1972). Shaw Brothers jumped into this genre with *Bamboo House of Dolls*, set in Japanese-occupied China, and it was a massive hit in Hong Kong, Europe, and North America.[45]

In 1974, only a few months after the commercial success of *Bamboo House of Dolls*, the German film producer Wolf C. Hartwig and the Austrian sexploitation director Ernst Hofbauer arrived in Hong Kong. Together with Run Run Shaw, they embarked on the German–Hong Kong coproduction *Virgins of the Seven Seas* (*Yang ji*, Ernst Hofbauer and Kuei Chih-Hung, 1974; also known as *The Bod Squad*). Hartwig and Hofbauer were well known for their adult film series *Schoolgirl Report* (*Schulmädchen-Report*), which consisted of thirteen films and ran through 1980. The series became known as the most successful German media product in terms of commercial value in the history of German cinema. The *Schoolgirl Reports* are estimated to have attracted over a hundred million viewers worldwide.[46] Part documentaries and part stage vignettes, based on a book by Günther Hunold, the *Schoolgirl Reports* are, Jennifer Fay argues, "pornographic exposés of the erotic life of Germany's middle-class adolescent girls."[47] Harwig and Hofbauer brought two of their "schoolgirls," Sonja Jeannine and Deborah Ralls, to the filming of *Virgins of the Seven Seas,* and Run Run Shaw signed additional contracts with two European softcore porn actresses, Diane Drube and Gillian Bray. Tove also joined the production.

The sex films and Cantonese comedies were, however, exclusively for Hong Kong audiences and were not suitable for Hong Kong's traditional Southeast Asian market. Laos and Vietnam were closed due to the communist victory in the Vietnam War. Indonesia imposed an import quota on Hong Kong pictures. Singapore separated from Malaysia in 1965 to become an independent and sovereign state. Malaysia tightened up its censorship restrictions. This "crisis within and without," Grace Leung and Joseph Chan argue, "caused Hong Kong cinema to become even more commercial and entertainment-oriented to meet the tastes of different markets."[48] As Stephanie Po-yin Chung explains, Shaw Brothers had to "tailor-make" its films to comply with the various censorship policies: "The moderate version would be reserved for the Hong Kong market, while the mild and hot versions were tailored for the market in Southeast Asia and United States/Europe/Japan respectively."[49] The Hong Kong film industry had to find a solution to survive. And soon the "solution" arrived, from an unexpected territory.

Nixon Shocks, *Five Fingers of Death,* and Hollywood

The early 1970s saw a metamorphosis that transformed Asia, the United States, and the world. During the détente in the 1970s, the US government was improving its relations with the USSR and with China. On February 12, 1972, Richard Nixon (1913–94; in office 1969–74) arrived in Beijing, the first US president ever to visit China. Nixon's move was largely motivated by the failure of the United States' Vietnam intervention. This unexpected "earthquake" was a major turning point in the Cold War tension between the United States and the communist states. For more than two decades, according to Odd Arne Westad, Washington "had been telling the Japanese, the Koreans, and the Southeast Asians that the Americans were in Asia to protect them against the expansionist plans of Chinese Communists."[50] Now, all of sudden, the Asians saw a smiling US president shaking hands with the Chinese leader. This was indeed a "shock" to most of America's Cold War allies in Asia—South Korea, Hong Kong, Taiwan, and, most of all, Japan.

In the realm of the film industry in Asia, the once affluent FPA network was on the brink of collapse. By the early 1960s, Southeast Asia had largely vanished from the Asian Film Festival's line-ups, although that was where the FPA had begun. Most Southeast Asian film producers expressed discontent with the federation. After South Korea's second turn as host, in 1966, when Shaw Brothers' *The Blue and the Black* (*Lan yu hei*, 1966) won the Best Picture award and South Korea, Taiwan, and Hong Kong shared most of the major awards, the Southeast Asian countries began to consider creating their own event. With the inauguration of the Association of Southeast Asian Nations (ASEAN) in 1967, Indonesia, Malaysia, the Philippines, and Thailand initiated an ASEAN subcommittee on film. That group staged the first ASEAN Film Festival in 1972. Daiei, the most powerful and influential motion picture studio in Asia in the 1950s, declared bankruptcy in 1971 after countless box office failures and bad decisions threw the studio into a deep financial crisis. Nagata, who had initiated the FPA, left the studio the following year. With Nagata's retirement and Daiei's impoverishment, Japan withdrew from the FPA committee completely in 1972. In that same year, the Asian Film Festival was held in Seoul as a noncompetition event. Japan sent only film prints, and no industry personnel attended. During the festival, Hong Kong, Taiwanese, and even some South Korean producers and executives seriously considered canceling the festival, as no regional industry moguls were left except Shaw. Even Run Run Shaw, now the most powerful film executive in the region, was losing his passion for the FPA. Indeed, while most of the FPA member studios were collapsing, Shaw Brothers had found a new market outside its comfort zone—the United States—with the success of its medium-budget kung fu film *Five Fingers of Death*.

Certainly, *Five Fingers of Death*'s success in the United States, as well as in Europe and the Middle East, came as a total surprise to Shaw and the Hong Kong film industry. *Five Fingers of Death*, directed by Chŏng Ch'ang-hwa, was a mediocre production at best by Shaw's standards and came in outside the top twenty in 1972's year-end box office returns, far behind Shaw's comedies and adult films such as *The Warlord* (*Tou ming zhuang*, 1972), *Legends of Lust* (*Feng yue qi tan*, Li Han-hsiang, 1972), and *Intimate Confessions of a Chinese Courtesan* (*Ai nu*, Chor Yuen, 1972). For Shaw, films like *Five Fingers of Death* were second-rate, medium-budget genre films that attracted mostly male audiences in Hong Kong and Southeast Asia. The worldwide "kung fu craze," however, arose out of the blue to globalize the Hong Kong film industry.[51] This was not what the Hong Kong film industry had anticipated. For Shaw Brothers, therefore, the period presented great opportunities to leap forward.

When *Five Fingers of Death* was distributed to the global media marketplace in 1973, the American film industry, and more specifically Warner

Brothers, was facing a radical transformation. During the late 1960s, the American film industry had entered the age of conglomerates. The studio system that had dominated Hollywood filmmaking changed dramatically in the 1960s in ways that profoundly affected the '70s. Lester D. Friedman explains, "Film attendance in the United States fell to an all-time low at the start of the decade (15.8 million in 1971) while production costs were rising (from 1.9 million in 1972 to 8.9 million in 1979)."[52] By the late 1960s, motion picture companies had been "either taken over by huge multifaceted corporations, absorbed into burgeoning entertainment conglomerates, or became conglomerates through diversification."[53] Gulf & Western took over Paramount in 1966, and Trans America merged with United Artists in 1967. Hollywood's longstanding studio system was disassembled, and filmmaking became the purview of the media conglomerates that now control the entire globe.[54] Approaches to foreign markets, budgets, and the previous studio system mode of production were transformed drastically, and runaway production became increasingly necessary.

Runaway production has a long history, dating back at least as early as the immediate postwar period in Europe. Subcontracting and coproducing low-budget exploitation films with European film production companies, particularly Italian, Spanish, and German companies, became an important tactic for reducing risk and managing the growing American film industry's global market during the 1960s. Italy and Spain proved "to have the right combination of studio facilities, scenic locales, and cheap, sometimes non-union labor to attract numerous large-scale epics," as well as modest-budget Western genre films that were termed "spaghetti Westerns" in the 1960s.[55] Ben Goldsmith and Tom O'Regan point out that motion picture studios in Europe, particularly Cinecittà in Italy, were capable of such massive-scale genre films and were effectively managed.[56] American coproductions with European studios started after World War II, Heffernan argues, due to "the efforts of war-ravaged countries, including Italy and England, to block theater receipts from the major US studios in an effort to prevent large amounts of currency from leaving their decimated economies."[57]

Coproduction was the most logical way to take greenbacks out of these countries, as in many European countries American studios were blocked from spending overseas earnings back home. Therefore, relatively small companies, most representatively American International Pictures (AIP), invested capital they had earned in foreign markets into local production in the form of coproductions. This gave AIP and other companies multiple advantages, including the ability to keep costs down, particularly for labor, while spending more on production quality. As a matter of fact, those runaway productions were very successful in both the American and European markets during the 1960s.[58] By the late 1960s, though, labor costs in Italy, Germany, and Spain were no longer "cheap" enough for the American studios. Language barriers and government red tape led to much longer shooting schedules, and thus the number of overseas productions decreased significantly.[59] Hong Kong soon emerged as an alternative destination. American producers rushed to Hong Kong because kung fu films, by the early 1970s, were the most rewarding moneymakers they could find. Shortly after the introduction of Hong Kong kung fu flicks to the American market by AIP and National General Pictures (NGP), Warner Brothers, now officially a subsidiary of Warner Communication Inc. (WCI), entered this business in the early 1970s.

In 1967, Jack L. Warner of Warner Brothers had sold the company to Seven Arts Ltd., which had already bought the television rights of over a hundred of Warner Brothers' post-1948 films for USD 84 million. Seven Arts Ltd., a Canadian company, represented the changing entertainment industry of this period. The company distributed the films of major studios to American and Canadian television networks and stations. Because American television networks (ABC, NBC, and CBS) had found that feature films presented during prime time could gain a larger percentage of the viewing public than could regular television programs, there was a dramatic increase in the amount of money the networks were willing to pay to lease motion pictures.[60] In 1961, the average price for leasing a motion picture to a television network was USD 150,000 for two airings. By 1968, the price was USD 800,000.[61] The new Warner Brothers-Seven Arts was acquired on July 9, 1969, by Kinney National Services, Inc., a total "outsider" to the entertainment business, engaged primarily in the business of car rentals, parking lots, construction, and funeral homes.[62] Before buying Warner Brothers-Seven Arts, the president of Kinney, Steve Ross, had already purchased the Ashley Famous Agency, National Periodical Publications, the Licensing Corporation of America, and Panavision. Warner Bros.-Seven Arts had also acquired the Atlantic Recording Corporation before the company's buyout. This newly constructed company, therefore, was ready to build a de facto entertainment conglomerate.

Within a couple of years, Kinney had devoured still more entertainment and leisure-related companies, including three large cable television operations, Sterling Publications, and Elektra Corporation. By 1971, Kinney had formed Warner Cable, Warner Books, WEA Corporation (Warner/Elektra/Atlantic), and Warner Brothers, and in 1972, Kinney was split into two entirely separate corporations: National Kinney and WCI. Steve Ross was elected to head WCI, which was divided into four divisions: film, music, television, and publishing.[63] Now, as merely a weak subsidiary, Warner Brothers was supported by WCI's record music and television operations. It became the producer of "software for the music, television, publishing, and electronic games companies allied with it in WCI," as Gustafson explains.[64] Therefore, a hit film could lead to a television program by Warner Television and could make even more profits from WEA (the music division), as in the case of *Alice Doesn't Live Here Anymore* (Martin Scorsese, 1974), which was followed by the successful TV series *Alice* (1976–85); and the multi-platinum music records of *Super Fly*, which were also published as paperback novels and a comic book.

Five Fingers of Death clearly represents the changing structure of the American film industry and Warner Brothers' new business direction. Several months before landing in American movie theaters, *Five Fingers of Death* had already shown an impressive performance on Warner Brothers' international distribution circuit in European countries such as Italy, Germany, and Britain, as well as in Middle Eastern countries, including Lebanon, Iran, and Egypt. Mark Werba wrote in *Variety*, "They [kung fu films] have now swept across the Orient and Middle East and are scoring in European markets."[65] In addition, Warner Television's successful TV series *Kung Fu* convinced Warner Brothers to distribute *Five Fingers of Death* in the American market as the studio's first "made in Hong Kong" product. By the time Warner Brothers picked up the film in 1973, the studio was already producing the first Warner Brothers–Hong Kong (Golden Harvest/Concord pictures) coproduction film *Enter the Dragon* (Robert Clouse, 1973), along with two blaxploitation films, *Cleopatra Jones* (Jack Starrett, 1973) and *Super Fly TNT* (Ron O'Neal, 1973).[66] Warner Television was regularly producing the TV series *Kung Fu* for ABC-TV. The first episode had aired on August 15, 1972, for ABC-TV's made-for-television movie show "Movie of the Week."[67] The Caucasian actor David Carradine played Kwai Chang Caine, a biracial (American/Chinese) Shaolin Monk. *Kung Fu* was a highly successful network primetime show, and by the third season the show had broadcast a total of sixty-two episodes.

Before kung fu came to America, its way was paved by a popular TV series called *The Green Hornet* (ABC, 1966–67). ABC had previously aired a show called *Hong Kong* (1960–61), and due to the show's popularity, *The Green Hornet* was successfully produced and broadcast by the same network. *The Green Hornet* was particularly important because the protagonist, the brave newspaper publisher Britt Reid (played by Van Williams), always fought crime with his "valet" Kato, a secret martial arts expert played by the legendary Bruce Lee. After the show's relative success, Bruce Lee wanted to be a lead actor in an American TV show. He assisted in the development of the martial arts project *The Warrior* (a title later changed to *Kung Fu*), hoping to get a major role on the show. However, according to Kareem Abdul-Jabbar, who wrote a biography of Bruce Lee, he was denied the lead role in *Kung Fu* because of "the ingrained racism of network television."[68] Deeply disappointed, Bruce Lee left America and went to Hong Kong, where he starred in a number of martial arts films, including *The Big Boss* (1971), *Fist of Fury* (1971), and *Way of the Dragon* (1972), and became an international star.

Clearly, Warner Brothers had noticed the growing popularity of kung fu culture in the United States. Books, art exhibitions, comic books, and street fashions indicated the public's fascination. In particular, African American, Asian American, and Hispanic youths, mostly residing in major urban centers such as Philadelphia, Los Angeles, New York, and Chicago, became strong supporters of kung fu cinema. Before major studios like Warner Brothers entered this business, as mentioned above, AIP, NGP, and other small to midsized distributors caught onto the trend. However, most Hong Kong cinema was still exhibited in Chinatown theaters. By the mid-1960s, there were more than two dozen Shaw Brothers theaters in New York, San Francisco, Los Angeles, and other cities. As Chinese culture became more integrated into mainstream American culture during the late 1960s and early '70s, most Hong Kong–imported films were given subtitles in English and Chinese. By the late '60s, Shaw Brothers was producing films for audiences around the world, although the majority of viewers were still ethnic Chinese.[69] Therefore, Warner Brothers' decision to distribute *Five Fingers of Death* was not a one-time event. It was based on carefully prepared marketing research and strategies. The latest Hong Kong–import films were targeted at both neighborhood theaters in African American communities and the wider market through appeals to the exploitation audience.[70]

On March 21, 1973, Warner Brothers opened *Five Fingers of Death* in thirty-five locations, including New York, San Francisco, and Los Angeles. The first reviews of the film were mixed. *Variety* said that the film was "exquisitely-filmed and packed with colorful production values; the direction by Cheng Chang Ho is powerful"; it predicted that the film would provoke a widespread response, "particularly in light of the success of ABC-TV's *Kung Fu* series."[71] The *New York Times* critic Roger Greenspun had a different view. He criticized the film for being "all too extravagant, too gratuitously wild," and even proposed that it was "entirely possible to take it as a joke."[72] *Five Fingers of Death* debuted at number one at the domestic box office on April 4. The film was exhibited in the three major cities in one first-run theater and fifty-three showcases and grossed USD 696,000 in its first week of screening. *Five Fingers of Death* eventually returned an unexpected USD 4.6 million in rentals to Warner Brothers.[73] *Variety* concluded that the film's unexpected success was because it had managed to attract action-oriented fans, both Black and white, as well as "camp followers who find the dubbing and excessive mayhem food for giggles," and commented that the success of *Five Fingers of Death* evoked "last year's [1972] *Super Fly* phenomenon."[74] Ultimately, *Variety*, like the *New York Times*, attributed the film's phenomenal reception to the recent commercial successes of blaxploitation films. However, *Five Fingers of Death*'s reception was far stronger than the trade magazine's analysis indicated. Tom Costner, who had observed the Manhattan audiences' reaction, stated, "I don't think I've ever heard an audience yell louder when the good guys struck blows against evil and injustice. Oddly enough, the audience in the first-run house on Broadway was more unified against the wrongdoers than a 42nd Street audience I later observed."[75] He claimed that people needed a fantasy escape from the daily pressures of life, and that the recent success of *The French Connection* (William Friedkin, 1971) and *Super Fly* could be discussed in the same way as that of *Five Fingers of Death*.

Enter the Dragon, a coproduction of Warner Brothers, Golden Harvest, and Bruce Lee's own Concord Pictures, was released in the United States on August 25, 1973. Warner Brothers released the film in New York a week before its wide release, and the film grossed a whopping USD 104,312 in its first three days.[76] In a change of position, the *New York Times* delivered a positive review. Howard Thomson wrote that *Enter the Dragon* was "expertly made and well-meshed," and the real surprise was that "this caboose cash-in was made so well, unlike its imported predecessors."[77] By the end of the review, he was praising the "crispy dialogues" of Michael Allin's script and the direction of Robert Clouse while looking down on the "essentially shoddy productions" of Hong Kong imported films.[78] With the help of positive reviews and Warner Brothers' aggressive marketing strategies, *Enter the Dragon* expanded into eleven cities, including Los Angeles, New York, San Francisco, Chicago, Detroit, and Philadelphia, and screened in twelve first-run and eleven showcase theaters in its second week of release. *Enter the Dragon* grossed USD 802,280 and ranked number one on *Variety*'s domestic box office chart. September and October of 1973 could be said to represent the peak of kung fu cinema in the history of American film culture. As David

Desser traces in great detail, kung fu films dominated the top position in five out of these eight weeks.[79] *Enter the Dragon*, *Lady Kung Fu* (*He qi dao*; also known as *Hapkido*, Huang Feng, 1972), *Shanghai Killer* (*Zhui ji*, also known as *The Chase*, Wong Tin Lam, 1971), and *Deadly China Doll* (*Hei lu*, Huang Feng, 1973) all ranked first on the charts, and by the end of the year, *Enter the Dragon* had passed the ten-million-dollar mark in domestic rentals.

As the first American-made kung fu film, *Enter the Dragon* took a different path than did its "made in Hong Kong" predecessors. Warner Brothers tried to reach a bigger audience, seeking to appeal to white filmgoers as well as the genre's stable patrons: African Americans and Hispanics. *Variety* attributed the film's success to its international cast (Black, white, and "Oriental"), its storyline, which was better than those of the dubbed "Chinese-made action-ers," and "a prestigious campaign from WB."[80] Warner Brothers' promotional campaign was an unusual effort. Ernie Grossman, the head of Warner Brothers' publicity department, used free karate classes, illustrated flip books, comic books, posters, news releases, radio and TV spots, and interviews.[81] In addition, Bruce Lee's sudden death helped to increase the film's word-of-mouth advertisement. All of the major US publications, such as *Esquire*, *Time*, *The Wall Street Journal*, and *Newsweek*, and a number of popular magazines covered the "unexpected" death of Bruce Lee.

The Inter-Asian Division of Cultural Labor

Shaw Brothers, Golden Harvest, and small independent film productions in Hong Kong were busy producing kung fu films to meet the ever-increasing global demand. However, the demand far exceeded the local film industry's capacity, and consequently what I call the "inter-Asian division of cultural labor" proceeded at an unprecedented rate beginning in 1974. In other words, Hong Kong film producers urgently needed subcontractors who had many years of experience in making kung fu films and were reliably quick to complete projects. They also needed more male performers who knew how to kick and female performers who were willing to take off their clothes. The money came from Euro-American companies, and Hong Kong film executives also had funds to wire. Thus, South Korea and Taiwan entered this unparalleled race to manufacture standardized kung fu products.[82] Giovanni Arrighi argues that the surge of nationalism under the Cold War regime created the "conditions for fierce inter-Asian competition between relatively low-wage industrialized and higher-income countries."[83] In the film industry, these conditions were in full force. During the mid-1970s, South Korea and Taiwan exploited their low wages and skilled labor, which attracted Hong Kong film executives, especially because the city-state was a relatively high-income colony and, most important, could transmit US dollars to each studio with no intervention. As a result, between 1974 and 1976, over three hundred kung fu films were produced in Hong Kong, one third of which were never released in Hong Kong.[84]

Not only major studios but also minor and independent companies in Hong Kong, Taiwan, and South Korea actively participated in the race. Although South Korea was not particularly known for martial arts films, several directors and actors began working eagerly in the Hong Kong film industry, including Chŏng Ch'ang-hwa, Nam Sŏk-hun (Namkung Hsun), and Hwang Chŏng-ri (Hwang Jang Lee). Kim Si-hyŏn, a South Korea–based action film director, evoked the period's extraordinary practices:

> There were some "brokers" in Seoul who had networks with Hong Kong. For example, my film *Black Spider* (*Hŭkkŏmi*, 1975) was exported to Hong Kong for USD 36,000. After the film's export, many of my action films [Taekwondo pictures, according to him] were pre-sold to Hong Kong. Overall, I had received USD 3,000–5,000 first, then Hong Kong productions paid the rest of USD 25,000–30,000 upon the films' completion. . . . Once or twice, Hong Kong kung fu stars like Carter Wong came to appear in my pictures but not often. He was a very expensive star. Therefore, we hired Korean actors and gave them "Hong Kong-style" pseudonyms.[85]

Accordingly, the South Korean film industry in the mid-1970s faced a great need for martial arts performers for both local and overseas markets. Since the country did not have its own cinematic tradition of this kind and therefore lacked a pool of martial arts actors, between 1974 and 1976, a group of Korean emigrants returned to South Korea to work in the film industry. They were all Taekwondo experts who had owned Taekwondo centers in North America and even in France: Rhee Jhoon Goo, Han Yong-ch'ŏ, and Kim Ung-kyŏng (Bobby Kim). Bobby Kim, known as "Korea's Charles Bronson," had owned three Taekwondo centers in Colorado. He signed a contract with T'aech'ang production in 1974. Publicized as Bruce Lee's friend, Kim proclaimed that his only aim was "to export South Korean cinema and acquire foreign currencies."[86] With the presence of "real" martial arts experts from overseas, the South Korean film industry discovered the immense popularity of action films in the local market. Due to the strict import quota, Korean audiences had until then had very limited opportunities to experience Hong Kong–produced kung fu films. At first, only a select few films were introduced to the South Korean market. Bruce Lee's *The Big Boss* and *Fist of Fury* outperformed other foreign films and broke the record for imported films in South Korea. Yi Tu-yong, Ko Yŏng-nam, Kim Si-hyŏn, and Kim Hyo-ch'ŏn began to churn out action films for the local market. In 1974 alone, the South Korean film industry released twenty-six martial arts films, about 20 percent of the total output of South Korean cinema in that year. Most of them were not even distributed in the domestic market. Hwang Chŏng-ri, Hwang In-sik, Kwŏn Yŏng-mun, and Wang Ho (also known as Casanova Wong) stood out as actors, and they made their way to Hong Kong. Ng See-yuen, a former Shaw Brothers executive, recruited Hwang Chŏng-ri and cast him in his debut film as a director: *The Secret Rivals* (*Nan quan bei tui*, 1976), produced by Ng's newly launched Seasonal Film Corporation in 1975. After the success of the film, Hwang earned fame in Hong Kong and stayed there for seven more years.[87] This division of labor maintained itself well, but eventually decreased in the late 1970s when the enthusiasm for kung fu films gradually evaporated in the global market, disappearing altogether in the mid-1980s.

After the Craze

By 1976, the global kung fu craze was showing signs of a significant decline. Kung fu films, which had replaced the major Hollywood studios' B-movies, suddenly faced indifference from their core audiences in the global market. Raymond Chow remarked in 1973, "The market will be flooded with kung fu films, and the initial curiosity may be killed by too many mediocre movies."[88] This fear was justified. As Chow aptly predicted, too many hastily dubbed, inferior kung fu films that failed to satisfy their audiences led to the genre's entire disappearance in the late 1970s. Most important, the biggest market for "made in Hong Kong" kung fu films, the American film industry, entered the age of blockbusters and multiplexes. Theaters in metropolitan areas closed down one by one.

In the Hong Kong local market, *Jumping Ash* (*Tiao hui*, Leong Po-chih, 1976), a crime thriller, was a hit, and the public was eager to see more of the realistic and local-centered films that old dinosaurs like Shaw Brothers could not supply. The New Wave directors Ann Hui, Tsui Hark, and Patrick Tam changed the industry altogether. The Shaw Brothers directors Chor Yuen and Lau Kar-leung reincarnated the 1960s martial arts film by adapting

Gu Long's martial arts literature—Yuen's *Killer Clans* (*Liu xing hu die jian*, 1976) and *The Magic Blade* (*Tian ya ming yue dao*, 1976)—and creating new cycles of Shaolin—Lau's *The 36th Chamber of Shaolin* (*Shao Lin san shi liu fang*, 1976) and *Executioners from Shaolin* (*Hong xi guan*, 1977). Nevertheless, Shaw Brothers' glory days were undoubtedly gone. Shaw's best asset, Gordon Liu Chia-hui, was no match for Golden Harvest's Jackie Chan, who dominated the entire Asian market throughout the 1980s. In contrast to Shaw's gradual demise in the motion picture industry, Chow's ambitions continued to grow, and Golden Harvest established a special department to make English-language films.[89] This department yielded *The Amsterdam Kill* (Robert Clouse, 1977), *The Boys in Company C* (Sydney J. Fury, 1978), and in 1980, with the worldwide fame of Jackie Chan, *Battle Creek Brawl* (Robert Clouse).[90] Chow, after taking a huge loss with these big-budget "global" projects, decided to focus on the regional market instead. Indeed, Golden Harvest found a major market for Jackie Chan: Japan. Chan's *Police Story* (*Jing cha gu shi*, 1985) became a box office sensation in Japan, and every Jackie Chan film made a huge profit in Asia, including in Japan, Taiwan, South Korea, and Southeast Asia.

Shaw Brothers, in contrast, lacked the vision that Chow possessed. Mona Fong, who had taken Chow's position at Shaw Brothers when he left, was not aware of the rapidly changing film business in Europe and America, and her decision to coproduce films with B-movie production companies in Europe eventually undermined the company's reputation and global outreach.[91] Between 1974 and 1976, Shaw Brothers coproduced *Legend of the Seven Golden Vampires* (Roy Ward Baker, 1974) and *Shatter* (also called *Call Him Mr. Shatter*, Monte Hellman, 1974) with the prestigious British horror film studio Hammer Pictures.[92] Warner Bros.' *Cleopatra Jones and the Casino of Gold* (Charles Bail, 1975) was shot at the facilities of Shaw Brothers.[93] Additional coproductions with Western companies included *Virgins of the Seven Seas, Supermen against the Orient* (*Che botte strippo strappo stroppio*, Bitto Albertini, 1974), *Superman against the Amazon* (*Superuomini, Superdonne, Superbotte*, Alfonso Brescia, 1974; also known as *Super Stooges vs. the Wonder Women*), *This Time I'll Make You Rich* (*Questa volta ti faccio ricco!*, Gianfranco Parolini, 1974), and *Mighty Peking Man* (*Xing xing wang*, Ho Meng-hua, 1976). Shaw Brothers even coproduced a kung fu–Western, *Blood Money* (*Là dove non batte il sole*, Anthony Dawson, 1975; also known as *The Stranger and the Gunfighter*) with Carlo Ponti, an Italian media mogul who cast Lee Van Cliff and Lo Lieh in this precursor of the Jackie Chan–Owen Wilson vehicle *Shanghai Knights* (David Dobkin, 2003).[94] Chua Lam, Shaw Brothers' overseas production director, said in an interview, "At that time, these foreign companies only wanted to find a reliable production company in Hong Kong for collaboration. Under the agreement, Shaw was responsible for all local production fees and held the Southeast Asian copyright."[95]

Shaw's global projects, nevertheless, performed poorly in both the local and global markets, and none of them made a splash at the local box office.[96] Shaw Brothers' worst disaster was the Shaw-AIP science fiction disaster film *Meteor* (Ronald Neame, 1979). On the surface, this USD 16 million blockbuster seemed to have everything it needed to be a successful summer product. The veteran commander Ronald Neame, who had directed *Poseidon Adventure* (1972) and *Odessa File* (1974), was hired to complete it. Sean Connery and Natalie Wood were the leading stars. But the film became the year's biggest box office flop. Another of Shaw's major investments in Hollywood, Ridley Scott's *Blade Runner* (1982), failed to recoup Shaw's shares. Run Run Shaw subsequently stopped venturing out to the West, and Shaw Brothers ceased its motion picture production entirely a few years later.

By the end of the decade, most of the erstwhile major studios no longer produced films. Shin Films, once one of Shaw's regional partners and competitors in the 1960s and 1970s, had closed its business in 1975 due to government pressure. And all of the film industry sectors in South Korea faced a rapid decline of the market, partly due to the increasing popularity of television. Similarly, the Taiwanese film industry suffered from overabundant "low-quality" martial arts films and melodramas that allowed local audiences' attention to wander to foreign movies.

The age of the motion picture studio in Asia, or of what this book has called the "Asian studio network," was over.

Epilogue

From Asia to Asia-Pacific

Any international film festival that is 40 years old should by now have acquired respect and recognition from filmmakers, media and filmgoers. So how come the Asia-Pacific film festival, which began in 1954, has yet to earn a distinctive position on the global fest circuit?

—Marselli Sumarno ("Asia-Pacific Film Festival
in Jakarta," *Variety*, July 17, 1995)

Mao Zedong died on September 9, 1976. With Mao's death, the ten-year history of the Cultural Revolution (1966–76) in China came to a close. Mao's China, as Chen Jian claims, entered the Cold War as "a revolutionary country."[1] During the Cold War, what Odd Arne Westad calls "an international system of states" was often marked by the tension between the two countering superpowers—the United States and the Soviet Union.[2] But in Asia, Mao's China occupied a central position. Within a few months of Mao's funeral, Hua Guofeng removed the Gang of Four (*siren bang*), a leftist political group composed of four powerful Chinese Communist Party (CCP) members: Zhang Chunqiao, Wang Hongwen, Yao Wenyuan, and Mao's wife Jiang Qing. The Cultural Revolution ended in 1976 with their arrest. Hua subsequently served as the chairman of the Chinese Communist Party and chairman of the Central Military Commission. But Hua's power did not last long. Deng Xiaoping (1904–97) ascended in the late 1970s to become China's supreme leader. Deng Xiaoping's policy was characterized by economic reform, modernization, and liberalization, and China, under Deng Xiaoping, benefited tremendously from its strategic alliance with the United States in terms of both security and development programs.[3] With the nation's political changes, Chinese cinema developed rapidly in the new era.[4] Filmmakers were able to denounce "the brutality of the Gang of Four during the Cultural Revolution," Yingjin Zhang explains, and they tested their newfound freedom by "exploring previously taboo or sensitive subjects and genres such as political persecution, female sexuality and martial arts."[5] Several new film studios were established, and the film school reopened its doors to *zhiqing* (educated young people), who during the Cultural Revolution era had been sent to rural areas to be "reeducated." In 1978, 153 students, including Zhang Yimou, Tian Zhuangzhuang, and Chen Kaige, attended the reopened Beijing Film Academy. This reopening marked the beginning of China's Fifth Generation cinema, the first postwar film movement in China to place Chinese cinema on the map of world cinema.[6]

The late 1970s brought major transformations in the regional film cultures and industries. In June 1977, the Hong Kong International Film Festival was launched at the City Hall. It was established by the Hong Kong Urban Council. Thirty-seven films were screened during the two-week period, including films by Wim Wenders, Satyajit Ray, Roberto Rossellini, Francois Truffaut, and King Hu. A year later, the International Federation of Film Producers Association (IFFPA) granted the festival its international status.[7] Soon, it had become, in Stephen Teo's words, Asia's first film festival "devoted not to the commercial interests of the industry but to cinema as film culture and art."[8]

In September 1978, Australia hosted its first Asian Film Festival. Sydney was the festival city. Australia had joined the FPA in 1975. It was John McQuaid, the South Australian Film Corporation's commissioner, whose passionate leadership pushed Australia to participate in the FPA. A year later, Busan, a southern port city of South Korea, hosted the Asian Film Festival for the first time. There two Australian submissions, *Picnic at Hanging Rock* (Peter Weir, 1975) and the short film *Leisure* (Bruce Petty, 1976), won multiple awards.[9] After this recognition at the Busan event, Australia became more enthusiastic about the FPA.[10] Two years later, Sydney hosted the festival. The opening ceremony took place in this harbor city's newly opened Opera House Concert Hall.[11] Ten countries—Australia, Thailand, India, Hong

Figure E.1. Official poster for the 24th Asian Film Festival in Sydney, Australia, 2–6 October 1978. National Film and Sound Archive of Australia, photo courtesy of the Federation of Motion Picture Producers in Asia-Pacific (FPA).

Kong, Indonesia, Malaysia, South Korea, Singapore, Taiwan, and Japan—sent films and delegates to Sydney.

It is worth nothing that until the 1970s, Australia had seen itself as "an outpost of the British race in an alien sea," in the words of the Australian diplomat Frederic W. Eggleston, and Asia had not been among the country's primary concerns.[12] Why, then, did Australia want to join the FPA? The answer is twofold. First, by 1967, Japan had displaced Britain as Australia's major trading partner. In 1969–70, 25 percent of Australian exports went to Japan.[13] Japan, now Australia's most important trading partner, launched an "Asia-Pacific policy." The policy was based on the concept that Japan and the advanced Pacific nations—the United States, Canada, Australia, and New Zealand—would foster economic development in Southeast Asia's developing countries. As discussed in chapter 2, Japan's "return" to Southeast Asia had roots in the mid-1950s. In 1956, the *Far Eastern Economic Review* reported, "Japan today is in fact not doing significantly better than before the War, in Asian trade. Japan's relatively weakness is particularly marked in respect of the countries of South and Southeast Asia. . . . The principal countries of that area are still mainly linked, in trade as in other matters, with the Western powers which formerly were their rulers."[14] Japan led the creation of the Asian Development Bank (ADB), an Asian counterpart of the World Bank, in 1966. The idea of the ADB was that development projects in Southeast Asia could be supported by a new financial institution for the region. Miki Takeo, the Japanese foreign minister (1966–68) and the driving force behind Japan's Asia-Pacific policy, imagined Japan as a "bridge" between Asia and the Pacific.[15] In Australia, the Gough Whitlam government (1972–75) saw Asia as a source of migrants and as a crucial region to which Australia should acknowledge that it belonged. Australia, accordingly, embraced the regional identity of the Asia-Pacific.[16]

Second, by the same logic, the Australian film industry began envisioning an expansion of its market to Asia in the early 1970s. The Australian film industry's first attempt to collaborate with its Asian counterparts was *The Man from Hong Kong* (Brian Trenchard-Smith, 1975; also known as *The Dragon Flies*). This was the first Australia–Hong Kong coproduction film.[17] Certainly, McQuaid and other industry executives hoped to bring Asian productions to Australia for location shooting and to encourage them to use Australia's postproduction facilities.[18] These executives regarded their hosting of the Asian Film Festival, several hundred Asian film producers, directors, and technicians ready to notice the status of the Australian film industry, as a rare opportunity for the emerging industry.[19]

With the presence of Australia and New Zealand (which joined the FPA in 1976), the FPA had to amend its constitution. During the Asian Film Festival in 1980, held in Yogyakarta, Indonesia, all of the FPA members agreed to change the name of the annual film festival. Turino Djunaedy, a renowned Indonesian film director and the chair of the Organization Committee, suggested including "the Pacific" in the organization since the FPA had "Pacific" members—Australia and New Zealand. It is worth noting that Indonesia, in 1974, had established the ASEAN Motion Picture Producers Association (AMPP). At the first meeting, an Indonesian delegate described the purpose and aim of the AMPP: "To promote the interests of the motion picture industries in the ASEAN countries, to elevate the artistic standards of motion pictures, and to ensure the dissemination and interchange of culture in the region through motion pictures,—thereby contributing to the development of the spirit of ASEAN solidarity."[20] The Indonesian delegates' proposal therefore had to be understood as the expression of the Southeast Asian film executives' will to transform the identity of the FPA and reduce the power of the Hong Kong producers. Manuel de Leon, a long-standing figure in the FPA, noted, "The FPA originally used the words 'Southeast Asia,' which was only later changed to 'Asia.' The original constitution, made in Manila in 1954, was amended in Hong Kong in 1956." At the end of the board meeting in Yogyakarta, they decided to finalize the name change issue a year later, at the twenty-seventh festival in Manila.[21]

The Manila event, however, did not take place. It is not clear why, but at least one thing is sure: the entire Filipino film industry had to struggle with the country's first lady, Imelda Marcos (b. 1929), and her ambitious project, the First Manila International Film Festival. She dreamed of a festival that would turn Manila into the "Cannes of the East."[22] In May, when the 27th Asian Film Festival was originally planned to be held, Mrs. Marcos proclaimed the construction of a gigantic "Film Center," a nine-story replica of the Greek Pantheon. The tragedy that befell the Manila Film Center is now well known. On November 17, 1981, the scaffolding on the sixth floor of the building collapsed, burying two dozen workers under tons of rubble. Construction, however, did not stop. The project manager decided to cover the bodies over with cement in order to hold the festival on time.[23] Mrs. Marcos invited more than three hundred guests, including George Hamilton, Peter Ustinov, Jeremy Irons, and Priscilla Presley. She threw parties at the presidential palace, the Malacanang, and staged a lavish opening party on January 18, 1982. President Ferdinand Marcos (1917–89; in office 1965–86) gave the dedication speech.[24] The First Manila International Film Festival showed films from thirty-nine countries. At the end of the festival, India's *36 Chowringhee Lane* (Aparna Sen, 1981) won the Best Picture award.

Nine months after the Manila International Film Festival, Kuala Lumpur, Malaysia, hosted the 27th Asian Film Festival in 1982, after a one-year hiatus. Ten member countries—Thailand, India, Hong Kong, Indonesia, South Korea, Taiwan, Australia, Japan, New Zealand, and Malaysia—participated and forty feature films were shown over six days. At the festival, the board members unanimously decided to change the Federation's Name from "the Federation of Motion Picture Producers in Asia" to "the Federation of Motion Picture Producers in Asia-Pacific." Hence, the Asian Film Festival also changed its name to the Asia-Pacific Film Festival.[25] The first event with the new name was held in Taipei from November 15 to 19, 1983. Ichikawa Kon's *The Makioka Sisters (Sasame-yuki,* 1983) won the Best Picture prize.

By the time the FPA underwent its major identity transformation, from "Asia" to "Asia-Pacific," an US-initiated film festival that aimed at bringing films from Asia and the Pacific had been launched in Honolulu, Hawaii—America's "Pacific" outpost. The Hawaii International Film Festival (HIFF) was established in 1981, the year the former actor Ronald Reagan (1981–89) won the US presidential election in a race against Jimmy Carter (1977–81). Reagan became the fortieth president of the United States. Following the Soviet war in Afghanistan, Reagan dropped the Nixon-Carter administration's policy of détente and, together with the UK's prime minister Margaret Thatcher (1979–90), escalated the Cold War tension between the United States and the Soviets. The Reagan government proceeded to offer financial and logistical support to the anticommunist opposition in Europe and the Middle East while consolidating its "friendship" with allies in the Asia-Pacific. HIFF's mother institution, the East-West Center (EWC), was one of the many organizations, research centers, and think tanks that the Reagan administration supported and actively used to advance the interests of the United States.

The EWC, a nonprofit educational institute adjacent to the University of Hawaii at Manoa, had long been affiliated with the United States' activities in the Asia-Pacific region. The brainchild of Lyndon Johnson (1963–69), then vice-president of the United States, the EWC was established in Hawaii in 1960. Johnson asked in 1959, "Why don't we foster truly international centers of learning where the world's best and most mature minds can meet and exchange ideas? . . . The first such center should be established in Hawaii to attract scholars and students from the East and West."[26] The EWC was

Figure E.2. The 5th Hawaii International Film Festival (HIFF) was held on November 26–30, 1985. Chen Kaige's *Yellow Earth* (*Huang Tudi*, 1984), introduced by Paul Clark, was screened at the festival. First row (left to right): Paul Clark, Zhang Yimou, and Chen Kaige. Second row (center): Jeanette Paulson Hereniko, the East-West Center's community relations officer, educational specialist, and director of HIFF. East West Center, Honolulu, Hawaii. Photo courtesy of Jeanette Paulson Hereniko.

therefore created to promote "better relations and understanding between the United States and the people of Asian and the Pacific."[27] The EWC's Institute of Culture and Communication (ICC), as Mary Bitterman (a former director of the ICC) remembers, placed a strong emphasis on the arts. John Charlot, who taught Hawaiian and Polynesian religions at the University of Hawaii, headed the arts group. Jeanette Paulson Hereniko, the ICC's community relations officer and an educational specialist, proposed the idea of launching a film festival that would spotlight Asian and Pacific Islander films.[28] Within a year, under the theme of "When Strangers Meet," HIFF started as a small community event that screened only ten films from Brazil, Australia, New Zealand, China, Sri Lanka, India, Japan, and the United States. All of the screenings and symposia were free and open to the public. Its aim was, as Hawaii's governor George R. Ariyoshi stated, to foster "friendship and understanding among the people of Asia, the Pacific, and America, and to improve cross-cultural interchange through the medium of film."²⁹ The ICC's second unit focused on the humanities, and Wimal Dissanayake, then an assistant director of the ICC, highlighted the contributions of writers, art historians, philosophers, and scholars of the region. Paul Clark, a New Zealand–born historian of modern China, led a journalism group.³⁰ Apart from the festival director Hereniko, it was Wimal Dissanayake, John Charlot, and Paul Clark who actively programmed, coordinated, and managed the festival.

If TAF was initiated as an institution to fight against the communist bloc in Asia, and especially in China, the EWC's aim was to serve the United States' interests in the Asia-Pacific. HIFF was, therefore, fundamentally different from other international film festivals in America, at least during the 1980s. Throughout the 1980s, the EWC and its annual film festival were one of the most important venues for not only introducing Asian cinema to Americans but also gathering film artists, young scholars, and critics interested in the subject. Two decades after TAF's motion picture project aimed to introduce "ideologically appropriate" Asian films to American soil through the organization's close connections with the San Francisco International Film Festival, as discussed in the fifth chapter, HIFF emerged as what Markus Nornes calls the "conduit" for the most information about Asian film.³¹ "We emphasized bringing in film critics, scholars and filmmakers," Hereniko recalls. She continues: "We encouraged interaction between critics, filmmakers and audiences. There were vibrant discussions, cross cultural collaboration and fascinating after-film discussions between filmmakers and the audience after the films, as well as academic film symposiums exploring the content of the films we screened."³²

Thanks to the academics, HIFF organized academic conferences and symposia and published unusually thick and informative festival catalogues.³³ HIFF, in its early periods, introduced films from Vietnam, Sri Lanka, the Philippines, Indonesia, Malaysia, and South Korea to American film critics, scholars, and filmmakers. HIFF is also remembered as the festival where China's Fifth Generation cinema made its "official" US debut. Chen Kaige's *Yellow Earth* (*Huang tudi* 1984), introduced by Paul Clark, was screened in December 1985 at HIFF to an enthusiastic reception.³⁴ Clark first saw *Yellow Earth* at the Hong Kong International Film Festival in April 1985, where two of the Fifth Generation films—*Yellow Earth* and Tian Zhuangzhuang's *September* (*Jiu yue*, 1984)—were introduced to audiences outside China. Realizing that *Yellow Earth* might forever change cinema and the world's perception of China, the HIFF organizing team, as Hereniko remembers, "raised the money for airfare and got donated hotels to bring Zhang Yimou,

Gu Changwei, and Chen Kaige to show *Yellow Earth* to packed enthusiastic audiences."[35]

After Hong Kong's and Hawaii's notable successes in showcasing Asian cinema, Japan initiated its own prestigious international film festival, led by the Ministry of Economy, Trade and Industry. The ministry had been preparing for the Tsukuba Expo in 1985, Japan's third world's fair, following Expo '70 in Osaka and Expo '75 in Okinawa. To take advantage of potential synergies, the Tokyo International Film Festival was planned for 1985. Japanese film industry moguls took charge of the festival committee, just as they had with the Southeast Asian Film Festival in the 1950s. The collective intention of government and industry, however, was fundamentally different from what it had been in the past. From its inception, the Tokyo festival aimed to project itself as Japan's own "A-list" international film festival, comparable to Cannes and Venice and not limited to the realm of Asian cinema. Interestingly enough, in June 1985, the same year the Tokyo International Film Festival was inaugurated, Tokyo hosted the 30th Asia-Pacific Film Festival. The Japanese organizing committee members were the presidents of Toho, Toei, Nikkatsu, Shochiku, Daiei, Nippon Herald, and Fuji Film. South Korea's *Deep Blue Night* (*Kipko P'urŭn Pam*, Pae Ch'ang-ho, 1984) won Best Film. A famous "gala closing party" at the New Otani Hotel followed the award ceremony. The FPA handed out honors to four men for their roles in establishing the federation thirty years previously: Nagata Masaichi, Run Run Shaw, Manuel de Leon, and Prince Yugala. Nearly a decade after leaving the FPA, the now-retired Nagata received a trophy on behalf of the other recipients.[36] Three months later, Nagata died at his home in Tokyo. A year later, Run Run Shaw closed his film production unit completely.

The Tiananmen square protests in China ended tragically in June 1989. The Berlin Wall fell in November 1989. A few days later, the first meeting of the Asia-Pacific Economic Cooperation (APEC), an intergovernmental forum for the Pacific Rim member economies, was held in Canberra, the capital of Australia. China joined APEC together with Hong Kong and Taiwan in November 1991. Only a month later, the Cold War ended, both in ideology and in political form, when Mikhail Gorbachev signed the Soviet Union out of existence on December 26. The United States had won. Francis Fukuyama proclaimed that "the end of history" had arrived in the form of triumphant liberal democracy.[37] To China, the end of the Cold War came as a complete shock. Without the Soviet Union, China suddenly had to face the United States in a unipolar world. For most civilians elsewhere in Asia, likewise, the surrounding world changed dramatically. South Korea and China estab-lished full diplomatic relations in April 1992. Diplomatic relations between South Korea and Taiwan, two of the United States' strategic and ideological allies in Cold War Asia, were terminated shortly afterward. The Japanese economy ran into trouble in the early 1990s and entered a long recession and deflation, known as Japan's "lost decade." And Hong Kong, TAF's major battlefield in the 1950s and one of this book's major players, returned to China and became a Special Administrative Region (SAR) in 1997.

The FPA's presence in post–Cold War Asia has been diminishing since the 1980s. The FPA was the de facto Cold War film network in Asia. TAF's idea in initiating the FPA had been essentially to guard Asia—America's Asia—from Communist China's influence over overseas Chinese in Southeast Asia and to contain the region under US control. This initial aim was lost. In the new millennium, the FPA and its annual film festival carried little clout in Asia's thriving film cultures and industries.[38]

China, once the FPA's supreme enemy, emerged as the region's new "big brother." China had never joined the FPA. With the end of the Cold War, however, China opened its door to the regional film industries. In the late 1990s, China proposed the catchphrase "please come in" (qing jinlai), and many transnational companies, which Michael Keane aptly calls "willing col-laborators," took advantage of preferential policies to set up manufacturing processing facilities that exploited China's cheap labor.[39] China became the "world's factory." Cinema was no exception.

Only a year after Hong Kong's handover to China, Iseki Satoru, the CEO of Nippon Film Development and Finance, Inc., produced the Chen Kaige–directed China-Japan coproduction film The Emperor and the Assassin (Jing ke ci qin wang) in 1998.[40] In place of Hong Kong, likewise, China emerged as South Korea's coproduction partner. Anarchists (Yu Yŏng-sik, 1999) was South Korea's first cinematic collaboration with China.[41] The Chinese film industry developed much faster than industry analysts had predicted. In 2001, Zhang Yimou's martial arts extravaganza Hero (Ying Xiong, 2002) topped the US box office in 2004, earning over USD 50 million. Stephen Chow's Kung Fu Hustle (Gung fu, 2004) soon followed. Since 2004, China's national film studio China Film Group has been actively coproducing films with Hong Kong produc-tion companies, capital, and creative personnel. Indeed, the collaborations between the two regions were triggered by the introduction of the Closer Economic Partnership Arrangement (CEPA) in June 2003, which enabled Hong Kong film producers to access the Chinese market. With the launch of CEPA, the Hong Kong film industry, whose domestic market had shrunk drastically since the mid-1990s, finally saw signs of rehabilitation. Hong King cinema was given a new market whose potential seemed infinite. CEPA, Darrell William Davis wrote, sought to "integrate China, Hong Kong and Macau through a package of changes providing favorable conditions for products and services from the latter two."[42] The opening of the Chinese film market to the Hong Kong film industry attracted many Asian media players, and within just a couple of years, most major media conglomerates in Asia had joined the race to tap into the massive Chinese film market.[43]

China has now become the fastest-growing film market in the world, growing at an annual rate of more than 30 percent in the last half-decade. In 2016, China's total number of cinema screens exceeded those of the United States.[44] China is currently the American film industry's number one overseas market. Only China, Aaron Han Joon Magnan-Park writes, can rescue "a Hollywood film when it bombs domestically."[45] In large part because of the Chinese film market's development in the past decade, the Asia-Pacific annual box office gross total is USD 16.7 billion (2018), the largest across all continents/regions.[46] Moreover, high-quality local Asian products, mainly from powerful regional filmmaking forces such as Japan, South Korea, India and the rapidly emerging industries in Southeast Asia, have flowed outward to global film markets to connect the region with international audiences through commercial cinemas, art theaters, major international film festivals, and digital platforms. Filmmakers and producers around the world, including in the United States, Europe, and Asia, increasingly look to China to expand their audiences and find new coproduction partners.

Shaw Brothers, after a long hiatus in filmmaking that began in 1986, opened its newest and largest digital postproduction studio in Asia in Tseung Kwan O, Hong Kong in 2005. Strategically situated at the gateway to China, only thirty kilometers away from Shenzhen, this new studio aims to be a "post-production mecca for Hong Kong–China coproduction films."[47] In addition, Chinese media conglomerates have been recruiting regional talent, particularly technicians, performers, and creative personnel, and buying out film and media companies, theaters, and TV stations in the region and beyond. Asia's film industry as a whole is experiencing a significant transformation, spearheaded by the rapid development of Chinese cinema. The Chinese film industry, more confident than ever, no longer needs to rely on the investments and creative forces of foreign media companies. With the size and volume of its domestic market, the Chinese film industry dreams of constructing its own version of Hollywood, "Chinawood."[48]

Meanwhile, in February 2020, the South Korean director Bong Joon-ho's *Parasite* (*Kisaengch'ung*, 2019) became the first foreign language film to win Best Picture at the Oscars, and swept other major awards including Best Director, Screenplay, and International Feature, after winning the Palme d'Or at the Cannes in May 2019. At Cannes, the Korean Film Commission, under its new president, O Sŏk-kŭn, unveiled and launched an ambitious plan, the ASEAN–Republic of Korea Film Organization.[49] The ten ASEAN countries, including Indonesia, Malaysia, Thailand, Cambodia, Vietnam, Myanmar, the Philippines, and Singapore, are joining hands to create this pan-Asian film organization. Japan and China are not involved in the new network.[50] Busan, home of the Busan International Film Festival, will be its headquarters. The Busan International Film Festival will provide the platform where the ASEAN film artists, executives, and government officials meet, discuss, and collaborate each year.[51] While China dreams of Chinawood, South Korean cinema aspires to position itself as a hub of the ASEAN film industry. Will both South Korea and China achieve their dreams? Are we witnessing the birth of a new Asian cinema network in the age of neoliberalism? Only time will tell.

Appendix

Suggestions for Further Reading

US Foreign Aid and Philanthropic Organizations

Berman, Edward H. *The Influence of the Carnegie, Ford, and Rockefeller Foundations on American Foreign Policy: The Ideology of Philanthropy*. Albany: State University of New York Press, 1983.

Bremner, Robert H. *American Philanthropy*. Chicago: University of Chicago Press, 1960.

Fleishman, Joel L. *The Foundation: A Great American Secret; How Private Wealth is Changing the World*. New York: Public Affairs, 2007.

Zunz, Olivier. *Philanthropy in America: A History*. Princeton, NJ: Princeton University Press, 2012.

US Diplomacy and the Cultural Cold War

Ansari, Emily Abrams. *The Sound of a Superpower: Musical Americanism and the Cold War*. New York: Oxford University Press, 2018.

Castillo, Greg. *Cold War on the Home Front: The Soft Power of Midcentury Design*. Minneapolis: University of Minnesota Press, 2010.

Davenport, Lisa E. *Jazz Diplomacy: Promoting America in the Cold War Era*. Jackson: University Press of Mississippi, 2009.

Von Eschen, Penny M. *Satchmo Blows Up the World: Jazz Ambassadors Play the Cold War*. Cambridge: Harvard University Press, 2006.

Fosler-Lussier, Danielle. *Music in America's Cold War Diplomacy*. Oakland: University of California Press, 2015.

Kodat, Catherine Gunther. *Don't Act, Just Dance: The Metapolitics of Cold War Culture*. New Brunswick, NJ: Rutgers University Press, 2015.

Prevots, Naima. *Dance for Exports: Cultural Diplomacy and the Cold War*. Middletown: Wesleyan University Press, 1999.

Wagnleitner, Reinhold. *Coca-Colonization and the Cold War: The Cultural Mission of the United States in Austria after the Second World War*. Translated by Diana M. Wolf. Chapel Hill: University of North Carolina Press, 1994.

More recently, scholars have emphasized the ways sports influenced and were influenced by Cold War politics. See:

Parks, Jenifer. *The Olympic Games, the Soviet Sports Bureaucracy, and the Cold War: Red Sport, Red Tape*. Lanham: Lexington Books, 2017.

Redihan, Erin Elizabeth. *The Olympics and the Cold War, 1948–1968: Sport as Battleground in the U.S.-Soviet Rivalry*. Jefferson: McFarland & Company, 2017.

Rider, Tony C. *Cold War Games: Propaganda, the Olympics, and U.S. Foreign Policy*. Champaign: University of Illinois Press, 2016.

Rider, Toby C., and Kevin B. Witherspoon, eds. *Defending the American Way of Life: Sport, Culture, and the Cold War*. Fayetteville: University of Arkansas Press, 2018.

Witherspoon, Kevin B. *Before the Eyes of the World: Mexico and the 1968 Olympic Games*. Dekalb: Northern Illinois University Press, 2014.

US radio propaganda (Radio Free Europe/Radio Liberty) during the Truman-Eisenhower and the histories of the Voice of America (VOA) are well discussed in the following volumes:

Johnson, A. Ross. *Radio Free Europe and Radio Liberty: The CIA Years and Beyond*. Washington, DC: Woodrow Wilson Center, 2010.

Krugler, David F. *The Voice of America and the Domestic Propaganda Battles, 1945–1953*. Columbia: University of Missouri Press, 2000.

Machcewicz, Paweł. *Poland's War on Radio Free Europe, 1950–1989*. Washington, DC: Woodrow Wilson Center, 2014.

Puddington, Arch. *Broadcasting Freedom: The Cold War Triumph of Radio Free Europe and Radio Liberty*. Lexington: University Press of Kentucky, 2000.

Urban, George R. *Radio Free Europe and the Pursuit of Democracy: My War Within the Cold War*. New Haven: Yale University Press, 1997.

The Cold War in Asia

Aldrich, Richard J., Gary D. Rawnsley, and Ming-Yeh T. Rawnsley, eds. *The Clandestine Cold War in Asia, 1945–1965: Western Intelligence, Propaganda and Special Operations*. London: Frank Cass, 2005.

Ang, Cheng Guan. *Southeast Asia's Cold War: An Interpretive History*. Honolulu: University of Hawaii Press, 2018.

Chou, Grace Ai-Ling. *Confucianism, Colonialism, and the Cold War: Chinese Cultural Education and Hong Kong's New Asia College*. Leiden: Brill, 2011.

Cullather, Nick. *The Hungry World: America's Cold War Battle against Poverty in Asia*. Cambridge, MA: Harvard University Press; Reprint edition, 2013.

Elliott, Oliver. *The American Press and the Cold War: The Rise of Authoritarianism in South Korea, 1945–1954*. New York: Palgrave Macmillan, 2018.

Friedman, Jeremy. *Shadow Cold War: The Sino-Soviet Competition for the Third World*. Chapel Hill: University of North Carolina Press, 2015.

Goscha, Christopher E., and Christian F. Ostermann. *Connecting Histories: Decolonization and the Cold War in Southeast Asia, 1945–1962*. Stanford, CA: Stanford University Press, 2009.

Hajimu, Masuda. *Cold War Crucible: The Korean Conflict and the Postwar World*. Cambridge, MA: Harvard University Press, 2015.

Kim, Charles R. *Youth for Nation: Culture and Protest in Cold War South Korea*. Honolulu: University of Hawaii Press, 2017.

Koikari, Mire. *Cold War Encounters in US-Occupied Okinawa: Women, Militarized Domesticity, and Transnationalism in East Asia*. Cambridge: Cambridge University Press, 2015.

Kwon, Heonik. *The Other Cold War*. New York: Columbia University Press, 2010.

Lee, Steven H. *Outposts of Empire: Korea, Vietnam, and the Origins of the Cold War in Asia, 1949–1954*. Montreal: McGill-Queen's University Press, 1996.

Li, Xiaobing. *The Cold War in East Asia*. New York: Routledge, 2018.

McGarr, Paul M. *The Cold War in South Asia: Britain, the United States and the Indian Subcontinent, 1945–1965*. Cambridge: Cambridge University Press, 2013.

Miller, Jennifer M. *Cold War Democracy: The United States and Japan*. Cambridge, MA: Harvard University Press, 2019.

Mizuno, Hiromi, Aaron S. Moore, and John DiMoia, eds. *Engineering Asia: Technology, Colonial Development and the Cold War Order*. London: Bloomsbury, 2018.

Murfett, Malcolm H., ed. *Cold War Southeast Asia*. Singapore: Marshall Cavendish, 2012.

Ngoei, Wen-Qing. *Arc of Containment: Britain, the United States, and Anticommunism in Southeast Asia*. Ithaca, NY: Cornell University Press, 2019.

Oh, Arissa H. *To Save the Children of Korea: The Cold War Origins of International Adoption*. Stanford, CA: Stanford University Press, 2015.

Phillips, Matthew. *Thailand in the Cold War*. New York: Routledge, 2015.

Roberts, Priscilla, and John M. Carroll, eds. *Hong Kong in the Cold War*. Hong Kong: Hong Kong University Press, 2016.

Schaller, Michael. *The American Occupation of Japan: The Origins of the Cold War in Asia*. New York: Oxford University Press, 1987.

Vu, Tuong, and Wasana Wongsurawat, eds. *Dynamics of the Cold War in Asia: Ideology, Identity, and Culture*. New York: Palgrave Macmillan, 2009.

Zhou, Taomo. *Migration in the Time of Revolution: China, Indonesia, and the Cold War*. Ithaca: NY: Cornell University Press, 2019.

Hollywood and the Cultural Cold War

Carruthers, Susan L. *Cold War Captives: Imprisonment, Escape, and Brainwashing.* Berkeley: University of California Press, 2009.

Corber, Robert J. *Cold War Femme: Lesbianism, National Identity, and Hollywood Cinema.* Durham: Duke University Press, 2014.

Dick, Bernard F. *The Screen Is Red: Hollywood, Communism, and the Cold War.* Jackson: University Press of Mississippi, 2016.

Doherty, Thomas. *Cold War, Cool Medium: Television, McCarthyism, and American Culture.* New York: Columbia University Press, 2003.

——. *Show Trial: Hollywood, HUAC, and the Birth of the Blacklist.* New York: Columbia University Press, 2018.

Frost, Jennifer. *Producer of Controversy: Stanley Kramer, Hollywood Liberalism, and the Cold War.* Lexington: University Press of Kentucky, 2017.

Hoberman, Jim. *An Army of Phantoms: American Movies and the Making of the Cold War.* New York: The New Press, 2012.

Prime, Rebecca. *Hollywood Exiles in Europe: The Blacklist and Cold War Film Culture.* New Brunswick: Rutgers University Press, 2014.

Smith, Jeff. *Film Criticism, the Cold War, and the Blacklist: Reading the Hollywood Reds.* Berkeley: University of California Press, 2014.

Upton, Bryn. *Hollywood and the End of the Cold War: Signs of Cinematic Change.* Lanham: Rowman & Littlefield, 2014.

Asian Cinema and the Cultural Cold War

Fu, Poshek, and Man-Fung Yip, eds. *The Cold War and Asian Cinemas.* London: Routledge, 2020.

Hee, Wai Siam. *Remapping the Sinophone: The Cultural Production of Chinese-language Cinema in Singapore and Malaya Before and During the Cold War.* Hong Kong: Hong Kong University Press, 2019.

Hirano, Kyoko. *Mr. Smith Goes to Tokyo: Japanese Cinema Under the American Occupation, 1945–1952.* Washington: Smithsonian Institution Press, 1992.

Hughes, Theodore. *Literature and Film in Cold War South Korea: Freedom's Frontier.* New York: Columbia University Press, 2014.

Klein, Christina. *Cold War Cosmopolitanism: Period Style in 1950s Korean Cinema.* Berkeley: University of California Press, 2020.

Taylor, Jeremy E. *Rethinking Transnational Chinese Cinemas: The Amoy-dialect Film Industry in Cold War Asia.* London: Routledge, 2011.

Transnational History of Asian Cinema

Chan, Kenneth. *Remade in Hollywood: The Global Chinese Presence in Transnational Cinemas.* Hong Kong: Hong Kong University Press, 2009.

Chung, Hye Seung, and David Scott Diffrient. *Movie Migrations: Transnational Genre Flows and South Korean Cinema*. New Brunswick, NJ: Rutgers University Press, 2015).

DeBoer, Stephanie. *Coproducing Asia: Locating Japanese—Chinese Regional Film and Media*. Minneapolis: University of Minnesota Press, 2014.

Van der Heide, William. *Malaysian Cinema, Asian Film: Border Crossings and National Cultures*. Amsterdam: Amsterdam University Press, 2002.

Lu, Sheldon, ed. *Transnational Chinese Cinemas: Identity, Nationhood, Gender*. Honolulu: University of Hawaii Press, 1997.

Nornes, Abé Mark. *Cinema Babel: Translating Global Cinema*. Minneapolis: University of Minnesota Press, 2007.

Tezuka, Yoshiharu. *Japanese Cinema Goes Global: Filmworkers' Journeys*. Hong Kong: Hong Kong University Press, 2011.

Wang, Yiman. *Remaking Chinese Cinema: Through the Prism of Shanghai, Hong Kong, and Hollywood*. Honolulu: University of Hawaii Press, 2013.

Film Festivals in Asia

Ahn, SooJeong. *The Pusan International Film Festival, South Korean Cinema and Globalization*. Hong Kong: Hong Kong University Press, 2011.

Berry, Chris, and Luke Robinson, eds. *Chinese Film Festivals: Sites of Translation*. New York: Palgrave Macmillan, 2017.

Cazzaro, Davide, and Darcy Paquet. *BIFF x BIFF*. Busan: Busan International Film Festival, 2015.

Iordanova, Dina, and Ruby Cheung, eds. *Film Festival Yearbook 3: Film Festivals and East Asia*. St. Andrews: University of St. Andrews Press, 2011.

Notes

Introduction

1. *SOS Hong Kong* was released in Hong Kong on August 26, 1967, under a different title, *The International Secret Agent (Guo ji nu jian die)*.

2. See Jin-kyung Lee, "Surrogate Military, Subimperialism, and Masculinity: South Korea in the Vietnam War, 1965–73," *Positions: Asia Critique* 17, no. 3 (2009): 655–82.

3. For more about *SOS Hong Kong*, see Sangjoon Lee, "Destination Hong Kong: The Geopolitics of South Korean Espionage Films in the 1960s," *Journal of Korean Studies* 22, no. 1 (2017): 346–64.

4. Chŏng Chong-hyŏn, "'Taedonga' wa sŭp'ai—Kim Naesŏng changp'yŏn sosŏl 'T'aep'ung' ŭl t'onghae pon 'Taedonga' ŭi simsang chiri wa 'Chosŏn'" ["'The Greater East Asia" and spy-imaginative geography of "the Greater East Asia" and "Joseon" from the viewpoint of *Typhoon*], *Taejung sŏsa yŏn'gu* 15, no. 2 (2009): 211–47.

5. Quoted in Zbigniew Brzezinski, "The Politics of Underdevelopment," *World Politics* 9, no. 1 (1956): 55.

6. According to Bruce Cumings, "We [America] do run a territorial empire—the archipelago of somewhere between 737 and 860 overseas military installations around the world, with American military personnel operating in 153 countries, which most Americans know little if anything about—a kind of stealth empire." See Bruce Cumings, *Dominion from Sea to Sea: Pacific Ascendancy and American Power* (New Haven, CT: Yale University Press, 2010), 393.

7. For more about the Greater East Asian Film Sphere and its impact during (and after) Japan's imperial adventure, see Janine Hansen, "The New Earth: A German-Japanese Misalliance in Film," in *In Praise of Film Studies: Essays in Honor of Makino Mamoru*, ed. Aaron Gerow and Abé Mark

Nornes (Yokohama and Ann Arbor, MI: A Kinema Club Publication, 2001), 184–97; Brian Yecies and Ae-Gyung Shim, Korea's *Occupied Cinemas, 1893–1948* (London: Routledge, 2009); Hikari Hori, *Promiscuous Media: Film and Visual Culture in Imperial Japan, 1926–1945* (Ithaca, NY: Cornell University Press, 2017); Kate Taylor-Jones, *Divine Work, Japanese Colonial Cinema and Its Legacy* (New York: Bloomsbury, 2017); and Dong Hoon Kim, *Eclipsed Cinema: The Film Culture of Colonial Korea* (Edinburgh: Edinburgh University Press, 2017).

8. Abé Mark Nornes, "The Creation and Construction of Asian Cinema Redux," *Film History* 25, no. 1–2 (2013): 181.

9. Sangjoon Lee, "Creating an Anti-Communist Motion Picture Producers' Network in Asia: The Asia Foundation, Asia Pictures, and the Korean Motion Picture Cultural Association," *Historical Journal of Film, Radio and Television* 37, no. 3 (2017): 517–38.

10. The FPA changed its official name twice—from the Federation of Motion Picture Producers in Southeast Asia to the Federation of Motion Picture Producers in Asia in 1957; "Asia" then became "Asia Pacific" in 1983.

11. Cindy Hing-Yuk Wong, "Film Festivals and the Global Projection of Hong Kong Cinema," in *Hong Kong Film, Hollywood and the New Global Cinema: No Film Is an Island*, ed. Gina Marchetti and Tan See Kam (London: Routledge, 2007), 181; Poshek Fu, "The Shaw Brothers' Diasporic Cinema," in *China Forever: The Shaw Brothers and Diasporic Cinema*, ed. Poshek Fu (Urbana: University of Illinois Press, 2008), 11.

12. Kim Kwan-soo, "Asea yŏnghwaje" [Asian Film Festival], *Kyŏnghyang shinmun*, June 19, 1956, 6.

13. Kinnia Yau Shuk-ting, "Shaws' Japanese Collaboration and Competition as Seen Through the Asian Film Festival Evolution," in *The Shaw Screen: A Preliminary Study*, ed. Wong Ain-ling (Hong Kong: Hong Kong Film Archive, 2003), 279–91; Sangjoon Lee, "The Emergence of the Asian Film Festival: Cold War Asia and Japan's Re-entrance to the Regional Market in the 1950s," in *The Oxford Handbook of Japanese Cinema*, ed. Miyao Daisuke (Oxford: Oxford University Press, 2013), 232–50; and Sangjoon Lee, "It's 'Oscar' Time in Asia!: the Rise and Demise of the Asian Film Festival, 1954–1972," in *Coming Soon to a Festival Near You: Programming Film Festivals*, ed. Jeffrey Ruoff (St. Andrews: St. Andrews University Press, 2012), 173–87.

14. *Asia-Pacific Film Festival 50th Anniversary Catalogue* (Kuala Lumpur, Malaysia: Ministry of Culture, 2005).

15. Julian Stringer, who wrote a dissertation on film festivals in 2003, begins his introduction by citing Paul Willemen: "So little work has been published on the role of film festivals in film culture that no knowledge whatsoever of the basic criteria with which to assess festivals can be taken for granted. Not ever amongst readers of specialized film journals." (Paul Willemen, "Pesaro: The Limitations and Strengths of a Cultural Policy," *Framework: A Film Journal* 15/16/17 (Summer 1981): 96. Cited in Julian Stringer, "Regarding Film Festivals" (PhD diss., Indiana University, 2003), 1.) Stringer then claims that in the time between when Willemen's article appeared in 1981 and the time Stringer completed his dissertation, no significant works on film festivals had been written. Since then, film festival studies have blossomed. Most of the literature, however, still focuses on European film festivals. Works that take a cinema studies approach to film festivals in Asia are therefore sparse and scattered, and Asia remains one of the least researched areas in the field.

16. Kenneth Osgood, *Total Cold War: Eisenhower's Secret Propaganda Battle at Home and Abroad* (Lawrence: University Press of Kansas, 2006); Laura A. Belmonte, *Selling the American Way: U.S. Propaganda and the Cold War* (Philadelphia: University of Pensylvania Press, 2008).

17. Frances Stonor Saunders, *The Cultural Cold War: The CIA and the World of Arts and Letters* (New York: The New Press, 2001). It was originally published in the UK under the title *Who Paid the Piper?: The CIA and the Cultural Cold War* (London: Granta Books, 1999).

18. Greg Barnhisel, *Cold War Modernists: Art, Literature, and American Cultural Diplomacy* (New York: Columbia University Press, 2015).

19. Tony Shaw, *Hollywood's Cold War* (Amherst: University of Massachusetts Press, 2007); Tony Shaw, *British Cinema and the Cold War* (London: I.B. Tauris, 2006).

20. Andrew J. Falk, *Upstaging the Cold War: American Dissent and Cultural Diplomacy, 1940–1960* (Amherst: University of Massachusetts Press, 2010); John Sbardellati, *J. Edgar Hoover Goes to the Movies: The FBI and the Origins of Hollywood's Cold War* (Ithaca, NY: Cornell University Press, 2012).

21. See Reinhold Wagnleitner, "American Cultural Diplomacy, Hollywood, and the Cold War in Central Europe," *Rethinking Marxism* 7, no. 1 (Spring 1994): 31–47; Nehzih Erdogan and Dilek Kaya, "Institutional Intervention in the Distribution and Exhibition of Hollywood Films in Turkey," *Historical Journal of Film, Radio and Television* 22, no. 1 (2002): 47–59; Pablo Leon Aguinaga, "State-Corporate Relations, Film Trade and the Cold War: The Failure of MPEAA's Strategy in Spain," *Historical Journal of Film, Radio and Television* 29, no. 4 (2009): 483–504; and Jindriska Blahova, "A Merry Twinkle in Stalin's Eye: Eric Johnston, Hollywood, and Eastern Europe," *Film History* 22, no. 3 (2010): 347–59. Regarding Hollywood vs. the Soviet Union during the Cold War, see James H. Krukones, "The Unspooling of Artkino: Soviet Film Distribution in America, 1940–1975," *Historical Journal of Film, Radio and Television* 29, no. 1 (2009): 91–112 and Sergei Zhuk, "Hollywood's Insidious Charms: The Impact of American Cinema and Television on the Soviet Union During the Cold War," *Cold War History* 14, no. 4 (2014): 593–617.

22. Charles K. Armstrong, "The Cultural Cold War in Korea, 1945–1950," *Journal of Asian Studies* 62, no. 1 (2003): 71–99.

23. Although "globalization" has become a buzzword in contemporary film studies, Asian film history largely remains the standard approach for examining language, culture, and national identity in film culture. If I do not consider edited volumes, only a handful of book-length studies have scrutinized the border-crossing and transnational history of Asian cinema. See Transnational History of Asian Cinema in the appendix to this book.

Chapter 1. The Asia Foundation's Motion Picture Project

1. Charles M. Tanner, "Trip to Hollywood," Japan Tokyo-Movies 1953, Box 9, Asia Foundation Records, Hoover Institution Archive, Stanford University (hereafter AFR).

2. Alsop (1900–1979) was an advertising agent and agent to the stars. He was Judy Garland's manager during the 1940s and 1950s. Alsop was a member of the CIA's Psychological Warfare Workshop and had been sent by the agency to secure the film rights to *Animal Farm* from George Orwell's widow in 1950. See Shaw, *British Cinema and the Cold War*, 94.

3. Frances Stonor Saunders has argued that Alsop was an ex-CIA agent and had been working "undercover" at Paramount during the 1950s. David N. Eldridge, however, has accused Saunders of misinterpreting Alsop's role and status in the industry. Eldridge found that it was Luigi Luraschi whose role and influence at Paramount meshed "perfectly with the interests of the CIA." See Saunders, *The Cultural Cold War*, 290–91; David N. Eldridge, "'Dear Owen': The CIA, Luigi Luraschi and Hollywood, 1953," *Historical Journal of Film, Radio and Television* 20, no. 2 (2000): 149–96.

4. To avoid unnecessary confusion, this book will refer to the Asia Foundation unless the Committee for a Free Asia itself is the subject of the discussion.

5. Cho Tong-jae and Park Tae-jin, *Partner for Change: 50 Years of The Asia Foundation in Korea, 1954–2004* (Seoul, Korea: The Asia Foundation, 2004), 13.

6. Y. Frank Freeman, president of the MPAA and vice president of Paramount Pictures, wrote in a letter to Nagata, "MPAA would deem it an honor if your Federation would consider a suggestion for a special award to be given at your festival. We would be pleased to make this award to the producer of a film which you would select as best disseminating Asian culture and increasing understanding of Asia by the western nations." A Letter to Nagata from Freeman, April 8, 1954, Film Festivals General 1951/54, Box 14, AFR.

7. On DeMille's anticommunist activities, see Saunders, *The Cultural Cold War*, 288–90; Falk, *Upstaging the Cold War*, 116–67; Hugh Wilford, *The Mighty Wurlitzer: How the CIA Played America* (Cambridge, MA: Harvard University Press, 2008), 116–17; and David Caute, *The Dancer Defects: The Struggle for Cultural Supremacy During the Cold War* (Oxford: Oxford University Press, 2003), 177–81.

8. Cited in Caute, *The Dancer Defects*, 180.

9. "Cecil B. DeMille 1940–1959," February 5, 1952, Hedda Hopper Papers, Folder 1107, Box 46, Special Collections, Academy of Motion Pictures Arts and Sciences, Margaret Herrick Library, Los Angeles, California (hereafter AMPAS).

10. "Films and Shows of the First Festival," *Indian Review* 53 (April 1952): 151.

11. Enakshi Bhavnani, "The International Film Festival," *March of India* 4, no. 4 (March–April 1952): 5–7.

12. Panna Raiji praised *Yukiwarisoo* as one of the finest films screened during the festival. He wrote, "It is such an outstanding film that it is unfortunate that the entries from Japan were not numerous enough to enable one to form an idea of the usual standard of production in that country. If, however, this picture is any criterion, film art in Japan has, indeed, reached a high level of perfection." Panna Raiji, "Some Outstanding Films," *March of India* 4, no. 4 (March–April 1952): 8.

13. K. L. Khandpur, "First International Film Festival of India," in *70 Years of Indian Cinema (1913–1983)*, ed. T. M. Ramachandran (Bombay: CINEMA India-International, 1984), 581.

14. Kishore Valicha, *The Moving Image: A Study of Indian Cinema* (Hyderabad, India: Orient Longman, 1988), 127. For instance, Bimal Roy wrote during the festival, "I watched *The Bicycle Thieves* by Vittorio De Sica and on the way back kept thinking about it. Why can't we make such films?" Quoted in Manoj Srivastava, *Wide Angle: History of Indian Cinema* (Chennai, India: Norton Press, 2016), 21.

15. Tanner, "Trip to Hollywood," AFR. Raj Kapoor reminisced, "Three Italians visited the 1952 film festival in Bombay: Roberto Rossellini, Vittorio De Sica and Cesare Zavatini . . . Frank Capra was in India for the festival and I had long talk with him [sic]." Ritu Nanda, *Raj Kapoor: Speaks* (New Delhi, India: Viking Penguin Books India, 2002), 122.

16. Bhavnani, "The International Film Festival," 7.

17. Joseph McBride, *Frank Capra: The Catastrophe of Success* (Jackson: University Press of Mississippi, 2011), 591.

18. Khandpur, "First International Film Festival of India," 581.

19. Nitin Govil, *Orienting Hollywood: A Century of Film Culture Between Los Angeles and Bombay* (New York: NYU Press, 2015), 162.

20. Laura E. Ruberto and Kristi M. Wilson, "Introduction," in *Italian Neorealism and Global Cinema*, ed. Laura E. Ruberto and Kristi M. Wilson (Detroit, MI: Wayne State University Press, 2007), 22.

21. Two years later, in September 1954, the first Indian film festival opened in Moscow. For more about this festival, see Sudha Rajagopalan, "Emblematic of the Thaw: Early Indian Films in Soviet Cinemas," *South Asian Popular Culture* 4, no. 2 (2006): 83–100.

22. Frank Capra, *The Name above the Title: An Autobiography* (New York: Macmillan Company, 1971), 432.

23. "Cecil B. DeMille 1940–1959," AMPAS.

24. Tanner, "Trip to Hollywood," AFR.

25. Transcribed report of "Federation of Motion Picture Producers of Southeast Asia: Organization and Preparation Conference," November 17–19, 1953, Film Festivals General 1951/54, Box 14, AFR.

26. Foreign Affairs and National Defense Division, *The Asia Foundation: Past, Present, and Future. Official Report Prepared for the Committee on Foreign Relations United States Senate* (Washington, DC, 1983), 1.

27. Wilford, *The Mighty Wurlitzer*, 3–4.

28. Wallace Turner, "Asia Foundation got CIA Funds," *New York Times*, March 22, 1967, 1. See also Sol Stern, "A Short Account of International Student Politics and the Cold War with Particular Reference to the NSA, CIA, etc.," *Ramparts* 5, no. 9 (March 1967): 29–39.

29. Victor Marchetti and John D. Marks, *The CIA and the Cult of Intelligence* (New York: Knops, 1974), 172.

30. Robert Blum, "The Work of The Asia Foundation," *Public Affairs* 29, no. 1 (1956): 47.

31. Brayton Wilbur was a founder of the San Francisco–based Wilbur-Ellis Co. and served as its president until his son, Brayton Wilbur Jr., took over the company in 1988. Wilbur Jr. also served as chairman of the board of TAF in the 1970s, as well as director of the San Francisco Opera, a trustee of the Asian Art Museum, and the fifth president of the San Francisco Symphony. See "Brayton Wilbur, Sr.," The Asia Foundation website, accessed April 26, 2018, https://asiafoundation.org/people/brayton-wilbur-sr/.

32. "Background Memorandum," *Committee for a Free Asia Newsletter*, September 28, 1951, Committee for a Free Asia, Box 37, C.

33. Central Intelligence Agency, "Project DTPILLAR," November 9, 1950, available online via the CIA library at https://www.cia.gov/library/readingroom/docs/DTPILLAR%20%20%20 VOL.%202_0052.pdf, accessed February 8, 2020.

34. "Background Information: Committee for a Free Asia," February 19, 1953, Committee for a Free Asia, Box 37, Alfred Kohlberg Collection, Hoover Institution Archive, Stanford University (hereafter AKC).

35. DeWitt Clinton Poole Jr. was an American diplomat who was also a spymaster during the Russian Bolshevik revolution of 1917. He was known as an expert in anticommunist propaganda and psychological and political warfare. Born on October 28, 1885, at a US Army post near Vancouver, Washington, he was the consulate general in Moscow during the revolution. In his long political career, Poole served as director of the State Department's Division of Russian Affairs, chairman of the advisory board of the School of Public and International Affairs, the head of the Foreign Nationalities Branch (FNB), special representative of the US secretary of state to Germany, and a member of the CFE. From 1951 until he retired in April 1952, Poole was the president of the Free Europe University in Exile. See "DeWitt Poole Dies; Retired Diplomat," *New York Times*, September 4, 1952.

36. Robert T. Holt, *Radio Free Europe* (Minneapolis, MN: University of Minnesota Press, 1958), 11.

37. Elena Aronova, "The Congress for Cultural Freedom, *Minerva*, and the Quest for Instituting 'Science Studies' in the Age of Cold War," *Minerva* 50 (2012): 308.

38. Michael Hochgeschwender, however, claims that *Der Monat* was different from other CCF magazines, as *Der Monat* was not established by the CCF and the magazine was neither directly nor indirectly funded by the CCF (or the CIA). See Michael Hochgeschwender, "*Der Monat* and the Congress for Cultural Freedom: The High Tide of the Intellectual Cold War, 1948–1971," in *Campaigning Culture and the Global Cold War: The Journals of the Congress for Cultural Freedom*, ed. Giles Scott-Smith and Charlotte A. Lerg (London: Palgrave MacMillan, 2017), 71–89.

39. Elena Aronova, "The Congress for Cultural Freedom," 308.

40. Hugh Wilford, "'Unwitting Asset?': British Intellectuals and the Congress for Cultural Freedom," *Twentieth Century British History* 11, no. 1 (2000): 43.

41. Holt, *Radio Free Europe*, 3–4.

42. Arch Puddington, *Broadcasting Freedom: The Cold War Triumph of Radio Free Europe and Radio Liberty* (Lexington, University Press of Kentucky, 2000), 20-32

43. "Questions and Answers," March 13, 1951, Committee for a Free Asia, Box 37, AKC.

44. I would like to sincerely thank Christina Klein, who kindly shared the existence of the DTPILLAR documents with me.

45. Frank G. Wisner was "chief of OSS operations in the central Balkans during the latter stages of the war and the man responsible for implementing the CIA's earliest covert operations." Wilford, *The Mighty Wurlitzer*, 19.

46. Central Intelligence Agency, "Project DTPILLAR," November 9, 1950.

47. The Office of Policy Coordination (OPC) was a United States covert psychological operations organization, created in 1948. OPC was merged with the CIA in 1951.

48. Central Intelligence Agency, "Project DTPILLAR," November 9, 1950.

49. "Committee for a Free Asia, Programs and Planning," September 26, 1951, available via Archive.org at https://archive.org/details/DTPILLARVOL.10040, accessed February 8, 2020.

50. Inderjeet Parmar, *Foundations of the American Century: The Ford, Carnegie, and Rockefeller Foundations in the Rise of American Power* (New York: Columbia University Press), 2012, 124.

51. "A Personal Statement on Your Memorandum of July 12th, concerning Appointment of a resident for Committee for a Free Asia," July 20, 1951, Committee for a Free Asia, Box 37, AKC.

52. "Committee for a Free Asia, Programs and Planning."

53. "The temporary closing of the London financial market after the eruption of the First World War made New York the center of international finance . . . European money flowed into New York markets, and America gradually replaced Britain as the largest financial power in the world. . . . The National City Bank of New York was inaugurated in 1915, after acquiring majority shares of the International Banking Corporation, and rapidly became one of the largest banks in Shanghai" (152–53). Zhaojin Li, *A History of Modern Shanghai Banking: The Rise and Decline of China's Finance Capitalism* (London: Routledge, 2003), 152–53. Li's book is the fascinating history of Shanghai's modern banking from the early twentieth century to the founding of the republic in 1949.

54. "Background Memorandum."

55. In a memorandum for the assistant director for policy coordination, whose name is erased on the declassified document, Greene's secretary Leila White provided security guidelines for recruiting new officers: "The officers of DTPILLAR [CFA] and other employees who will have a knowledge of the fact that this is a CIA sponsored organization and that CIA funds are being utilized for the operation of this organization will require a covert security clearance from I&SS in advance of their employment and in advance of their knowledge of this information." "Recommended Financial Plan for OPC Proprietary Project DTPILLAR," March 1, 1951, available online via the CIA library at https://www.cia.gov/library/readingroom/docs/DTPILLAR%20%20%20 VOL.%201_0097.pdf, accessed February 8, 2020.

56. Interestingly enough, Brayton Wilbur served as a trustee of Lingnan University of Canton from 1951 to 1954. For more about Lingnan University, see Steve Tung Au, *Lingnan Spirit Forever— A Mission in Transition, 1951–1990: From the Trustees of Lingnan University to the Lingnan Foundation* (New Haven, CT: Lingnan Foundation, 2002), available online at http://commons.ln.edu.hk/cgi/viewcontent.cgi?article=1029&context=lingnan_history_bks. "Committee For A Free Asia," dates unknown, available online via the CIA library, https://www.cia.gov/library/readingroom/docs/DTPILLAR%20%20%20VOL.%201_0001.pdf, accessed February 8, 2020.

57. Richard H. Cummings, *Radio Free Europe's "Crusade for Freedom": Rallying Americans Behind Cold War Broadcasting, 1950–1960* (Jefferson, NC: McFarland and Company, 2010), 52.

58. Greg Barnhisel points out that VOA focused little on art and culture, "filling most of its airtime with news, descriptions of American politics and society, and anti-Communist propaganda." See Greg Barnhisel, *Cold War Modernists*, 217.

59. "Questions and Answers"; "Radio Free Asia," November 20, 1951, Committee for a Free Asia, Box 37, AKC.

60. Cummings, *Radio Free Europe's Crusade for Freedom*, 52.

61. "Elwood Made Director of Radio Free Asia," *Palo Alto Times*, July 20, 1951.

62. "News From Radio Free Asia," September 2, 1951, Committee for a Free Asia, Box 37, AKC.

63. "Background Information: Committee for a Free Asia."

64. "John W. Elwood Tells: How Crusade for Freedom Monies Aid Europe, Asia," *Palo Alto Times*, March 1, 1952.

65. A Letter from Philip Horton to Allen Dulles, June 6, 1951, available online via Archive.org, https://archive.org/stream/DTPILLAR/DTPILLAR%20%20%20VOL.%201_0069#page/n0/mode/2up, accessed February 8, 2020.

66. Cummings, *Radio Free Europe's Crusade for Freedom*, 98.

67. "CFA Budget for FY 1955," June 25, 1954, available online via the CIA library, https://www.cia.gov/library/readingroom/docs/DTPILLAR%20%20%20VOL.%202_0034.pdf, accessed February 8, 2020.

68. "The Committee for a Free Asia," January 2, 1952, available online via Archive.org, https://archive.org/stream/DTPILLAR/DTPILLAR%20%20%20VOL.%201_0017#page/n0/mode/2up, accessed February 8, 2020.

69. After graduating from Swarthmore College in 1921, Valentine received his master's degree from the University of Pennsylvania in 1922. He was awarded LLD degrees from Syracuse, Amherst, and Union Universities (1935); Rutgers (1936); Swarthmore (1937); Denison University (1940); Lake Forrest College (1942); Allegheny College (1943); and Colgate (1944). He held an LHD from Hubbard College (1936) and a DLitt from Alfred University (1937). Before coming to Rochester, Valentine was a professor in the History, Arts, and Letters Department of Yale University (1932–35) ("Background Data: Alan Valentine," Information from the Committee for a Free Asia, December 11, 1951, Committee for a Free Asia, Box 37, AKC).

70. A Letter From Wilbur to Allen Dulles, June 13, 1951, Committee for a Free Asia, Box 37, AKC.

71. George Greene, "Dear Dick," November 29, 1951, available online via the CIA library, https://www.cia.gov/library/readingroom/docs/DTPILLAR%20%20%20VOL.%201_0029.pdf, accessed February 8, 2020.

72. Paul G. Pierpaoli, Jr., *Truman and Korea: The Political Culture of the Early Cold War* (Columbia: University of Missouri Press, 1999),73.

73. "News from The Committee for a Free Asia," December 11, 1951, Committee for a Free Asia (1951–1953), Box 4, Inez G. Richardson Collection, Hoover Institution Archive, Stanford University.

74. "Comparison Progress as of January 1, 1952 and August 1, 1952," August 1, 1952, Committee for a Free Asia, Box 37, AKC.

75. The field office representatives were Delmer M. Brown (Hong Kong), Robert B. Sheeks (Kuala Lumpur), Marvin A. McAlister (Rangoon), Fred A. Schuckman (Manila), Noel F. Busch (Tokyo), Samuel H. Rickard (Karachi), John Glover (Colombo), and Ward D. Smith (Taipei). "Administrative Memorandum No. 1: Reorganization," Committee for a Free Asia, February 19, 1953, Committee for a Free Asia folder, Box 37, AKC.

76. "CFA Budget for FY 1955."

77. For example, Delmer Brown, professor of Japanese studies at the University of California, Berkeley, served as the Tokyo representative in 1954–55. His replacement, Robert Hall, was another Japanese studies scholar at the University of Michigan, Ann Arbor. Brown's predecessor was Noel Busch, a veteran *Time-Life* journalist.

78. F. Sionil Jose, "50 Years of the Asia Foundation," *Philippines Daily Inquirer*, October 20, 2003, F2.

79. "CFA Budget for FY 1955."

80. "Asia Foundation Monthly Report," October 24, 1953, Box 1, Robert Blum Papers, Manuscripts and Archives, Yale University Library (hereafter RBP).

81. "Press Release," September 15, 1952, Committee for a Free Asia, Box 37, AKC.

82. In 1956, Valentine wrote a memoir titled *Trial Balance*. During the 1960s and '70s, Valentine wrote numerous academic and literary works, including *Lord North* (1967) and *The British Establishment, 1760–1784: An Eighteenth-Century Biographical Dictionary* (1970). Valentine died on July 14, 1980.

83. Alan Valentine, untitled, August 12, 1952, available online via the CIA library, https://www.cia.gov/library/readingroom/docs/DTPILLAR%20%20%20VOL.%201_0071.pdf, accessed February 8, 2020.

84. A Letter from Alan Valentine to General Walter B. Smith, September 15, 1952, John M. and Barbara Keil University Archivist and Rochester Collections, University of Rochester.

85. Alan Valentine, "Analysis of CFA Future," September 15, 1952, John M. and Barbara Keil University Archivist and Rochester Collections, University of Rochester.

86. "CFA Budget for FY 1955."

87. "CFA Budget for FY 1955."

88. Kenneth Osgood, *Total Cold War*, 48.

89. Kenneth Osgood, *Total Cold War*, 50.

90. Oddly enough, the Asia Foundation's website does not include the CFA, or the foundation's first president, Alan Valentine, in its official history. According to the website, "In 1954, a group of forward-thinking citizens who shared a strong interest in Asia, distinguished personal achievements, and dedicated public service established The Asia Foundation—a private, nongovernmental organization devoted to promoting democracy, rule of law, and market-based development in post-war Asia." "History," The Asia Foundation website, accessed June 21, 2019, https://asiafoundation.org/about/history/.

91. "Foundation Officers: Robert Blum," *The Asia Foundation Program Bulletin*, December 1958, Box 2, RBP.

92. Steve Weissman and John Shock, "CIAsia Foundation," *Pacific Research and World Empire Telegram* 3, no. 6 (September—October 1972): 3–4.

93. Charles Burress, "James L. Stewart—Longtime Liaison to Asia," *San Francisco Chronicle*, January 29, 2006.

94. Blum, "The Work of The Asia Foundation," 46.

95. "Second Revised Administrative Plan. Covert Action Staff Proprietary DTPILLAR," August 29, 1963, available online via Archive.org, https://archive.org/stream/DTPILLAR/DTPILLAR%20%20%20VOL.%203_0022#page/n0/mode/2up, accessed February 8, 2020.

96. Frances Stoner Saunders states that James Michener's long career "writing blockbusters with such modest titles as *Poland, Alaska, Texas,* and *Space* was punctuated by a spell with the Agency. In the mid-1950s, Michener used his career as a writer as cover for his work in eliminating radicals who had infiltrated one of the CIA's Asia operations." Saunders, *The Cultural Cold War,* 207. For more about Michener's Cold War activities, see Christina Klein's chapter "How to Be an

American Abroad: James Michener's The Voice of Asia and Postwar Mass Tourism" in her book *Cold War Orientalism: Asia in the Middlebrow Imagination, 1945–1961* (Berkeley: University of California Press, 2003), 100–142.

97. The first film that CFA fully financed was a thirty-minute, 16 mm color documentary film titled *Truth Shall Make Men Free*. It was made by the San Francisco–based Alfred T. Palmer Production in 1952. "Scenario for: Truth Will Make Men Free," Radio RFA First Program Data, dates unknown, Box 13, AFR.

98. Richard P. Conlon was an officer in the US Foreign Service in China, Korea, and Washington. He left in 1952 to become director of plans for the CFA. In 1955, he left to form his own company, Conlon Associates, which provided consulting services to the government and industry on international trade and investment in Asia.

99. John Glover, "Long Range Motion Picture Project," September 18, 1952, C-51.4 Plans—Motion Pictures, Box 9, AFR.

100. This film was also known as *Buddhist World Brotherhood*.

101. Glover, "Long Range Motion Picture Project."

102. "Background Information: Committee for a Free Asia."

103. "Background Information: Committee for a Free Asia."

104. Conlon delineated three approaches used by the communists: (1) dissemination of Russian and other communist or pro-communist films, (2) infiltration of the local motion picture production industries, and (3) infiltration and control of motion picture distribution apparatus. Richard P. Conlon, "Basic Position Paper CFA—Motion Picture Program," March 24, 1953, C-51.4 Plans—Motion Pictures, Box 9, AFR.

105. Conlon, "Basic Position Paper CFA—Motion Picture Program."

106. Conlon, "Basic Position Paper CFA—Motion Picture Program."

107. Soon-jin Lee, a Korean film historian, has written a detailed account of Charles Tanner's contribution to the post-independence South Korean film industry. See Soon-jin Lee, "1950 nyŏndae han'guk yŏnghwa sanŏp kwa migug ŭi wŏnjo: ashia jaedan ŭi chŏng-nŭng ch'wal yŏngso chosŏng ŭl chungshim ŭro" [Korean Film industry of the 1950s and American aid: The case of Asia Foundation's support for Jeongnung Production Studios], *Han'guk'ak yŏn'gu* [The journal of Korean studies] 43 (November 2016): 173–204. Tanner simply exchanged "his officer's uniform for business clothes, moving from the Army one day to the State Department, without losing a day's work," according to his daughter Robin Johnson-Tanner; Johnson-Tanner, email interview with the author, March 26, 2013. When the Korean War broke out, Tanner moved to Manila, then served with USIS in Tokyo for two years. In 1953, Tanner, his wife Dorie, and their baby girl moved to San Francisco, where his job at TAF was waiting. See "Charles M. Tanner Timeline," Covenant Players, https://www.covenantplayers.org/charles-m-tanner-timeline, accessed March 11, 2020.

108. "Staff Biography: John Miller," July 8, 1952, John Miller, Box 39, AFR.

109. Noel F. Busch, *Fallen Sun: A Report on Japan* (New York: Appleton Century Crofts, Inc., 1948).

110. Thomas W. Ennis, "Noel Busch, Author and Correspondent for *Life Magazine*," *New York Times*, September 11, 1985.

111. U Nu, *The People Win Through* (Rangoon: Society for Extension of Democratic Ideals, 1952), 1.

112. Richard Butwell, *U Nu of Burma* (Stanford, CA: Stanford University Press, 1963), 81.

113. U Nu, *The People Win Through*, 56.

114. Memorandum to Ray T. Maddocks from Glover, July 30, 1952, Movies General, Box 9, AFR.

115. "Cascade Pictures of California, Inc.," May 22, 1953, Cascade Pictures, Box 9, AFR.

116. Michael Charney, "U Nu, China and the 'Burmese' Cold War: Propaganda in Burma in the 1950s," in *The Cold War in Asia: The Battle for Hearts and Minds*, ed. Zheng Yangwen, Hong Liu, and Michael Szonyi (Leiden: Brill 2010), 50–53.

117. A letter to Eric Johnston, March 16, 1954, Japan Writer Project H-7 1953–54, Box 9, AFR.

118. Richard P. Conlon, "Basic Position Paper TAF-Motion Picture Program," March 24, 1953, Japan Writer Project H-7 1953–54, Box 9, AFR.

119. Blum's letter to Kenneth Clark (Vice President of MPAA), January 25, 1955, Gangelin-Paul-Correspondences, Box 9, AFR.

120. Maung Maung Ta (1926–2015) made his acting debut with *The People Win Through*. From 1955 to the 1980s, he was a highly successful actor who starred in over forty feature films.

121. "Premiere's Play Being Filmed—Hollywood Enthusiastic," March 23, 1953, Rebellion, Box 10, AFR.

122. Tanner, "Screening of Cascade's *Rebellion*," July 29, 1953, Media Audio-Visual Movies Rebellion (General 1952–1953), Box 10, AFR.

123. Richard P. Conlon, *"Rebellion or People Win Through* Showing," July 29, 1953, Rebellion, Box 10, AFR.

124. Tanner's Letter to Stewart, September 28, 1953, Media Audio-Visual Movies Rebellion (General 1954), Box 10, AFR.

125. Charney, *The Cold War in Asia*, 49.

126. "The People Win Through," *Burma Weekly Bulletin* 2, no. 39 (December 30, 1953): 1.

127. Richard Dyer MacCann, "To Counter Communist Propaganda," *Christian Science Monitor*, December 24, 1953.

128. Richard Dyer MacCann was born in Wichita, Kansas, in 1920 and attended the University of Kansas, where he received his BA in political science in 1940. After an MA at Stanford University in 1942 and three years of service in the United States and Europe during World War II, he completed a PhD in government at Harvard in 1951. His dissertation, "Documentary Film and Democratic Government," led him to a growing concern about communication and public opinion in the democratic process and to a special interest in the motion picture. He accepted a position as a staff correspondent in Los Angeles for the *Christian Science Monitor*, specializing in film and television reporting in 1951. After teaching at USC, he joined the faculty of the University of Iowa as professor in charge of the PhD program in film in the Department of Speech and Dramatic Art. He was one of the early editors of *Cinema Journal*. He was also the author of *Hollywood in Transition* (Boston: Houghton Mifflin, 1962), *Film and Society* (New York: Scribner, 1964), and *The People's Films: A Political History of U.S. Government Motion Pictures* (New York: Hastings House, 1973).

129. A memorandum to Stewart, May 3, 1954, Movies General/Hollywood "For the Record," Box 9, AFR.

130. Luigi Luraschi's letter to Stewart, March 10, 1955, Tradition/Asia Pictures/HK, Box 9, AFR.

131. Luigi Luraschi's letter to Stewart, March 10, 1955.

132. A memorandum to Stewart, May 3, 1954.

133. Joseph M. Kitagawa, "Buddhism and Asian Politics," *Asian Survey* 2, no. 5 (July 1962): 6.

134. Joseph M. Kitagawa, *Religion in Japanese History* (New York: Columbia University Press, 1966), 295.

135. Kitagawa, "Buddhism and Asian Politics," 6.

136. Marvin G. McAlister's Letter to John Grover, December 30, 1952, MEDIA Audio-Visual Cascade Pictures Burma Program, Box 9, AFR.

137. The total amount the CFA paid to Cascade for the script was USD 45,551.02.

138. Tanner's letter to Stewart, "Tathagata the Wayfarer: The Story of Gautama Buddha," August 17, 1953, Media Audio-Visual Movies Tathagata the Wayfarer (Life of Buddha), Box 10, AFR.

139. Tanner's letter to Stewart, August 17, 1953.

140. James W. McFarlane's letter to CFA, September 23, 1953, Media Audio-Visual Movies Tathagata the Wayfarer (Life of Buddha), Box 10, AFR.

141. Charles M. Tanner, "Discussion with James McFarlane on the Buddha Script," September 28, 1953, Media Audio-Visual Movies Tathagata the Wayfarer (Life of Buddha), Box 10, AFR.

142. Eugene Ford, *Cold War Monks: Buddhism and America's Secret Strategy in Southeast Asia* (New Haven: Yale University Press, 2017), 32.

143. Ford, *Cold War Monks*, 29.

144. Malalasekera received his PhD in literature from London School of Oriental Studies, the previous name of the SOAS (School of Oriental and African Studies), University of London.

145. G. P. Malalasekera, "The Buddha Film—The Truth About It," *Buddhist* 24, no. 8 (December 1953): 113.

146. Malalasekera, "The Buddha Film—The Truth About It."

147. "Not Bought Over by American Film Co," *Ceylon Daily News*, September 25, 1953.

148. "Preliminary Discussion on Film *The Life of Buddha*," October 2, 1953, Media Audio-Visual Movies Tathagata the Wayfarer (Life of Buddha), Box 10, AFR.

149. Preliminary Discussion on Film *The Life of Buddha*."

150. Tanner's Letter to James Stewart, September 28, 1953, Media Audio-Visual Movies Rebellion (General 1952–1953), Box 10, AFR.

151. Charles M. Tanner, "C-112 (Ceylon-Buddha Film)," November 3, 1953, Media Audio-Visual Movies Tathagata the Wayfarer (Life of Buddha), Box 10, AFR.

152. Robert Hardy Andrews' letter to Robert R. McBride of CFA, September 4, 1954, Media Audio-Visual Movies Tathagata the Wayfarer (Life of Buddha), Box 10, AFR.

153. "Isherwood's long and undistinguished career as a Hollywood screenwriter, scarcely touched on in his almost exclusively autobiographical oeuvre, and little discussed by his critics and biographers, sapped his talent and energy and left no memorable films by way of compensation. But he wasn't in it for the money, and nor was screenwriting an exercise designed, as he put it in *Christopher and His Kind* (1976), 'to subdue his nature temporarily' for the deferred benefit of his novels. Isherwood earnestly wanted to be a filmmaker, but as he told Gilbert Adair late in his life, 'something would always go wrong'" (Henry K. Miller, "Other Town to Tinseltown," *Times Literary Supplement*, March 22, 2017, https://www.the-tls.co.uk/articles/public/christopher-isherwood-cinema).

154. Mon Soe Min, "A Christian Company and the Buddha Film," *Burman*, March 3, 1955.

155. Ven. G. Anoma, "Buddhists, Awake Against Buddha Film," *Burman*, March 1, 1955. In line with this, one reader's letter to the *New Times of Burma* asked, "How can any film-star who is a mere *Pu-htu-zin* (who has a good morality and makes devoted attempts at meditation) with a one-hundred-per cent materialistic outlook, possibly emulate the facial expressions or the movements of an *Arhat* (one who is worthy)—let alone those of the Blessed One, the Holy One and the Supremely Enlightened One? At the same time, can a member of the holy *Sangna* (Buddhist Order) raise a finger or stand in the way of Metro-Goldwin-Meyer and their associates endeavoring to earn a livelihood on a project, wholesome or unwholesome?" U Pu, "Filming of The Life of Lord Buddha," *New Times of Burma*, March 19, 1955.

156. Ven. G. Anoma, *Burman*, March 1, 1955.

157. Mon Soe Min, *Burman*, March 3, 1955.

158. "Controversy Over Filming of Lord Buddha," *New Times of Burma*, April 10, 1955.

159. Robert Hardy Andrews' letter to Margaret E. Pollard of The Asia Foundation, November 29, 1955, Media Audio-Visual Movies Tathagata the Wayfarer (Life of Buddha), Box 10, AFR.

160. The first Hollywood-involved film about the life of Buddha came out in 1972. *Siddhartha*, directed by Conrad Rooks, was a coproduction of India and the United States. Twenty years

later, in 1993, the Italian maestro Bernardo Bertolucci directed a big budget Italy-France-UK-US coproduction film, *Little Buddha*, in which Keanu Reeves plays Siddhartha.

161. "Asia Foundation Monthly Report," April 9, 1954, Box 1, RBP.

162. "Executive Committee Report," May 5, 1954, Box 1, RBP.

163. Odd Arne Westad, *The Cold War: A World History* (London: Penguin Books, 2017), 138.

164. John W. Dower, *Japan in War and Peace: Selected Essays* (New York: New Press, 1993), 155.

165. Bruce Cumings, "Japan's Position in the World System," in *Postwar Japan as History*, ed. Andrew Gordon (Berkeley: University of California Press, 1993), 34.

166. Shunya Yoshimi and David Buist, "America as Desire and Violence: Americanization in Postwar Japan and Asia during the Cold War," *Inter-Asian Cultural Studies* 4, no. 3 (2003): 442.

167. W. W. Rostow, *An American Policy in Asia* (New York: John Wiley & Sons, 1955), 5.

168. W. W. Rostow, *Eisenhower, Kennedy, and Foreign Aid* (Austin: University of Texas Press, 1985), 85–98.

169. Akira Suehiro, "The Road to Economic Re-entry: Japan's Policy toward Southeast Asian Development in the 1950s and 1960s," *Social Science Japan Journal* 2, no. 1 (1999): 87.

Chapter 2. The FPA, US Propaganda, and Postwar Japanese Cinema

1. Kimura Takechiyo had no career in the film industry prior to joining Daiei. Born in April 1910, Kimura graduated from the jurisprudence department of Tokyo Imperial University in 1937, immediately joined the Ministry of Foreign Affairs, and was dispatched to the Japanese Legation in Mexico. After serving as secretary to the Privy Council and secretary to the home minister of the Japanese government, he became the executive secretary to the president of Daiei Studio. See The Federation of Motion Picture Producers in Southeast Asia, *Report on the 3rd Annual Film Festival of Southeast Asia*, Hong Kong June 12–16, 1956, 19.

2. Blum, "Executive Committee Report," May 5, 1954, Box 1, RBP.

3. Christopher Howard argues, "Post-Occupation Japanese cinema's new-found freedom to address previously taboo subjects was met by international press criticism claiming that significant sections of the Japanese film industry were abusing this autonomy to promote 'anti-American' values." Christopher Howard, "Re-Orienting Japanese Cinema: Cold War Criticism of 'Anti-American' Films," *Historical Journal of Film, Radio and Television* 36, no. 4 (2016): 529–30.

4. A letter to Dave Penn, April 24, 1954, Japan Writer Project H-7, Box 9, AFR.

5. Richard L-G. Deverall, "Red Propaganda in Japan's Movies," *America: National Catholic Weekly Review* 88 (November 1953): 174. Richard L-G. Deverall (1911–80) was born in Brooklyn, New York, and educated at Villanova College, where he received a BS in Sociology. After working with organized labor in Detroit, Deverall worked with the Office of War Information as a special advisor on labor matters. During the war, he was stationed in postwar Japan in a military capacity until 1948. Deverall was the Asia representative of the Trade Union Committee of the American Federation of Labor (AFL) from 1949 to the middle of 1952. Deverall then held the same position in Japan, headquartered in Tokyo, from the middle of 1952 to 1955. Lastly, Deverall served as the AFL-CIO's special assistant to the assistant general secretary of the International Confederation of Free Trade Unions (ICFTU) in Brussels, Belgium. For more about the AFL's anticommunist campaign in Japan and Deverall's role, see Christopher Gerteis, "Labor's Cold Warriors: The American Federation of Labor and 'Free Trade Unionism' in Cold War Japan," *Journal of American-East Asian Relations* 12, no. 3 (2003): 207–24.

6. Shindo Kaneto began shooting just a month after the end of the US occupation, finishing the movie in time for an August 6 world premiere. Ironically, *Children of the Atomic Bomb* was criti-

cized as insufficiently anti-American by Japan's left-wing teachers' union. *Children of the Atomic Bomb* was entered in the 1953 Cannes International Film Festival under the title of *Children of Hiroshima*. See Jim Hoberman, "Surviving the Bomb in *Children of Hiroshima*," *The Village Voice*, April 20, 2011, https://www.villagevoice.com/2011/04/20/surviving-the-bomb-in-children-of-hiroshima/.

7. "After graduating from Swarthmore College . . . in 1951, Theodore R. Conant (b. 1926) worked briefly as a film technician in New York and was invited to participate in a United Nations-funded film that portrayed the plight of South Koreans during the Korean War. During the final phase of the war, Conant was recruited to work with the BBC on their Christmas Empire program from Korea, as well as the exchange of wounded prisoners. He stayed on to help record a UN and BBC radio program series on Korean reconstruction. He subsequently became the acting head of the United Nations Korean Reconstruction Agency (UNKRA) Film Unit and while in Korea privately produced and directed several documentaries on different aspects of Korean culture. He later accepted a position as a filmmaker and sound recording engineer at Syracuse University under contract with the U.S. Aid Mission. Conant worked to upgrade the technical capacity of the Korean Office of Public Information. He was working in the Capitol Compound in 1960 when student demonstrations broke out and witnessed at close hand the fall of Syngman Rhee and the faltering efforts to create a new regime." "Theodore R. Conant Biography," The Conant Collection, Center for Korean Studies Collections, The University of Hawai'i, accessed April 26, 2018, http://ckslib.manoa.hawaii.edu/archives-and-manuscripts-collections/theodore-r-conant-collection/.

8. Theodore R. Conant, "Anti-American Films in Japan: Since the Occupation's End the Leftists Have Exploited Japanese Resentment of Defeat," *Films in Review* 5, no. 1 (January 1954): 8.

9. A letter to Dave Penn, April 24, 1954.

10. Victor Riesel, "Pro-Red Movies Aim to Discredit US in Japan," *Oakland Tribune*, March 24, 1954: 26.

11. The CIE was a suborganization of General Headquarters. The CIE controlled the entire film industry in Japan during the US occupation period.

12. A report to Noel Busch, November 24, 1952, Japan Writer Project H-7, Box 9, AFR.

13. Noel Busch, "Preliminary Notes on a Japan Moving Picture Program," June 5, 1953, Japan Writer Project H-7, Box 9, AFR.

14. John Miller, "Report on First Film Festival in Southeast Asia," May 31, 1954, Film Festivals General 1951/54, Box 14, AFR.

15. "Transcript report of Federation of Motion Picture Producers of Southeast Asia: Organization and Preparation Conference, November 17–19, 1953." Film Festivals General 1951/54, Box 14, AFR.

16. For more about the Malay Film Production, see Raphaël Millet, *Singapore Cinema* (Singapore: Editions Didier Millet, 2006) and Jan Uhde and Yvonne Ng Uhde, *Latent Image: Film in Singapore* (London: Oxford University Press, 2000).

17. Lamberto V. Avellana, director of *Huk in a New Life*, made two notable films during the 1950s—*Anak Dalita* (1953) and *Badjao* (1957). For more about Avellana, see Francisco Benitez's "Filming Philippine Modernity during the Cold War: The Case of Lamberto Avellana," in *Cultures at War*, 21–44. For more about *Badjao*, see Aileen Toohey, "Badjao: Cinematic Representations of Difference in the Philippines," *Journal of Southeast Asian Studies* 36, no. 2 (2005): 281–312.

18. Yomota Inuhioko, *Ilbon yŏnghwa ŭi ihae* [Understanding Japanese cinema], trans. Pak Chŏn-yŏl (Seoul, South Korea: Hyeonamsa, 2001); Donald Richie and Joseph Anderson, *The Japanese Film: Art and Industry*, expanded ed. (Princeton, NJ: Princeton University Press, 1982); Peter B. High, *The Imperial Screen: Japanese Film Culture in the Fifteen Years' War, 1931–1945* (Madison: University of Wisconsin Press, 2003), 320; *Report on the 3rd Annual Film Festival of Southeast Asia*, 38.

19. The intriguing story of Nagata Masaichi's overnight success is well documented in High, *The Imperial Screen*, 314–21.

20. See Mitsuyo Wada-Marciano, *The Production of Modernity in Japanese Cinema: Shochiku Kamata Style in the 1920s and 1930s* (PhD diss., University of Iowa, 2000), 205–11.

21. Christopher Howard, "Beyond *Jidai-geki*: Daiei Studios and the Study of Transnational Japanese Cinema," *Journal of Japanese and Korean Cinema* 3, no. 1 (2012): 6.

22. Howard, "Beyond *Jidai-geki*, 7.

23. It was Giuliana Stramigiolo, an Italian professor at Tokyo University of Foreign Languages, who recommended *Rashomon* to the Venice International Film Festival. Nagata didn't like *Rashomon*. He saw "no value" in *Rashomon*. He even "walked out of its screening with the single word, *wakaran*, a rude expression meaning incomprehensible." Andrew Horvat, "Rashomon Perceived: The Challenge of Forging a Transnationally Shared View of Kurosawa's Legacy," in *Rashomon Effects: Kurosawa, Rashomon and Their Legacies*, ed. Blair Davis, Robert Anderson, and Jan Walls (New York: Routledge, 2016), 46. Richie and Anderson, as well as Kurosawa Akira's own autobiography, have also illustrated it in detail. See Richie and Anderson, *The Japanese Film*, 229–32; Akira Kurosawa, *Something Like an Autobiography*, trans. Audie Bock (New York: Vantage Books: 1982), 180–87.

24. Curtis Harrington, "Film Festival at Cannes," *Quarterly of Film, Radio and Television* 7, no. 1 (1952): 32.

25. For instance, as will be discussed in chapter 5, Run Run Shaw tried Cannes and the San Francisco International Film Festival in hopes of gaining a "prestigious name tag" from the West. In line with this, Ho Hyŏn-ch'an, a renowned film critic in South Korea, claimed that South Korean cinema "should go to Venice and win the prize as Japan did a decade ago . . . to be recognized and receive awards, Korean cinema should put forward our local color in tandem with Asian themes that could appeal to westerners." Ho Hyŏn-ch'an, "Penisŭ ro kanŭn han'guk yŏnghwa" [South Korean cinema on the road to Venice], *Shilbŏ Sŭk'ŭrin* [Silver screen] (August 1965): 65; see also "The Colorful Cannes Film Festival," *Nan Guo Dian Ying* [Southern screen] 28 (June 1960): 30–33; "Shaw Brothers into World Market," *Nan Guo Dian Ying* [Southern screen] 65 (July 1963): 3–4.

26. Hirano, *Mr. Smith Goes to Tokyo*, 208–9.

27. For more about Kawakita and Zhang's wartime collaborations, see Fu, "The Ambiguity of Entertainment."

28. For more about the production history of *Anatahan*, see Sachiko Mizuno, "The Saga of *Anatahan* and Japan," *Spectator* 29, no. 2 (Fall 2009): 9–24.

29. Kitamura, *Screening Enlightenment*, 180.

30. Quoted in Hirano, *Mr. Smith Goes to Tokyo*, 38.

31. Peter Duus, *Modern Japan* (Boston: Houghton Mifflin Company, 1998), 253, 275.

32. Kyoko Hirano, "Japan," in *World Cinema Since 1945*, ed. William Luhr (New York: Ungar, 1987), 380.

33. Yoshimoto Mitsuhiro, *Kurosawa: Film Studies and Japanese Cinema* (Durham, NC: Duke University Press, 2000), 118.

34. Clearly, the film does not show any ideological conflict. Instead, the film simplifies and emphasizes the confrontations of two characters with Japanese militarism and their struggle to impede the Japanese government's war. Interestingly, the film arbitrarily distorts "real" history, creating, as Inuhiko asserts, a new "myth": that the common Japanese was deceived by militarism. See Yomota Inuhioko, *Ilbon yŏnghwa ŭi ihae*, 149.

35. Yoshimoto, *Kurosawa*, 118.

36. Keiko I. MacDonald, *Mizoguchi* (Boston: Twayne Publishers, 1984), 71.

37. See Duus, *Modern Japan*, 276–77.

38. Kitamura, *Screening Enlightenment*, 177.

39. For more about Nikkatsu's reentry into the market, see *Eiga Nenkan* (1955), 313–15; Mark Schilling, *No Borders, No Limits: Nikkatsu Action Cinema* (Farleigh: FAB Press, 2007), 12–29.

40. "Success Abroad Bring[s] Boom to Movie Export," *Nippon Times*, May 16, 1954, 5–6.

41. "Success Abroad Bring[s] Boom to Movie Export," 6.

42. See Aaron Gerow, "Narrating the Nationality of a Cinema: The Case of Japanese Prewar Film," in *The Culture of Japanese Fascism*, ed. Alan Talisman (Durham, NC: Duke University Press, 2009), 189; Aaron Gerow, *Visions of Japanese Modernity: Articulations of Cinema, Nation, and Spectatorship, 1895–1925* (Berkeley: University of California Press, 2010), 113–14.

43. "S. E. Asian Nations Take Part in Film Festival Here," *Nippon Times*, May 16, 1954, 5.

44. See *Eiga Nenkan* (1954), 54.

45. Yau, *Japanese and Hong Kong Film Industries*, 64.

46. The Japanese film industry introduced popular genre films to audiences in Asia. For example, *Radon* (*Sora no Daikaiju Radon*, Honda Ishiro, 1956), a monster film from Toho, was the most publicized film of the third Southeast Asian Film Festival in 1956, and Toho hosted a workshop on the latest filming technology during the festival. Richie and Anderson, *The Japanese Film*, 232–33.

47. For more on Japan's pan-Asian industrial complex and Ichikawa Sai's monograph *Ajia eiga no sozo oyobi kensetsu* [The creation and construction of Asian cinema] (1941), see Nornes, "The Creation and Construction of Asian Cinema Redux," 175–87.

48. Kinnia Shuk-ting Yau, "The Early Development of East Asian Cinema in a Regional Context," *Asian Studies Review* 33 (June 2009): 163.

49. Yau, "The Early Development of East Asian Cinema," 166.

50. Yau, "The Early Development of East Asian Cinema," 169.

51. Yau, "The Early Development of East Asian Cinema," 167.

52. *Kinema Junpo* 89 (May 1954): 63–64.

53. "The Second Exhibition of Film Technologies and Facilities," *Eiga Nenkan* (1955), 257–58.

54. See *Eiga Nenkan*, 1955, 1956, 1957.

55. *Report on the 3rd Annual Film Festival of Southeast Asia*, 11.

56. "Bring Outlook for Movie Festival; Better Films, Wider Market Foreseen," *Nippon Times*, May 16, 1954, 5.

57. Oba Mie, "Japan's Entry into ECAFE," in *Japanese Diplomacy in the 1950s*, ed. Iokibe Makoto, Caroline Rose, Tomaru Junko, and John Weste (New York and London: Routledge, 2008), 99.

58. E. E. Ward, "The Outlook for ECAFE," *Far Eastern Survey: American Institute of Pacific Relations* 18, no. 7 (April 6, 1949): 75.

59. *Nippon Times*, June 3, 1949.

60. Cited in Dower, *Japan in War and Peace*, 193.

61. James T. H. Tang, "From Empire Defense to Imperial Retreat: Britain's Postwar China Policy and the Decolonization of Hong Kong," *Modern Asian Studies* 28, no. 2 (1994): 319–20.

62. Cited in Tomaru Junko, "Japan in British Regional Policy towards Southeast Asia, 1945–1960," in *Japanese Diplomacy in the 1950s*, ed. Iokibe Makoto, Caroline Rose, Tomaru Junko, and John Weste (New York: Routledge, 2008), 58.

63. Tomaru, "Japan in British Regional Policy," 70.

64. Akira Suehiro, "The Road to Economic Re-entry: Japan's Policy toward Southeast Asian Development in the 1950s and 1960s," *Social Science Japan Journal* 2, no. 1 (1999): 88.

65. Suehiro, "The Road to Economic Re-entry," 88.

66. However, Yoshida's aim was not fulfilled, and his successor Kishi's grand tour of Southeast Asia in 1957 was also unsuccessful in producing significant results. The Japanese government failed to understand the realities faced by countries of the region, especially Indonesia, the Philippines, and Malaysia. Japan's reentry to the Southeast Asian market, after all, was primarily in the interest of Japan and the American government. Substantial progress in Japan's return to Asia, hence, was

made a decade later, with the establishment of the Asian Development Bank (ADB) in the mid '60s, in which Japan took the initiative.

67. Suehiro, "The Road to Economic Re-entry," 90.

68. Richie and Anderson, *The Japanese Film*, 229–30.

69. Quoted in *Asia-Pacific Film Festival 50th Anniversary Catalogue*, 11–12.

70. For more about the "flying geese" model, see Walter F. Hatch, *Asia's Flying Geese: How Regionalization Shapes Japan* (Ithaca, NY: Cornell University Press, 2010).

71. Kaname Akamatsu, "A Historical Pattern of Economic Growth in Developing Countries," *Developing Economies* 1, no. 1 (1962): 3–25.

72. A letter to William T. Fleming, January 5, 1954, Film Festivals General 1951/54, Box 14, AFR.

73. "Transcript report of Federation of Motion Picture Producers of Southeast Asia." All quotes in the section below related to the first conference in 1953 are from the report unless otherwise indicated.

74. Malik's company, Persari (established in 1951), is considered the third indigenous company—after Hiburan Mataram Stichting (1948) and Usmar Ismail's Perfini (Perusahaan Film National, 1950). Pesari quickly became one of the largest producers in Indonesia. See Krishna Sen, *Indonesian Cinema: Framing the New Order* (London and New Jersey: Zed Books, 1994), 20.

75. Sen, *Indonesian Cinema*, 21.

76. Busch, "Southeast Asian Federation of Motion Picture Producers," December 22, 1953, Film Festivals General 1951/54, Box 14, AFR.

77. Busch, "Southeast Asian Federation of Motion Picture Producers," December 22, 1953.

78. A letter to Fleming, January 5, 1954, Film Festivals General 1951/54, Box 14, AFR.

79. A letter to Blum, February 10, 1954, Film Festivals General 1951/54, Box 14, AFR.

80. A letter to Stewart from Robert B. Sheeks, December 30, 1953, Film Festivals General 1951/54, Box 14, AFR.

81. For more about the Malayan Film Unit, see Ian Aitken, *The British Official Film in South-East Asia: Malaya/Malaysia, Singapore and Hong Kong* (London: Palgrave Macmillan, 2016).

82. Thomas Hodge left the Malayan Film Unit and joined the Hong Kong branch of the Singapore-based Cathay Film Organization in 1957. He was the head of Cathay Film Services. For more about Hodge and his contribution to Hong Kong documentary films, see Ian Aitken and Michael Ingham, *Hong Kong Documentary Film* (Edinburgh: Edinburgh University Press, 2014), 71-100, and Ian Aitken, *The British Official Film in South-East Asia: Malaya/Malaysia, Singapore and Hong Kong* (London: Palgrave Macmillan, 2016), 45-85

83. A letter to Stewart from Robert B. Sheeks, April 9, 1954, Film Festivals General 1951/54, Box 14, AFR.

84. A letter to Eric Johnston (MPPA) from Blum, March 16, 1854, Hollywood-Correspondence, Box 9, AFR.

85. A letter to Dave Penn, April 24, 1954.

86. A letter to Blum from Busch, November 19, 1953, Writer Project (Japan), Box 9, AFR.

87. A letter to Busch from Tanner, dates unknown, Japan Writer Project H-7, Box 9, AFR.

88. A letter to Busch from Tanner, dates unknown.

89. "Writer's Project," dates unknown, Writer Project (Japan), Box 9, AFR.

90. A letter to Tanner, January 14, 1954, Japan Writer Project H-7, Box 9, AFR.

91. "Winston Miller to Japan in Ambassadorial Role," *Hollywood Reporter*, March 30, 1954, 7.

92. Miller's idea was basically the following: synopses of original stories were to be submitted to Miller, who would look them over to see if they would do; if he approved them, Miller would send the synopses to Daiei, where they would be translated into Japanese and scrutinized by Daiei's editorial board. If the synopses were accepted by Daiei, the authors would be paid a

handsome fee: from USD 500 to USD 2,000 per story. A letter to Stewart, May 4, 1954, The Japan Writer Project, Box 9, AFR.

93. "Attention! SWG Member," May 10, 1954, The Japan Writer Project, Box 9, AFR.

94. "Executive Committee Report," June 9, 1954, Box 1, RBP.

95. A letter to Stewart, May 4, 1954, Japan Writer Project H-7, Box 9, AFR.

96. A letter to Tanner, January 14, 1954, Japan Writer Project H-7, Box 9, AFR.

Chapter 3. It's Oscar Time in Asia!

1. On April 21, 1954, John Miller emphasized over the phone to Tanner that the Hollywood delegates should come as "diplomats rather than as guests of honor." Their attitude "should be that of diplomats representing the U.S. movie industry." April 21, 1954, Film Festivals General 1951/54, Box 14, AFR.

2. "Studio Publicity Directors Committee WE 3–7101 (Duke Wales)," May 18, 1954, Folder 149, Film Festivals P-Z, AMPAS.

3. "Memorandum," April 26, 1954, Movies General/Hollywood "For the Record," Box 9, AFR. Fourteen delegates attended the Uruguay festival, approved and sent out by Y. Frank Freeman, president of the MPAA and vice president of Paramount Pictures.

4. "Studio Publicity Directors Committee WE 3–7101 (Duke Wales)," January 5, 1955, Folder 149, Film Festivals P—Z, AMPAS.

5. Hervé Dumont, *Frank Borzage: The Life and Film of a Hollywood Romantic*, trans. Jonathan Kaplansky (Jefferson, NC: McFarland & Company, 2006), 342.

6. Dumont, *Frank Borzage*, 342.

7. "Studio Publicity Directors Committee WE 3–7101 (Duke Wales)."

8. *Eiga Nenkan* (1955), 54–60.

9. Usmar Ismail (1921–71) is generally considered the father of Indonesian cinema. He co-founded Persari Film with Malik. He was also known internationally for his film *Fighters for Freedom* (*Ped-juang*, 1961), which was entered into the second Moscow International Film Festival in 1961.

10. Quoted in Miller's letter to Blum, June 18, 1955, FMPPSEA 2nd, Box 16, AFR.

11. The Federation of Motion Picture Producers in Southeast Asia, *The First Film Festival in Southeast Asia Catalogue*, May 8–20, 1954, Tokyo, Japan.

12. Thomas Elsaesser, "Film Festival Networks: The New Topographies of Cinema in Europe," in *European Cinema: Face to Face with Hollywood* (Amsterdam: Amsterdam University Press, 2005), 89–90.

13. Fred Roos, "Venice Film Festival 1957," *Quarterly of Film, Radio and Television* 11, no. 3 (1957): 242.

14. A new system, centered on the festival director, appeared in the aftermath of the auteur theory phenomenon that swept most European countries during the early 1960s. It was in the 1970s that Rotterdam and other cities emerged as the sites of new festivals that were not rooted in a project of national or geopolitical interest. Instead, as Marijke de Valck writes, they were founded on the belief that "film festivals ought to take responsibility for programming themselves and dedicate the services to the benefit of quality cinema." See Marijke de Valck, *Film Festivals: From European Geopolitics to Global Cinephilia* (Amsterdam: Amsterdam University Press, 2007), 165.

15. "Big Five Film Companies Here Headed by Capable Leaders," *Nippon Times*, May 16, 1954, 7.

16. "Daiei Film *Golden Demon* Judged Best Asia Movie," *Nippon Times*, May 20, 1954, 1.

17. "Daiei Film *Golden Demon* Judged Best Asia Movie."

18. "For the Record," June 24, 1954, Hollywood—"For the Record," Box 9, AFR.

19. FPA, *The First Film Festival in Southeast Asia Catalogue.*

20. *Santi-Vina* has long been a "lost" classic of Thai cinema. The problems started immediately after the Southeast Asian Film Festival in 1954. After learning that he would have to pay a large sum of money in customs duties to take the film back to Thailand, Pestonji decided to ship it to London. He was later informed that the film had been damaged during the voyage, and he died in 1970 believing that his award-winning film was lost forever. In 2012, Sanchai Chotirosseranee, the deputy director of the Thai Film Archive, received an e-mail from Alongkot Maiduang, a film critic working on his PhD who had found the original sound negatives and at least some of the color picture negatives at the British Film Institute in London. The Thai Film Archive continued searching for a print in better condition and finally found one at the Gosfilmofond in Russia in 2013. The fully restored *Santi-Vina* was shown at the 69th Cannes International Film Festival in 2016. For more about the discovery of *Santi-Vina* and the story of the film's restoration, see Sanchai Chotirosseranee, "Finding Santi-Vina," *Journal of Film Preservation* 96 (April 2017): 107–12; Donsaron Kovitvanitcha, "Resurrecting a Legend," *Nation*, May 24, 2016, http://www.nationmulti media.com/life/Resurrecting-a-legend-30286552.html.

21. *Far Eastern Film News*, May 21/28, 1953, 35.

22. Yau, *Japanese and Hong Kong Film Industries*, 68.

23. *Kinema Junpo* 90 (June 1954): 21.

24. "Daiei Film *Golden Demon* Judged Best Asia Movie," *Nippon Times*, May 20, 1954, 1.

25. Miller, "Report on First Film Festival in Southeast Asia."

26. Miller, "Report on First Film Festival in Southeast Asia."

27. Miller, "Report on First Film Festival in Southeast Asia."

28. Miller, "Report on First Film Festival in Southeast Asia."

29. Miller, "Report on First Film Festival in Southeast Asia."

30. A letter to Luraschi, June 16, 1954, Japan Tokyo-Movies, Box 9, AFR.

31. A letter to Tanner, July 12, 1954, Japan Tokyo-Movies, Box 9, AFR.

32. For more about Walter Wanger (1894–1968), see Matthew Bernstein, *Walter Wanger, Hollywood Independent* (Minneapolis: University of Minnesota Press, 2000).

33. Richie and Anderson, *The Japanese Film*, 232–33.

34. Quoted in Tino Balio, *The Foreign Film Renaissance on American Screens, 1946–1973* (Madison: University of Wisconsin Press, 2010), 121.

35. "Telephone Call to Duke Wales," June 30, 1954, Hollywood—"For the Record," Box 9, AFR.

36. "He [Edward Harrison] became a complete devotee of [Satyajit] Ray, visiting his shooting in 1961 and releasing all his work in the United States until his death in 1967." Andrew Robinson, *Satyajit Ray: The Inner Eye* (Berkeley: University of California Press, 1989), 103.

37. Balio, *The Foreign Film Renaissance on American Screens*, 121.

38. James Powers, "The Golden Demon," *Hollywood Reporter*, May 3, 1956.

39. "*Rashomon* Boom Spurred Film Industry and Opened a New Export Channel," *Asahi Evening News*, May 17, 1955, B5.

40. Richie and Anderson, *The Japanese Film*, 248.

41. "The Princess Yang Kwei-fei," *Motion Picture Daily*, September 14, 1956.

42. Nevertheless, Nagata continued producing "large scale spectacles and big outdoor" films until the early 1960s. Jasper Sharp discusses Nagata's attempts at adapting a new technology to suit Japanese production and exhibition practices. See Jasper Sharp, "*Buddha*: Selling an Asian Spectacle," *Journal of Japanese and Korean Cinema* 4, no. 1 (2012): 29–52.

43. M. Chase, "Conversation with Irving Maas of MPPA," September 15, 1953, Hollywood "For the Record," Box 9, AFR.

44. John Miller, "Film Stories for Daiei from Members of Screen Writers Guild," November 17, 1954, Japan Writer Project H-7 (Winston Miller), Box 9, AFR.

45. "Conversation with Irving Maas of MPPA."

46. *Escapade in Japan* is the story of an American boy who survives a plane crash in Japan. Under the misconception that the American boy is being chased by the police, Japanese children help him to escape. Deeply frustrated, Winston Miller stopped communicating with Nagata and sold the screenplay to RKO in 1955. Arthur Lubin directed the film, which was shot entirely in Kyoto, Nara, and Tokyo, in 1956. "Escapade in Japan," MPAA Production Code Administration Record, AMPAS. Charles S. Aronson, a *Motion Picture Daily* film critic, reviewed *Escapade in Japan.* He viewed this "simple but delightful" little piece positively: "The film serves most admirably to present the Japanese in a pleasant, friendly and altogether favorable light, an aspect of the presentation, in these days and times internationally which can be of real importance." Charles S. Aronson, "Escapade in Japan," *Motion Picture Daily*, September 19, 1957.

47. Philip Rowe died suddenly in 1955. Mary Walker stepped in as acting representative (1955–56). For more about Walker's life trajectory, see Lee Iacovoni Sorenson, "In Memorium: Mary Walker Mag Hasse (1911–2007)," *Forum: Newsletter of the Federation of American Women's Clubs Overseas Inc* (Winter 2007–8): 2.

48. TAF had paid South Korea's membership fee for the FPA, at least until 1958. See Jack E. James's letter to Lee Byung-il, November 24, 1958, Media Audio-Visual Films KMPCA, Box 280, AFR.

49. Philip C. Rowe, "Visit in Hong Kong of Korean Observers for the Second Film Festival in South East Asia," April 19, 1955, FMPPSEA 2nd Singapore, Box 15, AFR.

50. "2nd Film Festival Southeast Asia Singapore 1955 Press Release," April 21, 1955, FMPPSEA 2nd Singapore, Box 15, AFR.

51. Nine members of the People's Action Party were elected into the Central Executive Committee with Toh Chin Chye as chairman and Lee Kuan Yew as secretary-general.

52. "Second Southeast Asian Film Festival Open," *Far East Film News* 2, no. 47 (May 13, 1955): 1.

53. Tonu Marsh, "MacDonald May Declare Open Film Festival," *Singapore Standards*, March 12, 1955.

54. The Philippines: *Lapu-Lapu* (Lamberto V. Avellana, 1955, LVN), *Prinsipe Teñoso* (Gregorio Fernandez, 1954, LVN), *Ifugao* (Gerardo de Leon, 1954, Premiere), *Dalagang Ilokana* (Olive La Torre, 1954, Sampaguita), *Dumagit* (Armando Garces, 1954, Sampaguita); Singapore: *Kasih Menumpang* (L. Krishran, 1955, Cathay), *Saudara-Ku* (Laurie Friedman, 1955, Cathay), *Irama Kaseh* (Laurie Friedman, 1955, Cathay), *The First Four Hundred* (Malayan Film Unit), *Rubber from Malaya* (Malayan Film Unit), *Hassan's Homecoming* (Malayan Film Unit), *Youth in Action* (Malayan Film Unit), *Filem Merana* (B. N. Rao, 1955, Malay Film Production), *Hang Tuah* (Phani Majumdar, 1955, Malay Film Production); Indonesia: *After the Curfew* (Lewat Djam Malam, Usmar Ismail, Pesari-Perfini, 1954), *Tarmina* (Lily Sudjo, Pesari, 1955); Hong Kong: *Beyond the Grave* (Doe Ching, 1954, Shaw & Sons), *The Orphan Girl*, *The Heroine*; Macao: *The Long Road* (Eurico Ferrerra, Eurasia Films), Taiwan: *By the Hillside* (1955, CMPC), *Poppy Flower* (Yuan Chongmei, Taiwan Films, also known as *Opium Poppy*); Thailand: *The Brothers* (B. Yugala, Asvin Pictures).

55. "Indonesia Staged Festival to Select Entries," *Far East Film News* 2, no. 47 (May 13, 1955): 31.

56. A letter to James Stewart from John Miller, January 12, 1955, FMPPSEA 2nd, Box 16, AFR.

57. *Kyŏnghyang shinmun*, July 6, 1955, 5.

58. The first Asian Film Festival held in Indonesia was in 1970. It was held from June 16 to 19 in Jakarta. The best picture of that year was an Indonesian film: *What are You Looking for, Palupi?* (*Apa Yang Kau Cari, Palupi?*, Asrul Sani, 1970).

59. *Kyŏnghyang shinmun*, June 19, 1956, 6.

60. "Award Winners," *Far East Film News* 2, no. 49 (May 27, 1955): 9.

61. A letter to James Stewart from John Miller, January 12, 1955, FMPPSEA 2nd, Box 16, AFR.

62. Bleakley McDowell, "Jules and Miriam Bucher" (Master's thesis, New York University, 2015).

63. "Indonesian Studio to Get U.S. Grant," *Nippon Times*, May 16, 1954, 7.

64. Since the Colombo Plan was a United States-UK joint cooperative plan for economic development in the countries of South and Southeast Asia that, in the end, fostered America's authority over the region, particularly in the former British Far Eastern colonies (Malaya, Singapore, North Borneo, Sarawak, and Brunei), the plan, in addition to financial aid, laid weighty emphasis on education. See Antonin Basch, "The Colombo Plan: A Case of Regional Economic Cooperation," *International Organization* 9, no. 1 (1955): 1–18.

65. Sen, *Indonesian Cinema*, 24–25.

66. Miriam Bucher, "2nd Southeast Asian Film Festival, Singapore, May 14–21, 1955," June 6, 1955, FMPPSEA 2nd, Box 16, AFR.

67. Bucher, "2nd Southeast Asian Film Festival, Singapore, May 14–21, 1955."

68. FPA, *Report on the 3rd Annual Film Festival of Southeast Asia*, 34.

69. Kinnia Yau claims that it was Graham who insisted on renaming the event. See Yau, "Shaws' Japanese Collaboration and Competition," 279–91.

70. M. Chase and C. Edwards, "Southeast Asia Motion Picture Producers Federation and Festival," January 7, 1954, Film Festivals General 1951/54, Box 14, AFR.

71. "12 Representing Korea at Festival," Media Audio-Visual KMPCA General, Box 60, AFR.

72. Cho Tong-jae, "Report on the Korean Participation in the 4th Asian Film Festival," June 18, 1957, FMPPSEA 4th, Box 88, AFR.

73. A letter to Thompson from James, July 25, 1957, FMPPSEA 4th, Box 88, AFR.

74. William A. Seiter was a Hollywood director who made more than a hundred feature films and was especially noted for his musicals and light comedies. He is perhaps best remembered for one of the best Laurel and Hardy cycles, *Sons of the Desert* (1933), and the Ginger Rogers and Fred Astaire musical *Roberta* (1935). By the time Seiter attended the festival, he had already stopped directing theatrical features. He retired from directing in 1960.

75. "Verbal Report—William A. Seiter," October 4, 1956, FMPPSEA 3rd, Box 18, AFR.

76. John Miller, "Report on Second Film Festival in Southeast Asia, Singapore 1955," June 18, 1955, FMPPSEA 2nd, Box 16, AFR.

77. Lola Young, the daughter of Chinese and French parents, lived in Hong Kong and appeared in Cantonese films during the 1950s. After becoming the first Hong Kong star to enjoy a Filipino following, she starred in another Hong Kong–Philippines coproduction, *Treasure of General Yamashita* (Rolf Bayer and Chapman Ho, 1957), but retired afterward and went to Italy to study music. See Law and Bren, *Hong Kong Cinema*, 215.

78. Law and Bren, *Hong Kong Cinema*, 205–6.

79. "Affair in Ankuwat: Tragic Love of the King's Daughter," *Nan Guo Dian Ying* [Southern screen] 3 (February 1958): 36–37. For more about *Love with an Alien*, see Sangjoon Lee, "Seoul-Hong Kong-Macau: *Love with an Alien* (1957) and Postwar South Korea-Hong Kong Coproduction," in *Asia-Pacific Film Co-Productions: Theory, Industry and Aesthetics*, ed. Dal Yong Jin and Wendy Su (London: Routledge, 2019), 256–74.

80. FPA, *Report on the 3rd Annual Film Festival of Southeast Asia*, 119.

81. FPA, *Report on the 3rd Annual Film Festival of Southeast Asia*, 120.

82. Richie and Anderson, *The Japanese Film*, 248.

83. Peter J. Katzenstein, "Japan, Technology and Asian Regionalism in Comparative Perspective," in *The Resurgence of East Asia: 500, 150, and 50 Years Perspective*, ed. Giovanni Arrighi, Takeshi Hamashita and Mark Sheldon (London: Routledge, 2003), 214.

84. Aaron Moore expertly examines the ways Japanese intellectuals, bureaucrats, and engineers used "technology" to rally people in Japan and its colonies during Japan's wartime era.

See Aaron Moore, *Constructing East Asia: Technology, Ideology, and Empire in Japan's Wartime Era, 1931–1945* (Palo Alto, CA: Stanford University Press, 2015).

85. Guo-juin Hong, *Taiwan Cinema: A Contested Nation on Screen* (London: Palgrave Macmillan, 2011), 72.

86. FPA, *Report on the 3rd Annual Film Festival of Southeast Asia*, 120–21.

87. FPA, *Report on the 3rd Annual Film Festival of Southeast Asia*, 123.

88. FPA, *Report on the 3rd Annual Film Festival of Southeast Asia*, 124.

89. Indeed, educating film technicians was a very important issue in Asia during the 1950s and 1960s. For instance, K. L. Khandpur, the senior director of the film division in India, was very active throughout the 1950s. For him, educating and training film technicians in Asia were pivotal concerns that most film executives in the region shared throughout the 1950s and 1960s. He proposed two solutions at UNESCO's annual meeting in January 1960. Khandpur stated, "Since satisfactory training facilities are not now available in Southeast Asia, technicians of the region can be given adequate instruction (a) by arranging for them to train in western countries, or (b) by setting up comprehensive training schools within the region itself." Khandpur claimed that the latter was preferable and that the two more advanced countries, India and Japan, should act passionately to reeducate the rest of the Southeast Asian film technicians. K. L. Khandpur, "Problems of Training Film Technicians in South East Asia," *UNESCO Meeting on Development of Information Media in South East Asia*, Bangkok, January 18–30, 1960.

90. Cho Tong-jae, "Report on the Korean Participation in the 4th Asian Film Festival."

91. "Hong Kong's *Back Door*, Yu Ming Cop High Honors at Asian Film Fest," *Variety*, April 19, 1960, 11.

92. "Funds Used by Fiscal Year Since Initiation of Projects," unknown author and unknown date, Production Fund General, Box 171, AFR.

93. "Asia Pictures," February 3, 1959, Audio-Visual Movies Asia Pictures 1958/59, Box 171, AFR.

94. A letter to Stewart from Tanner, January 5, 1954, Film Festivals General 1951/54, Box 14, AFR.

95. *Eiga Nenkan* (1956), 55.

96. John Miller, "Recommendations for Future Asia Foundation Relationships with the Federation of Motion Picture Producers of Southeast Asia and Its Member Film Industries," June 16, 1955, FMPPSEA 2nd, Box 16, AFR.

97. "Asia Foundation Monthly Reports," February 11, 1955, Box 1, RBP.

Chapter 4. Constructing the Anticommunist Producers' Alliance

1. The Committee for a Free Asia Study Group, *A Symposium on the Political, Economic and Cultural Position of the Overseas Chinese*, The Committee for a Free Asia, August 15, 1953, 3.

2. Lu Yan, "Limits to Propaganda: Hong Kong's Leftist Media in the Cold War and Beyond," in *The Cold War in Asia: The Battle for Hearts and Minds*, edited by Zheng Yangwen, Hong Liu, and Michael Szonyi (Leiden: Brill 2010), 98.

3. "Asia Foundation Monthly Reports," October 24, 1953, Box 1, RBP

4. Robert D. Grey, "Analysis of Financial Situation," March 18, 1955, Media Audio-Visual Asia Pictures, Box 171, AFR.

5. John Miller, "The Chinese Mainland Film Offensive in Hong Kong and the Position of the Non-Communist Hong Kong Producer," May 21, 1957, MEDIA Audio-Visual Movies Asia Pictures, Box 9, AFR.

6. Poshek Fu, *Between Shanghai and Hong Kong: The Politics of Chinese Cinemas* (Palo Alto, CA: Stanford University Press, 2003), 4.

7. John Miller, "Review, Evaluation and Proposed Project Funding for Fiction Motion Picture Activity," June 25, 1953, MEDIA Audio-Visual Movies Asia Pictures, Box 9, AFR.

8. Charles Tanner, "Hong Kong Movie Production Project," July 14, 1953, MEDIA Audio-Visual Movies Asia Pictures, Box 9, AFR.

9. For a more detailed account of Chang Kuo-sin's "Tri-Dimensional Project for the Battle for People's Minds," see Charles Leary, "The Most Careful Arrangement for a Careful Fiction: A Short History of Asia Pictures," *Inter-Asian Cultural Studies* 13, no. 4 (2012), 548–58.

10. Leary, "The Most Careful Arrangement," 548–58.

11. National Southwestern Associated University (*Lianda*) was the war-time amalgamation of Peking University, Tsinghua University, and Nankai University.

12. Lau C. K, "Chang Kuo-sin: Patriot Who Stuck to the Truth," in Chang Kuo-sin, *Eight Months Behind the Bamboo Curtain: A Report on the First Eight Months of Communist Rule in China* (Kowloon: City University of Hong Kong Press, 2015), 15–25.

13. It was, according to Huang Yu, a "rare first-person account of China's transformation from capitalism to communism." See Huang Yu, "Foreword," in Chang Kuo-sin, *Eight Months Behind the Bamboo Curtain*. Curiously, the biographical sketch of Chang by Lau C. K. that appears in this reprinted version does not mention the Asia Foundation.

14. For more about Asia Press, see Chen Lingzi's MA thesis, "In the Midst of the Overt and Covert: Hong Kong Asia Press in the Cultural Cold War" (National University of Singapore, 2017).

15. Man-fung Yip, "Closely Watched Films: Surveillance and Postwar Hong Kong Leftist Cinema," in *Surveillance in Asian Cinema: Under Eastern Eyes*, ed. Karen Fang (New York: Routledge, 2017), 44.

16. Grey, "Analysis of Financial Situation."

17. Geraldine Fitch, "How a Young Chinese Is Battling the Communists with Books," *New Leader*, January 5, 1953.

18. "The Asia Pictures Limited," July 15, 1953, Tradition Asia Pictures (Hong Kong), Box 9, AFR.

19. "The Asia Pictures Limited."

20. Poshek Fu, "Modernity, Diasporic Capital, and 1950's Hong Kong Mandarin Cinema," *Jump Cut: A Review of Contemporary Media* 49 (Spring 2007). https://www.ejumpcut.org/archive/jc49.2007/Poshek/.

21. Yingjin Zhang, "National Cinema as Translocal Practice: Reflections on Chinese Film Historiography," in *The Chinese Cinema Book*, ed. Song Hwee Lim and Julian Ward (New York: Palgrave Macmillan, 2011), 21.

22. Chang Kuo-sin, "Motion Picture Project," January 8, 1953, Tradition Asia Pictures (Hong Kong), Box 9, AFR.

23. Chang, "Motion Picture Project," January 8, 1953.

24. *Asia Pictorial Collection*, Hong Kong University Library Special Collections, Hong Kong University library.

25. Grey, "Analysis of Financial Situation."

26. Chang, "Motion Picture Project," January 8, 1953.

27. Thomas D. Scott, "Motion Picture Project," January 16, 1953, MEDIA Audio-Visual Movies Asia Pictures, Box 9, AFR.

28. Chang, "Motion Picture Project," January 8, 1953.

29. Delmer M. Brown, "Motion Picture Project," April 1, 1954, MEDIA Audio-Visual Movies Asia Pictures, Box 9, AFR.

30. Brown, "Motion Picture Project," April 1, 1954.

31. Brown, "Motion Picture Project," April 1, 1954.

32. Brown, "Motion Picture Project," April 1, 1954.

33. Charles Tanner, "Asia Foundation Movie Critique," March 1, 1955, MEDIA Audio-Visual Movies Asia Pictures "Heroine," Box 9, AFR.

34. L. Z. Yuan, "Screening of 'The Heroine,'" March 3, 1955, MEDIA Audio-Visual Movies Asia Pictures "Heroine," Box 9, AFR.

35. Tanner, "Asia Foundation Movie Critique."

36. Borzage's Letter to Charles Tanner, March 3, 1955, MEDIA Audio-Visual Movies Asia Pictures "Heroine," Box 9, AFR.

37. Albert Deane's Letter to Tanner, March 2, 1955, MEDIA Audio-Visual Movies Asia Pictures "Heroine," Box 9, AFR.

38. Luigi Lurashi, "The Heroine," March 2, 1955, MEDIA Audio-Visual Movies Asia Pictures "Heroine," Box 9, AFR.

39. Chang Kuo-sin's Letter to Tanner, April 28, 1955, Media Audio-Visual Movies Asia Pictures 1955–57, Box 171, AFR

40. John Miller, "Review, Evaluation and Proposed Project Funding for Fiction Motion Picture Activity," June 25, 1954, Tradition Asia Pictures (Hong Kong), Box 9, AFR.

41. James T. Ivy, "Motion Picture Program," July 15, 1955, Media Audio-Visual Movies Asia Pictures 1955–57, Box 171, AFR.

42. Supporting Chang was a remarkably generous act on the part of TAF. For instance, the general budget for the Hong Kong office in 1954–55 was USD 436,372. The total expenditure of the Asia Press, including the two bookstores, was USD 81,108, and Asia Pictures spent USD 80,125. TAF thus allocated a total of USD 161,233, more than one third of the total budget, to the two companies operated by Chang.

43. "Quarterly Activity Reports: October 31—December 31, 1956," January 5, 1957, Media Audio-Visual Movies Asia Pictures 1955–57, Box 171, AFR.

44. Suh Sang-mok, "The Economy in Historical Perspective," in *Structural Adjustment in a Newly Industrialized Country: The Korean Experience*, ed. Vittorio Corbo and Sang-mok Suh (Baltimore: Johns Hopkins University Press, 1992), 7–10.

45. Charles Tanner, "Motion Picture Program for Korea," October 20, 1954, Media Audio-Visual Motion Picture 1956, Box 60, AFR.

46. S. R. Joey Long, "Winning Hearts and Minds: U.S. Psychological Warfare Operations in Singapore, 1955–1961," *Diplomatic History* 32, no. 5 (November 2008): 899.

47. Osgood, *Total Cold War*, 104.

48. Nicholas J. Cull, *The Cold War and the United States Information Agency: American Propaganda and Public Democracy, 1945–1989* (Cambridge: Cambridge University Press, 2008), 123.

49. Kim, using filming equipment belonging to USIS, produced *A Cross in Gunfire* (*P'ohwa sog ŭi shipjaga*) in 1955. In a film set in the middle of the Korean War, a South Korean lieutenant (Kim Chin-gyu) and his troops sacrificed their lives for the sake of wounded American soldiers who were isolated and attacked by the Chinese Army. The anti-Japanese rhetoric was promptly converted to an infusion of anticommunism, and by doing so Kim successfully proved his "reformed" political and ideological identity to postwar South Korean society. In the same year, Kim was unanimously elected the president of the Korean Motion Picture Producers Association.

50. A letter to Blum from Brown, July 13, 1955, Box 1, RBP.

51. The total budget for the fiscal year 1955/56 was USD 231,045 including salaries, allowances, and operating expenses. "Korea Budget Summary," Budget (Allocations & Aps) 1956/57, Box 59, AFR.

52. "Assistant to the Korean Motion Picture Industry," Korea Budget AP's & Allocations etc 1955/56, Box 59, AFR.

53. "Assistant to the Korean Motion Picture Industry."

54. Jae-young Cha and Chanhee Yeom, "1950nyŏn-tae chuhan mikongpowŏn ŭi kilokyŏnghwa wa mikuk ŭi imichi kuch'uk" [Documentary films of the USIS Korea in the 1950s for constructing American images], *Han'gugŏllonhakpo* [Korean journal of journalism and communication] 56, no. 1 (2012): 245.

55. Heo Eun, "Naengjŏn shidae migug ŭi minjok kukka hyŏng sŏng kaeip kwa hegemoni kuch'ug ŭi ch'oejŏnsŏn chuhan mi gongbowŏn yŏng hwa," [The intervention of the United States in the formation of the nation-state and the frontline in terms of the establishment of hegemony during the Cold War era: with a special focus on the films produced by the United States Information Service in Korea], *Han'guksa yŏn'gu* [Journal of Korean history] 155 (December 2011): 144.

56. Han Sang Kim, "Cold War and the Contested Identity Formation of Korean Filmmakers: On *Boxes of Death* and Kim Ki-yong's USIS Film," *Inter-Asian Cultural Studies* 14, no. 1 (2013): 551–63.

57. See "Media Publications General" file, Box 61, AFR. TAF's financial support to the selective magazines of South Korea during the period consisted of donating paper to the publishers. "Media Paper General," "Media Publications Literature & Arts Weekly Oh Young-jin," and "Media Publications Women's World" files, Box 61, AFR.

58. Memorandum from Laurence G. Thompson, TAF representative, to Choi Yu, Minister of Education, March 21, 1958, Kukka girogwŏn gwa taet'ongnyŏng girogwŏn [Nara Repository and Presidential Archives], Sŏngnam, South Korea.

59. Greg Barnhisel, "Cold Warriors of the Book: American Book Programs in the 1950s," *Book History* 13 (2010): 186–87.

60. Armstrong, "The Cultural Cold War in Korea," 72.

61. Chungmoo Choi, "The Magic and Violence of Modernization in Post-Colonial Korea," in *Post-Colonial Classics of Korean Cinema*, ed. Chungmoo Choi (Irvine: University of Irvine, 1998), 5.

62. Miriam Bratu Hansen, "The Mass Production of the Senses: Classical Cinema as Vernacular Modernism," *Modernism/Modernity* 6, no. 2 (1999): 59–77.

63. Charles Tanner, "Korea Publishing," February 24, 1954, Media Publications Literature & Arts Weekly Oh Young-jin, Box 61, AFR.

64. Tanner, "Motion Picture Program for Korea."

65. John Miller, "Documentary Film on Korea," October 26, 1955, Media Audio-Visual Films—John Miller, Box 60, AFR.

66. John Miller, "Assistant to the Korean Motion Picture Industry," February 11, 1956, Korean Motion Picture Industry General, Box 60, AFR.

67. A letter to Eric Johnston, March 16, 1954, Japan Writer Project H-7 1953–54, Box 9, AFR.

68. Robert Blum, "Notes on Visit to Korea (October 29–November 2, 1956)," General Trip to Korea—R. Blum, Box 61, AFR.

69. This significant historical record is now available. See Sangjoon Lee, "On 'The Korean Film Industry': The Asia Foundation, Korean Motion Picture Cultural Association, and John Miller, 1956," *Journal of Japanese and Korean Cinema* 7, no. 2 (2015): 95–112.

70. The budget (USD 50,000) was approved on January 26, 1956. Stewart justified this unusually large expenditure, writing, "These proposals are based on the recommendations of John Miller of the Tokyo office who conducted a two-week survey of the South Korean motion picture industry in January . . . A film industry is a cultural asset to a nation. The motion picture medium is not only a form of art and entertainment but is also an effective method of communicating ideas. In Korea the film is practically the only means of mass entertainment. Korean leaders feel there is a strong need to preserve and expand their national production with its own individual characteristics. The principal that people usually prefer films portraying their own culture in their own language appears to obtain in Korea." "Assistant to the Korean Motion Picture Industry."

71. *Tonga ilbo*, July 7, 1956.

72. Miller, "Assistant to the Korean Motion Picture Industry."

73. A Letter from Mary Walker to Chang Key-young [Chang Ki-yŏng], September 4, 1956, Media Audio-Visual KMPCA General, Box 60, AFR.

74. Lee, "On John Miller's 'The Korean Film Industry,'" 8. Miller's report was, as he himself wrote, "the first study of its kind that has been made by either a Korean or a foreigner." Miller (December 29, 1956) certainly wished to make his report available to the Ministry of Education or "someone close to President Rhee." It seems, however, that the report did not even leave the foundation's office. Lawrence G. Thompson, the representative of Seoul office who had succeeded Rowe, sent a letter to Blum (June 14, 1957). He wrote, "Many months ago John Miller informed us that he had requested the Home Office to make available copies of his report for distribution to certain people in Korea. To date we have never heard whether this is to be done. We have received a number of inquiries from people who had heard of the existence of the report, and some of them have read our first copy. The KMPCA expressed the intention of putting out a Korean translation, but this has so far not been done. It may be that by now the report is becoming too dated to be of future interest." See Miller, "Paper on the Korean Motion Picture Industry," December 29, 1956, Media Audio-Visual Film-John Miller, Box 60, AFR.

75. For more about *Madam Freedom* and the 1950s South Korean cinema, see Christina Klein, "*Madame Freedom* (1956): Spectatorship and the Modern Woman," in *Rediscovering Korean Cinema*, ed. Sangjoon Lee (Ann Arbor: University of Michigan Press, 2019): 118–31.

76. "Han'guk ch'oedae ŭi yŏnghwa sŭt'yudio anyang sŭt'yudio" [Korea's biggest motion picture studio: Anyang Studio], *Shin yŏnghwa* [New cinema] (December 1957), 8–10. The reported budget of the construction was a massive USD 250,000.

77. Miller, "Paper on the Korean Motion Picture Industry."

78. Miller, "Paper on the Korean Motion Picture Industry."

79. "Proposed Program Budget 57–58," February 1, 1957, Korea Budget AP's & Allocations etc 1957/58, Box 59, AFR.

80. Robert Blum, "Loan for Production of Korean Motion Picture," February 16, 1956, Media Audio-Visual Films (Lee Yong Min), Box 60, AFR.

81. *Tonga ilbo*, May 29, 1959.

82. Yi Min, "Han hong hapchak yŏnghwa igukchŏngwŏn" [Korea-China coproductions and *Love with an Alien*], *Shin yŏnghwa* [New cinema] (December 1957), 78.

83. Suh, "The Economy in Historical Perspective," 7–10.

84. In the introduction to *South Korean Golden Age Melodrama: Gender, Genre, and National Cinema* (Detroit: Wayne State University Press, 2005), Kathleen McHugh and Nancy Abelmann write: "In the immediate aftermath of the Korean War, the release of two enormously popular South Korean films, *Story of Chunhyang* (1955) and *Madame Freedom* (1956), signaled the beginning of what would come to be known as the Golden Age of South Korean cinema . . . During the brief period from 1955 to 1972, a number of South Korean directors produced a body of works as historically, aesthetically, and politically significant as that of other well-known national film movements such as Italian Neorealism, French New Wave, and New German Cinema" (2–3).

85. "Transmittal of Letter of Agreement," June 25, 1962, Media Audio-Visual Films Korean Motion picture Cultural Association KMPCA, Box 280, AFR.

86. Partick Judge, "Meeting with Ed Hardy and Chang," July 9, 1958, Media Audio-Visual Movies Asia Pictures 1958/59, Box 171, AFR.

87. Yip, "Closely Watched Films," 45.

88. John F. Sullivan, "Asia Pictures," February 3, 1959, Media Audio-Visual Movies Asia Pictures 1958/59, Box 171, AFR.

89. A letter from John Grange to Robert Blum, October 30, 1959, Publishers Asia Press Discussions (Asia Pictures), Box 172, AFR.

90. J. F. Richardson, "Turnover of the Asia Pictures, Limited and The Asia Press, Limited to Chang Kuo-sin," March 31, 1961, Publishers Asia Press Asia Pictures Turnover Corres, Box 172, AFR.

91. A letter from Chang Kuo-sin to John Grange, March 28, 1960, Publishers Asia Press Discussions (Asia Pictures), Box 172, AFR.

92. Letter from Chang Kuo-sin to John Grange, March 28, 1960.

93. Letter from Chang Kuo-sin to John Grange, March 28, 1960.

94. Robert Blum, "The Asia Foundation: Purposes and Program," *United Asia: International Magazine of Afro-Asian Affairs* 11, no. 5 (1959): 414.

95. Thomas W. Ennis, "Noel Busch, Author and Correspondent for *Life Magazine*," *New York Times*, September 11, 1985, 27.

96. John Miller's Letter to Blum, February 11, 1957, Media Audio-Visual Film-John Miller, Box 60, AFR.

97. Untitled letter, May 30, 1961, Folder 44, Box 4, Freda Utley Papers (1886–1978), Hoover Institution Archive, Stanford University.

Chapter 5. Projecting Asian Cinema to the World

1. A year later, Kim Ki-young directed *The Housemaid* (*Hanyŏ*, 1960). A huge box office success at the time of its release, *The Housemaid* swept the Best Korean Film Awards in 1960, receiving five major awards. Of the thirty-two films Kim directed between 1955 and 1995, *The Housemaid* remains the most famous, and is considered one of the best films ever made in South Korea.

2. For more on Kim Ki-young's *Boxes of Death* and the USIS network, see Han Sang Kim, "Cold War and the Contested Identity Formation of Korean Filmmakers."

3. *The San Francisco Examiner*, October 19, 1961.

4. Romano Tozzi, "San Francisco's 4th Festival," *Films in Review* 6, no. 10 (December 1961): 607–8.

5. Romano Tozzi, "San Francisco's 3rd Festival," *Films in Review* 6, no. 1 (January 1961): 18.

6. de Valck, *Film Festivals*, 14.

7. de Valck, *Film Festivals*, 165.

8. Cindy Hing-Yuk Wong, *Film Festivals: Culture, People, and Power on the Global Screen* (New Brunswick, NJ: Rutgers University Press, 2011), 11. For more about the Karlovy Vary film festival's ideological apparatus and festival programming, see Regina Câmara, "From Karlovy Vary to Cannes: Brazilian Cinema Nuovo at European Film Festivals in the 1960s," in *Cultural Transfer and Political Conflicts: Film Festivals in the Cold War*, ed. Andreas Kötzing and Caroline Moine (Göttingen, Germany: V&R Unipress, 2017), 63–76.

9. Heide Fehrenback, *Cinema in Democratizing Germany: Reconstructing National Identity after Hitler* (Chapel Hill: University of North Carolina Press, 1995), 234–35.

10. Fehrenback, *Cinema in Democratizing Germany*, 236.

11. Fehrenback, *Cinema in Democratizing Germany*, 234–35.

12. Andreas Kötzing, "Cultural and Film Policy in the Cold War: The Film Festivals of Oberhausen and Leipzig and German-German Relations," in *Cultural Transfer and Political Conflicts: Film Festivals in the Cold War*, 32–33.

13. Cynthia Grenier, "The Festival Scene, 1960: Berlin, Karlovy-Vary, Venice," *Film Quarterly* 14, no. 2 (Winter 1960): 24.

14. Harold Zellerbach (1894–1978) was born in San Francisco on March 25, 1894, the son of Isadore and Jennie Baruh Zellerbach. He attended the University of California at Berkeley and earned his bachelor's degree in economics at the University of Pennsylvania in 1917. He was a top executive for fifty years of the Crown Zellerbach Corporation, a paper company started by his grandfather in 1870. See "Harold Lionel Zellerbach, 83, Dies: An Industrialist and Patron of Arts," *New York Times*, January 31, 1978, 30.

15. *San Francisco Examiner*, November 1, 1959.

16. J. I. Pimsleur, "The Man Who Has the World on a Shoestring," *San Francisco Sunday Chronicle*, October 16, 1960.

17. Traude Gómez, "The Glamour, the Stars and the Films that Kicked Off the San Francisco Film Festival in 1957," *San Francisco International Film Festival: The First to Fifty*, accessed March 19, 2020, http://history.sffs.org/our_history/how_sfiff_started.php.

18. "S.F. to Stage Film Festival This Fall," *San Francisco Examiner*, September 9, 1957.

19. "Film Festival Aide Touring Europe Now," *San Francisco Chronicle*, October 15, 1957.

20. Warren Harris, "See S.F. Film Festival Big Goodwill Booster," *Motion Picture Daily*, October 28, 1957.

21. "In Paris with Gene Moskowitz," *Variety*, October 24, 1957.

22. Emilia Hodel, "On *The Last Warrior*," *San Francisco News*, December 11, 1957.

23. "Japan Movie Drama Rates 'Magnificent,'" *Oakland Tribune*, December 12, 1957.

24. "*Pather Panchali*," *San Francisco Chronicle*, December 10, 1957.

25. Gavin Lambert, "Film Festival in San Francisco," *Film Quarterly* 12, no. 1 (Autumn 1958): 24.

26. Lambert, "Film Festival in San Francisco," 24.

27. "S.F. Hosts First US Film Festival," *San Francisco Examiner*, December 5, 1957.

28. Charles Einfeld, "U.S. Needs Film Fest in Typical City, Not Miami or D.C.," *Variety*, July 1, 1959.

29. Bob Thomas, "Film Festival for Hollywood Doubted," *Associated Press*, November 5, 1962.

30. Stanley Eichelbaum, "Mystery of Missing Hollywood Movies," source unidentified, November 3, 1961, San Francisco Film Festival Collection, AMPAS.

31. Eichelbaum, "Mystery of Missing Hollywood Movies."

32. "Why US Snubs Frisco Festival," *Variety*, November 4, 1959.

33. Borzage had also served on a jury of the Grand Festival Internacional Cinemagrafico in Buenos Aires, along with Mary Pickford, just one month before the Southeast Asian Film Festival. Pickford herself attended SFIFF in 1960. "Studio Publicity Directors Committee WE 3–7101 (Duke Wales)," Film Festivals P-Z, Folder 149, AMPAS.

34. "San Francisco's Festival. . . . the US is Not Represented," *Film Daily*, October 28, 1958.

35. "Why Isn't Hollywood in the Film Festival?" *San Francisco Chronicle*, November 5, 1958.

36. Romano Tozzi, "San Francisco's 4th Festival," 599–60.

37. Murray Schumach, "Zinnemann Urges Festival Support," *New York Times*, November 17, 1961.

38. "More to Running an Art House than Booking a Bardot Picture," *Box Office*, July 20, 1959.

39. Balio, *The Foreign Film Renaissance on American Screens*, 129.

40. Donald Richie and Joseph Anderson, "Traditional Theatre and the Film in Japan," *Film Quarterly* 12, no. 1 (Autumn 1958): 2–9. Within one year, Richie and Anderson published the first English-language comprehensive history of Japanese cinema, *The Japanese Film: Art and Industry*. *Film Quarterly* was first published in 1945 as *Hollywood Quarterly*. The University of California Press was the publisher, and its first editorial board included John Howard Lawson, Franklin Fearing, and the writer-director Abraham Polonsky. It was renamed the *Quarterly of Film, Radio, and Television* in 1951, and became *Film Quarterly* in 1958.

41. Henry Hart, "New York's Japanese Film Festival," *Films in Review* 8, no. 3 (March 1957): 101.

42. Margaret Pollard, "Fifth Asian Film Festival," March 24, 1958, Film Festival 5th Manila, Box 90, AFR.

43. Richard J. Miller, "San Francisco International Film Festival," July 28, 1958, Film Festival Intl. San Francisco, Box 90, AFR.

44. Miller, "San Francisco International Film Festival."

45. Pollard, "Fifth Asian Film Festival."

46. Pollard, "Fifth Asian Film Festival."

47. Margaret Pollard, "Filipino Academy of Movie Arts and Sciences," April 14, 1958, Film Festival 5th Manila, Box 90, AFR.

48. Harry H. Pierson, "San Francisco International Film Festival," September 12, 1958, Film Festival Intl. San Francisco, Box 90, AFR. This document lists Kukrit Pramoj as a director, but he was a narrator.

49. Cho Tong-jae, "Korean Participation in the San Francisco Film Festival," September 22, 1958, Film Festival Intl. San Francisco, Box 90, AFR.

50. USD 10,000 was converted to HKD 60,000. According to John Gange, TAF's Hong Kong representative, the total budget of *Nobody's Child* was HKD 285,000. John Gange, "Kuo Phone Film Co, Loan (AP-6011)," August 3, 1960, Media Audio-Visual Movies A Poor Child "Nobody's Child," Box 171, AFR. TAF had been reducing its assistance in the motion picture program in Asia, as mentioned earlier, and USD 10,000 was the maximum amount of support the current TAF office could provide. Pat Judge, "Loan for *A Poor Child*," February 28, 1958, Media Audio-Visual Movies Production Fund General, Box 171, AFR.

51. Paul Fonoroff, "Nobody's Child," *South China Morning Post*, March 31, 2013.

52. Chris Berry remarked, after watching the restored film for the first time at the 16th Far East Film Festival in Udine, Italy, in 2014: "A Mandarin-language film made in Hong Kong but set in mainland China, it [*Nobody's Child*] expresses both the nostalgia for home felt by refugees from Communism who had taken up residence in Hong Kong and also their awful memories of flight in the scenes set in snowy winter and shot in Hokkaido, Japan." Chris Berry, "Hanging on in There: Hong Kong Popular Cinema Featured at the 16th Far East Film Festival," *Senses of Cinema*, June 2014, http://sensesofcinema.com/2014/festival-reports/hanging-on-in-there-hong-kong-popular-cinema-featured-at-the-16th-far-east-film-festival.

53. Judge, "Loan for *A Poor Child*."

54. Judge, "Loan for *A Poor Child*."

55. Angel On Ki Shing, "The Star as Cultural Icon: The Case of Josephine Siao Fong Fong" (master's thesis, University of Hong Kong, 2000), 11–12.

56. William Smyly, "Hong Kong's Shirley Temple Finishes Her Film," *China Mail*, July 5, 1958, 1.

57. Chung Hsia, "Siao Fang Fang, The Mandarin Movie Prodigy Who Returns to the Free World," *World Today* 142 (February 1, 1958), Media Audio-Visual Movies Production Fund General, Box 171, AFR.

58. Judge, "Loan for *A Poor Child*."

59. Chung, "Siao Fang Fang."

60. Chung, "Siao Fang Fang."

61. Emilia Hodel, "Gala Ball to Climax SF Film Festival," *San Francisco News*, November 5, 1958.

62. Cited in "Hong Kong Film Called Primitive," *South China Morning Post*, November 12, 1958, 12.

63. L.Z. Yuan, "Nobody's Child," November 13, 1958, Media Audio-Visual Movies Production Fund General, Box 171, AFR.

64. Yuan, "Nobody's Child."

65. Yuan, "Nobody's Child."

66. Chu Hsu-hun, "Working Situation April-July 1959," dates unknown, Media Audio-Visual Movies Production Fund General, Box 171, AFR.

67. Ramona Curry, "Bridging the Pacific with Love Eterne," in *China Forever: The Shaw Brothers and Diasporic Cinema*, ed. Poshek Fu (Urbana: University of Illinois Press, 2008), 184.

68. Tozzi, "San Francisco's 3rd Festival," 25.

69. "The Colorful Cannes Film Festival," *Nan Guo Dian Ying* [Southern screen] 29 (July 1960): 30–33; "Shaws March into World Market," *Nan Guo Dian Ying* [Southern screen] 65 (July 1963): 2–3.

70. Tozzi, "San Francisco's 4th Festival," 603–4.

71. "Two Fine Festival Films," *San Francisco Examiner*, October 28, 1960.

72. Kim So-dong's Letter to Robert Sheeks, August 11, 1960, Film Festival Intl. San Francisco, Box 233, AFR.

73. James stated, "We discovered that Mr. Kim, who has encountered numerous financial difficulties recently, has moved his office—to a location we have not yet discovered—and sold his house—we do not know his new address. It is now too late to help or advise Mr. Kim, I'm afraid. I doubt that he would have the money even to have English subtitles added. It's too bad. *The Gambler* [*The Money*] is one of the better pictures made here recently. It comes pretty close to telling the brutal truth about Korean farm life, so close, in fact that the Ministry of Education last year refused to approve it for export." Jack E. James, Letter to Blum, September 6, 1960, Film Festival Intl. San Francisco, Box 233, AFR.

74. Stephen Uhalley Jr. was a marine veteran of the Korean War and was an officer of the Asia Foundation from 1960 to 1967. He left TAF after receiving his doctoral degree in modern Chinese history from UC Berkeley in 1967. Later he became the first director of the Center for Asia and Pacific Studies at the University of Hawaii. He was one of the founding associates for the East-West Center at the university. Uhalley Jr. was the author of *A History of the Chinese Communist Party* (Stanford University Press, 1988).

75. Stephen Uhalley, Jr., "International Film Festival," September 20, 1960, Film Festival Intl. San Francisco, Box 233, AFR.

76. Martin Russell, "Matinee Premieres of Two Far Eastern Films," *Variety*, November 6, 1962.

77. Michael S. Willis, "The Evergreen," *Variety*, November 7, 1962.

78. Kelly Y. Jeong, "*Aimless Bullet* (1961): Postwar Dystopia, Canonicity, and Cinema Realism," in *Rediscovering Korean Cinema*, ed. Sangjoon Lee (Ann Arbor: University of Michigan Press, 2019), 161.

79. *San Francisco Examiner*, November 7, 1963.

80. Richard Dyer MacCann, "Films and Film Training in the Republic of Korea," *Journal of the University Film Producers Association*, 16, no. 1 (1964), 17.

81. "The Aimless Bullet," *San Francisco Chronicle*, November 12, 1963.

82. "Festival Film: Inside Story—Why 'Bullet' was Entered at Frisco," *Film Daily*, November 12, 1963.

83. "Festival Film: Inside Story."

84. "Unusual Films from Yugoslavia and Korea," *San Francisco Chronicle*, November 7, 1963.

85. *Aimless Bullet* was ranked as the second best Korean film, after Kim Ki-young's *The Housemaid* (*Hanyŏ*, 1961), according to Korean Film Archive's 100 Korean Films, selected by critics, journalists, filmmakers, and scholars in South Korea in 2013. See Han'guk yŏngsang jaryowŏn [Korean film archive], *Han'guk yŏnghwa 100sŏn: 'ch'ŏngch'un ŭi shipjharo'esŏ 'p'iet'a'kkaji* [100 Korean films: From *Turning Point of the Youngsters* to *Pieta*], Han'guk yŏngsang jaryowŏn [Korean film archive] (2013).

86. Beginning in the late 1980s, a new cinema from South Korea emerged, collectively called by Western critics, journalists, and scholars "the Korean New Wave" (analogous to the "Hong Kong New Wave" of the late 1970s and "New Taiwan Cinema" of the mid-1980s). See Isolde Standish, "Korean Cinema and the New Realism: Text and Context," *East-West Film Journal* 7,

no. 2 (1993): 54–80; Moon Jae-cheol, "The Meaning of Newness in Korean Cinema: Korean New Wave and After," *Korea Journal* (Spring 2008): 36–59.

87. *The 9th San Francisco International Film Festival Program*, 1965, San Francisco Film Festival Collection, AMPAS.

88. The Film Society of Lincoln Center, *New York Film Festival Programs: 1963–1975* (New York: Arno Press, 1976), 10.

89. Susan Sontag, "The Decay of Cinema," *New York Times Magazine*, February 25, 1996, 60–61.

90. Rahul Hamid, "From Urban Bohemia to Euro Glamour: The Establishment and Early Years of the New York Film Festival," in *Film Festival Yearbook 1: The Festival Circuit*, ed. Dina Iordanova and Regan Rhyne (St Andrews: St Andrews University Press, 2009), 67–81.

91. See Film Society of Lincoln Center, *New York Film Festival.*

92. Hamid, "New York Film Festival."

93. Walter Blum, "Irving Levin: Pills, Brickbats and a Certain Fame Are the Rewards of the Boss of the S. F. International Film Festival," *San Francisco Examiner*, October 4, 1964.

94. Theodore Bredt, "On Films and Festivals," *San Francisco Chronicle*, October 27, 1963.

95. Bob Thomas, "Film Festival for Hollywood Doubted," *Associated Press*, November 5, 1962.

96. Blum, "Irving Levin."

97. John Miller, "Report on First Film Festival in Southeast Asia," May 31, 1954, FMPPSEA 1st Japan, Box 14, AFR.

98. A letter to Stewart from Robert B. Sheeks, April 9, 1954, FMPPSEA 1st Japan, Box 14, AFR. Sheeks stressed, at the end of his letter to Stewart, "We treat our work with Hodge and this Festival as confidential."

99. Miller, "Report on First Film Festival in Southeast Asia."

100. "Hong Kong's 'Back Door,' Yu Ming Cop High Honors at Asian Film Fest," *Variety*, April 19, 1960.

101. Law and Bren, *Hong Kong Cinema*, 167.

102. Yau, "Shaws' Japanese Collaboration and Competition," 279.

103. "'Oscar' Time in Asia: Sixth Asian Film Festival," *Nan Guo Dian Ying* [Southern screen] 15 (May 1959): 15.

104. "Glittering Sixth Asian Film Festival," *Nan Guo Dian Ying* [Southern screen] 16 (June 1959): 5.

105. Quoted in Yau, "Shaws' Japanese Collaboration and Competition," 282.

106. See Brian Yecies and Ae-Gyung Shim, "Asian Interchange: Korean-Hong Kong Co-Productions of the 1960s," *Journal of Japanese and Korean Cinema* 4, no. 1 (2012): 15–28.

107. Grace Ng, "Li Han Hsiang's Long Men Zhen," in *Li Han-Hsiang, Storyteller*, ed. Wong Ain-Ling (Hong Kong: Hong Kong Film Archive, 2007), 138–57.

Chapter 6. The Rise and Demise of a Developmental State Studio

1. Zbigniew Brzezinski, "Japan's Global Engagement," *Foreign Affairs* 50 (1971–72): 270–82; Brzezinski, *The Choice: Global Domination or Global Leadership* (New York: Basic Books, 2004).

2. Tino Balio, '"Struggles for Control," in *The American Film Industry*, ed. Tino Balio (Madison: University of Wisconsin Press, 1985), 122.

3. Janet Staiger, "The Package-Unit System: Unit Management After 1955," in *The Classical Hollywood Cinema: Film Production and Mode of Production to 1960*, eds. David Bordwell, Janet Staiger, and Kristin Thompson (New York: Columbia University Press, 1985).

4. Balio, '"Struggles for Control," 91–92.

5. Balio, ' "Struggles for Control," 123.

6. Michael Storper, "The Transition to Flexible Specialization in the US Film Industry: External Economies, the Division of Labour, and the Crossing of Industrial Divides," *Cambridge Journal of Economics* 13, no. 2 (June 1989): 275.

7. Cho Chun-hyŏng, ed., *Oral History Project 2008: Shin Films* (Seoul, Korea: Korean Film Archive, 2008), 129–30.

8. Ironically, the collective desire to establish vertically integrated motion picture studios in Asia during the 1960s materialized as Hollywood itself was moving from mass production methods to a post-Fordist form of production organization, what Michael Storper terms "flexible production." See Storper, "The Transition to Flexible Specialization," 273.

9. "Cultural proximity," according to Joseph Straubhaar, is a comparative advantage factor based on cultural similarities that go beyond language to include such elements as dress, nonverbal communication, humor, religion, music, and narrative style. Joseph D. Straubhaar, "Beyond Media Imperialism: Asymmetrical Interdependence and Cultural Proximity," *Critical Studies in Media Communication* 8, no. 1 (1991): 39–59.

10. The film historian Kyoko Hirano draws attention to three factors in this fall: the emergence and popularity of television, the failure of major studios to produce interesting or entertaining films, and their absurd management structure. Hirano, "Japan," 410.

11. *Sŏul shinmun*, January 10, 1962, 3.

12. The 1960s in South Korea began with two political upheavals: the April Revolution of 1960 and the May 16 coup of 1961. The April Revolution was started by citizens to condemn electoral corruption and to overthrow the dictatorship of Syngman Rhee. The revolution brought about important changes in the film industry, one of which was a temporary lifting of censorship. Instead, the Motion Picture Code of Ethics Committee, launched in July 1960 by people in the industry, conducted voluntary reviews. This committee had to suspend its activities only eight months after its establishment in August 1960, following the military coup led by general Park Chung Hee on May 16, 1961. For a more detailed discussion of South Korean cinema during the transitional period between the April Revolution and the coup, see Ham Ch'ung-bŏm, "hŏ jŏng kwado jŏngbu shigi han'guk yŏnghwa-gye yŏn'gu" [A study on the South Korean cinema in the period of the Heo-jeong interim administration: Focused on the 4.19 revolution], *Sunch'ŏnhyang inmun kwahak nonch'ong* [Sunch'ŏnhyang studies of humanities and science] 26 (2010): 67–93. See also Lee Soon-jin, "naengjŏn ch'ejeŭi munhwanolli wa han'guk yŏnghwa ŭi chonjaebangshik—yŏnghwa ŭi kŏmyŏl gwajŏng ŭl chungshim ŭro" [Cultural Logic of the Cold War System and Operation of South Korean Cinema On Censorship Practices of *A Stray Bullet*], *Kiŏk kwa chŏnmang* [Memory and future vision] 29 (Winter 2013): 374–423.

13. *Tonga ilbo*, May 14, 1962, 3.

14. *Tonga ilbo*, May 10, 1962, 3.

15. *Kyŏnghyang shinmun*, May 13, 1962, 3.

16. *Nippon Times*, May 15, 1962.

17. *Kyŏnghyang shinmun*, April 17, 1962, 4.

18. *The Houseguest and My Mother* was also selected as the South Korean entry for the Best Foreign Language Film at the 35th Academy Awards in 1963. It was not accepted as a nominee.

19. *Chosŏn ilbo*, May 23, 1963, 4.

20. *Chosŏn ilbo*, May 23, 1963, 4.

21. *Sŏul shinmun*, April 10, 1963, 4.

22. *Han'gug ilbo*, April 4, 1963, 5.

23. *Chosŏn ilbo*, April 18, 1963, 4.

24. *Chosŏn ilbo*, April 19, 1963, 5.

25. *Tonga ilbo*, April 19, 1963, 7.

26. "10th Film Festival in Asia," *Nan Guo Dian Ying* [Southern screen] 64 (June 1963): 5–8.

27. *Sŏul shinmun*, July 2, 1964, 5. *The Red Muffler* received two more awards at the 1964 festival: Best Actor (Sin Yŏngkyun) and Best Editing. "Further Festival Laurels for Shaws," *Nan Guo Dian Ying* [Southern screen] 78 (August 1964): 5–8. Shin Sang-ok received the Best Director award again in 1965 with his film *Rice* (*Ssal*, 1963). The 1965 Asian Film Festival was held in Kyoto, Japan, from May 10 to 15. *Tonga ilbo*, May 14, 1965, 3.

28. *Chosŏn ilbo*, April 19, 1963, 5.

29. Alice H. Amsden, "Diffusion of Development: The Late Industrializing Model and Greater East Asia," *American Economic Review* 81, no. 2 (May 1991): 283.

30. See Robert Wade, *Governing the Market: Economic Theory and the Role of Government in East Asian Industrialization* (Princeton, NJ: Princeton University Press, 1990); Woo Jung-Eun, *Racing to the Swift: State and Finance in Korean Industrialization* (New York: Columbia University Press, 1991); Meredith Woo-Cumings, ed., *The Developmental State* (Ithaca, NY: Cornell University Press, 1999); T. J. Pempel, ed., *The Politics of the Asian Economic Crisis* (Ithaca, NY: Cornell University Press, 1999); Peter B. Evans, Dietrich Rueschemeyer, and Theda Skocpol, eds., *Bringing the State Back In* (Cambridge: Cambridge University Press, 1985); Chalmers Johnson, *MITI and the Japanese Miracle: The Growth of Industrial Policy, 1925–1975* (Stanford, CA: Stanford University Press, 1982); and Alice H. Amsden's two books: *Asia's Next Giant: South Korea and Late Industrialization* (New York: Oxford University Press, 1989) and *Escape from Empire: The Developing World's Journey through Heaven and Hell* (Cambridge, MA: MIT Press, 2007).

31. Ha-Joon Chang, *The East Asian Development Experience: The Miracle, the Crisis and the Future* (London: Zed Books, 2006), 18.

32. Chang, *The East Asian Development Experience*

33. Dietrich Rueschemeyer and Peter B. Evans, "The State and Economic Transformation: Toward an Analysis of the Conditions Underlying Effective Intervention," in Evans, Rueschemeyer, and Skocpol, ed., *Bringing the State Back In*, 44.

34. Johnson, *MITI and the Japanese Miracle*, 18.

35. Johnson, *MITI and the Japanese Miracle*, 19.

36. Wade, *Governing the Market: Economic Theory and the Role of Government in East Asian Industrialization*; Amsden, *Asia's Next Giant: South Korea and Late Industrialization*; Linda Weiss and John Hobson, *States and Economic Development: A Comparative Historical Analysis* (Cambridge: Polity Press, 1995); and Woo-Cumings, *The Developmental State*.

37. Frederic C. Deyo, *Beneath the Miracle: Labor Subordination in the New Asian Industrialism* (Berkeley: University of California Press, 1989).

38. Shin Films has been discussed as a victim of the coercive and brutal tyrant Park Chung Hee and his militarized developmental state. For instance, Cho Hŭi-mun, a Korean film historian, asserts, "Shin Films was developed with the help of Shin's talent and passion but had to suffer from the government's irrational film policy that forced the industrialization and mismanagement of the whole system, and finally disappeared in the history." See Cho Hŭi-mun, "Han'guk yŏnghwa kiŏp'wa ŭi kanŭngsŏng gwa han'gye shinp'illŭm" [Shin Fims: The possibility and limitation of the corporatization of Korean cinema], *Yŏnghwa yŏn'gu* [Film studies] 14 (2006): 436.

39. Yi Hyŏng-p'yo, interview with the author, August 8, 2008.

40. Pak Haeng-ch'ŏl, interview with the author, July 31, 2008.

41. Stephanie Po-yin Chung, "The Industrial Evolution of a Fraternal Enterprise: The Shaw Brothers and the Shaw Organization," in *The Shaw Screen: A Preliminary Study* (Hong Kong: Hong Kong Film Archive, 2003), 2.

42. Chung, "The Industrial Evolution of a Fraternal Enterprise," 66–68.

43. Shin Sang-ok, "Naŭi yŏnghwa gyŏngnyŏk" [About my film career], *Naeoe yŏnghwa* (October 1965): 24.

44. Cho Chun-hyŏng, *Yŏnghwa jegug shinp'illŭm* [Shin Films: The movie empire] (Seoul, Korea: Korean Film Archive, 2009), 81–82.

45. Cho, *Yŏnghwa jegug shinp'illŭm*, 118.

46. Ch'oe Kyŏng-ok, interview with the author, October 2, 2008.

47. Pak Chi-yŏn, "Yŏnghwa bŏp chejŏng esŏ je-sach'a kaejŏng-gi kkaji ŭi yŏnghwa jŏngch'aek (1961 ~ 1984 nyŏn)" [From the liberation to the 1960s' film policy], in *Han'guk yŏnghwa jŏngch'aeksa* [A history of Korean film policy], ed. Kim Tong-ho, (Seoul, Korea: Nanam Publications, 2004), 194–95.

48. Yi Yŏng-il, *Han'guk yŏnghwa jŏnsa* [The complete history of Korean cinema] (Seoul, Korea: Sodo, 2004), 288.

49. Yi Hyŏng-p'yo, interview with the author, 2008.

50. *Chosŏn ilbo*, August 31, 1965, 5.

51. Five films were imported and distributed in 1964. They were three American films (*Donovan's Reef, The Nun's Story, Zulu*), an Italy-France coproduction (*Las Fida*), and an Italian film (*Il Gobbo*). See *Han'guk yŏnghwa charyo p'yŏllam* [The complete index of Korean film materials] (Seoul, Korea: Korean Motion Picture Promotion Corporation, 1976), 109–35.

52. *Han'gug ilbo*, August 30, 1962, 5.

53. Pak, "Yŏnghwa bŏp chejŏng esŏ je-sach'a kaejŏng-gi kkaji ŭi yŏnghwa jŏngch'aek," 208–17.

54. *Tonga ilbo*, January 8, 1963, 5.

55. Pak, "Yŏnghwa bŏp chejŏng esŏ je-sach'a kaejŏng-gi kkaji ŭi yŏnghwa jŏngch'aek," 208–17.

56. "Run Run Shaw Heads Hong Kong Film Delegation," *Nan Guo Dian Ying* [Southern screen] 51 (May 1962): 2–3.

57. *Kyŏnghyang shinmun*, May 10, 1962, 5.

58. *Nippon Times*, May 15, 1954.

59. "Che ku-hoe ashia yŏnghwaje kyŏlsan" [Wrapping up the festival: The 9th Asian Film Festival], *Yeonghwa Segye* [Film world] (June 1962): 89–93.

60. "Never Before on the Chinese Screen-Big Battle Scenes," *Nan Guo Dian Ying* [Southern screen] 49 (March 1962): 6–8.

61. "Joint Shaw-Taiwan productions," *Nan Guo Dian Ying* [Southern screen] 54 (July 1962): 12–13.

62. Wong Ka-hee, Shaw Brothers' physical production manager, provided the confidential contract documents between Shin and Shaw. The contract was officially signed by Alfred S. K. Lau (Shaw) and Shin Sang-ok (Shin) on September 25, 1962.

63. Interview with Wong Ka-hee, January 8, 2008.

64. The presale was a common practice for Shaw Brothers, since the company had always relied on markets other than Hong Kong. Shaw Brothers commonly signed three-year theatrical release contracts with overseas distributors. Therefore, even before *Last Woman of Shang* was released, Shaw, through the film's foreign release contract, could accumulate approximately two thirds of the film's budget. Law and Bren, *Hong Kong Cinema: A Cross Cultural View*, 188; Wong Ka-hee, interview with the author.

65. Linda Lin Dai, the film's heroine and Shaw's top actress, had killed herself on July 14, a month before the film's release. She was only 29. Run Run Shaw prepared the premiere as a memorial event, inviting a long list of stars, politicians, and a Hong Kong governor. "Movie Queen's Tragic Death," *Nan Guo Dian Ying* [Southern screen] 79 (September 1964): 6–8; "Tribute to Lin Dai," *Nan Guo Dian Ying* [Southern screen] 79 (September 1964): 13-19.

66. "Governor Sees Lin Dai Film," *Nan Guo Dian Ying* [Southern screen] 80 (October 1964): 14–17.

67. Interestingly enough, *Last Woman of Shang* was the first commercial release of a Shaw Brothers film in America. It was released at the 55th Street Playhouse in Manhattan in December 1964. This 253-seat theater, run by B. S. Moss Circuit, had been booked by Frank Lee, the US distributor for the Shaw Brothers Studio in Hong Kong, in order to release the Shaw films to highly sophisticated and selective New York audiences. The 55th Street Playhouse represented Shaw' strategic turn to the mainstream American market. But *Last Woman of Shang* was relentlessly ridiculed by New York cinephiles. Bosley Crowther, one of the most powerful film critics at the time, reviewed it harshly in the *New York Times*. He wrote, "Don't be surprised when you discover that you're looking at a Chinese costume film in a style of staging and acting that might be described as pre-Columbian DeMille. The film is a great big Oriental pageant, clothed in elegant sets and bright costumes, all in commendable color, with about as much dramatic form and pace as a third-rate Italian muscle-opera celebrating the exploits of the son of Hercules." See Howard Thompson, "Mandarin Films to Be Seen Here," *New York Times*, December 9, 1964; Bosley Crowther, "Screen: Hong Kong's Run Run Shaw," *New York Times*, December 15, 1964.

68. "Shaw Brothers' Glorious Achievements in 1963," *Nan Guo Dian Ying* [Southern screen] 71 (January 1964): 41.

69. "Li Li-hua as Goddess of Mercy," *Nan Guo Dian Ying* [Southern screen] 83 (January 1965): 30–33.

70. *Sŏul shinmun*, September 17, 1966, 5.

71. Cho, *Oral History Project*, 2008, 82.

72. In the early 1960s, Shaw tried a new method, making multiple language versions using different actors. As Hollywood did during the early 1930s, in 1965, Shaw Brothers hired local actors for each market. "Hong Kong, Manila, Singapore," *Nan Guo Dian Ying* [Southern screen] 86 (April 1965): 16.

73. "Screen Queens are Film Friends," *Nan Guo Dian Ying* [Southern screen] 102 (August 1966): 78–79.

74. *Chosŏn ilbo*, September 13, 1966, 5.

75. *Sŏul shinmun*, September 8, 1966.

76. "Run Run Shaw: World's Busiest Producer," *Nan Guo Dian Ying* [Southern screen] 87 (May 1965): 2–5.

77. Shin Films imported spaghetti Westerns, Shaw Brothers' *wuxia* films and Golden Harvest's Kung Fu series, Italian genre films, and New American cinema during the studio's import business period from 1964 to 1975. *The Golden Swallow* (*Jin Yan Zi*, Chang Cheh, 1968) attracted 300,000 viewers in 1968, and *Summertime Killer* (Antonio Isasi-Isasmendi, 1972), an Italian thriller, scored 360,000 in 1973. See Sangjoon Lee, "Martial Arts Craze in Korea: Cultural Translation of Martial Arts Film and Literature in the 1960s," *East Asian Cultural Heritage and Films*, ed. Kinnia Yau Shuk-ting (Palgrave/Macmillan, 2012), 173–95. Foreign film imports were indeed a highly profitable business in which success was almost guaranteed, whereas domestic production was extremely unpredictable and had many variables. See *The Complete Index of Korean Film Materials*, 115–52.

78. Ch'oe, interview with the author, 2008.

79. Cho, *Yŏnghwa jegug shinp'illŭm*.

80. *Chosŏn ilbo* reported that the film would be "produced as a full-color trilogy, directed by Shin Sang-ok with Japanese all-star casting such as Hasegawa Kazuo and Katsu Shintaro." *Chosŏn ilbo*, February 24, 1966, 5.

81. *Kyŏnghyang shinmun*, February 14, 1966, 5.

82. Kim Mi-hyŏn, ed., *Han'guk yŏnghwasa* [Korean film history] (Seoul: Communication Books, 2005), 175–77.

83. Shin Sang-ok, "Sŏdullŏya hal kiŏp'wa" [We should move forward to industrialize the film industry], *Daehan ilbo*, April 2, 1966, 5.

84. Shin Sang-ok, *Nan Yeonghwayeotda* [I was movie] (Seoul: Random House Korea, 2007).

85. However, despite the judgment, the department of publicity sanctioned the right to distribute the film on July 30. As a result, *Journey to the West* was finally released on September 6 at two theaters in Seoul. Right after the film's theatrical release, Shin Films entered its long stagnation. See *Tonga ilbo*, July 20, 1966, 3; *Kyunghyang Shimun*, July 20, 1966, 7; *Chosŏn ilbo*, July 21, 1966, 5.

86. "Hong Kong to Hold Festival," *Nan Guo Dian Ying* [Southern screen] 100 (June 1966): 2–7.

87. *Kyŏnghyang shinmun*, May 11, 1966, 5.

88. In 1952, Murao Kaoru was commissioned by TAF to compile a list of communist leaders of the motion picture industry in Japan. Yamamoto Satsuo was included in the list. See the second chapter of this book. For more about his life, see Yamamoto Satsuo, *My Life as a Filmmaker*, trans. Chia-ning Chang (Ann Arbor: University of Michigan Press, 2017).

89. An Pyŏng-sŏp, "Asea yŏnghwaje sŭk'aendŭl" [Asian Film Festival scandal], *Shin Tonga* (August 1966): 30–32.

90. See Jin-kyung Lee, "Surrogate Military, Subimperialism, and Masculinity," 655–56.

91. According to a 1970 article by Se Jin Kim, there were three main opinions on this matter. First, it was argued that pulling out 49,000 elite troops would jeopardize the security of the country. Second, the opposition raised the question of the cost of military involvement in terms of both human lives and finances. Third, the policy to expand military participation was alleged to be an insidious plot between the government and big business interests. Se Jin Kim, "South Korea's Involvement in Vietnam and Its Economic and Political Impact," *Asian Survey* 10, no. 6 (June 1970): 524–25.

92. Shin, *Nan Yeonghwayeotda*, 193.

93. Pak Haeng-ch'ŏl, interview with the author.

94. Pak Haeng-ch'ŏl, interview with the author. Shaw Brothers, especially when they needed snowy landscapes in their films' settings, came to Korea and worked with Shin Films during the latter half of the decade and through the 1970s.

95. Ch'oe, interview with the author.

96. Shin, *Nan Yeonghwayeotda*, 74–75.

97. Wong, interview with the author, 2008.

98. Shin saw *Come Drink with Me* (*Da Zui Xia*, King Hu, 1966) at the 1966 Asian Film Festival in Seoul and instantly recognized the film's commercial value. *Come Drink with Me* was officially distributed at the Paramount theater in Seoul in April 1967, under the title of *Pangnangŭi kyŏlt'u* (Duel of the Drifters), and instantaneously reached the position of number one foreign film of the year. This was the first Hong Kong *wuxia* film ever released in South Korea, and the film drew a record-breaking 300,000 patrons in Seoul alone while igniting fierce debates on the negative effects of violence and the low-culture status of *muhyeop* (martial arts) films and literature among the nation's intellectuals. Shin, accordingly, imported *Come Drink with Me*, *Magnificent Trio* (*Bian Cheng San Xia*, Chang Cheh, 1966), *The One-Armed Swordsman*, *The Golden Swallow*, and *Return of the One-Armed Swordsman* (*Du bi dou wang*, Chang Cheh, 1969). See Lee, "Martial Arts Craze in Korea," 189.

99. "*Love Eterne* Craze," *Nan Guo Dian Ying* [Southern Screen] 65 (July 1963): 50–51.

100. David Bordwell, Janet Staiger, and Kristin Thompson, *The Classical Hollywood Cinema: Film Style and Mode of Production to 1960* (New York: Columbia University Press, 1985), 94. Staiger named and examined the model while discussing an early Hollywood film director and executive, Thomas Ince, and his short-lived motion picture studio, the Thomas Ince studio. What Shin and Li shared with Ince was his primary emphasis on the script and the centralization of power and decision-making. Like Ince, who was also a film director, both Shin and Li were filmmakers. Ince's shortcomings were more or less identical to those of Shin and Li.

101. Emilie Yueh-yu Yeh, "Taiwan: The Transnational Battlefield of Cathay and Shaws," in *The Cathay Story*, ed. Wong Ain-ling (Hong Kong: Hong Kong Film Archive, 2002), 143.

102. Yingjin Zhang, *Chinese National Cinema* (London: Routledge, 2004), 137–38.

103. Stephanie Po-yin Chung, "A Southeast Asian Tycoon and His Movie Dream: Loke Wan Tho and MP&GI," in Wong Ain-ling, ed., *The Cathay Story*, 45.

104. Yeh, "Taiwan: The Transnational Battlefield of Cathay and Shaws," 145.

105. Yeh, "Taiwan: The Transnational Battlefield of Cathay and Shaws," 145.

106. Emilie Yueh-yu Yeh, "Taiwan: Popular Cinema's Disappearing Act," in *Contemporary Asian Cinema: Popular Culture in a Global Frame*, ed. Anne Tereska Ciecko (Oxford: Berg, 2006), 161.

107. Hong, *Taiwan Cinema*, 73.

108. For more on the Kuomintang government's cultural policy toward Mandarinizing Taiwanese cinema, see Hector Rodriguez, "The Cinema in Taiwan: Identity and Political Legitimacy" (PhD diss., New York University, 1995).

109. Emilie Yueh-yu Yeh and Darrell William Davis, *Taiwanese Film Directors: A Treasure Island* (New York: Columbia University Press, 2005), 44.

110. Yeh and Davis, *Taiwanese Film Directors*, 42–47. After the official closure of GMP, Li rejoined Shaw Brothers in 1971. Instantaneously, Li verified himself as a million-dollar director with *The Warlord* (*Da jun fa*, Li Han-hsiang, 1972).

111. The central producer system centralized "the control of production under the management of a producer, a work position distinct from staff directors . . . the modern manager of a well-organized mass production system which was now necessary to produce the quality multiple-reel film." Bordwell, Staiger, and Thompson, *The Classical Hollywood Cinema*, 134. Shin Films adopted this system due to the government's first MPL, which required each studio to release at least fifteen films per year.

112. Shin, *I Was Movie*, 20.

113. Pak, "Yŏnghwa bŏp chejŏng esŏ je-sach'a kaejŏng-gi kkaji ŭi yŏnghwa jŏngch'aek," 164–65.

114. "Kkum ŭi kongjang shinp'illŭm iyagi" [Story of a dream factory: Shin Films], *Yŏnghwa japchi* [Film magazine] (August 1970): 126–27.

115. Chin, interview with the author, 2008.

116. Chin, interview with the author.

117. *Tonga ilbo*, February 10, 1971, 6.

118. Chin, interview with the author.

119. Ch'oe, interview with the author.

120. *Chosŏn ilbo*, September 7, 1973, 5; *Kyŏnghyang shinmun*, September 7, 1973, 6, "Li Chun Kau As Seen By Huang Fung," *Golden Movie News* (April 1973): 44–45; "Taekwondo Heroes," *Golden Movie News* (July 1973): 34–47 and 60–61.

121. See Yi Yŏn-ho, "Shin sang-ok, tangshin ŭn nugu shimnikka?" [Shin Sang-ok, who are you?], *KINO* 120 (1997): 120–27.

122. Kim Kap-ŭi, interview with the author, August 22, 2008.

123. Kim Kap-ŭi, interview with the author.

124. Cho, *Yŏnghwa jegug shinp'illŭm*, 193–98. See also Steven Chung, *Split Screen Cinema: Shin Sang-ok and Postwar Cinema* (Minneapolis: University of Minnesota Press, 2014). This monograph contains a chapter on Shin's career in North Korea. For a more recent study of Shin's film career in North Korea, see Gabor Sebo, "A Study on the Impact of Shin Sang-ok on North Korean Cinema" (PhD dissertation, Korea University, 2018).

125. See Johannes Schönherr, *North Korean Cinema: A History* (Jefferson, NC: McFarland & Company, 2012), 99–101.

126. Kim Jong Il, *Yŏnghwa yesullon* [On the art of the cinema] (Pyongyang: Workers' Party of Korea Publishing House, 1973).

127. The story of Kim Jong Il's bizarre abduction of Shin and Ch'oe has been examined in the documentary *The Lovers and the Despot* (Robert Cannan and Ross Adam, 2016). Paul Fischer's *A Kim Jong-Il Production: The Extraordinary True Story of a Kidnapped Filmmaker, His Star Actress, and a Young Dictator's Rise to Power* (Flatiron Books, 2015) is also helpful in mapping out Kim Jong Il's ambitions in cinema and Shin's contribution to the 1980s North Korean film industry.

Chapter 7. Hong Kong, Hollywood, and the End of the Network

1. Steve Fore, "Golden Harvest Films and the Hong Kong Movie Industry in the Realm of Globalization," *The Velvet Light Trap* 34 (Fall 1994): 42.

2. Michael Curtin, "Media Capital: Toward the Study of Spatial Flows," *International Journal of Cultural Studies* 6, no. 2 (2003): 205.

3. Curtin, "Media Capital," 222.

4. Catherine R. Schenk, *Hong Kong as an International Financial Centre: Emergence and Development 1945–65* (London: Routledge, 2001), 137.

5. Stephanie Po-Yin Chung, "Moguls of the Chinese Cinema: The Story of the Shaw Brothers in Shanghai, Hong Kong and Singapore, 1924–2002," *Modern Asian Studies* 41, no. 1 (2007): 66.

6. Chung, "The Industrial Evolution of a Fraternal Enterprise," 2.

7. Chung, "Moguls of the Chinese Cinema," 669.

8. "Shaw's Cinema Net in Singapore and Malaysia," *Nan Guo Dian Ying* [Southern screen] 2 (January 1957): 3.

9. Shaw Malay Production was established in 1939. By 1957, the studio had churned out over a hundred films, mostly in local languages. For more about the studio, see Millet, *Singapore Cinema* and Uhde and Uhde, *Latent Image*.

10. Kean Fan Lim, "Transnational Collaborations, Local Competitiveness: Mapping the Geographies of Filmmaking in/through Hong Kong," *Geografiska Annaler*, Series B. Human Geography 88, no. 3 (2006): 346.

11. "Shaw's Cinema Net," 2–5.

12. "Shaw Adds 22 New Theatres in Two Years," *Nan Guo Dian Ying* [Southern screen] 21 (September 1958): 6–9.

13. "Shaw Adds 3 New Theatres to Chain in February," *Nan Guo Dian Ying* [Southern screen] 25 (February 1959): 3–4.

14. "Shaw's Chain of Theatres," *Nan Guo Dian Ying* [Southern screen] 47 (January 1962): 62–63.

15. Poshek Fu, "Hong Kong and Singapore: A History of the Cathay Cinema," in *The Cathay Story*, 66.

16. See "Miss Kikuko," *Guo Ji Dian Ying* [International screen] (December 1955): 14–19; "Merry-Go-Round," *Guo Ji Dian Ying* [International screen] (January 1956): 14–15; "Motion Pictures Produced on International Cooperation Standard," *Guo Ji Dian Ying* [International screen] (January 1956): 4–5.

17. Stephanie DeBoer discusses the first two parts of the trilogy in the first chapter of her book *Coproducing Asia*, 1–24.

18. "Miss Yu Ming, the Reigning Movie Queen of Asia," *Guo Ji Dian Ying* [International screen] (June 1960): 11–14; "Yu Ming Interviewed by Tokyo Newsmen," *Guo Ji Dian Ying* [International

screen] (December 1961): 17–18; "Yu Ming Filming in Japan," *Guo Ji Dian Ying* [International screen] (May 1962): 27; "Wild Welcoming for Yu Ming," *Guo Ji Dian Ying* [International screen] (May 1962): 28–29; "A Letter from Lucilla Yu Ming," *Guo Ji Dian Ying* [International screen] (May 1963): 21–24.

19. "Shaw's New Studio Opened," *Nan Guo Dian Ying* [Southern screen] (January 1962): 30–33; "Visit Shaw's Movie Town with Ling Po," *Nan Guo Dian Ying* [Southern screen] (January 1963): 30–35.

20. "Shaw Studio in 1968," *Nan Guo Dian Ying* [Southern screen] (January 1969): 3–4.

21. Poshek Fu, "The 1960s: Modernity, Youth Culture, and Hong Kong Cantonese Cinema," in *The Cinema of Hong Kong: History, Art, Identity*, ed. Poshek Fu and David Desser (Cambridge: Cambridge University Press, 2000), 81–82.

22. Poshek Fu, "The 1960s," 73–74.

23. Tan See Kam, "Shaw Brothers' *Bangpian*: Global Bondmania, Cosmopolitan Dreaming and Cultural Nationalism," *Screen* 56, no. 2 (Summer 2015): 207.

24. "Airlines in Asia: Cathay Pacific," *Far Eastern Economic Review*, August 11, 1960, 331–33.

25. Leung Ping-kwan, "Urban Cinema and the Cultural Identity," in Fu and Desser, *The Cinema of Hong Kong*, 377.

26. Poshek Fu, "The 1960s," 81–82.

27. Kinnia Yau Shuk-ting and June Pui-wah, "Transnational Collaborations and Activities of Shaw Brothers and Golden Harvest: An Interview with Chua Lam," in *Hong Kong Cinema Retrospective: Border Crossings in Hong Kong Cinema* (Hong Kong: Hong Kong Film Archive, 2000), 140.

28. During the 1960s in Hong Kong, Japanese film had a high profile and a loyal upper middle-class audience, especially compared to the core audiences for Hong Kong cinema (students and the lower white-collar class). See Emilie Yueh-yu Yeh and Darrell William Davis, "Japan Hong-screen: Pan-Asian Cinemas and Flexible Accumulation," *Historical Journal of Film, Radio, and Television*, 22, no. 1 (2002): 61–82.

29. For more about Inoue's Hong Kong career, see Darrell William Davis and Emilie Yueh-yu Yeh, "Inoue at Shaws," in *The Shaw Screen: A Preliminary Study*, edited by Wong Ain-ling (Hong Kong: Hong Kong Film Archive, 2003), 255–71.

30. "Spycatcher Pei-pei's Deadly Mission," *Nan Guo Dian Ying* [Southern screen] (May 1966): 4–5.

31. "Japanese Directs Society Exposé," *Nan Guo Dian Ying* [Southern screen] (June 1966): 28–31.

32. See "*Interpol*," *Nan Guo Dian Ying* [Southern screen] (November 1966): 24–25; "Jenny in Love Triangle," *Nan Guo Dian Ying* [Southern screen] (August 1968): 30–33.

33. "*Asiapol*," *Nan Guo Dian Ying* [Southern screen] (January 1967): 50. Shaw also recruited action-genre directors from South Korea. After the impressive box-office returns of *Special Agent X-7* in Hong Kong, Chŏng Ch'ang-hwa joined Shaw Brothers in 1968. For more about Chŏng Ch'ang-hwa's Hong Kong career, see Aaron Han Joon Magnan-Park, "Restoring the Transnational from the Abyss of Ethnonational Film Historiography: The Case of Chung Chang Wha," *Journal of Korean Studies* 16, no. 2 (Fall 2011): 249–83. See also Sangjoon Lee, "Chŏng Ch'ang-hwa kamdok kwa ashia hapchak yŏnghwa ŭi shidae" [Chŏng Ch'ang-hwa and the Age of Inter-Asian Co-production], *Yŏnghwa ch'ŏn'guk* [Cinema paradise] 21 (August 2011): 28–31.

34. In 1956, the young Ishihara Shintaro's novel *Season of the Sun* (*Taiyo no kisetsu*) won the Akutagawa prize, the most prestigious and conservative literature award in Japan. With its description of rich, bored, and vicious characters, the novel produced a cultural sensation. Inspired by Ishihara's novels, journalists created the term *taiyozoku* (sun tribe), which was given to a postwar generation who "hung around beaches during the summer vacation." Sato Tadao, *Currents in Japanese Cinema*. trans. Gregory Barrett (Tokyo and New York: Kodansha International, 1982), 212.

35. Michael Raine sees the early career of Ishihara Yujiro as symptomatic of the social and aesthetic conditions of contemporary Japanese mass culture. See Michael Raine, "Ishihara Yujiro: Youth, Celebrity, and the Male Body in late-1950s Japan," in *Word and Image in Japanese Cinema*, ed. Dennis Washburn and Carole Cavanaugh (Cambridge: Cambridge University Press, 2010), 202–25.

36. Kinnia Yau Shuk-ting, "Interview with Umetsugu Inoue," in *Border Crossings in Hong Kong Cinema*, 145–46.

37. Shaw Brothers did perceive its Southeast Asian market as still having a strong anti-Japanese sentiment that could be a barrier to distributing its films under the Japanese directors' names. Therefore, Shaw required these Japanese directors to use Chinese names. Although Inoue insisted on maintaining his name, the rest of the directors were credited under Chinese names. Yau, "Interview with Umetsugu Inoue," 146.

38. Zhang, *Chinese National Cinema*, 180.

39. James Kung and Zhang Yueai, "Hong Kong Cinema and Television in the 1970s: A Perspective," *A Study of Hong Kong Cinema in the Seventies*, the 8th Hong Kong International Film Festival (Hong Kong: The Urban Council, 1984), 14.

40. Kung and Zhang, "Hong Kong Cinema and Television in the 1970s," 14.

41. Kung and Zhang, "Hong Kong Cinema and Television in the 1970s," 14.

42. Hong Kong Film Archive, *Oral History Series 3: Director Chor Yuen* (Hong Kong: Hong Kong Film Archive, 2006).

43. Hui, however, left Shaw in 1974 to launch his own independent production, the Hui Film Company, with Raymond Chow's Golden Harvest. Throughout the 1970s, Hui wrote, directed, and starred in a series of very successful Cantonese comedy films, such as *Games Gamblers Play* (*Gui ma shuang xing*, 1974), *The Last Message* (*Tian cai yu bai chi*, 1975), and *The Private Eyes* (*Ban jin ba liang*, 1976).

44. The film tells the story of a Chinese Hong Kong man (Tsung Hua) who is an overseas businessman in Denmark and falls in love with a Danish woman with a very liberal sexual desires (Birte Tove). However, despite Tove's aggressive and passionate attempts to seduce Hua, he eventually marries a conservative Chinese woman (Li Ching). "With Love from Denmark," *Nan Guo Dian Ying* [Southern screen] (March 1973).

45. "Bamboo House of Dolls," *Nan Guo Dian Ying* [Southern screen] (January 1974): 55–62; "Bamboo House of Dolls," *Nan Guo Dian Ying* [Southern screen] (October–November 1973): 55–62.

46. Jennifer Fay, "The *Schoolgirl Reports* and the Guilty Pleasure of History," in *Alternative Europe: Eurotrash and Exploitation Cinemas Since 1945*, ed. Ernest Mathijs and Xavier Mendik (London: Wallflower Press, 2004), 39–52.

47. Fay, "The *Schoolgirl Reports* and the Guilty Pleasure of History," 40–42. Although it had elements of the *"Aufklärungsfilme"* (sex education films) of the 1960s, *Schoolgirl Reports* are clearly exploitative in their presentations of young females' sexual desires. With the series' unprecedented success, West Germany became the world's leading softcore porn producer.

48. Grace L.K. Leung and Joseph M. Chan, "The Hong Kong Cinema and Overseas Market, a Historical Review 1950–1995," in *Hong Kong Cinema Retrospective: Fifty Years of Electric Shadows* (Hong Kong: The Urban Council, 1997): 143–51.

49. "Moguls of the Chinese Cinema," 675.

50. Westad, *The Cold War*, 412.

51. David Desser has made an effort to historicize this phenomenon, which was, in fact, the consequence of the rapid reformation of the global film industry, the influx of European "cheap" entertainment films (e.g., spaghetti Westerns and French comedies), and the transitory void of American-made action cinema. See David Desser, "The Kung Fu Craze: Hong Kong Cinema's First American Reception," in Fu and Desser, *The Cinema of Hong Kong*, 19–43.

52. Lester D. Friedman, "Introduction: Movies and the 1970s," in *American Cinema of the 1970s: Themes and Variations*, ed. Lester D. Friedman (New Brunswick, NJ: Rutgers University Press, 2007), 2.

53. Tino Balio, *United Artists: The Company That Changed the Film Industry* (Madison: University of Wisconsin Press, 1987), 303.

54. Friedman, "Introduction," 3.

55. Sheldon Hall and Steve Neale, *Epics, Spectacles, and Blockbusters: A Hollywood History* (Detroit, MI: Wayne State University Press, 2010), 107.

56. Ben Goldsmith and Tom O'Regan, *The Film Studio: Film Production in the Global Economy* (Lanham, MD: Rowman and Littlefield, 2005), 11–13.

57. Kevin Heffernan, *Ghouls, Gimmicks, and Gold: Horror Films and the American Movie Business, 1953–1968* (Durham, NC: Duke University Press, 2004), 136.

58. Heffernan, *Ghouls, Gimmicks, and Gold*, 135–36.

59. Paul Monaco, *The Sixties: 1960–1969, History of the American Cinema* (Berkeley: University of California Press, 2001), 15.

60. Robert Gustafson, "What's Happening to Our Pix Biz? From Warner Bros. to Warner Communications Inc.," in *The American Film Industry*, edited by Tino Balio (Madison: University of Wisconsin Press, 1985), 575.

61. David J. Londoner, "The Changing Economics of Entertainment," in Balio, *The American Film Industry*, 607.

62. Gustafson, "What's Happening to Our Pix Biz?" 576.

63. Gustafson, "What's Happening to Our Pix Biz?" 582–83.

64. Gustafson, "What's Happening to Our Pix Biz?" 575.

65. Mark Werba, "Kung-Fu: Instant Box Office," *Variety*, March 7, 1973, 7.

66. "Film Production Pulse," *Variety*, March 7, 1973, 28.

67. P. Flanigan, "Kung Fu Krazy or the Invention of the 'Chop Suey Eastern'," *Cineaste* 6, no. 3 (1974): 8–10.

68. Quoted in Darrel Y. Hamamoto, *Monitored Peril: Asian Americans and the Politics of TV Representation* (Minneapolis: University of Minnesota Press, 1994), 60–61.

69. Neela Banerjee, "Chinese Theatre Threatened," *AsianWeek.com*, November 17, 2000, http://www.asianweeks.com/2000_11_17/bay3_greatstartheatre.html.

70. Kevin Heffernan, "Inner-City Exhibition and the Genre Film: Distributing *Night of the Living Dead* (1968)," *Cinema Journal* 41, no. 3 (2002), 61.

71. "Five Fingers of Death," *Variety*, March 21, 1973, 12.

72. "Swish! Thwack! Kung Fu Films Make It," *New York Times*, June 16, 1973, 14.

73. David A. Cook, *Lost Illusions: American Cinema in the Shadow of Watergate and Vietnam, 1970–1979* (Berkeley: University of California Press, 2002), 266.

74. *Variety*, March 28, 1973, 8.

75. Tom Costner, "Hong Kong's Answer to 007," *Village Voice*, May 17, 1973, 92.

76. *Variety*, August 29, 1973, 8.

77. Howard Thompson, "'Enter Dragon,' Hollywood Style," *New York Times*, August 18, 1973, 26:1.

78. Thompson, "'Enter Dragon,' Hollywood Style," 26:1.

79. Desser, "The Kung Fu Craze," 19–43.

80. "Road to 'Dragon' and $10-Mil," *Variety*, September 19, 1973, 16.

81. Flanigan, "Kung Fu Krazy or the Invention of the 'Chop Suey Eastern'" *Cineaste* 6, no. 3 (1974): 9.

82. "Hong Kong Filmmaker Huang Feng Says 'Korea is Ideal for Shooting Kung Fu Films,'" *Han'gug ilbo*, June 12, 1978, 5.

83. Giovanni Arrighi, "States, Market, and Capitalism, East and West," *Positions* 15, no. 2 (2007): 260. For more on Arrighi's critical works regarding the postwar and Cold War resurgences of East Asia from the perspective of world systems, see Giovanni Arrighi, Takeshi Hamashita, and Mark Sheldon, eds., *The Resurgence of East Asia: 500, 150, and 50 Years Perspective* (London: Routledge, 2003).

84. Leung and Chan, "The Hong Kong Cinema and Overseas Market," 136–51.

85. Chŏng Chong-hwa, "Aeksyŏn yŏnghwa mandŭlgi: kim shi-hyŏn kamdog int'ŏbyu" [Making action cinema: An interview with Kim Si-hyeon], *Yŏnghwa ŏnŏ* [Film language], 4 (Spring 2004).

86. "Chaemi gyop'o aeksyŏn bae-u bolly kim-i han'guk yŏnghwa ŭi such'ul-ŭl ikkŭnda" [Korean American action star Bobby Kim will lead Korean cinema's exports], *Yŏnghwa japchi* [Film magazine] (September 1975): 102.

87. Chu Sŏng-ch'ŏl, "Tŏ nŭkki chŏn-e mŏtchin yŏn'gi poyŏjwŏyaji" [I would like to show the audience some great acting before I get too old], *Cine 21*, March 5, 2009.

88. "Swish! Thwack!," 14.

89. "GH Will Keep Up Its Quality," *Golden Movie News*, January 1978, 19.

90. Mike Walsh, "Hong Kong Goes International: The Case of Golden Harvest," in *Hong Kong Film, Hollywood and the New Global Cinema: No Film Is an Island*, ed. Gina Marchetti and Tan See Kam (London: Routledge, 2007), 167–76; M. C. Tobias, *Flashbacks: Hong Kong Cinema after Bruce Lee* (Gulliver Books, 1979), 69–86.

91. Chŏng Ch'ang-hwa, interview with the author, June 2008.

92. *Variety*, December 19, 1973, 17. However, the first coproduction with a Western film studio dated back to 1966, when the British company Tower Films produced *Samuru* and *Five Golden Dragons* with the help of Shaw Brothers. See also "The Legend of Seven Golden Vampires," *Nan Guo Dian Ying* [Southern screen] (November–December 1973): 13–14; "Shatter," *Nan Guo Dian Ying* [Southern screen] (March 1974): 40–43. For more about *Legend of the Seven Golden Vampires*, see Sangjoon Lee, "Dracula, Vampires, and Kung Fu Fighters: *The Legend of the Seven Golden Vampires* and Transnational Horror Co-production in 1970s Hong Kong," in *Transnational Horror Cinema: Bodies of Excess and the Global Grotesque*, eds. Sophia Siddique Harvey and Raphael Raphael (Palgrave/MacMillan, January 2017), 65–80.

93. "Cleopatra Jones Meets the Dragon Lady," *Nan Guo Dian Ying* [Southern screen] (September 1974): 17–21; "An Insight into Shaw's Movie Town," *Nan Guo Dian Ying* [Southern screen] (October 1974): 14–17.

94. "Shaws Giant Co-production with Carlo Ponti," *Nan Guo Dian Ying* [Southern screen] (May 1974): 18–33.

95. Kinnia Yau Shuk-ting, "Transnational Collaborations and Activities of Shaw Brothers and Golden Harvest: An Interview with Chua Lam," in *Hong Kong Cinema Retrospective*, 141.

96. According to the year-end chart of 1974, *Virgins of the Seven Seas* was 32nd, *Mini-Skirt Gang* was 34th, and *The Legend of Seven Golden Vampires* was 39th. 1975 was even worse. *Blood Money* was 61st, *Cleopatra Jones and the Casino of Gold* was 65th, and *Supermen Against the Amazon* was merely 90th in the year's top 100. See Chen Qingwei, *Xianggang dianying gongye jiegon ji shichang fengxi* [The structure and marketing analysis of the Hong Kong film industry] (Hong Kong, 2000): 425–82.

Epilogue

1. Chen Jian, *Mao's China and the Cold War* (Chapel Hill: University of North Carolina Press, 2001), 277.

2. Westad, *The Cold War*, 617.

3. Westad, *The Cold War*, 24.

4. Chris Berry's *Post Socialist Cinema in Post-Mao China: The Cultural Revolution after the Cultural Revolution* (London: Routledge, 2004) scrutinizes about eighty films that were produced during the Cultural Revolution.

5. Zhang, *Chinese National Cinema*, 225–26.

6. According to Harry H. Kuoshu's account, film scholars commonly divide Chinese filmmakers into five generations (although some count the so-called Sixth Generation filmmakers in this traditional grouping): the pioneers of the 1920s (the first generation); the leftist filmmakers of the 1930s and 1940s (the second); the early PRC cinema of the 1950s (the third); from the early 1960s to the post-Mao late 1970s (the fourth); the post-Mao cinematic new wave that trained at the Beijing Film Academy (the fifth); and a group of young filmmakers who emerged in the 1990s and depart radically from the Fifth Generation filmmakers by focusing on contemporary Chinese youth culture and society (the sixth). Some of the most celebrated Fifth Generation film directors are Zhang Yimou, Chen Kaige, and Tien Zhuangzhuang. See Harry H. Kuoshu, *Celluloid China: Cinematic Encounters with Culture and Society* (Carbondale: Southern Illinois University Press, 2002), 2–3.

7. Ruby Cheung, "Ever-changing Readjustments: The Political Economy of the Hong Kong International Film Festival (HKIFF)," *New Review of Film and Television Studies* 14, no. 1 (2016), 64.

8. Stephen Teo, "Asian Film Festivals and their Diminishing Glitter Domes: An Appraisal of PIFF, SIFF and HKIFF," in *Dekalog 3: On Film Festivals*, ed. Richard Porton (London: Wallflower Press, 2009), 109.

9. *Picnic at Hanging Rock* received two awards: one for Excellent Philanthropic Film and the other for Rachel Roberts as Best Actress. An Excellent Creative Film award went to *Leisure*. McQuaid received the trophies on behalf of the Aussie recipients. "Asian Film Festival," *Filmnews*, August 1, 1976, 11.

10. In 1977, the Australian film industry dispatched an army of twenty delegates to the twenty-third annual event in Bangkok, Thailand, including Damien Stapleton (New South Wales Film Corporation), Frank Gardiner (Australian Film Commission), Murray Forest (Colourfilm), and ten people from the film industry in Queensland. Two Australian films, *The Getting of Wisdom* (Bruce Beresford, 1977) and *Summerfield* (Ken Hannam, 1977), were listed in the year's competition. "Aust. Representation at Asian Film Festival," *Filmnews*, October 1, 1977, 3.

11. Designed by the Danish architect Jørn Utzon, the Sydney Opera House was formally opened on October 20, 1973.

12. F. W. Eggleston, cited in Rodney Tiffen, *Diplomatic Deceits: Government, Media and East Timor* (Sydney: UNSW Press, 2001), 5.

13. Danielle Anderson, *Fifty Years of Australia's Trade* (Canberra, Department of Foreign Affairs and Trade, Australian Government Report, 2014), 3.

14. "United States Aid to Far Eastern Nations," *Far Eastern Economic Review*, June 6, 1957, 720.

15. Takashi Terada, "The Origins of Japan's APEC Policy: Foreign Minister Takeo Mikki's Asia-Pacific Policy and Current Implications," *Pacific Review* 11, no. 3 (1998): 337–63.

16. Regarding Australia's Asia-Pacific policy, see Ann Capling, "Twenty Years of Australia's Engagement with Asia," *Pacific Review* 21, no. 5 (2008): 601–22.

17. David Hannay, who worked for Greater Union in Australia, was the film's main producer. In Hong Kong, Golden Harvest provided its number one asset, the actor Jimmy Wang Yu. George Lazenby, a former James Bond actor who had signed a contract with Golden Harvest for a three-film deal, played a racist villain in this exploitative kung fu film. Beyond *The Man From Hong Kong*, Lazenby performed in *Stoner* (Huang Feng, 1974) and *A Queen's Ransom* (Ting Shan-his, 1976). Golden Harvest produced both films. For more about *The Man From Hong Kong*, see Stephen Teo, "Australia's Role in the Global Kung Fu Trend: *The Man from Hong Kong*," *Senses of Cinema* 62 (2001), accessed at http://sensesofcinema.com/2001/cteq/man_hk/.

18. Verina Glaessner, "Asia Festival," *Sight & Sound* 48 (Winter 1978): 28.

19. The 1970s also offered the Australian film industry the chance to regain some of its past prosperity. The Gorton government set up the Australian Film Development Corporation

(AFDC), the Experimental Film and Television Fund, and a national film education institution—the Australian Film and Television School (AFTS). The AFTS was located in Sydney and opened its doors in 1973. Gillian Armstrong, Phillip Noyce, and Chris Noonan were among the first cohort of twelve students in that year. Malcolm Fraser, another liberal leader, provided continued support to the film industry. During the Whitlam-Fraser era, Australian cinema emerged on the world cinema scene with such prominent auteurs as Peter Weir, Armstrong, Noyce, Bruce Beresford, Fred Schepisi, and George Miller. See Brian McFarlane, *Australian Cinema 1970–1985* (Melbourne: William Heinemann Australia, 1987), 20–21; Graham Shirley and Brian Adams, *Australian Cinema: The First Eighty Years* (Redfern, Australia: Currency Press, 1983), 242.

20. *Third Meeting of the ASEAN Sub-Committee on Film: Official Report* (Jakarta, Indonesia: November 1974).

21. "First Meeting of the FPA Board of Directors Held at Hotel Ambarrukmo Sheraton, Yogyakarta Indonesia 38th June 1980," dates unknown, Anthony Buckley Papers, 0622224: 0001, The 27th Asian Film Festival Folder, National Film and Sound Archive, Canberra, Australia.

22. Pamela G. Hollie, "Manila Film Festival Proves All-Out Spectacular," *New York Times*, February 7, 1982.

23. Leo Ortega Laparan, "The '81 Film Center Tragedy: When Mystery Turns Into Reality," *Manila Bulletin Research*, November 17, 2012.

24. Hollie, "Manila Film Festival."

25. "Constitution of the Federation of Motion Picture Producers in Asia-Pacific," dates unknown, Anthony Buckley Papers, 0622224: 0001, The 27th Asian Film Festival Folder, National Film and Sound Archive, Canberra, Australia.

26. Cited in John A Burns, "The Tenth Anniversary," *East-West Center Magazine*, Fall 1970, 4.

27. Institute of Culture and Communication, "Evolution of the Hawai'i International Film Festival," press release, October 12, 1985.

28. Mary Bitterman, interview by Karen Knudsen, September 15, 2008, interview narrative, East-West Center Oral History Project Collection, East-West Center, Honolulu, Hawaii, accessed at https://www.eastwestcenter.org/fileadmin/resources/ris/Oral_History/Bitterman/BITTERMAN_Mary_narrative--FinalProtectedCombo.pdf.

29. *The First Hawaii International Film Festival Program*, November 1–7, 1981.

30. Several years later, Paul Clark wrote the first comprehensive history of Chinese cinema, *Chinese Cinema: Culture and Politics since 1949* (Cambridge: Cambridge University Press, 1987)

31. Abé Mark Nornes, "Asian Film Festivals, Translation and the International Film Festival Short Circuit," in *Coming Soon to a Festival Near You: Programming Film Festivals*, ed. Jeffrey Ruoff (St. Andrews: St. Andrews University Press, 2012), 43.

32. Jeanette Paulson Hereniko, email interview with the author, May 18, 2016.

33. In 1986, the EWC had founded the *East-West Film Journal*, arguably the first American film journal devoted solely to the Asia-Pacific region as a whole. This short-lived film journal (the last issue was published in 1994) provided a forum in which Asian and Western cinemas could be introduced to and appreciated by a worldwide audience. Led by Dissanayake, Charlot, and Clark, the journal contained mostly articles based on presentations at conferences that the EWC and HIFF had co-organized. (Now) household names in the field of Asian cinema—Donald Richie, David Desser, Catherine Russell, Ning Ma, Keiko McDonald, Gina Marchetti, Chris Berry, Yoshimoto Mitsuhiro, Krishna Sen, Markus Nornes, and Yingjin Zhang—and film critics including Tony Rayns, Roger Ebert, Kenneth Turan, Stephen Teo, and Jonathan Rosenbaum contributed articles on East, Southeast, and South Asian cinemas.

34. Chris Berry wrote, "Few people outside China had seen many Chinese films, and even fewer claimed to understand or like them. . . . Within months all that changed when *Yellow Earth*

appeared at the Hong Kong Film Festival." Chris Berry, "Introduction," in *Perspectives on Chinese Cinema*, ed. Chris Berry (London: BFI Publishing, 1991), 1. Shortly after the success of *Yellow Earth*, Zhang Yimou won the Silver Bear at the Berlin Film Festival with his feature debut *Red Sorghum* (*Hong gaoliang*, 1987). Hou Hsiao-hsien has been a fixture on the international film festival circuit since his award at Venice in 1989 for *City of Sadness* (*Beiqing chengshi*). Edward Yang, Hou's peer, picked up a Silver Leopard at Locarno for *The Terrorizer* (*Kongbu fenzi*) in 1987. Together with Chen Kunhou, Hou and Yang would be known as leading figures of the Taiwan New Cinema (also known as New Taiwanese Cinema).

35. Hereniko, interview with the author.

36. "Asia Pacific Film Festival," *Variety*, June 11, 1985.

37. Francis Fukuyama, "The End of History," *National Interest* 16 (1989): 3–18.

38. Surprisingly, the FPA is still holding its annual event. The 58th Asia Pacific Film Festival was held in Taipei in September 2018. The award ceremony for the 58th edition took place at the Grand Mayfull Hotel in Taipei and was broadcasted live on Taiwanese TV. Sixteen countries and city-states sent delegates to the festival, including Malaysia, China, Japan, Macau, the Philippines, Indonesia, Vietnam, Pakistan, Iran, Bangladesh, Taiwan, Thailand, India, Nepal, Australia, Mongolia, and Russia. The Best Picture award went to the Australian drama *Lion* (Garth Davis, 2016), starring Dev Patel and Rooney Mara, and a Taiwanese director Midi Z won Best Director award for his critically acclaimed *The Road to Mandalay* (2016). Both films were produced in 2016. Despite the Taiwanese film industry's enthusiastic support, however, the fifty-eighth gathering attracted much less attention from the outside world than did its more scintillating competitors—the Busan International Film Festival and the Shanghai International Film Festival.

39. See Michael Keane, Brian Yecies, and Terry Flew, eds., *Willing Collaborators: Foreign Partners in Chinese Media* (Lanham, MD: Rowman & Littlefield, 2018); Michael Keane, "China's Digital Media Industries and the Challenge of Overseas Markets," *Journal of Chinese Cinemas* 13, no. 3 (Fall 2019), 244–56; and Michael Curtin, "What Makes Them Willing Collaborators? The Global Context of Chinese Motion Picture Co-productions," *Media International Australia* 159, no. 1 (May 2016): 63–72.

40. Stephanie DeBoer writes, "Iseki Satoru is the head of Nippon Development and Finance and is a producer with a wide range of commercial and independent productions to his credit. He worked as a film distributor in the 1980s and as the production manager of Akira Kurosawa's *Ran* in 1990. His transnational productions include such films as *Shadow of China* (Yanagimachi Mitsuo, 1990), *Smoke* (Wayne Wang, 1995), *A Little Life Opera* (Allen Fong, 1997), *Vampire Hunters* (Wellson Chin, 2002), and *Battle of Wits* (Javob Cheung, 2006)." Stephanie DeBoer, "Framing Tokyo Media Capital and Asian Co-Production," in *East Asian Cinemas: Regional Flows and Global Transformations*, ed. Vivian Lee (London: Palgrave Macmillan), 214.

41. *Anarchists* was not a planned coproduction. The producer Yi Chun-ik, who later became a prolific director himself, approached Shanghai Film Studio hoping to reduce the costs of this grand epic drama about Korean resistance fighters in Shanghai during Japanese colonial rule (1910–45). The Shanghai studio executives welcomed Yi's proposal, and the film was completed in 1999. *Anarchists* was not a box office success. It did, however, open a door to the Chinese film market. For more about China-South Korea cinema collaboration, see Sangjoon Lee, "The South Korean Film Industry and the Chinese Film Market," *Screen* 60, no. 2 (2019): 332–41.

42. Darrell William Davis, "Market and Marketization in the China Film Business," *Cinema Journal* 49, no. 3 (2010): 122.

43. A special dossier for *Screen*, "Reorienting Asian Cinema in the Age of the Chinese Film Market," includes five essays on the transformations of the regional film industry's practices, creative labor, artistic challenges, inter-Asian film coproduction, regional politics, and media memo-

ries juxtaposed with and in response to the Chinese film market's quantum leap. See Sangjoon Lee, ed., "Dossier: Reorienting Asian Cinema in the Age of the Chinese Film Market," *Screen* 60, no. 2 (Summer 2019): 298–350.

44. "China's Total Number of Cinema Screens Now Exceeds the US," *PWC China*, June 16, 2017, accessed at https://www.pwccn.com/en/press-room/press-releases/pr-160617.html.

45. Aaron Han Joon Magnan-Park, "The Global Failure of Cinematic Soft Power 'with Chinese Characteristics,'" *Asia Dialogue*, May 27, 2019. Accessed at https://theasiadialogue.com/2019/05/27/the-global-failure-of-cinematic-soft-power-with-chinese-characteristics/?fbclid=IwAR0jZ1u7 BWV2-JIrOALUURBjofzQll94JbZFWfCZU0Rb2s3tuunncZF1oUE.

46. Motion Picture Association of America, *Theatrical Market Statistics 2016*, March 2017, 7.

47. Wong Ka Hee, interview with the author, January 2008.

48. Most industry experts and market analysts predict that the size of the Chinese film market will surpass that of North America by 2022. Following the phenomenal commercial success of *Wolf Warrior 2* (*Zhan Lang 2*, Wu Jing), a domestic action blockbuster that was made in China in 2017 and grossed USD 874 million in China alone, other homegrown box office hit films have solidified the status of domestic films in the Chinese market, such as *Operation Red Sea* (*Honghai xindong*, Dante Lam, 2018), *Dying to Survive* (*Wo bus hi yao shen*, Wen Muye, 2018) and two mega-budget sci-fi films based on short stories by the celebrated writer Liu Cixin (*The Three-Body Problem*), *Crazy Alien* (Ning Hao, 2019) and *The Wandering Earth* (*Liulang diqiu*, Frant Gwo, 2019).

49. As a former head of the Busan Film Commission and a veteran film director, O Sŏk-kŭn helped create and solidify the Asian Film Commissions Network, launched in 2004, which is similarly comprised of Asian quasigovernmental organizations

50. "S. Korea Preparing to Set Up Joint Film Organization with ASEAN," *Yonhap News* Agency, May 21, 2019, accessed at https://en.yna.co.kr/view/AEN20190521002700315.

51. Patrick Frater and Sonia Kil, "Plans for Asian Film Center Given Launch in Busan," *Variety*, October 8, 2018, accessed at https://variety.com/2018/film/asia/plans-asian-film-center-launch-in-busan-1202971854/.

Bibliography

Archival Sites and Records in the United States

Academy of Motion Pictures Arts and Sciences (AMPAS), Margaret Herrick Library, Los Angeles, CA

Film Festivals P-Z
Hedda Hopper Papers
MPAA Production Code Administration Record
San Francisco Film Festival Collection

Alfred Kohlberg Collection (AKC), Hoover Institution Archive, Stanford University, CA
Asia Foundation Records (AFR), Hoover Institution Archive, Stanford University, CA
Conant Collection, C.V. Starr East Asian Library, Columbia University, NY
Freda Utley Papers (1886–1978), Hoover Institution Archive, Stanford University, CA
Hawaii International Film Festival Collection, Research Information Services Center, East West Center, University of Hawaii, HI
Inez G. Richardson Collection, Hoover Institution Archive, Stanford University, CA
Rare Books, Special Collections and Preservation Department, River Campus Libraries, University of Rochester, NY
Robert Blum Papers (RBP), Manuscripts and Archives, Yale University Library, CT

Archival Sites and Records in the Asia-Pacific

Anthony Buckley Papers, National Film and Sound Archive, Canberra, Australia.
Asia Pictorial Collection, Hong Kong University Library Special Collections, Hong Kong University Library, Hong Kong SAR
Asian Film Archive, Singapore
Hong Kong Film Archive, Hong Kong SAR
Korean Film Archive, South Korea
Lok Wan Tho Collection, National Archives of Singapore, Singapore
Nara Repository and Presidential Archives, South Korea
National Archives of Korea, South Korea
National Film Archive of Japan, Japan
National Library of Korea, South Korea
Seoul National University Library, South Korea

Magazines, Newspapers, and Almanacs

America: National Catholic Weekly Review
Asia Pictorial
Box Office
The Buddhist
Burma Weekly Bulletin
China Mail
China Yearbook
Chosŏn Ilbo [Chosŏn daily]
Daehan Ilbo [Daehan daily]
Daily Variety
East-West Center Magazine
Eiga Nenkan [Film almanac]
Far East Film News
Far Eastern Economic Review
Far Eastern Survey: American Institute of Pacific Relations
The Film Daily
Film Quarterly
Films in Review
Golden Movie News
Guo Ji Dian Ying [International screen]
Kinema Junpo [Cinema biweekly]
Kyŏnghyang shinmun [Kyŏnghyang daily]
Han'gug Ilbo [Han'gug daily]
The Indian Review
KINO
Manila Bulletin Research

The March of India
Motion Picture Daily
Naeoe Yŏnghwa [Cinema inside and outside]
Nan Guo Dian Ying [Southern screen]
The New Leader
The New York Times
Nippon Times
Oakland Tribune
Pacific Research and World Empire Telegram
The Quarterly of Film, Radio and Television
Ramparts
The San Francisco Chronicle
The San Francisco Examiner
San Francisco News
Screen Daily
Shilbŏ Sŭk'ŭrin [Silver screen]
Shin Tonga [New Tonga magazine]
Shin Yŏnghwa [New cinema]
Shina Ilbo [Shina daily]
Sight & Sound
Sŏul Shinmun [Sŏul daily]
South China Morning Post
Ssine 21 [Cine 21]
Time
Tonga Ilbo [Tonga daily]
Variety
The Village Voice
World Today
Yŏnghwa Ch'ŏn'guk [Cinema paradise]
Yŏnghwa Japchi [Film magazine]
Yŏnghwa Segye [Film world]

Personal Interviews

Cheng, Pei Pei, Ann Arbor, MI, USA, October 2012
Chin, Pong-jin, Seoul, South Korea, October 2008
Cho, Jun-hyoung, Seoul, South Korea, June 2007
Ch'oe, Kyŏng-ok, Seoul, South Korea, October 2008
Chŏng, Ch'ang-hwa, Seoul, South Korea, August 2008
Garcia, Roger, Xiamen, China, June 2019
Hereniko, Jeannette Paulson, May 2016 (e-mail interview)
Ho, Meng Hua, Hong Kong, August 2009
Johnson-Tanner, Bobbi M., April 2016 (e-mail interview)

Kim, Su-yong, Seoul, South Korea, August 2009

Law, Kar, Hong Kong, September 2007 and August 2009

Pak, Haeng-ch'ŏl, Bucheon, South Korea, July 2008 and May 2009

Wong, Ain-ling, Hong Kong, August 2008

Wong, Ka Hee, Hong Kong, January 2008

Yau, Shuk-ting Kinnia, Hong Kong, August 2008

Books and Essays

Aitken, Ian, and Michael Ingham. *Hong Kong Documentary Film*. Edinburgh: Edinburgh University Press, 2014.

Aitken, Ian. *The British Official Film in South-East Asia: Malaya/Malaysia, Singapore and Hong Kong*. London: Palgrave Macmillan, 2016.

Akamatsu, Kaname. "A Historical Pattern of Economic Growth in Developing Countries." *Developing Economies* 1, no. 1 (1962): 3–25.

Amsden, Alice H. *Asia's Next Giant: South Korea and Late Industrialization*. New York: Oxford University Press, 1989.

——. "Diffusion of Development: The Late Industrializing Model and Greater East Asia." *American Economic Review* 81, no. 2 (May 1991): 282–86.

——. *Escape from Empire: The Developing World's Journey through Heaven and Hell*. Cambridge, MA: MIT Press, 2007.

Anderson, Danielle. *Fifty Years of Australia's Trade*. Canberra: Department of Foreign Affairs and Trade, Australian Government Report, 2014.

Armstrong, Charles K. "The Cultural Cold War in Korea, 1945–1950." *Journal of Asian Studies* 62, no. 1 (February 2003): 71–99.

Aronova, Elena. "The Congress for Cultural Freedom, *Minerva*, and the Quest for Instituting 'Science Studies' in the Age of Cold War." *Minerva* 50 (2012): 307–37.

Arrighi, Giovanni. "States, Markets, and Capitalism, East and West." *Positions* 15, no. 2 (2007): 251–84.

Arrighi, Giovanni, Takeshi Hamashita, and Mark Sheldon, eds. *The Resurgence of East Asia: 500, 150, and 50 Year Perspectives*. London: Routledge, 2003.

Asia-Pacific Film Festival 50th Anniversary Catalogue. Kuala Lumpur, Malaysia: Ministry of Culture, 2005.

Au, Tung Steve. *Lingnan Spirit Forever—A Mission in Transition, 1951–1990: From the Trustees of Lingnan University to the Lingnan Foundation*. New Haven, CT: Lingnan Foundation, 2002.

Balio, Tino. *The Foreign Film Renaissance on American Screens, 1946–1973*. Madison: University of Wisconsin Press, 2010.

——. "Struggles for Control." In *The American Film Industry*, edited by Tino Balio, 103–32. Madison: University of Wisconsin Press, 1985.

——. *United Artists: The Company That Changed the Film Industry*. Madison: University of Wisconsin Press, 1987.

Barnhisel, Greg. *Cold War Modernists: Art, Literature, and American Cultural Diplomacy.* New York: Columbia University Press, 2015.

——. "Cold Warriors of the Book: American Book Programs in the 1950s." *Book History* 13 (2010): 186–87.

Basch, Antonin. "The Colombo Plan: A Case of Regional Economic Cooperation." *International Organization* 9, no. 1 (1955): 1–18.

Basket, Michael. *The Attractive Empire; Colonial Asia in Japanese Imperial Culture, 1931-1953.* Honolulu: University of Hawaii Press, 2008.

Belmonte, Laura A. *Selling the American Way: U.S. Propaganda and the Cold War.* Philadelphia: University of Pennsylvania Press, 2008.

Benitez, Francisco. "Filming Philippine Modernity During the Cold War: The Case of Lamberto Avellana." In *Cultures at War: The Cold War and Cultural Expression in Southeast Asia,* edited by Tony Day and Maya H. T. Liem, 21–44. Ithaca, NY: Cornell University Press, 2010.

Bernstein, Matthew. *Walter Wanger, Hollywood Independent.* Minneapolis: University of Minnesota Press, 2000.

Berry, Chris. "Introduction." In *Perspectives on Chinese Cinema,* edited by Chris Berry. London: BFI Publishing, 1991.

——. *Postsocialist Cinema in Post-Mao China: The Cultural Revolution after the Cultural Revolution.* London: Routledge, 2004.

Blum, Robert. "The Asia Foundation: Purposes and Program." *United Asia: International Magazine of Afro-Asian Affairs* 11, no. 5 (1959).

——. "The Work of The Asia Foundation." *Public Affairs* 29, no. 1 (1956): 46–56.

Bordwell, David, Janet Staiger, and Kristin Thompson. *The Classical Hollywood Cinema: Film Style and Mode of Production to 1960.* New York: Columbia University Press, 1985.

Brzezinski, Zbigniew. *The Choice: Global Domination or Global Leadership.* New York: Basic Books, 2004.

——. "Japan's Global Engagement." *Foreign Affairs* 50 (1971–72): 270–82.

——. "The Politics of Underdevelopment." *World Politics* 9, no. 1 (1956): 55–75.

Busch, Noel F. *Fallen Sun: A Report on Japan.* New York: Appleton Century Crofts, Inc., 1948.

Butwell, Richard. *U Nu of Burma.* Stanford, CA: Stanford University Press, 1963.

Câmara, Regina. "From Karlovy Vary to Cannes: Brazilian Cinema Nuovo at European Film Festivals in the 1960s." In *Cultural Transfer and Political Conflicts: Film Festivals in the Cold War,* edited by Andreas Kötzing and Caroline Moine, 63–76. Göttingen, Germany: V&R Unipress, 2017.

Capling, Ann. "Twenty Years of Australia's Engagement with Asia." *Pacific Review* 21, no. 5 (2008): 601–22.

Capra, Frank. *The Name above the Title: An Autobiography.* New York: Macmillan Company, 1971.

Caute, David. *The Dancer Defects: The Struggle for Cultural Supremacy During the Cold War.* Oxford: Oxford University Press, 2003.

Cha, Jae-young, and Yeom Chanhee. "1950nyŏn-tae chuhan mikongpowŏn ŭi kilokyŏnghwa wa mikuk ŭi imichi kuch'uk" [Documentary films of the USIS Korea in the 1950s for constructing American images], *Han'gugŏllonhakpo* [Korean journal of journalism and communication] 56, no. 1 (2012): 235–63.

Chang, Ha-Joon. *The East Asian Development Experience: The Miracle, the Crisis and the Future.* London: Zed Books, 2006.

Charney, Michael. "U Nu, China and the 'Burmese' Cold War: Propaganda in Burma in the 1950s." In *The Cold War in Asia: The Battle for Hearts and Minds,* edited by Zheng Yangwen, Hong Liu, and Michael Szonyi, 50–53. Leiden: Brill 2010.

Chen, Jian. *Mao's China and the Cold War.* Chapel Hill: University of North Carolina Press 2001.

Chen, Qingwei. *Xianggang dianying gongye jiegon ji shichang fengxi* [The structure and marketing analysis of the Hong Kong film industry]. Hong Kong: Dianying shuangzhoukan, 2000.

Cheung, Ruby. "Ever-changing Readjustments: The Political Economy of the Hong Kong International Film Festival (HKIFF)." *New Review of Film and Television Studies* 14, no. 1 (2016), 59-75.

Cho, Chun-hyŏng. *Yŏnghwa jegug shinp'illŭm* [Shin Films: The movie empire]. Seoul, Korea: Korean Film Archive, 2009.

Cho, Chun-hyŏng, ed. *Oral History Project 2008: Shin Films.* Seoul, Korea: Korean Film Archive, 2008.

Cho, Hŭi-mun. "Han'guk yŏnghwa kiŏp'wa ŭi kanŭngsŏng gwa han'gye shinp'illŭm" [Shin Films: The possibility and limitation of the corporatization of Korean cinema]. *Yŏnghwa yŏn'gu* [Film studies] 14 (2006): 421–38.

Cho, Tong-jae, and Park Tae-jin. *Partner for Change: 50 Years of The Asia Foundation in Korea, 1954–2004.* Seoul, Korea: The Asia Foundation, 2004.

Choi, Chungmoo. "The Magic and Violence of Modernization in Post-Colonial Korea." In *Post-Colonial Classics of Korean Cinema,* edited by Chungmoo Choi, 5–12. Irvine: University of California, 1998.

Chŏng, Chong-hwa. "Aeksyŏn yŏnghwa mandŭlgi: kim shi-hyŏn kamdog int'ŏbyu" [Making action cinema: An interview with Kim Si-hyeon]. *Yŏnghwa ŏnŏ* [Film language] 4 (Spring 2004).

Chŏng, Chong-hyŏn. "'Taedonga' wa sŭp'ai—Kim Naesŏng changp'yŏn sosŏl 'T'aep'ung' ŭl t'onghae pon 'Taedonga' ŭi simsang chiri wa 'Chosŏn'" ["'The Greater East Asia" and spy-imaginative geography of "the Greater East Asia" and "Joseon" from the viewpoint of *Typhoon*]. *Taejung sŏsa yŏn'gu* [Journal of popular narrative] 15, no. 2 (2009): 211–47.

Chotirosseranee, Sanchai. "Finding Santi-Vina." *Journal of Film Preservation* 96 (April 2017): 107–12.

Chung, Stephanie Po-yin. "The Industrial Evolution of a Fraternal Enterprise: The Shaw Brothers and the Shaw Organization." In *The Shaw Screen: A Preliminary Study,* edited by Wong Ain-ling, 1–18. Hong Kong: Hong Kong Film Archive, 2003.

——. "Moguls of the Chinese Cinema: The Story of the Shaw Brothers in Shanghai, Hong Kong and Singapore, 1924–2002." *Modern Asian Studies* 41, no. 1 (2007): 665–82.

——. "A Southeast Asian Tycoon and His Movie Dream: Loke Wan Tho and MP&GI." In *The Cathay Story,* edited by Wong Ain-ling, 36–51. Hong Kong: Hong Kong Film Archive, 2002.

Chung, Steven. *Split Screen Cinema: Shin Sang-ok and Postwar Cinema*. Minneapolis: University of Minnesota Press, 2014.

Clark, Paul. *Chinese Cinema: Culture and Politics Since 1949*. Cambridge: Cambridge University Press, 1987.

The Committee for Free Asia Study Group. *A Symposium on the Political, Economic and Cultural Position of the Overseas Chinese*. The Committee for Free Asia, August 15, 1953.

Cook, David A. *Lost Illusions: American Cinema in the Shadow of Watergate and Vietnam, 1970–1979*. Berkeley: University of California Press, 2002.

Cull, Nicholas J. *The Cold War and the United States Information Agency: American Propaganda and Public Democracy, 1945–1989*. Cambridge: Cambridge University Press, 2008.

Cumings, Bruce. "Japan's Position in the World System." In *Postwar Japan as History*, edited by Andrew Gordon, 34–63. Berkeley: University of California Press, 1993.

——. *Dominion from Sea to Sea: Pacific Ascendancy and American Power*. New Haven, CT: Yale University Press, 2010.

Cummings, Richard H. *Radio Free Europe's "Crusade for Freedom": Rallying Americans Behind Cold War Broadcasting, 1950–1960*. Jefferson, NC: McFarland and Company, 2010.

Curry, Ramona. "Bridging the Pacific with Love Eterne." In *China Forever: The Shaw Brothers and Diasporic Cinema,* edited by Poshek Fu, 174–98. Urbana: University of Illinois Press, 2008.

Curtin, Michael. "Media Capital: Towards the Study of Spatial Flows." *International Journal of Cultural Studies* 6, no. 2 (2003): 202–28.

——. "What Makes Them Willing Collaborators? The Global Context of Chinese Motion Picture Co-productions." *Media International Australia* 159, no. 1 (May 2016): 63–72.

Davis, D. W., and Emilie Yueh-yu Yeh. "Inoue at Shaws." In *The Shaw Screen: A Preliminary Study*, edited by Wong Ain-ling, 255–71. Hong Kong: Hong Kong Film Archive, 2003.

Davis, Darrell William. "Market and Marketization in the China Film Business." *Cinema Journal* 49, no. 3 (2010): 121–25.

Day, Tony, and Maya H. T. Liem, eds. *Cultures at War: The Cold War and Cultural Expression in Southeast Asia*. Ithaca, NY: Cornell University Press, 2010.

DeBoer, Stephanie. "Framing Tokyo Media Capital and Asian Co-Production." In *East Asian Cinemas: Regional Flows and Global Transformations*, edited by Vivian Lee, 213–34. London: Palgrave Macmillan.

Desser, David. "The Kung Fu Craze: Hong Kong Cinema's First American Reception." In *The Cinema of Hong Kong: History, Art, Identity*, edited by Poshek Fu and David Desser, 19–43. Cambridge: Cambridge University Press, 2000.

Deyo, Frederic C. *Beneath the Miracle: Labor Subordination in the New Asian Industrialism*. Berkeley: University of California Press, 1989.

Dower, John W. *Japan in War and Peace: Selected Essays*. New York: New Press, 1993.

Dumont, Hervé. *Frank Borzage: The Life and Film of a Hollywood Romantic*. Translated by Jonathan Kaplansky. Jefferson, NC: McFarland & Company, 2006.

Duus, Peter. *Modern Japan*. Boston: Houghton Mifflin Company, 1998.

Eldridge, David N. "'Dear Owen': The CIA, Luigi Luraschi and Hollywood, 1953." *Historical Journal of Film, Radio and Television* 20, no. 2 (2000): 149–96.

Elsaesser, Thomas. "Film Festival Networks: The New Topographies of Cinema in Europe." In *European Cinema: Face to Face with Hollywood*, 82–107. Amsterdam: Amsterdam University Press, 2005.

Evans, Peter B., Dietrich Rueschemeyer, and Theda Skocpol, eds. *Bringing the State Back In*. Cambridge: Cambridge University Press, 1985.

Falk, Andrew J. *Upstaging the Cold War: American Dissent and Cultural Diplomacy, 1940–1960*. Amherst: University of Massachusetts Press, 2010.

Fay, Jennifer. "The *Schoolgirl Reports* and the Guilty Pleasure of History." In *Alternative Europe: Eurotrash and Exploitation Cinemas Since 1945*, edited by Ernest Mathijs and Xavier Mendik, 39–52. London: Wallflower Press, 2004.

The Federation of Motion Picture Producers in Southeast Asia. *The First Film Festival in Southeast Asia Catalogue*, May 8–20, 1954, Tokyo, Japan.

——. *Report on the 3rd Annual Film Festival of Southeast Asia*, Hong Kong, June 12–16, 1956.

Fehrenback, Heide. *Cinema in Democratizing Germany: Reconstructing National Identity after Hitler*. Chapel Hill: University of North Carolina Press, 1995.

The Film Society of Lincoln Center. *New York Film Festival Programs: 1963–1975*. New York: Arno Press, 1976.

The First Hawaii International Film Festival Program. November 1–7, 1981, Hawaii International Film Festival Collection, East West Center Library, The University of Hawaii, HI.

Fischer, Paul. *A Kim Jong-Il Production: The Extraordinary True Story of a Kidnapped Filmmaker, His Star Actress, and a Young Dictator's Rise to Power*. New York: Flatiron Books, 2015.

Flanigan, P. "Kung Fu Krazy or the Invention of the 'Chop Suey Eastern.'" *Cineaste* 6, no. 3 (1974): 8–10.

Ford, Eugene. *Cold War Monks: Buddhism and America's Secret Strategy in Southeast Asia*. New Haven: Yale University Press, 2017.

Fore, Steve. "Golden Harvest Films and the Hong Kong Movie Industry in the Realm of Globalization." *Velvet Light Trap* 34 (Fall 1994): 40–58.

Foreign Affairs and National Defense Division. *The Asia Foundation: Past, Present, and Future. Official Report Prepared for the Committee on Foreign Relations United States Senate*. Washington, DC, 1983.

Friedman, Lester D. "Introduction: Movies and the 1970s." In *American Cinema of the 1970s: Themes and Variations*, edited by Lester D. Friedman, 1–23. New Brunswick, NJ: Rutgers University Press, 2007.

Fu, Poshek. "The 1960s: Modernity, Youth Culture, and Hong Kong Cantonese Cinema." In *The Cinema of Hong Kong: History, Art, Identity*. Edited by Poshek Fu and David Desser, 81–82. Cambridge: Cambridge University Press, 2000.

——. "The Ambiguity of Entertainment: Chinese Cinema in Japanese-Occupied Shanghai, 1941 to 1945." *Cinema Journal* 37, no. 1 (Autumn 1997): 66–84.

——. *Between Shanghai and Hong Kong: The Politics of Chinese Cinemas*. Stanford, CA: Stanford University Press, 2003.

——. "Hong Kong and Singapore: A History of the Cathay Cinema." In *The Cathay Story*, 60–75.

——. "Japanese Occupation, Shanghai Exiles, and Postwar Hong Kong Cinema." *China Quarterly* 194 (June 2008): 380–94.

———. "Modernity, Diasporic Capital, and 1950's Hong Kong Mandarin Cinema." *Jump Cut: A Review of Contemporary Media* 49 (Spring 2007). https://www.ejumpcut.org/archive/jc49.2007/Poshek/

———. "The Shaw Brothers' Diasporic Cinema." In *China Forever: The Shaw Brothers and Diasporic Cinema*, edited by Poshek Fu, 1–26. Urbana: University of Illinois Press, 2008.

Fukuyama, Francis. "The End of History." *National Interest* 16 (1989): 3–18.

Gerow, Aaron. "Narrating the Nation-ality of a Cinema: The Case of Japanese Prewar Film." In *The Culture of Japanese Fascism*, edited by Alan Talisman. Durham, NC: Duke University Press, 2009.

———. *Visions of Japanese Modernity: Articulations of Cinema, Nation, and Spectatorship, 1895–1925*. Berkeley: University of California Press, 2010.

Gerteis, Christopher. "Labor's Cold Warriors: The American Federation of Labor and 'Free Trade Unionism' in Cold War Japan." *Journal of American-East Asian Relations* 12, no. 3 (2003): 207–24.

Goldsmith, Ben, and Tom O'Regan. *The Film Studio: Film Production in the Global Economy*. Lanham, MD: Rowman and Littlefield, 2005.

Govil, Nitin. *Orienting Hollywood: A Century of Film Culture Between Los Angeles and Bombay*. New York: NYU Press, 2015.

Gustafson, Robert. "What's Happening to Our Pix Biz? From Warner Bros. to Warner Communications Inc." In *The American Film Industry*, edited by Tino Balio, 574–89. Madison: University of Wisconsin Press, 1985.

Hall, Sheldon, and Steve Neale. *Epics, Spectacles, and Blockbusters: A Hollywood History*. Detroit, MI: Wayne State University Press, 2010.

Ham, Ch'ung-bŏm. "hŏ jŏng kwado jŏngbu shigi han'guk yŏnghwa-gye yŏn'gu" [A study of South Korean cinema in the period of the Heo-jeong interim administration: Focused on the 4.19 revolution]. *Sunch'ŏnhyang inmun kwahak nonch'ong* [Sunch'ŏnhyang studies of humanities and science] 26 (2010): 67–93.

Hamamoto, Darrel Y. *Monitored Peril: Asian Americans and the Politics of TV Representation*. Minneapolis: University of Minnesota Press, 1994.

Hamid, Rahul. "From Urban Bohemia to Euro Glamour: The Establishment and Early Years of the New York Film Festival." In *Film Festival Yearbook 1: The Festival Circuit*, ed. Dina Iordanova and Regan Rhyne, 67–81. St. Andrews: St. Andrews University Press, 2009.

Han'guk yŏnghwa charyo p'yŏllam [The complete index of Korean film materials]. Seoul, Korea: Korean Motion Picture Promotion Corporation, 1976.

Han'guk yŏngsang jaryowŏn [Korean film archive]. *Han'guk yŏnghwa 100sŏn: 'ch'ŏngch'un ŭi shipjharo'esŏ 'p'iet'a'kkaji* [100 Korean films: From *Turning Point of the Youngsters* to *Pieta*]. Han'guk yŏngsang jaryowŏn [Korean film archive], 2013.

Hansen, Miriam Bratu. "The Mass Production of the Senses: Classical Cinema as Vernacular Modernism." *Modernism/Modernity* 6, no. 2 (1999): 59–77.

Hatch, Walter F. *Asia's Flying Geese: How Regionalization Shapes Japan*. Ithaca, NY: Cornell University Press, 2010.

Heffernan, Kevin. *Ghouls, Gimmicks, and Gold: Horror Films and the American Movie Business, 1953–1968*. Durham, NC: Duke University Press, 2004.

———. "Inner-City Exhibition and the Genre Film: Distributing *Night of the Living Dead* (1968)." *Cinema Journal* 41, no. 3 (2002): 59–77.

Heo, Eun. "Naengjŏn shidae migug ŭi minjok kukka hyŏng sŏng kaeip kwa hegemoni kuch'ug ŭi ch'oejŏnsŏn chuhan mi gongbowŏn yŏng hwa." [The intervention of the United States in the formation of the nation-state and the frontline in terms of the establishment of hegemony during the Cold War era: With a special focus on the films produced by the United States Information Service in Korea]. *Han'guksa yŏn'gu* [Journal of Korean history] 155 (December 2011): 139–69.

High, Peter B. *The Imperial Screen: Japanese Film Culture in the Fifteen Years' War, 1931–1945.* Madison: University of Wisconsin Press, 2003.

Hirano, Kyoko. "Japan." In *World Cinema Since 1945*, edited by William Luhr, 380–423. New York: Ungar, 1987.

Hochgeschwender, Michael. *"Der Monat* and the Congress for Cultural Freedom: The High Tide of the Intellectual Cold War, 1948–1971." In *Campaigning Culture and the Global Cold War: The Journals of the Congress for Cultural Freedom*, edited by Giles Scott-Smith and Charlotte A. Lerg, 71–89. London: Palgrave MacMillan, 2017.

Holt, Robert T. *Radio Free Europe.* Minneapolis: University of Minnesota Press, 1958.

Hong, Guo-juin. *Taiwan Cinema: A Contested Nation on Screen.* London: Palgrave Macmillan, 2011.

Hong Kong Film Archive. *Oral History Series 3: Director Chor Yuen.* Hong Kong: Hong Kong Film Archive, 2006.

Horvat, Andrew. "Rashomon Perceived: The Challenge of Forging a Transnationally Shared View of Kurosawa's Legacy." In *Rashomon Effects: Kurosawa, Rashomon and Their Legacies*, edited by Blair Davis, Robert Anderson, and Jan Walls, 43-55. New York: Routledge, 2016.

Howard, Christopher. "Beyond *Jidai-geki*: Daiei Studios and the Study of Transnational Japanese Cinema." *Journal of Japanese and Korean Cinema* 3, no. 1 (2012): 5–12.

——. "Re-Orienting Japanese Cinema: Cold War Criticism of 'Anti-American' Films." *Historical Journal of Film, Radio and Television* 36, no. 4 (2016): 529–30.

Huang, Yu. "Foreword." In Chang Kuo-sin, *Eight Months Behind the Bamboo Curtain: A Report on the First Eight Months of Communist Rule in China*, VI–VIII. Kowloon: City University of Hong Kong Press, 2015.

Jeong, Kelly Y. *"Aimless Bullet* (1961): Postwar Dystopia, Canonicity, and Cinema Realism." In *Rediscovering Korean Cinema*, edited by Sangjoon Lee, 160–72. Ann Arbor: University of Michigan Press, 2019.

Johnson, A. Ross. *Radio Free Europe and Radio Liberty: The CIA Years and Beyond.* Washington, DC: Woodrow Wilson Center, 2010.

Johnson, Chalmers. *MITI and the Japanese Miracle: The Growth of Industrial Policy, 1925–1975.* Stanford, CA: Stanford University Press, 1982.

Katzenstein, Peter J. "Japan, Technology and Asian Regionalism in Comparative Perspective." In *The Resurgence of East Asia: 500, 150, and 50 Years Perspective*, edited by Giovanni Arrighi, Takeshi Hamashita, and Mark Sheldon, 214–58. London: Routledge, 2003.

Keane, Michael. "China's Digital Media Industries and the Challenge of Overseas Markets." *Journal of Chinese Cinemas* 13, no. 3 (Fall 2019), 244–56.

Keane, Michael, Brian Yecies, and Terry Flew, eds. *Willing Collaborators: Foreign Partners in Chinese Media.* Lanham, MD: Rowman & Littlefield, 2018.

Khandpur, K. L. "Problems of Training Film Technicians in South East Asia." *UNESCO Meeting on Development of Information Media in South East Asia*, Bangkok, January 18–30, 1960.

———. "First International Film Festival of India." In *70 Years of Indian Cinema (1913–1983)*, edited by T. M. Ramachandran, 578–85. Bombay: CINEMA India-International, 1984.

Kim, Han Sang. "Cold War and the Contested Identity Formation of Korean Filmmakers: On *Boxes of Death* and Kim Ki-yong's USIS Film." *Inter-Asian Cultural Studies* 14, no. 1 (2013): 551–63.

Kim Jong Il. *Yŏnghwa yesullon* [On the art of the cinema]. Pyongyang: Workers' Party of Korea Publishing House, 1973.

Kim, Mi-hyŏn, ed. *Han'guk yŏnghwasa* [Korean film history]. Seoul: Communication Books, 2005.

Kim, Se Jin. "South Korea's Involvement in Vietnam and Its Economic and Political Impact." *Asian Survey* 10, no. 6 (June 1970): 524–25.

Kitagawa, Joseph M. "Buddhism and Asian Politics." *Asian Survey* 2, no. 5 (July 1962): 1–11.

———. *Religion in Japanese History*. New York: Columbia University Press, 1966.

Kitamura, Hiroshi. *Screening Enlightenment: Hollywood and the Cultural Reconstruction of Defeated Japan*. Ithaca, NY: Cornell University Press, 2010.

Klein, Christina. *Cold War Orientalism: Asia in the Middlebrow Imagination, 1945–1961*. Berkeley: University of California Press, 2003.

———. "*Madame Freedom* (1956): Spectatorship and the Modern Woman." In *Rediscovering Korean Cinema*, edited by Sangjoon Lee, 118–31. Ann Arbor: University of Michigan Press, 2019.

Kötzing, Andreas. "Cultural and Film Policy in the Cold War: The Film Festivals of Oberhausen and Leipzig and German-German Relations." In *Cultural Transfer and Political Conflicts: Film Festivals in the Cold War*, edited by Andreas Kötzing and Caroline Moine, 32–33. Göttingen, Germany: V&R Unipress, 2017.

Kung, James, and Zhang Yueai. "Hong Kong Cinema and Television in the 1970s: A Perspective." In *A Study of Hong Kong Cinema in the Seventies*, the 8th Hong Kong International Film Festival, 14–17. Hong Kong: The Urban Council, 1984.

Kuoshu, Harry H. *Celluloid China: Cinematic Encounters with Culture and Society*. Carbondale: Southern Illinois University Press, 2002.

Kurosawa, Akira. *Something Like an Autobiography*. Translated by Audie Bock. New York: Vantage Books: 1982.

Lau, C. K. "Chang Kuo-sin: Patriot Who Stuck to the Truth." In Chang Kuo-sin, *Eight Months Behind the Bamboo Curtain: A Report on the First Eight Months of Communist Rule in China*, 15–25. Kowloon: City University of Hong Kong Press, 2015.

Law, Kar, and Frank Bren. *Hong Kong Cinema: A Cross Cultural View*. London: Scarecrow, 2005.

Leary, Charles. "The Most Careful Arrangement for a Careful Fiction: A Short History of Asia Pictures." *Inter-Asian Cultural Studies* 13, no. 4 (2012): 548–58.

Lee, Jin-kyung. "Surrogate Military, Subimperialism, and Masculinity: South Korea in the Vietnam War, 1965–73." *Positions: Asia Critique* 17, no. 3 (2009): 655–82.

Lee, Sangjoon. "Chŏng Ch'ang-hwa kamdok kwa ashia hapchak yŏnghwa ŭi shidae" [Chŏng Ch'ang-hwa and the Age of Inter-Asian Co-production]. *Yŏnghwa ch'ŏn'guk* [Cinema paradise] 21 (August 2011): 28–31.

——. "Creating an Anti-Communist Motion Picture Producers' Network in Asia: The Asia Foundation, Asia Pictures, and the Korean Motion Picture Cultural Association." *Historical Journal of Film, Radio and Television* 37, no. 3 (2017): 517–38.

——. "Destination Hong Kong: The Geopolitics of South Korean Espionage Films in the 1960s." *Journal of Korean Studies* 22, no. 1 (2017): 346-364.

——. "Dracula, Vampires, and Kung Fu Fighters: The Legend of the Seven Golden Vampires and Transnational Horror Co-production in 1970s Hong Kong." In *Transnational Horror Cinema: Bodies of Excess and the Global Grotesque*, edited by Sophia Siddique Harvey and Raphael Raphael, 65-80. New York: Palgrave/MacMillan, 2017.

——. "The Emergence of the Asian Film Festival: Cold War Asia and Japan's Re-entrance to the Regional Market in the 1950s." In *The Oxford Handbook of Japanese Cinema*, edited by Miyao Daisuke, 232–50. Oxford: Oxford University Press, 2013.

——. "It's 'Oscar' Time in Asia! the Rise and Demise of the Asian Film Festival, 1954–1972." In *Coming Soon to a Festival Near You: Programming Film Festivals*, edited by Jeffrey Ruoff, 173–87. St. Andrews: St. Andrews University Press, 2012.

——. "Martial Arts Craze in Korea: Cultural Translation of Martial Arts Film and Literature in the 1960s." In *East Asian Cultural Heritage and Films*, edited by Kinnia Yau Shuk-ting, 173–95. New York: Palgrave/Macmillan, 2012.

——. "On 'The Korean Film Industry': The Asia Foundation, Korean Motion Picture Cultural Association, and John Miller, 1956." *Journal of Japanese and Korean Cinema* 7, no. 2 (2015): 95–112.

——. "Seoul-Hong Kong-Macau: *Love with an Alien* (1957) and Postwar South Korea-Hong Kong Coproduction." In *Asia-Pacific Film Co-Productions: Theory, Industry and Aesthetics*, edited by Dal Yong Jin and Wendy Su, 256–74. London: Routledge, 2019.

——. "The South Korean Film Industry and the Chinese Film Market." *Screen* 60, no. 2 (2019): 332–41.

Lee, Soon-jin. "1950 nyŏndae han'guk yŏnghwa sanŏp kwa migug ŭi wŏnjo: ashia jaedan ŭi chŏng-nŭng ch'wal yŏngso chosŏng ŭl chungshim ŭro" [Korean Film industry of the 1950s and American aid: The case of the Asia Foundation's support for Jeongnung Production Studios]. *Han'guk'ak yŏn'gu* [The journal of Korean studies] 43 (November 2016): 173–204.

——. "Naengjŏn ch'ejeŭi munhwanolli wa han'guk yŏnghwa ŭi chonjaebangshik—yŏnghwa ŭi kŏmyŏl gwajŏng ŭl chungshim ŭro" [Cultural logic of the Cold War system and operation of South Korean cinema on censorship practices of *A Stray Bullet*]. *Kiŏk kwa chŏnmang* [Memory and future vision] 29 (Winter 2013): 374–423.

Leung, Grace L.K., and Joseph M. Chan. "The Hong Kong Cinema and Overseas Market, a Historical Review 1950–1995." In *Hong Kong Cinema Retrospective: Fifty Years of Electric Shadows*, 143–51. Hong Kong: The Urban Council, 1997.

Leung, Ping-kwan. "Urban Cinema and the Cultural Identity." In *The Cinema of Hong Kong: History, Art, Identity*, edited by Poshek Fu and David Desser, 227–51. Cambridge: Cambridge University Press, 2000.

Li, Zhaojin. *A History of Modern Shanghai Banking: The Rise and Decline of China's Finance Capitalism*. London and New York: Routledge, 2003.

Lim, Kean Fan. "Transnational Collaborations, Local Competitiveness: Mapping the Geographies of Filmmaking in/through Hong Kong." *Geografiska Annaler*, Series B. Human Geography 88, no. 3 (2006): 337–57.

Lingzi, Chen. "In the Midst of the Overt and Covert: Hong Kong Asia Press in the Cultural Cold War." Master's thesis, National University of Singapore, 2017.

Londoner, David J. "The Changing Economics of Entertainment." In *The American Film Industry*, edited by Tino Balio, 603–11. Madison: University of Wisconsin Press, 1985.

Long, S. R. Joey. "Winning Hearts and Minds: U.S. Psychological Warfare Operations in Singapore, 1955–1961." *Diplomatic History* 32, no. 5 (November 2008): 899–930.

Lu, Yan. "Limits to Propaganda: Hong Kong's Leftist Media in the Cold War and Beyond." In *The Cold War in Asia: The Battle for Hearts and Minds*, edited by Zheng Yangwen, Hong Liu, and Michael Szonyi, 94–118.

MacCann, Richard Dyer. *Hollywood in Transition*. Boston: Houghton Mifflin, 1962.

——. *Film and Society*. New York: Scribner, 1964.

——. "Films and Film Training in the Republic of Korea." *Journal of the University Film Producers Association* 16, no. 1 (1964): 17.

——. *The People's Films: A Political History of U.S. Government Motion Pictures*. New York: Hastings House, 1973.

MacDonald, Keiko I. *Mizoguchi*. Boston: Twayne Publishers, 1984.

Magnan-Park, Aaron Han Joon. "Restoring the Transnational from the Abyss of Ethno-national Film Historiography: The Case of Chung Chang Wha." *Journal of Korean Studies* 16, no. 2 (Fall 2011): 249–83.

Marchetti, Victor, and John D. Marks. *The CIA and the Cult of Intelligence*. New York: Knopf, 1974.

McBride, Joseph. *Frank Capra: The Catastrophe of Success*. Jackson: University Press of Mississippi, 2011.

McDowell, Bleakley. "Jules and Miriam Bucher." Master's thesis, New York University, 2015.

McFarlane, Brian. *Australian Cinema 1970–1985*. Melbourne: William Heinemann Australia, 1987.

McHugh, Kathleen, and Nancy Abelmann. Introduction. In *South Korean Golden Age Melodrama: Gender, Genre, and National Cinema*, by Kathleen McHugh and Nancy Abelmann, 1–15. Detroit: Wayne State University Press, 2005.

Millet, Raphaël. *Singapore Cinema*. Singapore: Editions Didier Millet, 2006.

Mizuno, Sachiko. "*The Saga of Anatahan* and Japan." *Spectator* 29, no. 2 (Fall 2009): 9–24.

Monaco, Paul. *The Sixties: 1960–1969, History of the American Cinema*. Berkeley: University of California Press, 2001.

Moon, Jae-cheol. "The Meaning of Newness in Korean Cinema: Korean New Wave and After." *Korea Journal* (Spring 2008): 36–59.

Moore, Aaron. *Constructing East Asia: Technology, Ideology, and Empire in Japan's Wartime Era, 1931–1945*. Stanford, CA: Stanford University Press, 2015.

Nanda, Ritu. *Raj Kapoor Speaks*. New Delhi: Viking Penguin Books India, 2002.

Ng, Grace. "Li Han Hsiang's Long Men Zhen." In *Li Han-Hsiang, Storyteller*, edited by Wong Ain-Ling, 138–57. Hong Kong: Hong Kong Film Archive, 2007.

Nornes, Abé Mark. "The Creation and Construction of Asian Cinema Redux." *Film History* 25, no. 1–2 (2013): 175–87.

Oba, Mie. "Japan's Entry into ECAFE." In *Japanese Diplomacy in the 1950s*, edited by Iokibe Makoto, Caroline Rose, Tomaru Junko, and John Weste, 98–113. New York: Routledge, 2008.

Osgood, Kenneth. *Total Cold War: Eisenhower's Secret Propaganda Battle at Home and Abroad*. Lawrence: University Press of Kansas, 2006.

Pak, Chi-yŏn. "Yŏnghwa bŏp chejŏng esŏ je-sach'a kaejŏng-gi kkaji ŭi yŏnghwa jŏngch'aek (1961 ~ 1984 nyŏn)" [From the liberation to the 1960s' film policy], in *Han'guk yŏnghwa jŏngch'aeksa* [A history of Korean film policy], edited by Kim Tongho, 194–95. Seoul, Korea: Nanam Publications, 2004.

Parmar, Inderjeet. *Foundations of the American Century: The Ford, Carnegie, and Rockefeller Foundations in the Rise of American Power*. New York: Columbia University Press, 2012.

Pempel, T. J, ed. *The Politics of the Asian Economic Crisis*. Ithaca, NY: Cornell University Press, 1999.

Pierpaoli, Paul G., Jr., *Truman and Korea: The Political Culture of the Early Cold War*. Columbia: University of Missouri Press, 1999.

Puddington, Arch. *Broadcasting Freedom: The Cold War Triumph of Radio Free Europe and Radio Liberty*. Lexington, University Press of Kentucky, 2000.

Raine, Michael. "Ishihara Yujiro: Youth, Celebrity, and the Male Body in late-1950s Japan." In *Word and Image in Japanese Cinema*, edited by Dennis Washburn and Carole Cavanaugh, 202–25. Cambridge: Cambridge University Press, 2010.

Rajagopalan, Sudha. "Emblematic of the Thaw: Early Indian Films in Soviet Cinemas." *South Asian Popular Culture* 4, no. 2 (2006): 83–100.

Richie, Donald, and Joseph Anderson. *The Japanese Film: Art and Industry*, expanded ed. Princeton, NJ: Princeton University Press, 1982.

Robinson, Andrew. *Satyajit Ray: The Inner Eye*. Berkeley: University of California Press, 1989.

Rodriguez, Hector. "The Cinema in Taiwan: Identity and Political Legitimacy." PhD diss., New York University, 1995.

Rostow, W. W. *An American Policy in Asia*. New York: John Wiley & Sons, 1955.

——. *Eisenhower, Kennedy, and Foreign Aid*. Austin: University of Texas Press, 1985.

Ruberto, Laura E., and Kristi M. Wilson. "Introduction." In *Italian Neorealism and Global Cinema*, edited by Laura E. Ruberto and Kristi M. Wilson, 1–23. Detroit, MI: Wayne State University Press, 2007.

Rueschemeyer, Dietrich, and Evans, Peter B. "The State and Economic Transformation: Toward an Analysis of the Conditions Underlying Effective Intervention." In *Bringing the State Back In*, edited by Peter B. Evans, Dietrich Rueschemeyer, and Theda Skocpol, 44–76. Cambridge: Cambridge University Press, 1985

Sato, Tadao. *Currents in Japanese Cinema*. Translated by Gregory Barrett. Tokyo and New York: Kodansha International, 1982.

Saunders, Frances Stonor. *The Cultural Cold War: The CIA and the World of Arts and Letters*. New York: The New Press, 2001. Originally published in the UK as *Who Paid the Piper? The CIA and the Cultural Cold War*. London: Granta Books, 1999.

Sbardellati, John. *J. Edgar Hoover Goes to the Movies: The FBI and the Origins of Hollywood's Cold War*. Ithaca, NY: Cornell University Press, 2012.

Schenk, Catherine R. *Hong Kong as an International Financial Centre: Emergence and Development 1945–65*. London: Routledge, 2001.

Schilling, Mark. *No Borders, No Limits: Nikkatsu Action Cinema*. Farleigh: FAB Press, 2007.

Schönherr, Johannes. *North Korean Cinema: A History*. Jefferson, NC: McFarland & Company, 2012.

Sebo, Gabor. "A Study on the Impact of Shin Sang-ok on North Korean Cinema." PhD diss., Korea University, 2018.

Sen, Krishna. *Indonesian Cinema: Framing the New Order*. London: Zed Books, 1994.

Sharp, Jasper. "*Buddha*: Selling an Asian Spectacle." *Journal of Japanese and Korean Cinema* 4, no. 1 (2012): 29–52.

Shaw, Tony. *British Cinema and the Cold War*. London: I.B. Tauris, 2006.

——. *Hollywood's Cold War*. Amherst: University of Massachusetts Press, 2007.

Shin, Sang-ok, *Nan Yeonghwayeotda* [I was movie]. Seoul: Random House Korea, 2007.

Shing, Angel On Ki. "The Star as Cultural Icon: The Case of Josephine Siao Fong Fong." Master's thesis, University of Hong Kong, 2000.

Shirley, Graham, and Brian Adams. *Australian Cinema: The First Eighty Years*. Redfern, Australia: Currency Press, 1983.

Srivastava, Manoj. *Wide Angle: History of Indian Cinema*. Chennai, India: Norton Press, 2016.

Standish, Isolde. "Korean Cinema and the New Realism: Text and Context." *East-West Film Journal* 7, no. 2 (1993): 54–80.

Stephenson, Shelly. "'Her Traces Are Found Everywhere': Shanghai, Li Xianglan, and the 'Greater East Asian Film Sphere.'" In *Cinema and Urban Culture in Shanghai, 1922–1943*, edited by Yingjin Zhang, 222–45. Stanford, CA: Stanford University Press, 1999.

Storper, Michael. "The Transition to Flexible Specialisation in the US Film Industry: External Economies, the Division of Labour, and the Crossing of Industrial Divides." *Cambridge Journal of Economics* 13, no. 2 (June 1989): 273–305.

Straubhaar, Joseph D. "Beyond Media Imperialism: Asymmetrical Interdependence and Cultural Proximity." *Critical Studies in Media Communication* 8, no. 1 (1991): 39–59.

Stringer, Julian. "Regarding Film Festivals." PhD diss., Indiana University, 2003.

Suehiro, Akira. "The Road to Economic Re-entry: Japan's Policy toward Southeast Asian Development in the 1950s and 1960s." *Social Science Japan Journal* 2, no. 1 (1999): 85–105.

Suh, Sang-mok. "The Economy in Historical Perspective." In *Structural Adjustment in a Newly Industrialized Country: The Korean Experience*, edited by Vittorio Corbo and Sang-mok Suh, 6–34. Baltimore: Johns Hopkins University Press, 1992.

Tan, See Kam. "Shaw Brothers' *Bangpian*: Global Bondmania, Cosmopolitan Dreaming and Cultural Nationalism." *Screen* 56, no. 2 (Summer 2015): 195–213.

Tang, James T. H. "From Empire Defense to Imperial Retreat: Britain's Postwar China Policy and the Decolonization of Hong Kong." *Modern Asian Studies* 28, no. 2 (1994): 317–37.

Teo, Stephen. "Asian Film Festivals and their Diminishing Glitter Domes: An Appraisal of PIFF, SIFF and HKIFF." In *Dekalog 3: On Film Festivals*, edited by Richard Porton, 109–21. London: Wallflower Press, 2009.

——. "Australia's Role in the Global Kung Fu Trend: *The Man from Hong Kong*." *Senses of Cinema* 62 (2001). http://sensesofcinema.com/2001/cteq/man_hk/.

Terada, Takashi. "The Origins of Japan's APEC Policy: Foreign Minister Takeo Mikki's Asia-Pacific Policy and Current Implications." *Pacific Review* 11, no. 3 (1998): 337–63.

Third Meeting of the ASEAN Sub-Committee on Film: Official Report. Jakarta, Indonesia: November 1974.

Tiffen, Rodney. *Diplomatic Deceits: Government, Media and East Timor.* Sydney: UNSW Press, 2001.

Tobias, M. C. *Flashbacks: Hong Kong Cinema after Bruce Lee.* Gulliver Books, 1979.

Tomaru, Junko. "Japan in British Regional Policy towards Southeast Asia, 1945–1960." In *Japanese Diplomacy in the 1950s,* edited by Iokibe Makoto, Caroline Rose, Tomaru Junko, and John Weste, 55–75. New York: Routledge, 2008.

Toohey, Aileen. "Badjao: Cinematic Representations of Difference in the Philippines." *Journal of Southeast Asian Studies* 36, no. 2 (2005): 281–312.

U, Nu. *The People Win Through.* Rangoon: Society for Extension of Democratic Ideals, 1952.

Uhalley Jr., Stephen. *A History of the Chinese Communist Party.* Stanford, CA: Stanford University Press, 1988.

Uhde, Jan, and Yvonne Ng Uhde. *Latent Image: Film in Singapore.* London: Oxford University Press, 2000.

de Valck, Marijke. *Film Festivals: From European Geopolitics to Global Cinephilia.* Amsterdam: Amsterdam University Press, 2007.

Valicha, Kishore. *The Moving Image: A Study of Indian Cinema.* Hyderabad, India: Orient Longman, 1988.

Wada-Marciano, Mitsuyo. "The Production of Modernity in Japanese Cinema: Shochiku Kamata Style in the 1920s and 1930s." PhD diss., University of Iowa, 2000.

Wade, Robert. *Governing the Market: Economic Theory and the Role of Government in East Asian Industrialization.* Princeton, NJ: Princeton University Press, 1990.

Walsh, Mike. "Hong Kong Goes International: The Case of Golden Harvest." In *Hong Kong Film, Hollywood and the New Global Cinema: No Film Is an Island,* edited by Gina Marchetti and Tan See Kam, 167–76. London: Routledge, 2007.

Weiss, Linda, and John Hobson. *States and Economic Development: A Comparative Historical Analysis.* Cambridge: Polity Press, 1995.

Westad, Odd Arne. *The Cold War: A World History.* London: Penguin Books, 2017.

Wilford, Hugh. *The Mighty Wurlitzer: How the CIA Played America.* Cambridge, MA: Harvard University Press, 2008.

——. " 'Unwitting Assets?': British Intellectuals and the Congress for Cultural Freedom." *Twentieth Century British History* 11, no. 1 (2000): 42–60.

Willemen, Paul. "Pesaro: The Limitations and Strengths of a Cultural Policy." *Framework: A Film Journal* 15/16/17 (Summer 1981): 96–98.

Wong, Cindy Hing-Yuk. "Film Festivals and the Global Projection of Hong Kong Cinema." In *Hong Kong Film, Hollywood and the New Global Cinema: No Film Is an Island,* edited by Gina Marchetti and Tan See Kam, 177–92. London: Routledge, 2007.

——. *Film Festivals: Culture, People, and Power on the Global Screen.* New Brunswick, NJ: Rutgers University Press, 2011.

Woo, Jung-Eun. *Race to the Swift: State and Finance in Korean Industrialization.* New York: Columbia University Press, 1991.

Woo-Cumings, Meredith, ed. *The Developmental State*. Ithaca, NY: Cornell University Press, 1999.

Yamamoto, Satsuo. *My Life as a Filmmaker*. Translated by Chia-ning Chang. Ann Arbor: University of Michigan Press, 2017.

Yau, Shuk-ting Kinnia. "The Early Development of East Asian Cinema in a Regional Context." *Asian Studies Review* 33 (June 2009): 161–73.

———. "Interview with Umetsugu Inoue." In *Hong Kong Cinema Retrospective: Border Crossings in Hong Kong Cinema*, 145–46. Hong Kong: Hong Kong Film Archive, 2000.

———. *Japanese and Hong Kong Film Industries: Understanding the Origins of East Asian Film Networks*. London: Routledge, 2009.

———. "Shaws' Japanese Collaboration and Competition as Seen Through the Asian Film Festival Evolution." In *The Shaw Screen: A Preliminary Study*, edited by Wong Ain-ling, 279–91. Hong Kong: Hong Kong Film Archive, 2003.

———. "Transnational Collaborations and Activities of Shaw Brothers and Golden Harvest: An Interview with Chua Lam." *Hong Kong Cinema Retrospective: Border Crossings in Hong Kong Cinema*, 141. Hong Kong: Hong Kong Film Archive, 2000.

Yau, Shuk-ting Kinnia, and June Pui-wah. "Transnational Collaborations and Activities of Shaw Brothers and Golden Harvest: An Interview with Chua Lam." In *Hong Kong Cinema Retrospective: Border Crossings in Hong Kong Cinema*, 138–43. Hong Kong: Hong Kong Film Archive, 2000.

Yecies, Brian, and Ae-Gyung Shim. "Asian Interchange: Korean-Hong Kong Co-Productions of the 1960s." *Journal of Japanese and Korean Cinema* 4, no. 1 (2012): 15–28.

Yeh, Emilie Yueh-yu. "Taiwan: Popular Cinema's Disappearing Act." In *Contemporary Asian Cinema: Popular Culture in a Global Frame*, edited by Anne Tereska Ciecko, 156–68. Oxford: Berg, 2006.

———. "Taiwan: The Transnational Battlefield of Cathay and Shaws." In *The Cathay Story*, 142–49.

Yeh, Emilie Yueh-yu, and Darrell William Davis. "Japan Hongscreen: Pan-Asian Cinemas and Flexible Accumulation." *Historical Journal of Film, Radio, and Television*, 22, no. 1 (2002): 61–82.

———. *Taiwanese Film Directors: A Treasure Island*. New York: Columbia University Press, 2005.

Yi, Yŏng-il. *Han'guk yŏnghwa jŏnsa* [The complete history of Korean cinema]. Seoul, Korea: Sodo, 2004.

Yip, Man-fung. "Closely Watched Films: Surveillance and Postwar Hong Kong Leftist Cinema." In *Surveillance in Asian Cinema: Under Eastern Eyes*, edited by Karen Fang, 33–59. New York: Routledge, 2017.

Yomota, Inuhiko. *Ilbon yŏnghwa ŭi ihae* [Understanding Japanese cinema]. Translated by Pak Chŏn-yŏl. Seoul, South Korea: Hyeonamsa, 2001.

Yoshimi, Shunya, and David Buist. "'America' as Desire and Violence: Americanization in Postwar Japan and Asia during the Cold War." *Inter-Asia Cultural Studies* 4, no. 3 (2003): 433–50.

Yoshimoto, Mitsuhiro, *Kurosawa: Film Studies and Japanese Cinema*. Durham: Duke University Press, 2000.

Zhang, Yingjin. *Chinese National Cinema*. London: Routledge, 2004.

——. "National Cinema as Translocal Practice: Reflections on Chinese Film Historiography." In *The Chinese Cinema Book*, edited by Song Hwee Lim and Julian Ward, 17–25. New York: Palgrave Macmillan, 2011.

Zheng, Yangwen, Hong Liu, and Michael Szonyi, ed. *The Cold War in Asia: The Battle for Hearts and Minds*. Leiden: Brill, 2010.

Index

CPSIA information can be obtained
at www.ICGtesting.com
Printed in the USA
LVHW011034250322
714381LV00014B/521